M000211226

TAKING UP THE RUNES

TAKING UP THE RUNES

A Complete Guide to Using Runes
in Spells, Rituals, Divination, and Magic

DIANA L. PAXSON

WEISER BOOKS
San Francisco, CA / Newburyport, MA

First published in 2005 by
Red Wheel/Weiser, LLC
With offices at:
500 Third Street, Suite 230
San Francisco, CA 94107
www.redwheelweiser.com

Copyright © 2005 Diana L. Paxson
All rights reserved. No part of this publication may be reproduced or transmitted in
any form or by any means, electronic or mechanical, including photocopying,
recording, or by any information storage and retrieval system, without permission
in writing from Red Wheel/Weiser, LLC. Reviewers may quote brief passages.

ISBN: 978-1-57863-325-8

Library of Congress Cataloging-in-Publication Data

Paxson, Diana L.
  Taking up the runes : a complete guide to using runes in spells, rituals,
divination, and magic / Diana L. Paxson.
      p. cm.
  Includes bibliographical references.
  ISBN 1-57863-325-7
  1. Runes—Miscellanea. I. Title.
  BF1779.R86P39 2005
  133.3'3—dc22

                                    2005003630

Cover and book design by Anne Carter
Typeset in Janson and Meta
Cover photo © Getty Images

Printed in Canada
TCP
10 9 8 7 6

To the Rider of the Tree

CONTENTS

Acknowledgments   *ix*

Introduction   *1*

PART ONE

The Runes

CHAPTER

1	Taking Up the Runes	*17*
2	Fehu and Uruz	*29*
3	Thurisaz and Ansuz	*47*
4	Raidho and Kenaz	*67*
5	Gebo and Wunjo	*81*
6	Hagalaz and Naudhiz	*99*
7	Isa and Jera	*117*
8	Eihwaz and Perthro	*133*
9	Elhaz and Sowilo	*155*
10	Tiwaz and Berkano	*173*
11	Ehwaz and Mannaz	*195*
12	Laguz and Ingwaz	*215*
13	Dagaz and Othala	*231*
14	Bringing Back the Runes	*247*

PART TWO

The Rituals

Introduction   *261*

CHAPTER

1   Taking Up the Runes: A Ritual Journey   *263*

2   Fehu/Uruz: A Ritual for Abundance   *273*

3   Thurisaz/Ansuz: Thurs Spells   *283*

4   Raidho/Kenaz: The Fire Faring   *295*

5   Gebo/Wunjo: The Gift of Joy   *303*

6   Hagalaz/Naudhiz: Needfire   *311*

7   Isa/Jera: Melting the Ice   *323*

8   Eiwaz/Perthro: The Tree and the Well   *331*

9   Elhaz/Sowilo: Safe on the Sun Road   *341*

10   Tiwaz/Berkano: The Tree of Tyr   *353*

11   Ehwaz/Mannaz: A Ritual of Union   *361*

12   Laguz/Ingwaz: The Mysteries of
     Yngvi and Erde   *371*

13   Dagaz/Othala: Kinship and Awakening   *383*

14   Descending the Tree   *393*

15   A Runic Initiation   *403*

     Pronunciation Guide   *410*

     Bibliography   *412*

ACKNOWLEDGMENTS

The materials in this book were originally developed for the Rune Study class that I organized in 1989 and have repeated and refined several times in later years. Participants have included people with extensive academic or ritual backgrounds and people with none, but all have shared a fascination with the runes. This book is for those whose enthusiasm and comments inspired me to connect a great deal of miscellaneous material into (I hope) a coherent whole, especially Tom Johnson, whose generous sharing of research materials and expertise in Old Norse has made this a much more solid piece of work than it would otherwise have been, Dr. Stephan Grundy, for offering his encouragement, and his corrections and suggestions on a number of crucial details, and to Patrick Buck for proofreading.

This is also the place to formally acknowledge my debt to those who have led the way in the current rebirth of serious study of the runes as a system for spiritual development—especially to Edred Thorsson, founder of the Troth, whose book *Futhark* was the first discussion of the runes to combine sound scholarship with magical discipline; to Freya Aswynn, Drighten of the Rune Gild in the United Kingdom, whose devotion to Odin has enabled her to bring so much of his energy into the world, and to Kveldúlf Gundarsson, Warder of the Lore in the Troth, whose energy, insight, scholarship, and support have been of much assistance.

I am grateful to Leigh Ann Hussey for permission to include some material incorporated into the HAGALAZ/NAUDHIZ ritual, the invocation to Odin in the EIHWAZ/PERTHRO ritual, and the "Spindle" chant. Thanks to the estate of Paul Edwin Zimmer for permission to use material in the Yngvi/Erde rite, parts of some of the meditations, and the blessings on the horn and bread in the ANSUZ/THURISAZ ritual, and to Hilary Ayer for contributing the "To Stop Floods" spell in the same ritual. Thanks to Deborah Bender for letting me include the words to the "Bay Region Weather Round," to Laurel Mendes for "Blossom," and to Jim Graham for the original material in the Wolfbinding meditation.

I would also like to acknowledge my debt to the many members of Hrafnar and the Troth who have increased my understanding of heathen lore and practice, and to the participants in my rune classes whose interest, insights, and enthusiasm enriched our shared experience.

The Way of the Runes

Runes you must seek   and staves of counsel
Most mighty staves
Strongest staves
That Fimbulthulr [Mighty Speaker] stained   that the great gods
   fashioned
That were graven and spelled by Hrópt [one who prays].

("Hávamál": 141)

THE CURRENT RESURGENCE OF INTEREST in traditional spirituality encompasses the lore of many lands. The teachings of Native Americans have much to offer those who wish to live close to the earth; the Celtic path opens a way to the Otherworld; the orisha religions bring the deities to the human world. In this meeting of traditions, the religious ideas of the Germanic peoples have rarely been represented. Yet today we are seeing an awakening awareness of the spirituality of Northern Europe. The first evidence of that interest has been a sudden influx of books about the runes.

Many first encountered the runes in J. R. R. Tolkien's *Lord of the Rings* (although it must be noted that Tolkien, who knew the runes very well, shifted them around for his own reasons, so that, for instance, the *G* rune, for Gandalf, is represented by FEHU ᚠ rather than GEBO✕). Here was a sacred alphabet, elegant in form, with the allure of ancient mystery. Furthermore, it was a mystery that belonged to the North, to the old gods of the Anglo-Saxons and the Vikings, whose culture was the foundation of our own. In Old High German, the word *run*, or *runa*, means mystery, and those who seek secrets in the runes will not be disappointed. The Indo-European root for the word may be the same *reu* that appears in the names of the Hindu and Greek gods of the heavens, Va*run*a and Ou*ran*os, with a sense of supernatural sound. As a spiritual system, the runes are based on a marriage of sound and sense, the use of words to give conscious expression to intuitions that are beyond all human language, and to distill order from the chaos of experience.

But the runes are also a practical, flexible, and effective symbol system with a variety of uses that opens itself to the sincere seeker with amazing readiness.

The most obvious use of the runes is as a means of communication. They are indeed an alphabet—a system of symbols representing sounds that can be used to spell words. However, this usefulness does not account for their attraction. The Latin alphabet succeeded in becoming the medium of global communication even though, or perhaps because, its letters never acquired sacred significance. As a sacred alphabet, runes are much more like Hebrew letters, each having a meaning in itself that transcends its function as a representation of sound.

Like Hebrew letters, each rune has a name of its own and serves as a focus for a constellation of meanings, associations, and symbols. For this reason, the individual runes are powerful tools for meditation. A systematic study of each of them in turn can become an initiation, opening the psyche and integrating the personality. Such a survey also serves as an excellent general introduction to Northern European culture.

Today, the best-known application of rune lore is in divination. Chips or stones marked with the runes are drawn, cast, or laid out in patterns like tarot cards. The complexity of a reading may be affected by the fact that there are fewer runes than there are cards, but a good reader can uncover considerable depth. A tarot card carries more visual information than a rune chip, but like the runes, the cards are named. Reading tarot requires knowledge of the basic, generally accepted meaning of each card and interpretation of the symbolism being used in a given deck, in the light of the reader's own insight. When you read runes instead of cards, you do not have the help of the artist's symbolism in determining meaning. Instead, the simple rune form triggers associations in the consciousness of the interpreter directly. Furthermore, a set of runes can be improvised on chips of wood or slips of paper at need.

However, divination does not begin to exhaust the possibilities of rune lore. References in the Eddas, the sacred poetry of the North, make it clear that one major use for the runes was in constructing charms and spells. The runes can be used singly, combined as bindrunes, or employed in inscriptions. The techniques used by the rune wise for such operations are described fairly clearly. What is never stated, however, is which runes are to be used for which purposes. This, presumably, was the knowledge that was transmitted orally from teacher to pupil, or acquired via meditation or initiation or through direct inspiration from the gods.

Effective use of the runes requires both the old wisdom and the new. A sound grasp of traditional culture and mythology will enable the rune reader to draw on the power invested in runic symbols over the years. But all magic flows through the mind of the maker and must have meaning in terms of his or her personal symbol system as well. We live in a global culture, and where an archetype from another land seems to illuminate some aspect of a rune's meaning, it deserves consideration. The student must not only consciously study the meanings ascribed to the runes by earlier scholars, but must internalize them.

The runes are an expression of the spirituality of Northern Europe, but the culture in which they are currently flowering is diverse and pluralistic. Just as people of all ethnic origins may be attracted to Native American spirituality or the worship of the orishas, individuals from many backgrounds are becoming fascinated by the runes. There has been a great deal of discussion about the value of genetic links in accessing ethnic spiritual systems. Many people find that the magic of their own ancestors is easier to learn. I myself approach the Northern tradition with more confidence because I know that my foremothers did the same.

However, I know many genetically European individuals who are successfully practicing African, Native American, or Eastern traditions. Although followers of Santeria are likely to have Black or Hispanic ancestry, and participants in the Sun Dance must be Native American, there are many individuals who have a natural affinity for the religious practices of cultures with which they have no genetic connection. The gods look at the colors of our spirits, not of our skins. Today, spiritual traditions are becoming as exportable as ethnic foods. If our bodies, whose genetic link to our ancestors is undeniable, can digest egg rolls from China and chilies from Mexico, why is it so hard to believe that we can assimilate variety in nourishment for our souls?

The early Germanic peoples were not racist. When the migrating tribes met the Huns, they reacted to them as they would to any other tribe and fought or intermarried with them as policy required. The Vikings raided folk of all ethnic origins with equal enthusiasm and took slaves most often from Ireland. In "Völuspá" we are told that the first war in the world was between the Aesir and the Vanir. After a confrontation, it was settled not by conquest, but by alliance and treaty. If the Vanir were the gods of a pre- (or even, following J. P. Malory's theories, an "early") Indo-European earth religion who were adopted by the incoming tribes, then a willingness to adapt and assimilate new racial and cultural elements goes back to the origins of the Germanic people. Another theory holds that it was the worshippers of the Vanir who invaded, bringing with them a more advanced agricultural technology.

A belief in reincarnation is found among many of the early Indo-European peoples. Traces of it occur not only in India, where it became a major tenet of the religion, but among the Celts and in Scandinavia as well. Clans welcomed the spirits of the dead home partly in hopes of attracting them back to the wombs of their women to be reborn, but though it was expected that souls would reincarnate among their descendants, some Scandinavian folktales suggest this was not always so.

One theory current in occult circles is that in the twentieth century people from many races are reincarnating in different cultures in order to promote world understanding. This might explain, for instance, why some Third World people are taking so readily to Western ways and why many Americans are turning to Zen or shamanism. Be that as it may, the fact is that the runes speak to people of many ethnic backgrounds. I accept all those who have heard the call of the Northern gods as my companions on the Way.

ORIGINS

What is the source of this system that attracts us so? On the level of myth, the runes were given to us by Odin. In the "Hávamál" ("The Sayings of the High One"), Odin says,

> I know I was hanged   on the windy tree
> For nine full nights,
> Stabbed by a spear,   offered to Odin
> Sworn by myself to myself,
> Upon that tree   that no man knows
> From what roots it rises.
>
> No bread did they bear to me   nor horn handed;
> Into the deep I gazed—
> I took up the runes,   took them up, screaming,
> Then fell back again.
>
>   ("Hávamál": 138-39)

The myth behind the runes is one of sacrifice. The god whose name means "divine frenzy," "inspiration," or "ecstasy," was himself hanged and stabbed in the traditional fashion in which sacrifices were made to him, experiencing everything, offering everything for the moment of transcendence in which he could manifest into consciousness the words of power. As the shaman in cultures from Siberia to South America goes crying for a vision and brings back his power song to heal the people, the deity who walks between the worlds brings us the runes. In considering the runes' external history, we must not lose sight of their spiritual significance.

Historically, the first known runic inscriptions date from the second century CE (Common Era). Their sophistication argues that runes may have been in use for at least a century before that. Many, though not all, of the rune staves show a kinship with the equivalent letters in the Mediterranean alphabets, which suggests that the idea of such a symbol system, if not the system itself, may have been inspired by contact with the south. Various scholars have put forth convincing arguments for an origin among the Goths on the Danube, Romanized Germans in Raetia (Switzerland), or in Jutland, where the earliest inscriptions have been found (possibly the oldest example is the "Meldorf" brooch, which may date back to 50 CE).

One theory gives the runes an Etruscan inspiration, and puts their origin earlier still, or suggests that they were North Italic in origin, disseminated by the early Germanic Marcomanni or Herulian tribes. An intriguing possibility suggested by Paul Edwin Zimmer is that part of their inspiration comes from the Etruscan alphabet. Interestingly enough, one of the few Etruscan words for which we have a Latin translation is their word for the gods—*aisar* (Friedrich 1957, p. 138) which sounds a great deal like the Old Norse *aesir*. If there is indeed a connection, the most probable route for transmission would have been the overland amber routes to the Baltic, which had been used since the Bronze Age.

	ATTIC	LYDIAN	ETRUSCAN	OSCAN	LATIN
A	Ɐ Ɐ	𐤠	A	ⴸ	ᴧ ⋏ A
B	ß	𐤡	ⴖ Ⴆ ⴖ	ⴖ	ß B
C/G	∧		⅂ < C	>	< c Ⴀ
D	△	𐤣	◁ D	ꓤ	▷ D
E	⅌ Ⅎ E	𐤤	⅂ F E	Ⅎ	E ‖
F/W			⅂ E F	⅃	F ⌐'
Z/J	I	I	I		
H	日		日 日	日	H
TH	⊕		⊗ ⊕		
I	⅃ ⎮	⎮ ⎮	⎮	⎮ ⱶ	⎮
K	K	Ⱡ	Ⱡ K	Ⱡ	K
L	Γ ᒪ	⅂	⅃ ᒪ	⅃	ᒪ L
M	⋏	⋏	⋏ ⋏	Ⱶ	M
N	Ⴎ Ⴎ	Ⴎ	Ⴎ Ⴔ M	Ⴎ	N
X/SH	I	日 田			
O	○	○	○		○
P	Γ Γ Γ		⅂ P	Π	Γ P
R	▷ P D	٩	٩ P	Ⴇ	R R R
S	⟨ ⟨	?	⟨ ⱻ	⟨	⟨ S
T	T	T	T Ⴕ	T	T
U	Y V	Ⴤ	Ⴤ	V	v ⋁
PH	Φ Φ		Φ		
KH	X †		X		
PS/X			Ⴤ		

ANCIENT ALPHABETS

Adapted from figures
in "Alphabet"
*Encyclopedia
Britannica* Vol. I
pp. 680-81 (1958)

Ⴤ Also Corinth,
Miletus, Thera

If the inspiration was Western Greek, Siegfried Kutin suggests that a possible source was Pytheas, a geographer from the Greek colony of Massalia (Marseille), who was the first representative of Greek culture known to have made contact with a Germanic tribe. At the beginning of the fourth century BCE, Pytheas made a journey during which he investigated the western centers of the amber trade by visiting the Teutons, who held the holy amber isle of Abalos (probably Heligoland), and the Guttones near the mouth of the Vistula (Kutin 1977).

From all this, it should be clear that although we can call the runes ancient with some certainty, the details of their origins and evolution lie shrouded in mists as dense as those that veil the Baltic shores. Interpretation of the earliest inscriptions is equally problematic. R. I. Page quotes D. M. Wilson as saying "that for every inscription there shall be as many interpretations as there are scholars working on it"(Page 1987, p. 10).

Runes were inscribed on spearheads, brooches, shield bosses, wooden staves, combs, and later, memorial stones. Some of the inscriptions indicate the name of the owner or maker of the object, others appear to be magical inscriptions invoking luck or protection. Later on, runes were used for more ordinary communications, to identify or tally goods, and the like. As the Roman Church and European feudalism spread into the northern countries, so did the Latin alphabet. Soon Anglo-Saxon texts were being written in an odd mixture of runes and Latin letters. By the time the sagas were written down, the Latin alphabet had become the means of written communication, and when runes were used, it was generally for magical purposes.

The old Germanic runic alphabet, or *futhark* (a word formed from the sounds of the first six runes), consisted of twenty-four symbols written in a traditional order. The Anglo-Saxons added nine more to express additional sound combinations, while the Scandinavians eventually ended up with a simplified sixteen-stave futhark. There were numerous variations upon these basic themes, and even within one futhark the forms of the runes could vary. For convenience, the twenty-four runes may be divided into three "aetts," or eights, named for the runes with which they begin: Freyr's aett, Hagal's aett, and Tyr's aett.

THE PRINCIPAL FUTHARKS

#	Elder Futhark form/s name		Younger Futhark form/s name		Anglo-Saxon Futhorc form/s name		sound
1.	ᚠ	fehu	ᚠ	fé	ᚠ	feoh	F
2.	ᚢ	uruz	ᚢ	úr	ᚢ	úr	U
3.	ᚦ	thurisaz	ᚦ	thurs	ᚦ	thorn	th
4.	ᚨ	ansuz	ᚨ	áss	ᚨ	ós	A
5.	ᚱ	raidho	ᚱ	reidh	ᚱ	rad	R
6.	ᚲ	kenaz	ᚲ	kaun	ᚻ	ken	C/K
7.	ᚷ	gebo	-	-	ᚷ	gyfu	G
8.	ᚹ	wunjo	-	-	ᚹ	wynn	W
9.	ᚺ	hagalaz	ᚼ	hagall	ᚻ	haegl	H
10.	ᚾ	naudhiz	ᚾ	naudhr	ᚾ	nyd	N
11.	ᛁ	isa	ᛁ	íss	ᛁ	ís	I
12.	ᛃ	jera	ᛆ	ár	ᛄ	gér	Yuh
13.	ᛇ	eihwaz		yr	ᛇ	éoh	ei
14.	ᛈ	perthro	-	-	ᛈ	peordh	P
15.	ᛉ	elhaz	-	-	ᛉ	eolh	zh
16.	ᛋ	sowilo	ᛋ	sol	ᛋ	sigil	S
17.	ᛏ	tiwaz	ᛏ	týr	ᛏ	tír	T
18.	ᛒ	Berkano	ᛒ	bjarkan	ᛒ	beorc	B
19.	ᛗ	ehwaz	-	-	ᛗ	eh	eh
20.	ᛗ	mannaz	ᛘ	madhr	ᛗ	mann	M
21.	ᛚ	laguz	ᛚ	lögr	ᛚ	lagu	L
22.	ᛜ	ingwaz	-	-	ᛝ	ing	ng
23.	ᛞ	dagaz	-	-	ᛞ	daeg	D
24.	ᛟ	othala	-	-	ᛟ	éthel	O
25.					ᚪ	ac	a
26.					ᚫ	aesc	aah
27.					ᚣ	yr	u
28.					ᛡ	ior	io
29.					ᛠ	éar	ea
30.					ᛢ	cweorp	qu
31.					ᛣ	calc	k
32.					ᛥ	stán	st
33.					ᚸ	gár	g

NORTHERN CULTURE

Although the runes can be studied purely as a magical alphabet, to use them effectively for any purpose other than simple inscriptions it is necessary to understand not only their literal but their symbolic or spiritual meanings. This requires some familiarity with the religious ideas of the people who created them.

When the Romans first encountered the Teutonic tribes, they described the native deities by comparing them to their own. Wodan (Odin) was identified with the Roman Mercury; Tiwaz (Tyr) with Mars; and Thunar/Donar (Thor), the Thunderer, with Jupiter; while Frija (Frigg) filled the place of Venus. The correspondences between these deities are not nearly as tidy as the Romans would have liked to believe, but they do give us a point of reference.

The important thing to remember is that Odin was not only a psychopomp—a guide and god of the dead—but he was also the greatest of magicians, mighty in both witchcraft and word magic, and (perhaps because as a wanderer, he accompanied the tribes on their migrations and conquests) a god of kings and warriors and the poets who praised them. Tyr, the original sky god, remained god of judicial combat, and Thor retained his role as weather god and defender. Frigg, with her attendant demigoddesses, ruled as queen. In Scandinavia, the roles assigned to "Third Function" deities by Georges Dumézil (1973)—agriculture and crafts—were fulfilled by the Vanir, the lord Freyr, his sister Freyja (whose character is much closer to that of the Roman Venus), and their father, Njordh, the sea-god. Their presumed mother, Nerthus, was a goddess of the amber coast, who governed the fertility of man, beast, and land as she had done since the first European fields were sown. These gods and their functions are all represented in the runes.

The practice of Germanic religion seems to have allowed for considerable individual initiative. Each tribe or district was united by periodic festivals at which the gods were honored by processions, sacrifice, and communal feasting, but most religious practice was focused on protecting the individual farmstead and maintaining a harmonious relationship with the local land-spirits and guardian spirits of the family. The chief man of a district was responsible for both political and religious leadership (generally he was the one with the wealth to maintain a temple or sponsor the festivals), but individuals were free to devote themselves to particular deities.

Some people developed a private practice as spiritual professionals—healers or weatherworkers or seers. There is a strong shamanic element in many of the techniques described in the sagas. Other practices seem to be typical of the old European agricultural complex, elements of which survived in farming communities until the advent of the automobile. Women in particular were believed to be spiritually talented, and often enjoyed great prestige. The warrior cult of the berserker so familiar from comic books was practiced chiefly in times of extended warfare, or by the professional warriors. Old Norse is rich in words for both male and female spiritual specialists of all kinds.

In this book, Germanic religion, like the Northern gods, will be addressed primarily as it relates to the runes and their uses. However, there are many resources available to those who would like to explore this area further. In *Teutonic Religion*, Kveldúlf Gundarsson provides an excellent introduction to the deities and beliefs and basic rituals. Probably the most useful general introduction to Teutonic culture is *Gods and Myths of the Viking Age*, by H. R. Ellis-Davidson, or *Myths and Symbols of Pagan Europe* by the same author. Also recommended is *Our Troth*, published by the Troth, a nonracist national organization of individuals and kindreds practicing Germanic religion. Their Web site (www.thetroth.org) offers a wealth of information. For a full bibliography, see the end of this book.

The best way to become familiar with the spirit of the Norse gods and their mythology is to read and reread the Elder (or Poetic) and Younger (or Prose) Eddas. The most available translations are *The Poetic Edda*, translated by Lee M. Hollander, and the thirteenth-century Icelandic historian Snorri Sturluson's *Edda*, translated by Anthony Faulkes. The Icelandic sagas, and general books on Viking culture, such as *Everyday Life in the Viking Age* by Jacqueline Simpson, are also useful in providing a context. The more you can think like an ancient heathen, the better you will understand their runes, so you should read as much and as widely as you can.

In addition to becoming familiar with the primary source material on Northern culture, reading widely in contemporary runelore will also expand your understanding. The discussions of the runes in this book make reference to the principal authors, but you will benefit even more from reading them all yourself and coming to your own conclusions.

A good beginning would be Edred Thorsson's *Futhark*, *Runelore*, and *At the Well of Wyrd*. Tony Willis's *Runic Workbook* has good material on divination, and *Rune Games*, by Marijane Osborn and Stella Longland, gives an extensive discussion of the Anglo-Saxon runes. Freya Aswynn's *Leaves of Yggdrasil* (reissued as *Northern Mysteries and Magic*) covers the runes with more cultural references and feminine focus than most. I would also highly recommend Gundarsson's *Teutonic Magic*, not only for its information, but for its meditations. Other books on the subject continue to be published. For more suggestions, check out the bibliography at the end of this book. Read and compare.

EXPERIENCING THE RUNES

When Odin took up the runes, he took something from without, and brought it within. Only by making it a part of himself was he able to share it with others. This book is about making the runelore presented in the first part of each chapter so much a part of your own consciousness that you can use the runes as you use a tool fitted to your hand, or a language you know well. Meditation and study will take you only so far on this path. To walk the Way of the Runes, you must experience the runes as they manifest both in the part of Midgard that lies outside yourself and the worlds within.

Like most, I began learning about the runes by reading. I found them fascinating and sensed that there were a number of levels at which they could be used. Each one seemed to offer a tantalizing glimpse into the human psyche in general and Germanic culture in particular. I spent one summer meditating on the runes one by one, but still they eluded me. In the fall of 1987 I had an interesting encounter with Odin and began to work with him. It was clear that my education in Germanic religion must begin with the runes.

On the principle that the best way to learn something is to teach it, I asked my friends if they would like to study with me. I was extremely fortunate in the group of talented people who responded, including several poets and a graduate student in Scandinavian Studies. Their dedication kept me going when my own energies might have flagged, and their contributions enriched the rituals. As I had hoped, through the runes we gained access to the entire Germanic world. The classes I have taught since then have only deepened this understanding.

Although the group discussions are extremely rewarding, it has become clear that the degree to which participants benefit from the discussions and rituals is determined primarily by how much work they do between meetings. For this reason, although the materials presented in this book include instructions for creating a study group, most of the experiences and exercises can be used alone.

USING THIS BOOK

This book is not intended to be the one, true, and only approach to rune lore. It is a study guide that integrates material from a variety of sources. Each chapter in part 1 presents the name, shape, pronunciation, and meaning for two runes (also see the pronunciation guide on page 409). Our understanding of their meaning is derived first from their names and then from the Anglo-Saxon rune poem (which includes all the runes in the Elder Futhark plus several additional runes that are not discussed here) and the Icelandic and Norwegian rune poems (which cover only the staves in the Younger Futhark). Thus some of the runes have three sets of verses, while others have only one. However, even when a rune only appears in the Anglo-Saxon poem, the concepts for which it is a gateway may be found in the Eddas, sagas, and histories, and where I have found a relevant passage, I have included it. Since runic studies are an evolving discipline, I have also summarized the ways in which some of the most important modern writers on runelore interpret and use the runes as well as offering my own.

Understanding the runes also requires a knowledge of the spiritual and cultural context in which they developed and were used. The sections on each pair of runes are therefore followed by a section titled "Study and Experience" in which I discuss related myths, history, and customs. This section also contains suggestions for experiential and ritual work that will help you to internalize the runes' meanings.

In part 2 you will find rituals for group use based on each pair of runes. Of course there are other ways to arrange the material, by studying one rune at a time, for instance, or by addressing the runes in different combinations (a useful approach if you are working through the runes for a second or third time). Just as in divination, in which their meanings shift according to their arrangement, you will find that the runes cast new light upon each other's meanings with each new pairing.

You can choose to use this book in a number of ways. If you are working by yourself, you can study each rune at your own pace, reading the discussion, meditating on the rune, and doing as much of the ritual work as you can. However, you will find that your motivation increases if you can gather a number of like-minded friends and meet once a month to discuss the results of your studies and to complete your assimilation of the runes by doing the group rituals that appear in part 2.

You can practice the exercises during the meetings or choose to wait until you are familiar with the entire futhark before trying them. I strongly recommend that you do as many of the exercises and rituals as you can. Simply reading about the runes will only give you an intellectual appreciation. If you are to use them effectively, your runecraft must come from the heart.

SOURCES

The most popular and poetic translation of the Elder Edda is by Lee Hollander, and you may prefer to substitute his version for my translations when doing the rituals. Caroline Larrington gives a more literal translation.

Another useful version is the one by James Chisholm, which includes the Old Norse original. My usual source for the Younger Edda is the version by Anthony Faulkes. The translation I have used for the Norwegian and Icelandic rune poems is from 1887, found in Appendix B of *The Old English Rune Poem* by Maureen Halsall. The modern English versions of the verses from the Rune Poem itself, however, are my own translation. Except for those selections otherwise cited, songs, spells, and verses are my own.

Part 1

The Runes

Chapter 1

TAKING UP THE RUNES:
As an Individual
or Group

THE FIRST MEETING OF A RUNE STUDY GROUP, or the first time you set apart to formally begin your study of the runes, should be used for organization and orientation.

A possible first meeting outline is as follows:

1. Introductions, in which each person summarizes his/her background and reasons for wanting to study the runes.
2. Identify what resources are available and decide how to acquire additional materials.
3. Decide on how your study will be organized.
4. Summarize the history of the runes.
5. Discuss ways of working with the runes between meetings.
6. Ritual: Meditation, "Taking Up the Runes."
7. Celebration and grounding.

INTRODUCTIONS

If you are working alone, use this time to write down your understanding of what the runes are and your goals in studying them. You will find it very interesting to compare this description with your perceptions at the end of the course of study. In a group, everyone should be given the opportunity to (briefly) state what they are hoping to get out of the class.

RESOURCES

The group needs to find out what resources it has already and which books or other materials it should acquire. Clearly, everyone will need a copy of *Taking Up the Runes* and some of the other rune books. A bibliography that includes recommended materials on the runes appears at the end of this book. Some people may already own useful items that are not in the bibliography. If you are working with a group, the resource problem can be eased if each member buys some of the books and reports on relevant content at each meeting. I would, however, recommend that anyone seriously studying Germanic culture acquire copies of Ellis-Davidson's *Gods and Myths of Northern Europe* (reissued as *Gods and Myths of the Viking Age*) and the Elder and Younger *Eddas*. Everyone should also have a notebook in which to take notes on discussions, collect handouts, record the results of individual work, and so on.

ORGANIZATION

Decide the following questions now:

1. In what order will you work through the futhark?
2. When will you have your meetings or study times?
3. What will you do during meetings or study sessions? (Discussion, ritual, both, etc.)
4. Will one person lead the group, or should a different member take responsibility each time?
5. Do you want to encourage people to wear any kind of distinctive clothing?

Scheduling

Our rune study groups have found it most convenient to start at the beginning of the futhark and address two runes each at a monthly meeting, thus covering all twenty-four, with introduction and graduation, in fourteen months. This section is organized into "meetings" on that assumption, with suggestions for discussion and texts for group rituals, as well as activities and rites for a student working alone.

There is something to be said for both approaches. The solo student can set his or her own pace; however, working with a group, even a small one, helps keep you focused and motivated. Working alone, you are free to concentrate on the aspects of the runes you find most interesting. On the other hand, having to accommodate everyone's interests may result in a more balanced coverage of the subjects, and the insights of other group members can be illuminating.

Obviously this is not the only way to go about it. The information can be used by an individual as a guide to meditation and reflection, and with some adaptations, the group rituals, as well as the solo rites, can be worked alone. Certainly, anyone intending to lead a rune study group should work through the book ahead of time. If you are studying alone, you may find it possible to go through the course more quickly—at the rate of one rune a week, for instance. You will also derive some benefit from simply reading the book.

Some may prefer to have a separate meeting to discuss each rune and develop a ritual for each one, or do the rituals presented here every other meeting. Others may decide to use Thorsson's concentric diagram of the runes (on p. 74 of *Futhark*) as a guide and work from the inside of the circle out, or from the outside of the circle in. Any two runes drawn at random will

illuminate each other. You may decide to work through the futhark from
FEHU to OTHALA the first time, and choose some other arrangement for
a second round. If you do choose another approach, the rituals included in
this section can be used for inspiration.

Obviously the most appropriate day for such meetings or for rune work in
general is Wednesday (Wodan's Day), but weekend meetings will allow you
more time.

Dress

Whether you are working alone or with a group, you may find that dressing
appropriately helps you to shift into a Norse mode of consciousness. The
psychology of costume is well known. We dress up for an evening out, or put
on running shoes to go hiking, and find ourselves already getting into the
mood of the thing simply by getting ready. The association of a given action
with a certain mode of dress or even a piece of jewelry can help condition the
mind and speed up the process of shifting gears to begin your task. You will
find that if you always put on, for instance, a copper disk engraved around
the edge with the futhark when you are about to work with the runes, simply slipping the necklace over your head will help you to concentrate. Some
groups go a bit farther and create Norse-style tunics to wear at rituals, while
others favor a pendant or necklace with an appropriate T-shirt.

If you would like to do some sewing, my book *Germanic Costume* includes
history, illustration, and patterns. It is available from The Troth, Box 472,
Berkeley, CA 94701 for $10.

HISTORY

The group leader should summarize the history and development of the runes
found in the "Origins" section on page 4 of the Introduction to this book. Add
material from any other sources you may have, especially *Runes*, by Page, and
Thorsson's *Runelore*. Read them yourself if you are working alone.

At the end of the discussion, or during the potluck that follows the ritual,
remind everyone that the runes to be studied next month are FEHU and
URUZ. Each person will need to bring a bank deposit slip to class for the ritual. They should prepare by reading the discussions of these runes in their
rune books and following up as many of the suggestions for further reading
and experience as they can. If you are working alone, you may begin reading
the study section for FEHU/URUZ as soon as you have finished the ritual in
this chapter.

BETWEEN MEETINGS

Rune-related activities to be done between meetings include reading, setting up an altar, meditation, making and consecrating your own rune staves, and seeking experiences that relate to the runes. Keep a file or notebook in which you record your experiences after each exercise.

Altars

A rune altar can be as simple as a section of dresser or shelf covered with a plain cloth on which you set a candle or votive light, cards on which you have drawn the runes you are working with, the disks or staves of those runes, and any appropriate pictures or other items, such as a head of grain or statuette of a cow for FEHU, a picture of an aurochs for URUZ, and so on. Norse god images are becoming available from companies such as Mythic Images and JBL, and pictures can be photocopied from books of mythology or from the libretto of Wagner's *Ring of the Nibelungs*, illustrated by Arthur Rackham (These are now in the public domain. Copies can be downloaded from the Troth Web site, *www.thetroth.org*).

Meditation

The runes must not only be studied, but internalized. Before beginning meditation with the runes, you need to learn to relax and focus your attention. To relax, sit in a balanced position which can be maintained without muscular tension or any effort of will. A good choice is a comfortable straight chair in which you can sit with your palms resting upon your knees. Those who are flexible or have experience in Eastern forms of meditation may find that sitting cross-legged works as well. Before sitting down, stretch to loosen your muscles.

Deepen your focus by counting your breaths. With practice, you can condition yourself to enter a focused state through a specific breathing pattern. I have found that breathing in to a slow count of four, holding for two beats, letting the breath out to the count of four and pausing for two more beats works well.

Another method is to use the runic yoga system called stadhagaldr, developed by Thorsson and based on the theories of Kummer and Marby, in which the runester forms the rune shapes with his or her body. This system is fully described in Thorsson's first book, *Futhark*.

Inscribing

One way to internalize the runes is to physically inscribe them on your body. This is a good way to begin a runic meditation. You can scratch the rune on your skin with a fingernail or inscribe runes with consecrated oil (something like oil of wintergreen or cinnamon that leaves a tingle on the skin), with water, or with saliva. When working with the runes one at a time, you can draw them on your forehead over the "third eye," at the base of the throat, over the solar plexus, or on the palms of your hands. Take a moment to feel the shape of the rune upon your skin. As the sensation fades, draw it inward and absorb the rune shape into your own essence.

Envisioning

As you study each rune, draw or paint it (usually in red on a white background) large enough to be seen clearly from a few feet away, and set it up where you can contemplate it. This rune card can be used as the starting point for a number of visual exercises.

1. Stare at the rune card intently; then cover it with a blank piece of paper and wait for its complementary image to appear there.

2. Stare at the rune card for a few moments; then shut your eyes and visualize it against a blank background.

3. Once you can maintain the image internally, imagine it pulsing with light and then changing color. Practice transforming it from one color to another until you can do this at will.

4. Hold the image of the rune in your mind. Visualize it first pulsing, then expanding, until it becomes a doorway. At first you may do no more than look through the door and note what you see, then shrink the rune to close it again. As you look through this door, quiet your mind and allow images to appear. Do not try to force the vision, or worry about whether you are seeing the "right" things.

With more practice, you can step through the doorway and explore the world to which the rune is the portal. But remember to pay attention to where you are going and memorize the landmarks. You will be more comfortable if you can retrace your steps precisely in reverse order. If you become disturbed or frightened by anything you see, visualize the rune again and snap back through it into your body. An additional protection is to visualize or draw the rune ELHAZ (ᛉ) between you and anything disturbing.

Intoning

Runes are both sounds and symbols. Intoning the runes is the first step in spellwork—*galdr*, or incantation. To internalize the sound of the rune, sing it. The early 20th-century Armanen tradition of runic study developed a technique known as runic yodeling, which conjures up bizarre images of wizards in lederhosen perching on mountaintops as they warble runes. Nonetheless, the idea is a good one, although I prefer a sonorous and sustained intonation in the style of Hindu mantra singing rather than a shout. Your chanting does not need to be loud, and unless you are working outdoors or alone in the house, it is best to aim for intensity rather than volume. Hindu tradition identifies several levels of chanting, ranging from chanting aloud to the prayer of the heart, in which the mental vibration of the mantra unites the worshipper with the god. The runes can be intoned in all of these ways. For an impressive demonstration of the potential in runic galdr, listen to the CDs produced by Aswynn.

To chant a rune, visualize it, take a deep belly-breath, and let the outflow of the air carry the sound. Choose a note that falls comfortably within the middle range of your voice. Usually the vowel sounds will be held longest, but save enough breath to finish up the final consonants.

You may find that different runes demand different notes, up and down the scale. You will certainly discover that various sounds vibrate in different places in your body. You can also learn to direct this vibration to different areas. Some runes relate naturally to certain parts of the body—ANSUZ to the mouth and throat, for instance. This principle also has applications in healing. A rune sound can become the first part of a meditation. Continue intoning the rune, visualizing it pulsing in time to the vibrations of your voice, until the rune is all that you can see and hear. Bring the chanting to a climax and then let it fade.

Ingesting

A method which works well as the end of a meditation sequence and can also be used in group ritual is to inscribe the rune on something that you eat or drink. In the sagas, the usual method is to write the runes on a piece of wood or bone and scrape them off into a drink. Other delivery systems include writing the rune on a piece of paper in a water-soluble, nontoxic substance such as juice, and washing it off into a beverage. Writing a rune on a piece of crystallized sugar is a possibility, as is scratching it into a cake of hard choco-late and scraping it off. Runes can be drawn in liquid, sprinkled into it, or inscribed in the air and projected into it with the energy from the palm of the hand.

Runes can be eaten as well as drunk. Aswynn reports getting good results when she first studied the runes by eating cakes with the runes inscribed on them. They can be scratched into a cookie or cracker, set into it with raisins, drawn on it with frosting, juice, honey, etc., or the dough can be molded into the shape of the rune.

Whether you are eating or drinking, it is important to do so with intention and attention. As you consume the rune-inscribed food or drink, visualize the rune and feel its energy expanding through your system.

Crafting Runes

Rune sets made from stones, chips, or cards are now widely available. However, while you are studying the runes you will find it useful to make or at least to consecrate your own. The advantage of the runes over other divinatory systems is that this is relatively easy. In fact, if you are caught somewhere without your set and you need to do a reading, you can easily make some from pieces of cardboard. When you make your own runes, your energy goes into them and they will respond to your need.

According to the Roman writer Tacitus, the ancient Germans cast lots made of fruitwood for divination (*Germania*, trans. 1942). Norwegian folk tradition as reported by Jane Sibley (1989) includes divination with a set of rune sticks about four inches long. Osborn and Longland (1964) recommend making a practice set from wooden tongue depressors. However, today the most common form for runes is that of small pieces which can be drawn, laid out, or mixed up easily, and are of a convenient size to carry in a pouch.

The most common materials for rune sets are wood and stone. They can also be made out of metal, clay, or bone. My first set was made from plasticine baked in my oven, which preserved my fingerprints in the surface. If you have a good saw, you can cut round cross-sections from a branch to make rune disks. Oak, ash, rowan, yew, beech, and birch are all sacred trees. Fruitwood can be used as well. Cross-sections of antler are another possibility. If you cut the wood from a living tree, remember to explain to the tree what you are doing and ask its permission; thank the tree and offer some of your blood or saliva to the stump after you have cut your branch. Ideally, wood for magical purposes should be cut during a waxing moon.

A section about an inch and a half in diameter and a quarter-inch thick is a convenient size. The bark can be left on or removed. Another option is to buy a bag of wood "buttons" from a woodworking or fine lumber store. These are the round disks of wood inset in furniture to cover countersunk screws, about the size and shape of checkers, made of natural hardwood such as beech, birch, or oak. Stones are heavier to carry, but have a good feel. Some people have made runestones by engraving the polished rocks sold for games of Go. Another source is water-smoothed "skipping" stones found on the beach or in streambeds.

The Eddas contain references to scratching or incising, carving, and burning the runes. For carving, woodworkers' tools, a graving tool, or a small, sharp penknife can be used. Runes can also be burned into wood or bone with a wood-burning tool. Electric engraving tools meant for inscribing serial numbers on metal to prevent theft are available cheaply from hardware stores and can be used on metal, bone, or stone. The inscriptions on Scandinavian runestones were often colored red, and it seems probable that the references to coloring, dyeing, or staining the runes refer to this practice. Painting the runes after you have incised them will also make them more visible.

If you already have a set of consecrated runes, you may choose instead to create a wand or staff on which the runes are graven as your work for this study.

Consecrating Your Runes

You can consecrate your runes in a number of ways. The red color used to stain the runes on Viking runestones suggests blood, a primary source of magical energy. In folk magic, all bodily fluids are considered powerful. Ethical considerations aside, these days it is not generally practical to use the blood of animals, but the one source of blood we are free to use is our own. Women have an advantage here, since moon blood is especially powerful, but pricking one's finger with a sterile needle will provide enough blood to stain one or two runes. Mixing your saliva with the red paint with which you will go over the incised runes will also create a physical connection. Water-based acrylic paint wears well. You can use a dry cake of watercolor or powdered poster color, or grind your own pigment from stone.

Here's one way to bless the runes you are making. Make sure you will not be disturbed and collect your materials. Lay out a clean white cloth with a candle and matches, salt, and a small bowl of water. You will also need the rune/s you are consecrating, an incising tool, pigment, brush, and/or a needle, and (if your runes are wooden) furniture wax or another sealant. Perform this ceremony during a waxing moon, or (if you are a woman) when your moon blood is flowing, or on a Wednesday:

1. Carry the lit candle clockwise around the space to *sain* (sanctify and purify) it. Say something like:

> Life light, sun bright,
> with sacred fire I sain this site!

2. Invoke Odin as master and giver of the runes, and Earth (Erda) as Mother and source of your materials, since the purpose of this rite is to evoke the spiritual pattern expressed by the rune into manifestation in the physical wood or stone.

3. Set the rune disk on top of the salt in the dish. Settle yourself comfortably and focus as you do when preparing for meditation.

4. Draw the rune on your forehead, chant its name, and visualize it vividly, continuing until awareness of this rune and its meaning drives out all else. Take up the disk, and as you continue to murmur the rune name, incise it. Add your blood or saliva to the pigment and color the rune, stating that you are doing this as an offering and a link, so that the rune will speak truth to you. When the rune disk has been inscribed and stained, hold it against your heart or forehead or between your palms, breathe on it, etc., while impressing upon it the image of the rune you have visualized.

5. Name the rune, using your own words or a charm like the following, based on the description of the awakening of humankind in "Völuspá" 18.

> Child of (name the wood or stone)
> I claim you,
> With *Önd* I awaken you,
> With *Odhr* I inspire you,
> With *Lá* and *Læti* and *Litr* I enliven you,
> As the sons of Bor gave life to humankind.
> As this water sprinkles you,
> To you this name I fasten;
> From henceforward (Rune name)
> shall you be.

Önd is spirit, the breath of life; *Odhr* is inspiration, or sense; and *Lá*, *Læti*, and *Litr* are shape, movement, and health; sometimes translated as soul, sense, and being. Sprinkling with water was used in pre-Christian naming rituals in the North.

6. If the runestave is made of wood, or a watersoluble paint is being used, it should be finished by sealing it with wax or a coat of thin lacquer; though this may be done later. When you have completed the naming rite, thank the gods and open the sacred space by turning counterclockwise.

7. Keep your runes in their own bag, preferably made from a natural material such as linen, wool, or leather. You may also keep in the bag a casting cloth of plain white silk, linen, or cotton.

THE GROUP RITUAL

The central part of the ritual for this meeting (which you will find on page 263 in the second part of this book) is a pathworking, or guided meditation, describing a journey to the Worldtree to encounter the runes. If you are working alone, you may want to read the meditation onto a tape and play it during your ritual. Allow about four long beats between the in and out breaths at the beginning, and pause where there are gaps. You may then also sing the futhark song included with the ritual.

Chapter 2

FEHU and URUZ

FEHU AND URUZ WORK WELL AS A PAIR because they both have to do with the manifestation of productive energy. In the case of FEHU, this force is primarily directed toward growth and wealth, luck and love, while URUZ is both more powerful and more abstract, governing physical health, or even the manifestation of divine energies on the physical plane.

THE FIRST RUNE: ᚠ FEHU

Pronunciation: "FAY-hu"
Meaning: Wealth (Cattle)

FEHU is herds and fertile fields
Freely, Freyr finds wealth for friends.

The Ancient Meanings

"Wealth" is the first and most basic meaning for the first rune in the futhark in all the old rune poems. It was the origin of the English word "fee." However, the word itself originally meant livestock, especially cattle. Latin made the same associations—our word "pecuniary" comes from the Latin *pecus*, a cow—demonstrating that for the early Indo-Europeans, wealth was not only transferable, but could move under its own power. Like the Celts, the early Germanic peoples were a cattle culture. Dairy products were a staple of the diet. The most valued beasts were kept through the winter in one end of the communal longhouse. The animals which could not be fed until spring were sacrificed to honor the gods and feed the people. One way or another, wealth was counted in cows.

However, prosperity can be a mixed blessing. The Anglo-Saxon rune poem is the most sanguine:

> ᚠ *[feoh] byþ frofur   fira gehwylcum;*
> (Wealth be by all very much welcomed;)
> *sceal ðeah manna gehwyle   miclun hyt daelan*
> (Each man shall deal it out freely,)
> *gif he wile for drihtne   domes hleotan.*
> (If he will from the Lord get approval.)

In the Norwegian rune poem, the fact that wealth is not always a blessing is also made quite clear.

> ᚠ *[Fé] vaeldr fraénda róge;*
> (Wealth causes trouble among relatives;)
> *føðesk ulfr í skóge.*
> (The wolf is raised in the forest.)

And the Icelandic poem agrees:

> ᚠ *[Fé] er fraenda róg*
> (Wealth is trouble among relatives)
> *ok flaeðar viti*
> (and fire of the sea)
> *ok grafseiðs gata.*
> (and path of the serpent.)

Probably the most dramatic example of wealth causing trouble among relatives in Germanic literature is the story of the treasure that Siegfried wins from Fafnir (who has taken the form of a dragon to guard it). It has already caused several deaths before he gets it, and impelled by greed, his wife's brothers finally kill him. Their refusal to reveal its hiding place leads to their deaths in the end. In the *Nibelungenlied*, Siegfried's murderer, Hagen, finally dumps the gold into the Rhine, an exploit still celebrated by a statue in the city of Worms.

Perhaps the advice offered in the Anglo-Saxon poem can help one avoid the problems predicted in the Northern verses. If wealth is shared while its owner is still living, there will be nothing for the heirs to fight over. In Iron Age society, generosity was the greatest of virtues. In the "Hávamál," several verses underline the connection between cattle-wealth and the right use of prosperity.

> Full-stocked folds   had Fitjung's sons,
> Who bear now a beggar's staff;
> Wealth is brief   as the wink of an eye,
> Of friends, 'tis most false.
> The unwise man,   if he should get
> Wealth or woman's love,
> His arrogance grows   but not his sense—
> On he goes, deep in delusion.

> ("Hávamál": 78-79)

The moral is clear—wealth is to be guarded, but not hoarded. Nor should it lull one into a false sense of security. Welcome though it may be, it must be taken as a gift of the gods. Neither the fruits of the earth nor the love of others can ever be owned (the last verse implies a special warning not to treat women as property!). They are loaned to us only, to be used productively and shared with others. True riches are the wealth the soul gains from a life well-lived.

Modern Meanings

Meanings ascribed to this rune by modern commentators range from the mystical to the practical. Willis believes that the kind of wealth represented by cattle is that which grows when cared for, which can produce more money when wisely invested, but that the rune sometimes means the need to conserve resources. Thorsson, on the other hand, sees in the rune motion and expansion of power, mobility, luck, and fertility.

It seems logical to associate this rune with the Norse deities of wealth and prosperity, Freyr and Freyja, whose names begin with the same sound. Their names mean "Lord" and "Lady" in Old Norse, and one wonders if the "Lord" in the Anglo-Saxon rune poem originally referred to a similar figure (the term, *drihtne* refers to the leader of a war-band, and both Freyr and Freyja had a warrior aspect as well).

Freyr and Freyja are the second generation of the Vanir, the other clan of gods. They govern the fertility of the land and the creatures that live upon it, especially the increase of flocks and herds. As fertility deities, their influence extends naturally into the area of love, on the one hand, and commerce, on the other. In this context, Aswynn suggests that the rune should also be connected with Njordh, god of commerce on the sea.

In earliest times, Freyr's animal may have been the deer (the "horned beasts" herded by Robin Hood). Certainly the rune has the appearance of the antler, which will be Freyr's only weapon at Ragnárok, the final battle with the Giants. Freyr's sword was the payment given to Skirnir to win the giant-maid Gerd as the god's bride. She finally agreed to tryst with him at the sacred barley field. Clearly the complex of motifs associated with the Vanir is rich in associations with fertility, and bread and beef are still the staple foods of the Northern Hemisphere.

Today, wealth is represented not by cattle, but by money, which is also a symbolic form of energy. Money gives power, but it becomes useless if it is conserved too tightly. For the community to prosper, money and energy have to move on.

If horned beasts belong to Freyr, gold is an attribute of Freyja. Her best-known possession is the necklace Brisingamen, acquired by exchanging sexual energy for the skill of the dwarf smiths. When she searched the world for her lost lover, she was said to have wept tears of gold. The first episode in the conflict between the Aesir and the Vanir occurs when a Gullveig ("Intoxication of Gold"), who is usually considered an aspect of Freyja, enters the hall of the High One.

> The war I remember,   the first in the world,
> When Gullveig with spears was gashed
> And in the hall of Hár she was burned.
> Three times burned,   three times reborn,
> Often and again,   yet ever she lives.

("Völuspá": 21)

After this demonstration, the gods decide that making a treaty with the Vanir is the better part of valor, and Freyr and Freyja go to Asgard in the exchange of hostages. Is Gullveig inherently dangerous, or are the problems caused by the gods' hostility? The power represented by Gullveig is a basic human drive, and although greed can cause serious problems, when gold delights instead of destroying, even its enjoyment can be a positive thing. To be productive, the force of FEHU must be kept in motion by the exchange of GEBO or the harvesting of JERA.

Gundarsson points out that the word "fire" is often used in kennings for gold, as in "fire of the dragon's bed" or "fire of the creek." At certain times a flame was believed to burn above burial mounds in which treasure was hid. Whether in the form of gold (symbolizing and facilitating the exchange of energy among living things) or the sexual energy that is the immediate cause of physical fertility, FEHU carries a fiery power. It can represent the life force, or *hamingja*.

Interpreting and Using FEHU

FEHU is always a rune of productivity, though the context may vary. Spiritual or artistic creativity, physical fertility, or the ability to create or to maintain wealth can be indicated, or it may signify an improvement in one's finances or health. If FEHU is surrounded by runes of caution, it may indicate a need to conserve physical or emotional resources, or suggest poverty and an inability to use the resources at hand. If you are using FEHU in a spell or invocation, be sure to specify which kind of fertility you mean, or you may find that it is your "flocks and herds" (especially cats) that are increasing instead of your bank account. Inscribe this rune in gold ink on your checkbook. In spells, pair this rune with GEBO to promote exchange.

FEHU is also one of the runes used in gardening, when you are trying to encourage your plants to flower and grow. Write it on a stave (or on the back of the plastic tag with the name of the plant that comes stuck in the flowerpot) and stick it into the ground. Other runes that can be used for this purpose are: URUZ, JERA, and INGWAZ, for reasons which will be obvious when we come to discuss them.

FEHU can be used in any work having to do with the Vanir in general, or with Freyr or Freyja. Inscribe it on the forehead to increase attractiveness and sexual vigor (but formulate your intention clearly so that you will get love rather than fertility, unless, of course, you are trying to conceive). FEHU is one of the runes used to invoke passion, productivity, and prosperity in a couple being married.

When FEHU appears in a rune reading, it can refer to any of the above, depending on the nature of the question and the runes that surround it. For instance, if it was the first rune in a group of three drawn to illuminate someone's present situation, it would probably indicate that the activities implied by the other two would prosper. For example, FEHU, MANNAZ, and OTHALA would be a very good combination for someone about to set up a new household. It is generally considered to be a fortunate rune.

THE SECOND RUNE: ᚢ URUZ

Pronunciation: "OO-rooz"
Meaning: Aurochs (Wild Ox)

URUZ, Aurochs, urges earthward
Spirit strength to shape creation.

The Ancient Meanings

Continental and Scandinavian sources differ on the meaning of this rune, but most modern commentators have followed the Germanic interpretation, which is that URUZ refers to a wild member of the cattle family—an aurochs, the wild cow, or perhaps a bison (the European woods bison, or wisent). Northern meanings are less conclusive. The Norwegian rune poem gives the word the meaning "slag," while the Icelandic makes it "rain" or "drizzle." In German, *Ur* is also a prefix designating something as original or primordial.

The Anglo-Saxon rune poem gives the clearest description.

> ᚢ*[ur] byþ anmod ond oferhyrned,*(Aurochs is fearless and greatly horned,)
> *felafrecne deor, feohteþ mid hornum*
> (A very fierce beast, it fights with its horns.)
> *mære morstapa; þæt is modig wuht.*
> (A famous roamer of the moor, it is a very courageous animal.)

Here, the beast referred to is definitely the aurochs, the ancient, wild, long-horned black ox of Europe, which could measure as much as six feet at the shoulder. Tacitus refers to killing a wild cow as a rite of passage among the young men of the third-century Germanic tribes. The aurochs is portrayed in Paleolithic cave paintings, and survived in Europe until 1627, when the last known animal was killed in Poland.

The Icelandic rune poem gives a different interpretation.

> ᚢ*[úr] er skyja gratr*
> (Drizzle is weeping of the clouds)
> *ok sakara þerrir*
> (and destruction of the hay-harvest)
> *ok hirðhis hatr.*
> (and abhorrence of the herdsman.)

In this version, we have what appears to be a straightforward description of what happens when it rains at the wrong moment during the growing season. The Norwegian rune poem quoted below is even more obscure. Is the movement of reindeer over the snow being compared to the way slag rises to the top of molten iron, or are the two statements parallel interpretations of the word *Ur?* If the latter, at least we have in the reindeer another large, horned beast to add to the collection.

ᚢ *[úr] er af illu jarne:*
(Slag comes from poor iron:)
opt løypr ræinn á hjarne.
(Often the reindeer runs over the hard-frozen snow.)

At first glance, all of these interpretations would seem to be to be contradictory. However, a synthesis of modern commentators leads to some ingenious interpretations involving the ways in which wild energy can be brought into manifestation.

Modern Meanings

All of the modern writers on the subject follow the aurochs interpretation for the meaning of this rune. For Thorsson, URUZ is Audhumla, the primal cow who was born when the cosmic fire met the primal ice. Her licking released the first being, Buri, from the ice, and her milk fed the giant Ymir, from whose body the world was made. Thus, URUZ is the archetype, the pattern of creation whose energy shapes matter, the wild force of creation. He notes that the horns of the ox point up, but the rune points down, releasing spiritual energy into manifestation.

Gundarsson relates the "slag" and "drizzle" of the Scandinavian rune poems to the endless process of patterning, cleansing, and reshaping that is the work of URUZ. It is the power drawn up by the Worldtree only to be released back into the Well of Urdh. This twin power of shaping and nourishment is symbolized by the two beasts that graze on the upper limbs of the Tree, the goat Heidhrun, who gives enough mead to satisfy all Valhalla's heroes, and the hart Eikthyrnir, from whose horns flow the liquid that fills the cauldron-well of Hvergelmir, source of all rivers.

Aswynn's interpretation also focuses on this rune as a source of primal earth energy, a creative force that breaks down old forms and builds up new ones. For her, it also has implications of courage and endurance, and the correct application of aggressive energy. She feels that this energy is a vital part of the healing process.

The opinion of Willis is similar. He interprets the rune to indicate the use of energy and courage to move into a new state or position or to make a change and identifies the rune as one of vitality, health, and fighting spirit.

Osborn and Longland point out that with URUZ, the domestic cattle of FEHU have become wild oxen, fiercely defending their territory. They remind us that horned helmets were worn for religious ceremonies (never in battle) during the early period (the curved horns on the helmets of Bronze

Age votive figures are shaped like those of the aurochs), and they suggest that horns signify the penetration of the other world. In URUZ, the momentum of FEHU can be harnessed to advantage.

A closer look at the Norse creation mythology reveals some interesting conjunctions of imagery. In the Younger Edda ("The Deluding of Gylfi"), Snorri tells us that the various worlds, or states of being, came into existence gradually. Before Midgard (our Earth) was made, Muspelheim, the world of fire, and misty Niflheim existed. When the rivers flowing out of Niflheim "came so far from their source that the yeasty venom accompanying them hardened like slag, it turned into ice. Then . . . a drizzling rain that arose from the venom poured over it and cooled into rime."

A little later we learn that where the frost met the warmth of Muspel it thawed and became the primal giant Ymir and also the cow called Audhumla, who licked away the rime to reveal the first god. In the Younger Edda, we therefore find the slag and drizzle of the Scandinavian rune poems transformed into the archetypal cow of the Anglo-Saxon poem.

Students of Kabbalah will note that many of the characteristics of this rune are reminiscent of Chokmah and Binah, the second and third sephiroth on the Tree of Life. Chokmah is the Divine Wisdom/first vibration/Word, that acts upon the inert matter of Binah to produce creation (as the active fire and inert ice combine to produce Audhumla, who releases the forces that will shape the world. The horns of the ox form a U, producing the sound of the rune. Interestingly enough, the first letter of the Hebrew alphabet is Aleph, the ox (although probably the domestic variety).

Horns were a common feature in early temples—actual bull's horns in Neolithic goddess shrines and the stone "horns of the altar" in Crete and the Near East. They are usually interpreted as representing the male principle, although female wild cattle are also horned. Celtic art includes both horned gods and horned goddesses. Horned headdresses had a ceremonial significance in many cultures, including Sumerian and Egyptian. Bronze-age votive figurines discovered in Scandinavia sometimes have horned helmets, and Celtic horned helms have been found; however, there is no evidence that horned helmets of the sort popularized by cartoons were ever worn by the Vikings in war.

The American equivalent of the aurochs is the longhorn cow, or possibly the bison. The symbolism of the rune is, in fact, strongly reminiscent of Plains Indian concepts of "Grandfather Buffalo." Buffalo was the major source of food and materials for the plains tribes, not owned, but hunted on equal terms. White Buffalo Calf Woman gave the Sioux their sacred pipe and basic religious law. In Africa the wilder aspects of this energy are suggested by the water buffalo path of the orisha Oya. Note also the similarity in the shape of the rune to the traditional representation of Nut, the Egyptian sky goddess who arches over the earth, supporting herself on her hands and feet. Drops of milk from her breasts formed the Milky Way, and her cosmic maternity is like that of the cow Audhumla.

URUZ is the result of a series of transformations that take place in the liminal space where opposites meet. From the chaos of creation, order emerges, personified by the Divine Cow, but it is an order that depends on the tension of opposites. URUZ is energy and sustenance that has to be fought for, and it provides the energy to defend and preserve one's community. However, in a natural society there is a cooperative and religious relationship between hunter and prey; each takes risks for survival, and the hunt is a transformative experience for both. When the uplifted horns of the wild ox sink earthward, the wild energy is changed into available resources, and there is food for both body and soul. This is also the energy that is used in healing, a powerful flow that revitalizes the patient by strengthening the will to live.

Interpreting and Using URUZ

In some contexts, this could be a rune of manifestation—physical resources becoming available, spiritual energy producing results, or the need to organize and pattern energy so that it will be usable. Its position may say something about the physical energy or health of the subject. It could also imply the need to take an active role in getting or protecting resources, including nutrition, and if necessary, to take risks, to be willing to change. In a negative position it might mean that there is difficulty in making a change or a need to get rid of the past. URUZ works to help other forces to manifest. Magically, URUZ is the act of pouring out an offering from the sacred horn. As a rune associated with the slow melting of glacial ice, it may indicate a need to pay attention to the direction in which one is expending one's energy.

In spellwork, URUZ can be used to increase energy or to make potential available, drawn on the forehead, for instance, when one is tired. It helps the powers of other runes to manifest on the physical plane. Combined with FEHU, it promotes growth and prosperity; combined with LAGUZ, it would get things moving or perhaps bring rain. Combined with TIWAZ, it could help bring swift justice.

FEHU AND URUZ: STUDY AND EXPERIENCE

How we can experience the power of these two runes in our lives? How, for instance, does one manifest the prosperity of FEHU? The principles of sympathetic magic would suggest that acting as if you have abundance will encourage it to appear. Obviously one must exercise some discretion—do not go into debt on the assumption that buying a new car will help you to win the lottery! You might, however, manage to get dressed up and go out to dinner, or treat yourself to a hot tub or a massage. Pamper yourself. Do something sensuous. Better still, reevaluate your life to identify areas of abundance you may not have been aware of. Are you rich in friends? In health? In creativity? Money in the bank is not the only kind of prosperity.

To explore URUZ, read about the Norse creation myth in Ellis-Davidson's *Gods and Myths of the Viking Age* or in the Younger Edda (at the beginning of "The Deluding of Gylfi"), and compare it to modern cosmology. Look back at your own beginnings. What is the earliest thing you can remember? At what point do the mists that hide your past begin to thin? Try to identify the events in your life that have contributed most to making you the person you are today. Experience the strength of URUZ by engaging in some strenuous physical activity. Go hiking on a stormy day and pit yourself against the elements. Evaluate your own state of health and make plans to improve it. Draw the URUZ rune on your forehead for energy.

Studying and meditating on appropriate aspects of Norse mythology and culture will also help you to understand these runes. To begin, let's look at the Vanir.

The Vanir

In the prologue to the Younger Edda, Snorri Sturluson tells how the Aesir migrated from the Near East through Germany to Scandinavia. Whether this represents some memory of a Bronze Age movement northward or only the arrival of new ideas and technology from the south has been debated. The Scandinavian archaeological record indicates cultural changes, but relatively little physical change in the population from the first settlements in the Mesolithic on.

On the other hand, there was considerable movement on the Continent— the Goths, for instance, are first heard of living just above the Black Sea. Snorri identifies Odin's original realm as Troy (!), and his history of the Aesir may well preserve some memory of continental migrations, just as the Old Norse version of the Siegfried story, *Volsungasaga* tells the story of the war between the Burgundians and the Huns.

References to the conflict between the Aesir and Vanir in "Völuspá" (21–23) may reflect the process by which the religions of the migrating Germanic tribes and the sedentary folk they found were combined. In the story, a woman called Gullveig, who is believed to be one of the Vanir, comes to the hall of Odin; the gods spear her and three times attempt to burn her, but she survives. It is unclear whether the conflict in which the Vanir break the Aesir battle line occurs before or after Gullveig's visit, but as a result,

> Then came the Powers   to their judgement seats,
> The most holy gods,   and for this held council:
> Whether the Aesir should   were-gild pay
> Or all the gods   should the offerings share?

("Völuspá": 23)

The Aesir decide that since they can't even destroy the goddess, much less the Vanic army, they had better make an alliance, which is confirmed by an exchange of hostages. These hostages are the god Njordh and his children, Freyr and Freyja. According to Snorri, "He brought about a reconciliation between the gods and the Vanir."

Njordh is a god of prosperity with power over the sea. He protects merchants and fishermen. His name is cognate with that of Nerthus, a Germanic goddess described by Tacitus in his *Germania*. According to Roman observations, Nerthus was a goddess of abundance whose shrine was on an island, and whose image was borne in a cart around the countryside to promote a good growing season. Snorri also tells us that Freyr and Freyja are Njordh's children by his sister. I conclude that they must therefore be the offspring of the Germanic earth-goddess who, in the tradition of territorial goddesses, remained in her homeland when her consort moved northward.

In these two pairs we appear to have two generations of deities. Like Poseidon and Demeter, Njordh and Nerthus govern man's use of the fertility of the sea and the soil. A later myth emphasizes Njordh's connection to the earth by wedding him to the Jotun-maid Skadhi; however, her elemental mountains are less compatible with his realm than the sea-girt isle of Nerthus, and the marriage does not last. Freyr and Freyja appear to have more to do with animals—Freyr was honored by stallion fights and has as his weapon an antler, and one of Freyja's bynames is Syr, the Sow. Their personalities are fully developed, and they play a significant part in the legends of Asgard.

Freyr decided when there should be rain or sunshine and controlled the fruitfulness of the earth. He was invoked for peace, plenty, and the prosperity of men. Other Scandinavian fertility gods such as Frodhi and Ing may have been local forms of Freyr, or equivalent deities whose functions were later assimilated to the greater persona. Freyr's images show him with an erect phallus, and his sacred animals were the stallion and the golden boar, Gullinbursti, on which he rode. He also had a magical ship, Skithbladnir. His servant, the magically adept Skirnir, won for him as wife the beautiful Jotun-maiden Gerd. His palace is given as Alfheim, which makes him lord of the Alfar, the semidivine spirits of the ancestors who dwell beneath the earth in their mounds.

Freyja was, according to Snorri, "the most renowned of goddesses." She was a goddess of love and war, who chose half of the slain to dwell in Sessrumnir, the many-seated hall. Her husband was the shadowy figure Odh, who may in truth be Odin, to whom she taught the magic called seidh. Freyja had many names, Mardoll of the Sea, Horn the Weaver, *Gefn the Giver*, and Syr the Sow. Her chariot was drawn by cats, but at times she also rode one of her worshippers, Ottar, in the shape of a boar. In addition, she could fly in the form of a falcon. Her most treasured possession was the necklace Brisingamen, for which she paid the price of a night with the four dwarf smiths who made it. Freyja's epithet was "Vanadis," goddess of the Vanir, and as such, she may be considered the chief of the Disir, the female ancestral spirits who watched over the family.

In many ways Freyja recalls the great goddesses of love, war, and sovereignty of the early Middle East whose chariots were drawn by lions. But she also shows characteristics that are wilder. Of all the goddesses she has the greatest number of animal epithets and often seems to share their elemental nature. To many who worship her today, she is the lady of the beasts as well as the great lady who enjoys the love poetry of men.

A Ritual for Abundance

Whether or not you are working with others with whom you will join in the group ritual at the end of this section, you may want to do some individual ritual or spellwork with each rune. A solo ritual for prosperity, working with FEHU, could begin with the procedure for establishing sacred space provided for the group ritual, or you could simply carry a lighted candle around the room. For the actual working, you will need a bowl of fertile grain (or a mixture of grains, such as barley, wheat, rice, millet, oats, rye, etc.) and a pot of good soil. To make sure that some of those seeds will actually grow, you may want to include a packet of seeds sold for gardening.

Arrange all your materials on a linen cloth on a box or table—somewhere you can reach while sitting comfortably. Invoke Freyr and Freyja and offer them the grain. State very clearly that as each seed in the bowl, once planted, has the potential to multiply, you desire your own work to be fruitful and bring you abundance. Focus on the seeds and visualize them sprouting and flourishing, then visualize your own prosperity as customers, contracts, or some other appropriate form. Affirm that this will be so. Sing the rune into the bowl and draw it through the seeds with your finger. Then plant some of it (at least nine grains) in the pot. When you have finished, open the circle.

Since true prosperity can only occur in the context of a prosperous community, package the remainder of the seed mix to send to friends. Carefully tend the pot of grain that you have planted, and each time you water it, repeat your visualization. Collect the seed heads when the plants ripen and save them for luck pieces or to plant in later rituals.

A Love Spell

The Vanir, Freyja in particular, can also be invoked to bring love into your life. You will need a (preferably green) candle; a stick about three feet long (ideally of fruitwood cut during the waxing moon); a knife; flowers in a vase; some red yarn; a square of fine linen or silk about four inches on a side, needle, and thread; and a bowl of love herbs.

If there are no herb stores in your area, try a generous pinch each of sweet herbs such as lemon balm, basil, thyme, cardamom, cinnamon, cloves, and lavender—all culinary spices you can find at a grocery store—and some dried rose petals. If you do have access to an herb store, however, get one ounce each of several of the following, given by Scott Cunningham as having appropriate associations in British tradition: betony (Latin, *betonica officinalis*; Old English, *betonice*), seed of columbine (*aquilegia canadensis*, lion's herb), gentian (*gentiana lutea*, *mearealla*), lady's mantle (*alchemilla vulgaris*, bear's foot), lavender (*lavandula*, elf leaf), lobelia (*lobelia inflata*), meadowsweet (*spiraea filipendula*, bridewort), periwinkle (*vinca minor*, *maagdepalm*, blue button), southernwood (*artemisia abrotanum*, lad's love or maid's ruin, *aprotanie*), vervain (*verbena officinalis*, *æscthrote*), yarrow (*achillea millefolium*, *yearwe*), thyme, and almost any of the mint family. If you are a man, add juniper berries or rue (herb of grace, *rude*). Ideally, you should have nine kinds of herbs.

Arrange these things on a linen cloth. Carry the candle around the room to establish your sacred space, sit down, and spend a few moments relaxing and focusing, gazing at the flowers. Then close your eyes, and visualize the goddess. To many, she is all golden beauty, but she appears to others as dark—breathe her name softly, adding descriptive phrases—"Freyja, Lady of

Love, come to me, Freyja, queen of cats, come to me, Freyja, Brisingamen's bearer, Freyja, blessed in beauty, etc." until an image is clear.

When you have made contact with the goddess, tell her what is wrong with your love life. Ask her help in understanding what you truly need and how to obtain it; in her presence, you may see things differently. Do not, however, ask her to *make* the object of your affections love you. Relationships formed by force rarely last long or end well. What you should be asking for is to find someone with whom love will be mutually rewarding.

As soon as your need is clear, open your eyes, take the stick, and carve FEHU, ᚠ, for love; URUZ, ᚢ, to bring it into manifestation; NAUDHIZ, ᚾ, for the force of your fate; and JERA, ᛃ, that all may come to pass in its right season, on the bark, intoning each rune as you cut it. You may anoint the runes with a little of your saliva or blood when you are done. Take the flowers and tie them to the top of the stick with the red yarn.

Now pour the herbs into a mixing bowl. As each one goes in, chant its name and stir it with the rune-carved stick, saying, "Betony, [etc.] bring love to me." When all the herbs have been put into the bowl, draw the runes through them with the stick, then stir nine times, chanting:

> Runes root deep as plants in ground,
> Holy herbs to help be bound —
> Uruz, Nauðiz, Jera, Fé,
> Bring my own true love to me!

When you have done this, pour as much of the herbal mixture as will fit into the square of cloth and stitch it up into a closed packet. You may stitch or draw the runes on the cloth. Wear this pouch next to your skin until the next new moon, and after that on appropriate occasions, such as when going out on a promising date. After undoing your circle, take the remaining herbs and the stick to a wild place where the rising sun will fall upon it, dig a hole, and pour the herbs in, then set up the stick above it and go away without looking back.

A Spell for Strengthening

The first rite involving URUZ is one of awakening and affirmation. Basically, it involves indulging yourself in a healing bath. At a time when you can be sure you will not be interrupted, preferably just before you go to bed, purify your bathroom with the smoke of vervain, rosemary, or your favorite herbal incense. Turn out the bulb and light a few candles. Run the bathwater warm, but not overwhelmingly hot, and add a spoonful of salt for purification and a pint of infusion of mugwort or mint, or a few drops of rosemary oil (all strengthening herbs).

Lie down in the bath, and imagine that you are the primal ice being melted by the warmth of Muspel's fires. Let the scented water relax each limb. As the tension leaves each muscle, consciously release it. Float, needing nothing, wanting nothing. When the water begins to cool, get out of the tub.

Draw the URUZ rune on your forehead. Then take a rough towel and rub life back into your limbs. As you do so, imagine that it is the rough tongue of Audhumla, the great cow, licking you free from all that keeps you weak or frozen, as she did Ymir. As you dry each part of your body, say something like:

> This is my foot, strong to stand;
> (this is my mouth, strong in speech, etc.)
> By Auðumla freed,
> By Erda fed,
> By Loður led,
> Thus I reclaim it.

Erda is of course the earth goddess. Lodhur is one of the mysterious trinity of gods who gave life to humankind. His contribution was health and strength. When everything is dry, put on clean nightclothes, drink a cup of warm milk, go to bed, and sleep well.

A Spell to Dispel Illness

If the previous ritual is not enough to energize you, try the following procedure, which uses the energy of URUZ on health problems. Set up your sacred space and light a red candle. You will also need a hammer or stone with the URUZ rune drawn on it (or better still, a drinking horn), a bowl of ice cubes, and a clean cloth.

Begin by identifying those things that are standing in the way of good health for you, not only known health problems, but aspects of your lifestyle that may make it hard for you to stay healthy. Then pick up one of the cubes of ice and give it the name of the problem. If the difficulty is in a particular part of the body, touch the ice to the place until you feel the chill.

When you have named an evil, put the ice cube on the cloth on a hard surface and pick up the hammer, stone, or horn, point down. Wrap the cloth around the cube so pieces won't go flying, and smash the ice, saying something like:

> Ox, Ox, by stone and stock,
> By hoof and horn, remove this block!
> If it be in the limb, if it be in the skin,
> If it be in the blood, if it be in the bone,
> If it be in the head, if it be within,
> Stamp on it, trample it into the stone!

Repeat this process until all the blocks have been dealt with. After you have completed your working, dump the smashed ice at a crossroads or throw it into running water. This spell can also be used to break up other kinds of blocks and barriers. Be careful, however, as releasing this much energy can sometimes have an effect that is as traumatic as the problems it dispelled.

THE SECOND MEETING

The second meeting of a rune study group, like the first, is likely to be to some extent introductory, since the group will still be settling in, and this will be the first meeting at which you are actually discussing the runes. It will probably be useful to review the organizational decisions made at the first meeting and summarize the procedure for the evening. In general it works best to divide the meeting into two halves. The first half, of approximately an hour to an hour and a half, should be devoted to discussion. The group may want to try doing the stadhyr (runic yoga) described by Thorsson in *Futhark*, intoning the runes, or projecting the energy of each rune to a partner (palm to palm) at this time. After a break, the second part of the meeting can be devoted to the ritual.

Encourage participants to share their own interpretations and insights into their meanings. Those who have been reading other rune books can present the interpretations of the writers with whom they are working, and the group can try to identify where the sources agree and where they differ, and speculate on why. Look for "cognate" meanings—archetypal parallels from other cultures with which they may be familiar that illuminate the runes' meaning. This goes for an individual working alone as well, except that you will have to do it all yourself.

A good plan is to spend about a half hour exploring each rune, and then discuss the way they interact. For instance, in considering FEHU and URUZ together, one might look at the balance between generosity and conservation, or the relationship between the herd of domestic cattle and the single wild cow with its suggestions of controlled domesticated energy versus wild force. How does the physical fertility granted by FEHU differ from the primal energy that URUZ brings into manifestation?

Group members may also want to discuss ways in which the forces represented by these two runes can be experienced. You may find that as you study the runes each month their influence begins to affect your life.

Additional discussion can also be spent on aspects of Norse culture or mythology that relate to some issue brought up in the discussion of the runes. This would, for instance, be an excellent time to introduce the Vanir. In addition to the material in this section, you should look at the discussion of Freyr, Freyja, Erda, and the Vanir as a group in *Gods and Myths*.

After the discussion, or during the potluck that follows the ritual, remind everyone that the runes that will be studied next month are THURISAZ and ANSUZ. They should prepare by reading the discussions of these runes in the next chapter and following up as many of the suggestions for further reading and experience as they can.

The Group Ritual

If you are working with a group, the group ritual for these runes is on page 273. It incorporates imagery associated with the runes FEHU and URUZ to draw into manifestation the abundance and prosperity that are the gift of the Vanir. Everyone will need to bring a deposit slip from his or her checkbook or a piece of play money to the ritual.

Chapter 3

THURISAZ and ANSUZ

THE THIRD AND FOURTH RUNES IN THE FUTHARK are both associated with gods. THURISAZ is a rune of Thor, the defender, as well as that of the gigantic forces against which he defends. Thor is the son of Jordh—an elemental earth goddess. His father is Odin, master of all the powers of mind. Together they ward body and spirit. Both are extremely powerful, but their strengths are different.

THE THIRD RUNE: ᚦ THURISAZ

Pronunciation: "THUR-ee-sahz"
Meaning: Thurs, Thorn, Thor

**THURISAZ, the Thorn of Thor,
is Force that frees, or fights a foe!**

The Ancient Meanings

THURISAZ is the third rune of the futhark. The Norse and Icelandic rune
poems agree on the name—*thurs*—a word that is usually used to designate a
supernatural being (usually monstrous), especially a Jotun, one of the titanic
race who are both the ancestors and opponents of the Aesir. However, the
texts of these two poems seem to suggest a type of threat that is less mythic,
but perhaps more immediate, an evil caused by the kind of spirits that in later
generations were classed as "trolls," which haunted the wild.

The Norwegian rune poem tells us:

> ᚦ*[þurs] ældr kvenna Kvillu:*
> (Thurs causes illness in women:)
> *kátr værðr fár af illu.*
> (few rejoice at bad luck.)

While the Icelandic poem elaborates with:

> ᚦ*[þurs] er kvenna kvol*
> (Thurs is the torment of women,)
> *ok kletta bui*
> (and the dweller in the rocks/cliffs,)
> *ok varðrunar verr.*
> (and the man [husband?] of Vardh-runa.)

The significance of the name "Vardhruna," which translates literally as "warding rune," is not known, although it has been suggested that she is one of the Jotnar. The name could come from some lost piece of folklore, or the statement might refer to the magical relationship between spirits and the spells that protect against them. People of all cultures who live close to the land have a keen awareness of the spiritual dimensions of the life around them, a belief condemned by the medieval Church as witchcraft and dismissed by modern researchers as superstition. However, modern science is beginning to discover the dangers in assuming that we understand everything about the world around us. Surely it does no harm to honor the spirit in all things, and it may be a prerequisite to living in harmony.

Power is neutral, capable of being used for good or ill. In the Eddas, the thurses generally appear in a role antagonistic to the gods; the Jotnar, however, are in origin simply the primal powers of Nature. They are neither "good" nor "evil." They are simply "other."

Like the Norse verses, the Anglo-Saxon rune poem treats this rune as dangerous, but the interpretation it offers seems to have been logically derived from the shape of the rune:

> ▶ *[þorn] byþ ðearle scearp; þegna gehwylcum*
> (Thorn is most sharp, for every thane)
> *anfeng ys yfyl, ungemetun rethe*
> (who grasps it, it is harmful, exceeding cruel)
> *manna gehwylcum ðe him mid resteð.*
> (To every man who rests among them.)

One wonders whether the designation of this rune as the "thorn" might be an example of evolutionary etymology. Did the Christian Anglo-Saxon author of the rune poem alter a term that had become meaningless as the language changed by attempting to explain away as brambles the evil that the women of the Norse verses encountered among the rocks? Or was the writer changing a name that appeared to refer to the rejected pagan mythology into a familiar word?

Certainly, to fall among thorns is painful; however, in the ancient world thorns had a number of uses, both physical and magical. Various kinds of berries with thorny stems are a major source of fruit in the North. Brambles can be woven into barriers, and in folktales sometimes a thorn hedge is magically grown to create a protective barrier. Thorns were also used in magic. In the legend of Sigurd we are told:

> On the mountain   a valkyrie sleeps,
> about her flickers   the bane of trees;
> Ygg with the (sleep-) thorn   once did prick her,
> The flax-goddess (woman) felled.
>   A fighter other than the one he wished."
>
> ("Fafnirsmál": 43)

In his paper, "The Thing about Thorns," Stephen Glosecki (1992) has suggested that Grendel overwhelmed the men of Heorot by scratching a sleep-thorn into the beams of the hall, thus making them easy prey. The most direct reference to the use of the thurs rune in magic occurs in "Skírnismál," in the story of Skirnir's wooing of the giant-maid, Gerd, for Freyr, in which he says that she must wed a three-headed thurs called Hrimgrimnir if she will not marry the god, and finishes by the threat of a rune-spell:

> A 'thurs' rune I rist on you   and three more;
> to be desirous, depraved and lewd.
> But I can scratch out   what I scratched on
> If there prove to be no need.
>
> ("Skírnismál": 36)

This final threat is the clincher, and Gerd agrees to be Freyr's bride. The procedure referred to is probably the practice of scratching a runespell on a tree (and scraping it off to remove the spell). It is unclear whether the rune is being used here to represent the thurses to whose embraces Skirnir would condemn the giant-maid, or whether the rune's energy is intended to power the rest of the spell. Perhaps the sharp point of the thorn "injects" the power. In Germanic folk magic, thorns were sometimes used as the physical manifestation of "elf-shot."

Modern Meanings

Contemporary writers have struggled with the problem of how to manage the energy of this rune. Many interpret THURISAZ as the rune of Thor, or of Thor and of the thurses, or Jotnar, as well. In later mythology Thor is said to be the son of Odin, but his mother is Earth (Fjorgynn or Jordh), and his worship as a major deity was widespread and perhaps older than that of Odin. Earth as a primal elemental force is one of the elder generation of deities— the Jotnar (giants), who are the Norse equivalents of the Titans. Thor's primary function in the legends is to slay them, both male and female. His character in the Eddas expresses raw physical power that is used to defend both

Asgard and Midgard from the chaotic energies of the Jotnar. He tells the fer-
ryman:

> Many jötnar there would be   if all were let live,
> Little room in Midgard   would there be for men.
>
> ("Hárbarzljódh": 23)

It should be noted, however, that even Thor does not kill *all* the giants—only
enough of them so that men can survive. The raw power of Nature must be
balanced, not obliterated, and there is some evidence that the Jotnar also
received offerings, especially from those journeying in the wilderness.

According to Snorri, "might and strength were Thor's characteristics, by
these he dominates every living creature" (1987, "Gylfaginning": 10). Thor
was identified with Jupiter, because he is the god of thunder and the sacred
oak (like Zeus, son of Rhea). He can also be compared to the Hindu warrior
storm god Indra. Thor's kingdom is Thruthvangar, his hall, Bilskirnir; his
goats are named Tooth-gnasher and Gap-tooth, and his attributes are the
hammer, Mjollnir, the magic gauntlets with which he grips it, and his belt of
strength. He was often portrayed as red-bearded with exceptionally bright
and piercing eyes.

Thorsson states that the thurs rune represents pure action, potency, raw
power, and strength on the physical plane. It is the projectable form of
applied power, at once the polarized violence of the giants and the force of
Thor that defeats them, the power that releases built-up tension as the lightning releases the power of the storm. James Peterson's interpretation is that
the thurses, or Jotnar, represent elemental, unconscious, irrational, and
chthonic forces. Sibley states that the rune represents divine power active on
the physical plane, a link between the psychic and material realms. It is also
seen as a rune of chthonic, unstructured natural force. It represents those
powers that can grip and seize one with surprise and terror.

This power is also that of regeneration and fertility. During the Viking
period especially, Thor was the most popular of the Aesir. He was perceived
as being both powerful and dependable. Thor's pillars were set up flanking
the high seat in the hall. Oaths were sworn upon his gold or silver ring. He
brought the storms whose rain fed the crops and banished those powers that
would destroy them. His lightning fertilizes the soil by stimulating the for-
mation of nitrates. Thus he was the favorite deity of farmers. There are many
stories about his strength and prowess, often humorous. All his deeds are
done with gusto; he lives in the present and deals with problems forcefully
and immediately.

People wore an image of Thor's hammer for protection and made its sign to hallow food and drink and to bless the bride at a wedding. Aswynn feels that THURISAZ is the third dynamic aspect of the force of fertility introduced by FEHU and URUZ, the third stage in the process of creation described in the Younger Edda. It is therefore an expression of the Jotun-energy of Ymir, the being from whose substance the world was made. One of the forces that the thurs rune can release is the creative power of the libido. It is a symbol of masculine potency, which quickens life in the earth and the wombs of women. Perhaps this is why Petersen believes that the "torment of women" referred to in the Norwegian rune poem is the menstrual cycle, and Wardle identifies it with the pangs of childbirth.

Interpreting and Using THURISAZ

THURISAZ is one of the most powerful runes for use in magic, but as Aswynn points out, it must be handled carefully. Like nuclear power, it is a force that can heal or destroy. The rune also acts as a catalytic force when paired with others and can be added to empower a spell.

Drawing THURISAZ on a sharp object such as a fossil tooth or arrowhead (or an actual thorn) enables it to be used as a focus for the evil being drawn out in shamanic extraction magic (curing elf-shot) or to scratch a spell on something, such as someone's skin or a tree.

One use of this rune and of Thor energy in general is in weatherworking. Drawing it on one's forehead will increase energy, and intoning it as a mantra will help summon or align one with the forces that bring storms. Be careful, however, to study the normal weather patterns for the area and work to strengthen them, or you may contribute to a dangerous imbalance.

In runespells THURISAZ can be drawn to represent either Thor or the Jotnar. Be careful when invoking the latter, however, as their forces are alien to human thought processes, and extremely powerful. In the mythology, the gods interact with both Jotnar and humans, but there are no direct interactions between etins and men. The gods serve as a buffer between us and the raw forces of Nature, and Thor should be invoked as a balance whenever one is working with those powers. Drawing a "hedge" of thurs runes with the points turned outward creates a powerful protective warding.

In readings, Willis feels that the appearance of the thurs rune may mean good luck or assistance, or it may be a warning to take stock and consolidate before moving further or to seek professional advice before making decisions. Depending on the runes that accompany it, THURISAZ could be a warning not to rush into things like a charging billy goat. It can also indicate the presence or need for a condition of health and enthusiasm.

If the question being addressed is a practical one, Aswynn suggests that THURISAZ would indicate conflicts and complexities involving aggression, or possibly psychological problems. If the analysis is psychological, however, the rune might relate to the individual's strength of will and the will that opposes him. In a reading on relationships it might target areas of conflict. In a negative position, it might indicate a need to shake up the individual or situation, or destructive tendencies that must be recognized to be dealt with.

THE FOURTH RUNE: ᚠ ANSUZ

Pronunciation: "AHN-sooz"
Meaning: A God, Mouth

**ANSUZ, OS, is Odin's wisdom
Communicating ecstasy.**

The Ancient Meanings

The meanings ascribed to this rune in the old poems center around the concept of communication, extended to include the god who gave us the runes. The name of the rune in Old Norse is *As*, one of the Aesir, specifically their chieftain, Odin. In Anglo-Saxon the word *As*, "a god' has been Christianized to a Latin word that has almost the same sound—*Os*, or "mouth." According to the Anglo-Saxon rune poem:

> ᚠ *[Os] byþ ordfruma ælcre spræce,*
> (Mouth is the chieftain of all speech)
> *wisdomes wraþu ond witena frofur,*
> (mainstay of wisdom, comfort to wise ones)
> *and eorla gehwam eadnys ond tohiht.*
> (for every noble earl hope and happiness.)

In this description, the rune could refer either to language or its source. The structure of the verse seems to suggest the latter. This is made even more clear in the Icelandic poem, which states:

> ᚠ *[óss] er aldingautr*
> (Ase is the olden-father [Odin],)
> *ok asgarðs jofurr*
> (Asgard's chieftain,)
> *ok valhallar visi.*
> (and the leader of Valholl.)

On the other hand, the Norwegian rune poem interprets the meaning of "mouth" very differently.

> ᚠ *[óss] er fiestra færða*
> (River mouth is the way of most journeys:)
> *for, en skalpr er sværða.*
> (but a scabbard of swords.)

One can understand the second line as a reference to the power of words to calm violence, providing the wisdom for warriors referred to in the Anglo-Saxon poem; however, unless the first line of the Norwegian poem is a metaphor for the point of departure of a shamanic journey, it is tempting to dismiss it as a convenient rhyme!

The Elder Edda is rich in verses referring to the power of words. Words were the chief weapon at the Althing. Among the runes that Sigdrifa offers to Sigurd are the following:

> Speech-runes learn—that no one may seek
> To repay harm with hate;
> Well must you wind   and weave them
> And set them all together:
> When men for justice   are met at the Althing
> And all their leaders are there.
>
> ("Sigdrifumál": 13)

The poem called the "Hávamál," or the sayings of Hár, the High One, is a collection of proverbs attributed to Odin. Many of them warn against speaking too much, or unwisely. "'Tis readily found, when the runes thou ask . . . that 'tis wise to waste no words" (80). The advice against chattering suggests that the stereotype of the strong, silent Northman was an ideal rather than the average, especially when the mead horn was being passed around the hall.

According to the poem, the wise man does not boast, does not tease his table-mates at a feast, and he does not waste words talking to fools.

Unfortunately the poem allows a man more latitude in the matter of truthfulness when courting a woman. "Hávamál," (104–110) also includes the account of how Odin entered the hall of the giant, Suttung, and seduced his daughter Gunnlod, who allowed him to drain from the cauldron called Othroerir ("exciter of inspiration") the mead of poetry, which he then carried home to the gods and to humankind. The result was the gift of verse:

> Then I became fertile   and grew in wisdom,
> And waxed and did well:
> One word to another   word led on,
> One work to another work.
>
> ("Hávamál": 141)

Finally, it is in the poem of Hár that we find the verses describing how Odin discovered/manifested the runes (which I quoted at the beginning of the introduction). This passage leads into a list of runic spells. The fourth spell, is magic for freeing from fetters.

> That fourth I know, if foemen have
> Fettered me hand and foot;
> I chant a charm the chains to break,
> So the fetters will fly off my feet,
> And off of my hands the halter.
>
> ("Hávamál": 148)

The spell to bind a foe's will and slow his movements—the war-fetter—is often referred to in accounts of battles and appears to have been one of the skills in which human "Valkyries" such as Sváva and Sigrún in the Helgi lays were trained. Possibly the procedure included a shriek like that of the Irish raven-goddess, the Morrigan, whose cry unmanned the enemy. However, this verse appears to refer to the breaking of physical bond, and might be interpreted metaphorically as magic to free the tongue-tied and endow the dumb with eloquence.

It is worth noting how many Germanic words for magical practice refer to speech or song. The root of the word *spá* (see Scottish *spae*, English *speak*, German *spahen*) means to prophesy or foretell, and titles such as *spámadhr* and *spákona* (prophecy-man, prophecy-woman) are derived from it. The verb *vitka* meant to bewitch by singing a charm over and is related to words such as the Old Norse *vitki* and the English "witch" and "wizard." "Seidh" magic usually involves a spell, charm, or incantation. The title *thulr*, or "sage," came from the verb *thylja*, to chant or murmur. Its Old English cognate is *thyle*, usually translated as "speaker" or "orator." According to the Old Norse dictionary, the word *vardlokkur*, a "word-locking," or spell-song, may be related to the English "warlock," although this interpretation has been debated. Another set of words for magical incantation are related to the Old Norse *galdr*.

Modern Meanings

Agreement among the ancient interpretations of this rune has led to a general consensus among modern commentators that ANSUZ has to do with communication in general and Odin in particular. According to Thorsson, ANSUZ is the force of creation. *Odhr*, the root word of the name Odin, means "frenzy, inspired mental activity, inspiration." The poetic mead and its vessel are both called Othroerir (exciter of inspiration). This is the rune of the Word—song, poetry, and incantation. Osborn and Longland say that it governs the power of oratory, speech, and poetry, and Willis believes it is a rune of wisdom and knowledge, advice, and teaching. Peterson feels ANSUZ also indicates occult mastery and the sacrifices that entails. For Sibley it is divine power on the divine plane, acting in the spiritual or psychic domains.

Aswynn states that this rune represents consciousness, intelligence, communication, and reason. The Aesir represent the organizing intellectual force that balances the chaotic, chthonic energies of the Jotnar. It is a rune of the element of air, Odin's element, as the medium that carries sound, or even in its atmospheric aspects as wind and storm. ANSUZ is also the energy of prana, identified by the Germanic school of rune magic as "odic" force.

ANSUZ is the rune of the Aesir and of Odin, their chief, especially in his aspect as source of the inspired ecstasy of poetry. This inspiration was gained through the shamanic initiation referred to above in which he hung on the Worldtree and won the runes of wisdom. Odin also bought a drink of wisdom from the well of Mimir by sacrificing his eye. He acquired the mead of poetry by shape-changing and playing the part of the shamanic trickster (the full story is found in "Poetic Diction" in the Younger Edda). The story has certain suggestive features that recall the story of Taliesin and the cauldron of Cerridwen, in which the hero also wins wisdom from the cauldron guarded by the goddess, though in that case, the shape-changing follows the drink instead of preceding it.

In this aspect, Odin is certainly the god of mental powers—all those qualities associated with the element of air, with Mercury, and with the sphere of Hod in Kabbalah. As the High One, Odin gave the gift of *önd*, "spirit" or "breath." His wisdom, however, is ecstatic rather than intellectual. Assisting him are his ravens Huginn (Thought) and Muninn (Memory). When Odin travels the earth in disguise, he wears a broad-brimmed hat and a gray or blue cloak, and is fond of engaging the unwary in riddle games.

In the "Deluding of Gylfi" (Prose Edda), Odin lists alternative names and epithets that are used to refer to him in the literature. It is unclear whether the many names of the god developed because his true name had become too sacred for use or as the result of an attempt to cover all his aspects or simply as an expression of his love of language. An important device in Norse and Anglo-Saxon poetry is the kenning—a description of the thing instead of its proper name (a metaphor), which expresses a rich universe of relationships and perceptions. To understand ANSUZ is to tap into the meaning of language.

Interpreting and Using ANSUZ

In a reading, ANSUZ often indicates mental or creative activity in general and verbal in particular; wisdom, the need for it, also spiritual power as differentiated from physical, or action/development on the spiritual plane. On the physical plane, however, it may relate to problems with breathing or the lungs or the action of the wind.

Aswynn's interpretation for a practical reading are communication and transmission, or an indication of something with sources in the past. For a psychological profile, she suggests that the rune would indicate higher sources of inspiration from without or within. In a relationship, it would have to do with communication between the partners. In a negative position, ANSUZ can mean a separation from one's true spirit, communications problems, or spiritual imbalance.

When the rune appears in a spiritual context it may have to do with inspiration, with ecstatic experience, or with the action of the god Odin himself in the life of the querent or the world. It carries the force of consciousness itself, expanding awareness through the spoken symbols of the runes.

In the "Lay of Sigdrifa," we are told, "Mind-runes learn, if thou shalt become wiser than other men" ("Sigdrifumál": 14). The rune ANSUZ is the most powerful mind-rune of all. It can be chanted, inscribed, or projected to stimulate eloquence and mental activity, and is a good rune for writers or anyone working in creative or intellectual fields.

THURISAZ AND ANSUZ: STUDY AND EXPERIENCE

The Aesir

Studying the first two runes provided us with an opportunity to meet the Vanir. When we reach THURISAZ and ANSUZ, or *As*, which means "a god," or one of the Aesir, we must consider the Aesir, the other family of gods. In the later literature of the North, it is the Aesir who dominate the mythology. The conflict with the Vanir is told from their point of view, and the legends follow their adventures. In Snorri's euhemeristic account, the Aesir were a tribe in Asia Minor whose chieftain, Odin, was king of Troy. They moved north, pausing in various regions so that Odin could sire sons to found royal families, and ended finally in Scandinavia. In one sense this tale is the Norse equivalent of the stories in which Virgil or Geoffrey of Monmouth traces the origins of their nations back to Troy. It is possible, however, that it also reflects a folk memory of an ancient migration north-ward from Scythia to Scandinavia sometime in the Bronze Age.

Among the Norse, as in other cultures, mythology evolved in a continu-ing cycle of syncretism and diversification as clans joined and combined their legends, then split up to develop local variants once more. Germanic mythol-ogy bears a family resemblance (exhaustively explored by Dumézil and oth-ers) to the mythological structures of other Indo-European peoples. However, each region also had its local traditions and deities, whose cults were elaborated in times of separation and combined when a center of cul-tural and political authority developed once more.

Gods, like men, grow and change with the cultures in which they live. Odin, who appears to have begun as a shamanic deity, teacher of cosmic knowledge and master of magic, was the deity best fitted to help the Germanic peoples adjust to the new conditions and cultures they encoun-tered in their migrations, which may account for his eventual predominance.

If the Vanir are seen as the gods of the Neolithic agriculturalists, the Aesir may be considered (from an equally oversimplified perspective), as the deities of the pastoral tribes. Although Snorri presents them as two ethnic groups, it is possible that the predominance of one mythos or the other depended on the lifestyle of the people worshipping them rather than on their ethnicity. The Vanir are gods of the land. The earth mother, although identifiable as a single archetype, has as many local names as there are districts. The Aesir, on the other hand, tend to be function-gods who can migrate with the tribe when it moves on.

According to Dumézil (1973), Indo-European mythologies consist of deities who represent three fundamental principles: (1) maintaining cosmic and juridical order; (2) the exercise of physical prowess; and (3) the maintenance of physical well-being, for example, the functions of the Brahmins or druids, the functions of the kings and warriors, and the functions of the farmers. In the North, the first principle originally required a pair of deities, Odin and Tyr, although Odin later subsumed both aspects, while the second was represented by Thor and the third by the Vanir.

The character and function of Thor are discussed along with the THURISAZ rune. Odin is a more complex deity. His many names demonstrate his multiplicity of aspects. We have already encountered him as originator of the runes. The discussion of ANSUZ focuses on his role in regard to language. As we work our way through the futhark, we will encounter him in many guises.

The Giants

If the Aesir are the function-gods of human crafts, and the Vanir of agriculture, what of the natural forces with which both must deal? When one sifts through the overlay of dualistic mythology, it appears that in Germanic religion this principle may have been represented by the Jotnar—the Giants, or etin-kin. THURISAZ may be a rune of Thor, but Thor himself is the son of Jordh—Earth—identified as a giantess. The rune is clearly that of the thurs, the giant.

In Mediterranean mythology, the Titans play a role that may in its origins be similar. They are an earlier generation of deities, identified with natural forces—the sun, earth and heaven, the sea. In Greek myth, Mother Earth is the Titan, Gaia, while the goddess of the grain and the arts of agriculture is the Olympian Demeter. Zeus defeats Chronos—Father Time—in order to become king of heaven.

In the North, the theological structures are simpler, but I believe that one may identify a similar process of differentiation. The first beings to appear at the beginning of the world are Jotnar. Odin, Vili, and Vé are the sons of Bor, presumably also a Jotun, and it is from the body of the Jotun Ymir that the world is constructed. Throughout the mythology, the Jotnar serve not only as antagonists, but as sources of wisdom, and as a source of mates for the gods as well.

Njordh and Freyr marry the giantesses Skadhi and Gerd, and even Thor is the child of one giantess and sires a son on another, so clearly they are not always enemies. The Norse system seems to produce figures who provide their own balance. The Jotnar give birth to the force that controls them. One may view Thor as the result of the interaction of consciousness (Odin) with primal power. Some of the Jotnar, like Surt, appear only as antagonists, but others, like Utgard Loki, seem to represent primal, chthonic forces that may be dangerous, but are not inherently evil. There is some evidence that individual Jotnar were worshipped in some rural areas. They appear to have been primal powers of the natural world, disruptive or beneficent depending on the situation. Their chaotic energy balances the ordering powers of the gods.

Snorri provides an extensive list of Jotnar in "Poetic Diction." The major classes of Giants include the cliff-thurses, the rime-thurses, and the mist-thurses. They include great lords, such as Starkadr Aludrengr, the "exceedingly wise giant" who was the grandfather of the hero Starkad; Vafthruthnir, who taught Odin wisdom; Aurvandil the Bold; Aegir, who brews great cauldrons of ale to entertain the gods; and Suttung, from whom Odin stole the poetic mead. Loki is a liminal figure between Jotnar and Aesir, able to move in both realms.

Of course the major foes of the Aesir are also Jotnar. In these battles, Thor is the chief champion, slaying both giants and giantesses with gusto. Some of his chief opponents are Hrungnir, whose weapon was a whetstone; Thiazi, father of Skadhi; and Thrym, who stole Thor's hammer. His female foes are even more chthonic and ambiguous, and include Hyrokkin the wolf-rider, Greip, and Gjolp. Their destructions are recounted with gusto, and the tone in which these battles are described may be related to the general anxiety about everything female that developed as the Vikings came under the influence of Christianity.

From this perspective, Ragnarók—the war between the Aesir and the Jotnar that is destined to occur at the end of this age of the world—appears more as a combat between human structuring principles and unbalanced natural forces than a battle between cosmic good and cosmic evil. To deal with the Jotnar, we need to understand the primal and unconscious forces that empower or motivate us. Passions like hatred may be personified as fire-thurses, the Sons of Muspel. The rime-thurses may govern colder passions, like envy or despair.

Thurs-forces can be opposed by rethinking the situation—using words to reconceptualize the problem and structure one's thinking, or by drawing on one's own primal energies. The fourth rune-spell in "Hávamál," (stanza 148) which according to some systems corresponds to THURISAZ, can be considered an active spell by which Thor immobilizes his foes, while the fifth (stanza 149), for ANSUZ, is the spell by which Odin frees those whom the Jotnar have frozen. The choice of which to use depends on whether the threatening force is active or passive.

The group ritual for this chapter aims at bringing Jotun forces into balance and under control. However, in their own realm, they are sovereign and should be honored as natural powers. To work with the Jotnar, you must leave the protected walls of your garth and journey to Utgard—"outside the garth." These days truly wild places are hard to find, but any place where there are growing things, a natural park, a city park or even a vacant lot, is a step in the right direction, especially after dark, when the people go away and the other powers begin to stir.

Go prepared with offerings—biodegradable foodstuffs that can be left on the ground such as crackers and dried meats, dried fruit, and the like, and some milk. Find a secluded spot, and pour or lay out your offerings on the ground, being careful to remove all wrappings.

Sit for a little while in silence, listening to the sounds of the night. Feel the solidity of the earth that supports you and make your prayer to Earth Mother. Send her energy through your palms. One by one, honor the wild powers of the mountains and forests, the sky and the sea. Salute the great ones, the Jotnar, by name: Ymir, from whose bones the Earth was made; Kári, who rides the winds; Löge, elemental fire, and Aegir and Ran who rule the deeps. Seek for the power that rules the region in which you live, and see if it will send you an image and a name.

Honor the smaller spirits, the land wights, as well. Turn in each direction, and ask those beings who guard it to show themselves to you. In the sagas, shamans seeking to spy out Iceland saw it guarded by a dragon, a bird, a bull, and a rock giant, but in each locality the forms taken by the spirits are different. Usually, the shapes in which you perceive them will be those of local birds or animals. Whether or not you see them as creatures who will tell you their names, you can honor them as landvaettir, woods-roes, duergar, nackar, mer-folk, and vind-alfar.

When you have finished, leave quietly, without looking behind you. Remember to honor the spirits of Utgard whenever you are moving between the worlds.

Word and Will

ANSUZ is a rune of word-magic and communication. To experience it, exercises that sharpen the wits and train one in wordcraft are useful. Play games of verbal skill like Scrabble or do crossword puzzles. Tell riddles. While you are studying ANSUZ is the time to go to a reading or a play and practice writing poetry.

If time allows, one interesting exercise for a study group is "Word Wars." This is essentially a free-association game that primes the verbal pump and stimulates the flow of imagery that is the source of poetry. One begins by distributing twenty-four slips of paper, each of which bears a "seed word" that relates to one of the runes so that each person has one or more. These words are: *wealth, horn, strength, breath, wheel, fire, gift, joy, egg, need, cold, year, tree, play, elk, sun, spear, earth, horse, man, lake, power, day,* and *home.*

Together, the group begins to chant the spell. The first person says his or her word, and the next two fill in the blanks in the spell with whatever words they associate with it. The group then repeats the spell and the second person inserts his or her seed word, and the two people who follow free-associate two words, and so forth until all the seed words have been used. A drum beat may be used to help maintain the rhythm.

> **Sing the song and say the spell,**
> **Wodan's winnings from the well,**
> **The word is (seed word) and _____,**
> **and _____,**
> **Write the runes the tales to tell!**

Gealdor (Old Norse, Galdr), or "incantation," is the form of magic specifically associated with Odin. In the legends, all kinds of magic are likely to be accompanied by charms or spells, usually in poetic form, or using poetic techniques such as rhythm, rhyme, and repetition. The ritual for these runes provides one example of how such skills can be used in a magical working.

Germanic Verse Forms

Take this opportunity to study Germanic verse forms. Read *Beowulf* or other Anglo-Saxon poetry in a good verse translation—read it aloud until you have internalized the sounds and rhythms. If you feel really inspired, read Snorri Sturluson's "Poetic Diction" in the Prose Edda (the complete Penguin edition, translated by Anthony Faulkes). The more elaborate Old Norse verse forms may be more than you want to tackle, but a study of the kennings, or metaphors, will give you valuable insight into the workings of the Germanic mind.

The basic Germanic verse form is the four-beat, alliterative line. In Old English poetry, every line is divided into two half lines containing a minimum of four syllables. Two of these syllables in each half line carry a major stress, or beat, and at least one of the stressed syllables in the first half line

must begin with the same consonant sound as the first of the stressed syllables in the second. The form is especially effective if the two stressed syllables in the first half and the first stress of the second begin with the same
sound, as in this example from "The Battle of Maldon":

> *Hige sceal þe heardra, heorte þe cenre,*
> (Soul shall be harder, heart be keener,)
> *mod sceal þe mare, þe ure maegen lytlað.*
> (Courage shall be more, as our might lessens.)

(312–13)

The word translated as "soul" is cognate to the Norse *hug*, the source of the
name Huginn. The word for courage, *mod*, carries implications of will and
emotion, fighting spirit.

For some excellent examples in modern English, see the poetry of the
Rohirrim in J. R. R. Tolkien's *The Two Towers*. The music of the verse is
increased by additional consonance within words; the repeated "d" sounds of
"Riders" and "Theoden," the final "k" in "awake" and "dark." Note that it is
not necessarily the sound that begins a word, but that of the first accented
syllable, that counts.

Your verses may not be as perfect as Tolkien's, but you will find that with
practice the four-beat line comes quite easily. And as for alliteration, after
awhile it becomes almost impossible to avoid.

However, memorizing a dictionary will not make you a good communi-
cator, and knowing how to make verses is not necessarily the same thing as
writing poetry. To invoke the aid of Odin in wordcraft, you may perform the
following ritual.

Prepare, in your office or the room where you do most of your intellectual work, an altar for Odin. Use a black or dark blue altar cloth. You will also
need a candle (blue or white) and a drinking horn or goblet. For an image,
you can photocopy an illustration, or even use a figurine of a wizard, since
you are addressing the god in his aspect as Master of Wisdom. Also lay on
this altar books that you are studying, or the title page of whatever written
material you are working on. For the offering, prepare a flagon of hon-
eymead or a honey drink made by diluting honey with hot water to taste and
adding a little lemon juice and some cinnamon or other spices.

Prepare your sacred space as usual, light the candle, then pour the honey
drink from the flagon into your goblet or horn. Speak the following invocation which is taken from Paul Edwin Zimmer's collection *Wine of Kvasir*.

Invoking the aid of Odin our father
ᚠ *(Bless me ᚱᚾ.)*
And Bragi the bard-god, the brew of dwarves,
Poetry we pour, the potent drink.
Quaff now this cup of Kvasir's blood,
Remember the roving Rider of Yggdrasil
Stole the stuff to bestow on men.
The gallows-god in Gunnlod's bed
Won the wondrous wine of bards,
And in form of feather flew with the gift,
The magical mead, that men might sing!
Give thanks for the gift to Gauta-Tyr,
And raise now the praise of the Raven-god!

Now, look for a moment at your image, or close your eyes and build up the figure of the god from imagination. Picture him cloaked, with a hat whose brim hides one eye, leaning on a staff. Provide a suitable background, and look for the black shapes of Huginn and Muninn winging overhead.

When you have a clear image, articulate clearly the nature of the word-craft you need help with, whether it be personal communication, technical writing, or poetry. Ask for the gift of inspiration and word skill, ask the god to send Huginn and Muninn to help you with thought and memory.

When you have stated your case, thank the god. Then open your eyes, draw the ANSUZ rune on your forehead, and chant the rune aloud. Finish by taking a drink of the consecrated mead. The rest should be poured out on the earth in offering. As your project progresses, whenever you feel the need of help, light the candle and sit for a few minutes in front of the altar, opening yourself up to further inspiration.

THE THIRD MEETING

The third meeting of the rune group will probably follow the procedure established for the second. By this time the group should be settling down; most members should have acquired the basic resources and developed a pattern for individual study. In the discussion, try to get as much personal involvement as possible. Which activities or meditation practices did people try? How did they work? What is the range of individual reactions and what can we learn from them?

The Group Ritual

The ritual for the runes THURISAZ and ANSUZ is on page 283. It incorporates imagery associated with these runes and its purpose is to use the magical craft of ANSUZ to control the energy of THURISAZ, specifically in the area of weatherworking, whether you need more rain or less.

Chapter 4

RAIDHO AND KENAZ

YOUR STUDY OF THE RUNES IS NOW WELL UNDERWAY. As you follow this road, you are no doubt discovering that the work has a momentum of its own, and that the longer you work with the runes, the easier it becomes to get involved with each one. But you will also have discovered that your reactions to the various runes are not the same. They are all significant, and all useful, but their applications differ. You may find that a rune like THURISAZ is a powerful tool for working with energy, while KENAZ might seem milder. On the other hand, for another student the relative powers of these two runes might be the opposite. The meanings of the runes are constant, but to each user they resonate differently.

THE FIFTH RUNE: ᚱ RAIDHO

Pronunciation: "Rah-EED-ho"
Meaning: Ride (Cart)

Upon RAIDHO the road is ridden
To work and world around together.

The Ancient Meanings

All the old sources agree that the primary meaning of this rune is horse transportation, riding. The word *raidho* (or *radho*) is an old German spelling. In German and Old English *rad* is the word for wheel. In Old Norse, it would be *reidh*, whose meaning includes both the act of riding and the vehicle in which one rides. The Norse terms *trollreid* and *gandreid* mean traveling in the spirit world. In Old Norse, the word *rádh* means counsel, from the same root as the Old English *rede*. The Norse word *reidhi*, on the other hand, meant "wrath." In writing Old Norse, this rune was used for the "r" sound only in initial and medial positions. When it terminates a word, as in Freyr, the sound was actually somewhere between an "r" and a "z" and is spelled with the Elk rune ELHAZ, (ᛉ) when writing in the Elder Futhark, and with the Yew rune, YR, (ᛦ) when the Younger Futhark is used.

The old rune poems focus on riding astride, as in the Icelandic poem:

> ᚱ *[reið] er sitjandi sæla*
> (Riding is joy of the rider)

> *ok snuðig ferð*
> (and a speedy journey,)
> *ok jors erfði.*
> (and the labor of the horse.)

and the Norwegian:

> ᚱ *[Ræið] kvæða rossom væsta;*
> (Riding is said to be worst for horses;)
> *Reginn sló sværðet bæzta.*
> (Regin forged the best sword.)

Both verses are more sympathetic to the horse than to the rider. The second line in the Norwegian poem is a puzzle. In the *Volsungasaga*, Regin was the dwarf smith who fostered the hero Sigurd and raised him to kill the dragon Fafnir and recover the gold of Andvari. The "best" sword, referred to in the second line, is presumably Gram, given by Odin to Sigurd's father, Sigmund, later shattered by the god, and finally remade by Regin for his fosterling. Gundarsson suggests that this line shows the need to act at the "right" time.

The Anglo-Saxon rune poem elaborates on the same idea, as do the Norse poems, but even more vividly.

> ᚱ *[Rad] byþ on recyde rinca gehwylcum*
> (Riding is in the hall for a warrior)
> *sefte, ond swiþwæt ðamðe sitteþ ond ufan*
> (soft, more strenuous when astride)
> *meare mæganheardum   ofer milþaþas.*
> (A great stallion pounding the long mile paths.)

This verse especially conveys swift motion and a sense of purpose. As Osborn and Longland point out, the riding here is being done on a horse that is under human control. The distinction between the "soft" life in the hall and the more strenuous existence on the road suggests the need for hard experience and action. Riding long distances grants perspective. It has also been construed to mean a raid (which was often done on horseback, especially on the Scottish borders).

Modern Meanings

RAIDHO is at once the act of moving and the vehicle that contains what is moved. The turning of its wheels governs all rhythmic, cyclical actions.

Thorsson defines RAIDHO as the vehicle, and the road it takes, the Way. According to him it governs rhythmic action and organized activity (including institutions such as nations or religions), the forms of things. It is the rune of logic and proportion, of cognition, also the path of rightly ordered action—ritual working—the roadways by which one travels between the worlds. For Peterson, it is the chariot of the sun, travel, speedy (especially electronic) communication, the sun's vitality and potential brought into manifestation. It covers the creation and transmission of information and goods. It is also sometimes called the Wagon rune, and as such, may be ascribed to Aku-Thor, the charioteer, whose goat's hooves and wagon wheels go thundering across the world.

Aswynn suggests that the name of this rune is also cognate with the Gothic *raiht*, which means "right," perceiving the correct and just way to go. This was the way that the mounted knight of chivalry was expected to follow, and he had the power to defend the rights of others as well. She interprets the rune to indicate the need for personal responsibility, to decide what is right and to exercise control over what path one follows. The individual should control his or her ego as the horse is controlled by the rider. For her, RAIDHO is primarily a rune of divine order as well.

Gundarsson's discussion integrates the ideas of the sun wheel and the divine order by focusing on the function of solar measurement in defining the order of the year. As a rune of right order, the god to whom it relates would be Forseti. The Sanskrit *rita* is the *solarhringar* of Iceland, upon which are marked out the hours of the day or the seasons of the year. Certainly the correct functioning of earthly life depends on the journey of the sun. In either case, as he points out, the measurements are "right" because they are appropriate to the situation.

Perhaps the best discussion of Old Norse concepts of time and spatial relations is found in Kirsten Hastrup's *Culture and History in Medieval Iceland* (1985). Time was commonly calculated by observing the movement of the sun past natural features around the farmstead that served as "day-marks." Observation of the sun's rising therefore served to integrate the individual in both time and space. Right and wrong were defined by relationship and motion. Gundarsson suggests that in spiritual work, the horse being ridden is the *fylgja* (personal guiding spirit), and the rhythm of motion is the drumbeat that carries the spirit on its journeying. We will encounter this association again more strongly in our discussion of the Horse rune, EHWAZ.

One of the most remarkable achievements of Bronze Age Scandinavian art is the "Sun-wagon of Trundholm," a horse and wagon that support an exquisitely ornamented golden disk. Sun wheels, horses, and wagons are also inscribed on the stones of the Bronze Age grave of Kivik, in southern Sweden. In Norse mythology, many of the gods have wagons that their totem creatures draw. A ritual wagon was used to carry not only the Sun, but the gods when they visited their people. Tacitus describes this custom among the early Teutons in Denmark, where the deity in question was the earth goddess, Nerthus, and general truce held during her journey. There is a later description in the Old Norse book, *Flateyjarbok*, in which a wagon carried the image of Freyr, who was served by a priestess, around Sweden each autumn. Apparently the suddenly increased weight of the wagon indicated the god was present, and the phenomenon may have been used for divination. Whether the wagon carried the Lord or the Lady, the custom seems to have been part of the worship of the Vanir. Its progress ensured peace and plenty for the land.

The riding of a single steed, whether it carries a knight on his way to do justice or bears the shaman on his journey, is an individual act, requiring personal responsibility. A cart is a vehicle in which many can ride to the same place in the same way. RAIDHO is therefore not only a rune for the personal journey, but one that governs the organizational forms required for people to work together. Although that movement may involve repetition, these forms must keep moving to function. They are useful not for their own sake, but because they enable people to reach their goal.

Interpreting and Using RAIDHO

RAIDHO is particularly useful as a journey rune. It can be chanted for protection while traveling or inscribed on car charms, baggage, or letters to help them arrive safely at their destination, especially joined in a bindrune with ELHAZ. For Willis, it is primarily a rune of travel, indicating a journey or a message, or possibly negotiations or discussions. When paired with ANSUZ, it may indicate misleading or ambiguous messages or business dealings.

This rune may refer to organizations, people working together, structure, or forms. In the Anglo-Saxon rune row, it implies a horse, not a wagon, but in either case, it means movement. There is also an implication of communication, since messengers rode horseback. In a reading, it could mean any of the above, or change, going into a new situation, or having something new coming into your life from outside.

Other implications have to do with giving or receiving advice or counsel, with following directions or plans, or with change and movement in general. The appearance of this rune could indicate a movement that brings order to chaos. In a contrary sense, it might point to a change in direction.

THE SIXTH RUNE: ᚲ ᚴ ᚳ KENAZ

Pronunciation: "KEN-ahz"
Meaning: Torch

KENAZ kens creation's fire;
With torch transforming hearth and hall.

The Ancient Meanings

This rune name seems to have originated in the Old Germanic *kien*, meaning a pine or fir tree, which led to the Old English meaning of *cen*, a torch, whose simplest form was a pitchy knot of pine. The Anglo-Saxon rune poem describes the domestic uses of the pine torch. Osborn and Longland point out its emphasis on warmth, light, a protected environment. It is a rune of hearth and home, the safe setting in which even the noble warriors can take their ease.

> ᚳ *[Cen] byþ cwicera gehwam cuþ on fyre*
> ([Torch] to the living familiar aflame,)
> *blac on beorhtlic, byrneþ oftust*
> (Is blinding and brilliant, it burns most often)
> *ðær hi aeþelingas inne restaþ.*
> (Where royal folk within are resting.)

Although the Scandinavian poems give the rune a different meaning, images of fire and firelight are common in the Eddas. In the verses below, the first verse has the fire signifying hospitality. In the second, the image of one torch lighting another seems to signify what should happen when the guests are gathered and the conversation takes fire as speakers are inspired by each other's eloquence.

> Fire he needs   who now comes in,
> Cold to the knee;
> Food and clothes   are what a man needs
> Who fares over the icy fell.

("Hávamál": 2)

> Brand from brand kindles   until it's burned,
> Spark kindles from spark,
> Man becomes wise   by speaking to men,
> But gets dull, staying dumb.

("Hávamál": 57)

However, the German term for an evergreen was not carried over into Old Norse, which appears to have interpreted the rune name as the Norse word nearest in sound, *kaun*, meaning a boil or scab. This interpretation is reflected in the Norwegian rune poem:

> ᚲ *[Kaun] er barna bœlvan;*
> ([Sore] is fatal to children;)
> *bœl gørver nán fœlvan.*
> (Death makes a corpse pale.)

as well as in the Icelandic:

> ᚲ *[Kaun] er barna bol*
> ([Sore] is the bale of children)
> *ok bardaga for*
> (And a scourge,)
> *ok holdfua hus.*
> (And the house of rotten flesh.)

In both verses, the sore or ulcer is afflicting children and leads to death. Gundarsson attempts to reconcile the conflict between the meanings of the Anglo-Saxon and Norse verses by noting that in the earlier period, the bones of the dead were prepared for burial by allowing the flesh to decay in the "house of rotten flesh" (an unsealed mound), whereas later, it was burned away in the funeral pyre.

Modern Meanings

"Torch" seems the most useful interpretation for this rune, although heat is also implied by the root meaning, "sore." The simplest form of torch was simply a pitchy pine knot. Torches were made by binding together chips of wood with a mixture of tow and trimmings from flax and hemp and soaking them in some flammable material such as beeswax or resin. The English "keckie" was a hollow stem of cow parsley packed with tallow-soaked tow. Wardle gives the meaning of the rune as "pitchflare," relating it to the Norwegian word *kjønrøk*, "lampblack," and connecting the Gothic rune name *chozma* with the Greek *kausima*, "firewood."

Torches were used not only to light great halls, but to light the way in ritual. The Greek goddesses Hecate and Selena are commonly portrayed with torches in their hands. The rune could therefore signify both physical and spiritual enlightenment. Carrying fire around a property (presumably in the form of torches) was the traditional Norse ritual for claiming it, in both the legal and religious sense, to establish the boundaries of the odal ground.

Another popular interpretation identifies KENAZ with the fire of the forge. For Thorsson, it is a rune of creativity and craftsmanship, shaping things by control over fire, forcing dissolution of the old in order to reshape it. Thorsson cites the figure of Volund—the Wayland Smith of English tradition, and the semidivine smith of Germanic legend, who was captured and hamstrung by king Nidlod and forced to serve him. Eventually he took a terrible revenge and escaped with the aid of a pair of wings he had crafted. Aside from a reference in the Old English "Deor's Lament," the oldest surviving form of the story is the "Völundarkviða" in the Elder Edda. An excellent modern treatment of the theme is found in Michael Scott Rohan's trilogy, *The Winter of the World* (1989–90), especially Volume III: *The Hammer of the Sun*.

Gundarsson interprets the fire of KENAZ as the initiatory forge within which the shaman or king is purified and transformed. In his interpretation, initiation takes place in the forge of the smith, or the forge of the earth goddess, the mound. KENAZ is a rune "of unmaking for the sake of remaking." The fire within the mound also suggests the fire drake, the hidden power of wyrd—the potential destiny about which we will learn more when we study NAUDHIZ. Aswynn points out the relationship of the Anglo-Saxon rune name to the Germanic verb *kennen*, "to know" "surviving in Scots border dialect, as in "D'ye ken John Peel," for example, suggesting that one meaning of the rune is the torch of knowledge. However, it might also be related to the Dutch *kunst*, an art or craft, or even the Old English *cyning*, a king, the head of a group of "kin," expression of its consciousness and high priest of its mysteries. In the "Rigsthula," it is Heimdall who teaches the runes and the art of governing to his son Kon.

Einar Haugen (1985) suggests that the "Lay of Grimnir" represents a ritual of kingship. In the poem, King Geirrod imprisons Odin between two fires for eight nights without food or drink. On the ninth day the king's son gives him a horn of mead and is rewarded by receiving the sacred knowledge that he will need to function as ruler and high priest of his people and a prophecy, almost instantly fulfilled, that he will inherit his father's throne. Haugen speculates that the priest of Odin might have fasted between the hearthfires until he reached the requisite state of ecstasy in which to convey the knowledge necessary to initiate the new king.

Fire is also traditionally associated with sexuality ("carrying a torch," "burning with passion," etc.), and the sexual drive can be diverted into positive paths—spiritual or artistic fertility—or negatively, into violence. For Willis, KENAZ is body heat, vitality and stamina, recovery from illness or ill fortune, and positive action in sexual or other relationships, the gift of male life force, primal fire, creativity. According to Alfred Kallir (1980), the Old English *cennan* means "to beget, from the body or the mind," and may even be related to the root for "cunt." All this would support the sexual connotations that this rune has in much of the recent literature. A German tradition, picked up by Gundarsson, connects it with the goddess Freyja. The form of the torch itself is phallic; and the process of making fire with a fire drill can easily become a sexual metaphor.

One must not forget, however, that fire, whether physical or metaphoric, can destroy as well as enliven. Out of control, the hearthfire can burn down the forest. The seventh runespell in the "Hávamál" seems relevant here.

> I know a seventh (spell),   if I see a hall
> Over the feasters blazing,
> Burn it never so bright   yet I can control it—
> That galdor I can sing.
>
> ("Hávamál": 151)

Sometimes the consuming fire is itself the source of healing. The heat of a septic sore is the body's way of defending itself from infection. Cautery, or purification by fire, is a drastic, but effective means of eradicating evil.

KENAZ is the controlled fire of the forge or hearth, or the purifying, transforming, and sometimes consuming fire of the fever or the pyre. It is a potentially violent force, which through craft and knowledge can be brought under control. It is the fire of love, which can also be destructive, or the needfire that is kindled for protection.

Interpreting and Using KENAZ

If KENAZ is associated with runes of fertility or artistry in a reading or runespell, it probably will mean creative work; if it is combined with runes of strength, it may mean purifying force or uncontrolled passion. If the context is mystical, it might mean illumination. Gundarsson says it means controlled fire, destruction for the purposes of creation, or in a negative context, disintegration without reintegration or unguided shaping. For Peterson it means affliction, distress, something that will get worse if left unattended. Aswynn, on the other hand, associates it with clarity of thought, insight, and concentrated effort. It is used to throw light on difficult questions and illuminate the hidden causes of problems. It can be used in conjunction with RAIDHO and EHWAZ for spirit travel, to light the way, as a weapon or a light to attract good influences.

RAIDHO AND KENAZ: STUDY AND EXPERIENCE

The Right Road

RAIDHO is a rune that can be experienced physically as well as magically. In one sense, it is our spiritual path, in this case, the Northern Way. But it can also simply refer to traveling. The experience of physical movement can be appreciated for itself or internalized as a basis for meditation. When you go somewhere, even commuting to work, pay attention to the journey. What do you see from a bus that you don't from a car, and how is the experience of driving different from that of being driven? What kinds of skills and awareness are required to move safely through the world? What adjustments do you have to make as you enter a different environment? Are you the same person at work as at home?

If the journey is a longer one, the kind that requires planning and preparation, or involves an unfamiliar mode of transportation, this becomes even easier. Airplane flights are especially good opportunities for working with RAIDHO. Invoke Odin's eight-legged horse, Sleipnir, to help you get off the ground, and sign yourself with the protection rune, ELHAZ (Y), as well as RAIDHO (these two runes can be used to protect your baggage as well). A more traditional form of traveling is horseback riding. If you have never done so, this might be the time to take an introductory lesson, and as you ride, imagine yourself guiding the horse through the forests of a thousand years ago. If you prefer, go for a ride in a wagon. Make or decorate a miniature wagon in which to carry images of the gods at rituals.

Blessing Your Car

A personal ritual for working with RAIDHO is the car blessing. In the old days, protective magic was performed when one was going into a situation of danger—certainly driving a car in today's traffic qualifies! Your goal here is to protect the vehicle from all dangers, internal or external, and to ensure smooth and pleasant journeying. The rite will not take the place of regular upkeep and repair of worn-out parts, but it should give you road luck and ensure that problems only occur when and where you can deal with them.

If possible, precede the working by a thorough cleansing of the vehicle. Wash the car, clear out all the junk inside it, and sweep or vacuum. Moving counterclockwise, smudge the car with any pungent smoke, commanding all ill luck, confusion, and weakness to be gone.

Then, with whiskey, paint, or oil that you have blessed, draw on the hood of the car the rune ANSUZ, ᚨ, and say something like, "Odin, Worldwalker, ward my ways and lead me well." On the passenger-side door draw TIWAZ, ↑, and say, "Tyr the trusty, ward my right from all wights and woe." On the driver-side door draw THURISAZ, ᚦ, and say, "Donar, Defender, ward my left from all wights and woe." At the rear of the car draw MANNAZ, ᛗ, and say, "Heimdall, Father of Men, let no ill overtake me." Draw an ELHAZ rune ᛉ on the roof of the car for general protection. (For more elaborate runic inscriptions, see the discussion of bindrunes in the section on the rune GEBO.) Repeat these invocations aloud when driving in heavy traffic or difficult conditions.

In addition, you may sprinkle the car with water and give it a name, and invoke a car wight to guard it. A charm bag or crystal hanging from the mirror will provide a focus for the spirit to cling to. The runes given above may be inscribed on the tag of the ring on which you keep your car keys so that you invoke them whenever you start the car.

Sacred Fire

Working with KENAZ can also lead to some new skills. Listen to the sword-forging scene in Wagner's opera *Siegfried*. If an opportunity presents itself, watch a blacksmith at work, or learn about how metal is cast and forged. Learn to make a torch, or start a fire with a fire drill.

To make a torch, you will need a piece of pinewood, a handful of kindling, some scraps of natural cotton or linen fabric, a roll of jute twine, and some kind of tar or pitch (look for this in a paint store, but be sure and read the directions so that what you get is not explosive, just flammable, and make sure that the smoke is not poisonous). Split the end of the wood or simply bind the sticks to it, winding them with the fabric scraps and sticking them together with liberal amounts of pitch. Use the jute twine to hold the whole thing together. A somewhat simpler procedure would be to get a kit from a craft store and try dipping your own candles. Consecrate the torch or candle by signing it with KENAZ at various stages in construction and visualizing the brilliance and effect of its light.

In the sagas, there are references to claiming a piece of land by carrying fire around its boundaries, illuminating those borders identified in both human and spiritual realms. Carrying fire around an area is also one method of warding. Torchlight processions are still part of many folk celebrations, and candles are carried around churches to sanctify them even today.

While you are working with KENAZ, ward your home or living space by carrying a candle clockwise (deasil) around it, visualizing a circle of astral flame surrounding it as Odin drew Löge's fire from Brunhild's rock with his spear. As you move around the area to be warded, say something like:

With sacred flame I circle this space.
Needfire now protects this place!

The God/dess in the Cart

In many cultures, torchlight processions accompany the progress of a patron deity. The practice was known in ancient Egypt and can be seen in Catholic Saint's Day parades today. The Germanic version seems to have been especially associated with deities of the Vanir cult and probably predates the Indo-Europeans. Tacitus reports that the tribes of Germany's northern coast

> . . . unite in the worship of Hertha or Mother Earth; and suppose her to interfere in the affairs of men, and to visit the different nations. In an island of the ocean stands a sacred and inviolate grove, in which is a consecrated chariot, covered with a veil, which the priest alone is permitted to touch. He becomes conscious of the entrance of the goddess into this secret recess: and with profound veneration attends the vehicle, which is drawn by yoked cows. At this season all is joy; and in every place which the goddess deigns to visit is a sense of festivity. No wars are undertaken; arms are untouched; and every hostile weapon is shut up. Peace abroad and at home are then only known; then only loved; till at length the same priest reconducts the goddess, satiated with mortal intercourse, to her temple. The chariot, with its curtain, and if we may believe it, the goddess herself, then undergo ablution in a secret lake. (*Germania*: 40)

Elsewhere, Tacitus says that the goddess was carried in a galley, like Isis of the Ships. The Vanir ruled both earth and sea, and the boat and the wagon seem to have been ritually interchangeable. A highly decorated boat or wagon bed like those found in the woman's burial at Oseby may have been used. Danish evidence suggests that this tour took place in February at the beginning of the spring plowing.

A similar custom is reported in Sweden in the eleventh century. In the "Tale of Ogmund Bash" (McKinnell 1972), a young man called Gunnar Half-and-Half is forced to flee to Sweden and comes to a district where Freyr is worshipped. The priestess says Freyr dislikes Gunnar, but she and all the people there are quite pleased with him, so she invites him to "stay here over the winter and go to the feasts with Freyr and me when he goes to ensure good crops for the people" (p. 142).

When they do set out, they are caught by a snowstorm. Gunnar doesn't want to lead the carthorse, and the god comes out of the cart and fights with him. Gunnar is getting the worse of it until he decides to go back to being a Christian, at which point the god leaves the idol, and Gunnar breaks it. He gives the priestess the ultimatum of allowing him to disguise himself as the god or leaving her. The people are impressed that they have come in such weather, and that Freyr can now eat and drink with them. He doesn't speak much, will only accept gold, silver, and such (no sacrifices). He also gets the priestess pregnant.

> That was taken to be excellent, and the Swedes were now delighted with this god of theirs; the weather too was mild and all the crops so promising that nobody could remember the like. (McKinnell 1972, p. 143)

Eventually the word gets around, and King Olaf of Norway hears and suspects what has happened, "because the strongest heathen cults are when living men are worshipped," and sends a messenger to bring Gunnar home.

This account has several points of interest. Clearly the visit of even a bogus god imposed a truce upon the neighborhood. It seems to have taken place early in the growing season. In both cases, the deity is one of the Vanir and served by a priest of the opposite sex. The Swedish example makes it clear that an image of the deity was carried in the cart, but the reaction of both the people and King Olaf suggests that it was not unknown for the deity to be represented by, or even to speak through, a human being.

One more piece of evidence comes from the Goths in the fourth century (Burns 1984, pp. 146–47). In one of the few examples of active barbarian resistance to the spread of Christianity, King Athanaric ordered a cleansing of the soil by having a god statue carried through his territories. In each village, the god was greeted with a feast at which all present had to partake of the sacrifice. Christians, who were forbidden by their faith to share in such a meal, had the choice of death or fleeing to Roman territory.

The image of the decorated wagon emerging from the darkness of the forest escorted by riders bearing torches is a powerful one. The traditional pattern of habitation in the Germanic countries was one of scattered settlements—villages or clansteads governed by elders. The primary social structure was the family, and the demands of farm work and the difficulties of transportation made it hard for large numbers of people to gather for festivals. Instead, the festival came to the people.

The situation seems oddly similar to that of nineteenth-century rural America, where the religious needs of the people were met by circuit-riding preachers and traveling camp meetings. For the ancient Norse and Germans, the opportunity to feast and revel in the presence of the deity of peace and abundance must have had a powerful impact.

The Group Ritual

If working with a group, the ritual for RAIDHO and KENAZ can be found on page 295. It is based on the imagery of the torch and the deity in the cart.

Chapter 5

GEBO and WUNJO

WITH THE STUDY OF GEBO AND WUNJO you will have finished the first aett, or grouping, of the Elder Futhark and completed the first third of your study of the runes. Has the time seemed short? Each time I begin to work through the futhark the task looks immeasurable, and yet by this point in the journey I find it hard to believe that so much has been done.

Each aett of the futhark seems to finish with a rune of hope. At the end of the first aett, GEBO and WUNJO give us joy. Both of these runes are "good" in the sense that it is hard to find any negative meanings for them. But they are not as alike as they might at first appear. If you practice the stadhyr, analyze the differences in energy flow. Working with another person, send first the energy of one rune, and then of the other, and compare. Does the energy feel "hot" or "cool"? Dynamic or serene? What insights do these differences give you regarding the ways the runes can be used?

THE SEVENTH RUNE: ✕ GEBO

Pronunciation: "GHEB-o"
Meaning: Gift

**GEBO unites the gift and giver
In equal exchange of energy.**

The Ancient Meanings

In the Elder Futhark, the "G" rune is named *gebo*, a gift. The Old English name for this rune, *gyfu*, means a gift, or generosity. The "G" rune is not included in the Younger Futhark and hence does not appear in the Norwegian and Icelandic rune poems. The "g" sound is less common in the Scandinavian languages, which dropped the "ge-" prefix to verbs found in Gothic and Anglo-Saxon and retained in modern German early. In Norse inscriptions, *kaun* did double duty for the hard "g" and harder "k" sounds.

The importance of gifts in old Germanic society is well attested in Tacitus:

> No people are more addicted to social entertainments, or more liberal in
> the exercise of hospitality. To refuse any person whatever admittance
> under their roof, is accounted flagitious. . . . No one makes a distinction
> with respect to the rights of hospitality, between a stranger and an
> acquaintance. The departing guest is presented with whatever he may
> ask for; and with the same freedom a boon is desired in return. They are
> pleased with presents; but think no obligation incurred when they give
> or receive. (*Germania*: 21)

In fact, Burgundian law imposed a fine on anyone who refused hospitality to a
guest. The Anglo-Saxon rune poem fully supports the meaning of "gift"
ascribed to the rune in the Elder and Anglo-Saxon Futharks. The verses
describe the way in which the virtue of generosity, as highly valued in old
Germanic society as in other heroic cultures, was practiced. A standard epithet
for a king in early English poetry is "ring-giver," and it is the generosity of a
lord to his followers that earns their devotion. The verse suggests that this
virtue extends beyond the war band to a more generalized hospitality. Helping
the homeless was an ethical imperative in a society in which life was even more
uncertain than it is in our own.

> X *[Gyfu] gumena byþ gleng and herenys,*
> (Giving, to all men, brings credit and honor)
> *wraþu and wyrþscype, and wræcna gehwam*
> (help and worthiness—and to every outcast)
> *ar and ætwist ðe byþ oþra leas.*
> (is the estate and substance, that have naught else.)

Although the Younger Futhark does not include the "G" rune, Old Norse
literature, the "Hávamál" in particular, is well stocked with advice on the
subject of generosity. Just as generosity was a characteristic of a good lord,
being niggardly could cost a leader much of the repute he had won in
battle, especially if he slighted a bard. In "Grímnismál," the inhospitable
behavior of the king (even though it is based on mistaken information) leads
to disaster when he torments Odin instead of welcoming him! Many legends
in Germanic and other literatures show that the stranger should be welcomed as a representative of the gods, especially since a god is exactly what
he may turn out to be! The first part of the following verse parallels the
Anglo-Saxon, but continues with a counterexample.

> Those who are generous   and brave live best,
> And seldom nurse anxiety,
> But a fearful man   is frightened by all,
> And the miser mourns what he gives.

> ("Hávamál": 48)

In Icelandic society, generosity was a requirement for social standing. A district leader, or gothi, was required to host the seasonal sacrificial feasts and provide the wherewithal for the offerings. This value showed up most strongly in marriage customs. The delay between the betrothal and the marriage often mentioned in the sagas allowed the families concerned to gather the resources to throw a wedding feast that would establish the standing of the new couple and bring credit to their relatives. In Old Norse, the word *gipt* may refer not only to a simple gift, or a gift of nature (a natural talent) or income, but to a wedding, and a number of words associated with marriage incorporate it. *Giptar-mál*, or "gift-feast," is the word for the wedding feast, which, along with putting the bride and groom to bed together before witnesses, constituted legal marriage (as it did in ancient Celtic society as well). The essence of the ancient marriage custom is retained in the modern wedding reception. Gifts were exchanged by the families, presented to the guests to help them remember the occasion, and given by the groom to the bride the next morning.

The old Norse were not, however, totally trusting. In the later period, at least, there appeared to be a point after which generosity was considered foolishness. The Germanic mind had a fine sense of balance regarding such obligations. Both good and evil were to be repaid as equitably as possible, as reflected in the elaborate laws for the settling of blood feuds. In the "Grímnismál," King Geirrod's painful hospitality is requited when he stumbles and falls on his own sword. The Viking equivalent of the golden rule goes:

> With garb and with weapons   should friends gift each other;
> That, one can see for oneself.
> Those who give to each other   stay friends the longest,
> If they keep things going well.
>
> To his friends a man   shall always be a friend,
> And return gift for gift;
> Laughter for laughter   let him return
> And falshood for lies.
>
> ("Hávamál": 41–42)

This concern extended even to sacrificial offerings, which could also have a severe impact on a fragile economy. It appears that in the later period, at any rate, the Norse began to learn moderation.

> It's better not to pray   than to make too many offerings;
> One gift demands another,
> It's better not to send   than to sacrifice too much.
>
> ("Hávamál": 145)

Modern Meanings

Both ancient and modern references to GEBO and giving explore the implications of generosity and exchange. Everyone agrees that giving is good, but there seems to be some ambivalence regarding the value of unconditional offering versus the need for a careful balance in the exchange.

For Thorsson, the primary meaning of this rune is exchange. This includes giving, sharing, receiving of power; psychic joining of two or more people to create a physical or magical result or exchange between gods and humanity; or economic interaction. It may also involve sacrifice (including self-sacrifice). The triple gift of Odin is consciousness, life breath, and form. Thorsson also picks up on the marriage implications to give the rune a meaning of mystical marriage.

Gundarsson's discussion of sacrifice is particularly interesting, focusing on the initiatory function of self-sacrifice, from Odin's offering of himself to himself on the Worldtree to the vitki's sacrifice of him or herself as a prelude to transformation. His meditation on this rune is particularly powerful. He points out that in Norse religion, offerings are neither bribes to persuade the gods to help nor payment, but rather the symbol for an exchange of loyalties modeled on the relationship between an ancient king and his followers.

Osborn and Longland pick up on the meaning as indicated in the Anglo-Saxon poem and describe GYFU as a rune of giving out of generosity or to win renown, receiving in reciprocity or to establish dependence. It indicates an exchange of worth, and may be a way of including the outcast in the social structure. Peterson points out that the GYFU rune often appears in prosperity charms. Aswynn's discussion of the importance of balance and equality in exchange is especially useful.

In ancient times, generosity was one of the noblest of virtues. The purpose of wealth was not to be hoarded, but to be spread around society. It provided social lubrication; it was a way of recycling, the expression of "what goes around, comes around." Legally mandated programs of public support are emotionally unsatisfying for all parties and often inequitable or simply inefficient. In troubled times, individuals or groups working together must take responsibility for the community. But giving can be soured by unwillingness, both for giver and receiver. A gift can confer independence or prosperity on the receiver, or it can bind him into a cycle of dependence. The principle of balance must be applied at the psychological level, rather than at that of the ledger. Those who give should be grateful for the gifts that have put them in a position to be generous; those who receive should be provided with opportunities to pass the benefits on.

In general, GEBO is considered a rune of the Vanir, especially the goddess Gefion (associated with Frigga), or Gefn (an epithet of Freyja). Gefion was the name of the goddess worshipped at the royal center of Leire in Denmark. She may have been a goddess of agriculture, the "giver" of the fruits of the earth, one of the Matronae who gave gifts to humankind. It also suggests Freyr and Freyja's role in sexual exchange and prosperity. The XXX put at the end of a letter to indicate "love and kisses" is an invocation of the luck of the Vanir.

We need the gifts of the Vanir every day in order to survive. At the ecological level, the doctrine of exchange teaches that we must balance what we take from the earth with what we give in return. This means expressing our gratitude to the plants and animals whose lives enable us to live. It also means actively seeking ways to recycle and conserve, and supporting political and social programs that promote environmental responsibility.

This rune also governs more esoteric exchanges, especially exchanges of energy or magical power, whether between individuals or between humans and gods. The Norse concept of religious relationship is not one of subservience. Men and gods work together in order to serve and save the world (as the heroes will fight for Odin at Ragnarók). They empower us, but our belief strengthens them. Sacrifice consists of "making sacred"; the god sanctifies the item offered, which then returns to the donor either directly or spiritually. Odin's sacrifice of himself to himself can be seen as an integration of aspects; we do the same thing when we place our bodies and personalities at the service of our higher selves.

Thus, GEBO can also be usefully considered as a rune of Odin. In the Viking Age the Allfather's gifts were highly valued. Kings sacrificed for victory, and accused the god of treachery when a battle was lost. Their problem, I think, stems from a basic misunderstanding of the god's purposes. Odin is not concerned with the fate of kingdoms, but with that of the world. His myths demonstrate that he will sacrifice anything and anyone, including himself, to obtain knowledge and guide the transformation of the world. From his initiates he demands all they have, but he gives all of himself in return. He cannot be used, and those who offer themselves to him should beware, for his price may be terrible, and they will serve the god's purposes, not their own. But the gift he gives in return is ecstasy.

Interpreting and Using GEBO

Depending on the context, the diviner should consider all possible meanings for "gift" in a rune layout, including the gifts of the spirit, or a need to look at the nature of one's interactions with others, especially in the area of emotions. Another area to consider is the balance between aspects of an individual's life, or between the individual and his or her environment. The rune can also have an economic significance, however, relating to job relationships and results. Willis sees in the rune a union or partnership of some kind, an indication that the person will receive gifts or love, a wedding, unity of action and intention ("'tis a gift to be simple"?), or an indication of concern about a relationship.

GEBO might also refer to contracts, agreements, and alliances—legal or emotional. The individual may be about to receive material wealth or honor, or be called upon to give them to another. It could even represent involvement in nonprofit or charitable activities. Negative meanings include extravagance or stinginess, or problems with cash flow.

GEBO can be used as a general luck rune, doubled or tripled for emphasis. Combined with FEHU, it works for prosperity, and with INGWAZ, for fertility. Use it to consecrate gifts and offerings. Combined with ANSUZ, it can relate to the self-sacrifice that leads to enlightenment. It can also be used to create a link between other forces or in spells of integration or balancing.

THE EIGHTH RUNE: ᚹ WUNJO

Pronunciation: "WOON-yo"
Meaning: Joy

**WUNJO wins Wishfather's blessing,
Joy joins folk in family freedom.**

The Ancient Meanings

The meaning of the Gothic *wunjo* is "joy," or "bliss." In Old English, the meaning of *wynn* is the same. In Old Norse, the etymological equivalents of words beginning with *w* are spelled with a *v*, the letter named "vend" in the Icelandic alphabet. But this sound was spelled with *u*, because *w* does not appear in the Younger Futhark. The interpretation of the rune in the Anglo-Saxon rune poem portrays the Old English ideal of happiness—absence of trouble, adequate resources, and the power to protect them.

> ᚹ *[Wynn] bruceþ ðe can weana lyt,*
> (Joy is for one who knows little of woe,)
> *sares and sorge, and him sylfa haefþ*
> (pains and sorrows, and to him who has)
> *blæd and blysse and eac byrga geniht.*
> (power and bliss and buildings good enough.)

In the traditional "Boar's Head Carol," the Yule feast is dedicated to the "King of Bliss," a phrase that, in this context, could refer equally to the Christian deity or to Freyr, to whom the boar was dedicated. There are many references in Anglo-Saxon poetry to dwelling in bliss in the courts of heaven or in a king's hall. The god best associated with this rune might be Freyr, or according to a tradition mentioned by Aswynn, Ullr (the Anglo-Saxon Wuldor), or, following Jacob Grimm's interpretation, Odin.

Grimm provides an extensive analysis of the word *Wunsch* in his discussion of Wodan in chapter 6 of the first volume of *Teutonic Mythology* According to him.

> The sum total of well-being and blessedness, the fulness of all graces, seems in our ancient language to have been expressed by a single word, whose meaning has since been narrowed down; it was named wunsch (wish). This word is probably derived from "wunja," our wonne, bliss; wunisc, wunsc, perfection in whatever kind. (Grimm 1966, p. 138)

In thirteenth-century German poetry, *Wunsch* is personified as the agency by whom God creates. "We see Wish provided with hands, power, looks, diligence, art, blossom, fruit; he creates, shapes, produces master-pieces, etc." (Grimm 1966, p. 142) and in all regards seems interchangeable with God, from which Grimm concludes that these stock phrases were originally applied to a Germanic god, namely Wodan, whose Norse names include "Oski," the Fulfiller of Desires.

Other phrases support this identification. The "Oskmeyjar," or "wish-women" are the Valkyries (also translated as "adopted daughters"). The

German *wunschiligerta*, or "wishing-rod," may relate to Odin's epithet "Gondlir," or "bearer of the magic wand," and possibly also to the "glory twigs" of the Anglo-Saxon Nine Herbs charm. Grimm provides a great deal of support for an image of the ancient Germanic Wuotan that is considerably broader than that given him by the Norse, including functions of prosperity and fertility that farther north are reserved to the Vanir. As Gundarsson has pointed out, in Denmark and Sweden, folk practices in which the last sheaf is dedicated to Odin suggest that he was seen as a god of fertility. In "Hyndluljod" he is called a giver of gold, and King Heidhrekr sacrifices to him to break a famine. If Wodan/Odin originally had such an aspect, it would be part of his character as Wishfather, giver, like the Roman Mercury, of all good things.

In the "Lay of Sigdrifa," the Valkyrie, or Wishmaiden, begins teaching her wisdom to Sigurd by saying:

> Beer I bring thee,   thou 'tree-of-battle,'
> Mixed with might,   mingled with honor,
> Full of spells   and songs of power
> With goodly charms   and runes of joy.

> ("Sigdrifumál": 6)

Though WUNJO is not included in the Scandinavian rune poems, the Eddas also have something to say about happiness. In "Hávamál" it is the result of wisdom and a good reputation among men. Joy is also a reward of friendship—"man is the joy of man" ("Hávamál": 47). A man is blessed who lives fearlessly and does not waste time worrying. Wisdom in measure brings happiness, but too much knowledge can cause problems—" Seldom a heart will sing with joy if the owner be all too wise" ("Hávamál": 55). But best of all is simply to be alive.

Modern Meanings

More recent interpretations of WUNJO seem to be hampered by the rune's very straightforwardness and simplicity. Joy, happiness, and bliss are desired by all, yet by their nature, they are almost impossible to define.

Thorsson interprets the rune as representing a harmonization of diverse elements, joining, blending, binding; fellowship and union within the clan for the common good. Peterson, on the other hand, defines it as happiness, or spiritual ecstasy. For Osborn and Longland, it means joy as an ideal in a hard world, or the innocent joy of a child. Thorolf Wardle identifies the

Gothic *Wunjo* with the Old High German *Wunna*, a meadow, as well as the modern German *wonne* or "bliss," and identifies it as the billowing Bronze Age grassland over which the flourishing herds of the ancient Germanic tribes roamed. Certainly for a pastoral people, a flock of contentedly grazing beasts represents one kind of bliss.

Aswynn has an interesting interpretation of WUNJO as "the power or realization of the true will," which can bring the energy of THURISAZ (which it somewhat resembles) into consciousness. WUNJO's position as the final rune in the first aett represents the perfection of the process of creation to which she feels the runes in the first aett all refer.

Gundarsson also believes that WUNJO is a rune of will, the determination that maintains the vitki's enthusiasm for the work of magical attainment despite all discouragements, a weapon with which to battle sorrow and despair. Happiness is to be found within the security of a stronghold—the warded will, and the safe place surrounded by kin and friends. However, he points out that too much good fellowship can cause complacency or blindness to problems. WUNJO is a rune of healing, especially for emotional problems, or interpersonal conflicts. It can help the mind and body to work together and improve the mental state to aid the body in healing and strengthen the immune system at all levels.

One major meaning of the rune of joy seems to involve happiness in a social setting. This is not the solitary ecstasy of the seer, but a joy that comes from relationships, especially those relationships that involve linking people through familial, sexual, or emotional bonds. Even when it refers to creativity, it is the kind of artwork that serves a useful purpose. It evokes the kind of joy that one feels at a really good community festival or family party. This is the happiness idealized in Germanic poetry, the wise and well-balanced person surrounded by family and friends in the hall.

In studying this rune, one might do well to consider the meaning of Joseph Campbell's advice, "Follow your bliss!" But what is bliss? What do you really want, long for, desire? There are plenty of gurus about who are eager to tell us what we ought to wish for, but every wish is an act of magic, and should be considered carefully. Fairy tales are full of cautionary tales about people who make wishes without thinking through the consequences. As Marion Zimmer Bradley was fond of saying, "Be careful what you ask for, you may get it."

In Scandinavian folk belief, one person's willed or even involuntary desire can have a powerful effect on the soul of another. Ill-wishing a person or an animal can cause illness or death. Sickness can also result if one is the object of uncontrolled love longing (*elsk*). Especially when fueled by a strong emotion, the human will has great power.

The mystics of all faiths have taught that the goal of religious practice is joy—the bliss of union with the deity. For the Germanic warrior, Valhalla was an idealized version of the happy company gathered in the hall, and bliss in the afterlife equaled the perfecting of the joy sought in this one. We see the gods differently than did our ancestors, but we know that they are real, and when we welcome them to feast with us in the sumbel (a formal ritual in which gods and hereos are toasted), their presence brings a joy that combines the traditional vision of the kindred feasting in the hall with the experience of communion with the Divine.

There is another kind of joy in the search for wisdom, especially when one can share the quest with companions found upon the way. There is the joy that comes upon one unawares, the gift of the gods, and there is the joy that is willed: to find beauty in a world that sometimes seems determined to deny it, to love whether or not love is returned, and to go into battle laughing with joy in your ability to face the challenge whether you win or lose.

Interpreting and Using WUNJO

In a reading, WUNJO suggests a positive interpretation of the surrounding runes. It may refer to success in love relationships or happiness in any kind of shared activity, especially work; spiritually it indicates integration of personality or forces. More generally, it indicates joy and happiness, good news, a good outcome, joy in the work of one's hands, craftwork, or emotional ties or affection. WUNJO can indicate, or promote, harmony, joy, prosperity, and friendship and can be used as a general purpose luck rune. Draw WUNJO on your forehead to lift a depression. In a negative position, its hazards are stagnation, strife, and alienation.

WUNJO governs the making of bindrunes, which are essentially aesthetic combinations of runes, like monograms, that have a magical purpose. Bindrunes are created and built up in much the same way as magical sigils. They are formed by selecting appropriate runes for the problem and making double use of as many as possible of their lines. Bindrunes may express a concept and/or include a word. They are basically conceptual anagrams.

GEBO AND WUNJO: STUDY AND EXPERIENCE

Gifts and Givers

GEBO is one of the easiest runes to put into practice. Giving is an active verb, and a little thought will show you a multitude of ways to experience GEBO's exchange. The act of giving can take place on the personal, social, and environmental levels, culminating in an exchange of energy with the gods.

On the personal level, we give gifts to our friends. Gifts are exchanged in the ritual, but you might also take this opportunity to give something to those you love. The gift does not necessarily have to cost money. Write an unexpected letter to an old friend or relative. Tell someone thank you, or that you love her. You cannot assume that people are telepathic, but even if your friends know how you feel, it's good to hear it put into words. Take a friend out to lunch. Give someone flowers. Paying your debts is a gift of a kind. Return borrowed books, pay your bills.

On the social level, GEBO can be experienced by giving to those you do not know. Walk down the street with a pocketful of change and give something to each homeless person you meet. When feasts were given in the ancient tribes, one planned to feed everyone, and having food available for wanderers was part of the hospitality. A modern equivalent is to ask people to bring canned foods to the ritual and then deliver the food to the local shelter. Ancient peoples passed on extra clothing as well as food. This might be the time to go through your closets and take things you no longer use to the Salvation Army or an equivalent organization.

At the environmental level, we can explore ways to give back to Mother Earth some of what we take from her each day. Make a donation to the environmental action group of your choice. Plant a tree. If you are already recycling, find some new way to conserve or reuse resources.

Another part of giving is being able to receive with joy. Give the gift of allowing someone to do something for you—if someone pays you a compliment, receive it without protest. Honor the giver by believing in his or her respect for you. Let someone take you out to lunch. Make a list of things that people have given you in the past. Take a walk in the nearest wild park and really look around you, appreciating the things that Mother Earth gives us without charge. Give something to yourself: a massage, a bubble bath, a chocolate bar.

Studying GEBO offers you an opportunity to analyze what you get in material, emotional, and spiritual support, and what you give. To whom do you give? From whom do you receive? Giving and receiving may be coming from different directions, but does it all balance out? If not, take another look at what you are doing, and seek ways to even up the exchange.

This process can be ritualized by throwing a "fairy godmother" party for a friend. This can be a unique way to celebrate a birthday, but no excuse is required beyond the recipient's need. The format of the ritual/party is based on those fairy tales in which the fairies (lineal descendants of the Disir, those female spirits who continued to protect their descendants) give gifts at the naming of a child.

This will take some planning, because the point is not to give gifts that are pretty or expensive, but gifts, whether physical or spiritual, that the recipient truly needs. To do so, you will have to objectively consider your subject's situation—meditate, holding his/her image in your awareness, or perhaps spend some time together in which you lead the conversation around to the question of gifts/needs and really listen to what is said.

Clean as you would for a party, and purify as you would before a ritual. Decorations add to the festivity, or you can place candles about the room. Put the recipient in the place of honor and present the gifts. These can be symbolic—a bloodstone for courage, for instance, or a picture of a new car. You can also give energy, or promises of help where needed. "Give" runes and the powers they carry by drawing them on the recipient's forehead or wherever else seems appropriate (TIWAZ along the backbone, for instance, to straighten the spine).

Finish by giving your friend a new name indicating some quality that will be helpful: "Victory-bringer," for instance, or "Clear-thinker." The pagan custom (even in pre-Christian times) was to sprinkle the newborn with water to seal the naming. If this is uncomfortable, give the recipient a drink of mead, crown him/her with a birthday crown, or in some other way signify the naming.

This gift-giving process can also be accomplished at a distance through a meditation in which you visualize the recipient receiving your gifts and being transformed by them.

Bindrunes

The study of GEBO and WUNJO, with all their implications of connection and exchange, is a good preparation for learning to create bindrunes. Bindrunes are essentially runic monograms—a way of combining runes that is both aesthetic and magical.

Whether you are carving or drawing, each rune must be drawn separately, even if some of the strokes are repeated. Intone the name of the rune as it is drawn. Bindrunes can be drawn on doors or windowsills to aid in warding houses; on cars or luggage; on amulets, weapons, or tools. Bindrunes drawn on the body are also used in healing. Thorsson has a good discussion with examples in *Futhark*. Page includes several examples, some in conjunction with runic inscriptions, which illustrate how they were used. Some examples appear below.

Examples of Bindrunes:

X + ᚠ =   good luck or
          spiritual power

↑ + Y + ᚦ = protection

↑ + ᛈ + X + ᛉ = love magic
              formula

M + ᛁ + R = spiritual journey

X + ᛈ = gift of joy

↑ + ᛇ + R = justice

R + Y or, ᛋ + Y = protection for
                   luggage or mail

ᚠ + Y = protect computer

R + R + R = speed

X + ᚠ = 'gau'/ Go!

Joy

When all things are in balance, one of the results is joy. Despite, or perhaps just because joy cannot be described but only experienced, it is very difficult to discuss it. For each person the experience of bliss will be somewhat different. One person's image may be dancing in a sunlit glade. For another it may be like standing in a brisk wind on a mountaintop, or letting the wind whirl you away. For others, it is the state of being that is achieved in *samadhi*: radiant light or divine darkness, in which one exists without need for words. I call WUNJO a rune of Odin because this ecstasy lies at the root of his name. Bliss is his greatest gift to humankind.

But those who have sought bliss report that it cannot be addressed directly. According to some, it can be achieved by focusing completely on an action: cutting wood and drawing water, running, dancing, or even swordplay. Sometimes it is enough to direct one's attention to "a few of my favorite things." Joy, like true love, is elusive when pursued. It is not necessary to seek it on a mountaintop. As the Anglo-Saxon verses imply, it can be found just as readily among good companions around one's own fire.

WUNJO is to a great degree a matter of focus. In order to "follow one's bliss," you must first identify it. What do you really want to do with your life? What gets you naturally high? When you find your purpose, you will also find joy.

Given the above, it is difficult to prescribe a ritual that will enable you to experience joy. However, the regular practice of meditation is probably the best way to achieve it. Mysticism is rather like sex—you can read any amount of glowing description, but the only way to really understand what it's all about is to go out and do it. And even then it helps if you practice. A number of excellent books on the subject are available, drawn from various cultures. The most highly developed material of this kind comes from the Hindu and Tibetan traditions.

The basic principles governing the physiology and psychology of meditation transcend traditions. An adaptation appropriate to Norse practice could work as follows.

Choose a place in which you will be uninterrupted, and a time at which you are still alert and yet can afford to relax. Secure your space by carrying a candle around it. You may also invoke the dwarves Austri, Sudhri, Vestri, and Northri to guard the directions. If you wish, add an invocation to whatever god or goddess you feel closest to, or a prayer to Odin Wishfather, giver of önd, the holy breath.

Then set the candle on a cleared space or an altar and turn out the lights. Most people find it most comfortable to sit upright in a chair that supports the back and arms, although those who are more flexible may sit cross-legged or in whatever other position they can sustain comfortably for an extended time.

Identify and relax each muscle group in turn. When you have done so, regularize your breathing by counting in for four beats, hold two, then out four, hold two, and so forth. Repeat this until your mind is centered and focused. You may find it helpful to simply practice relaxing and focusing for a few days before you continue with the rest of the procedure.

When you are able to relax at will, focus your attention on the candle flame. Contemplate it, appreciate it, and let any other thoughts that come into your mind simply float away (it does no good to order yourself not to think about the blue monkey—instead, recognize it, and then gently shunt it aside). When the candle flame fills both inner and outer vision, close your eyes and imagine that flame forming itself into the figure of the rune—ᚹ. Let the rune grow larger and larger until you can walk into it. Feel its warmth and brilliance surrounding and permeating you until you are conscious of nothing except the Light.

Allow the experience to conclude naturally—do not worry about being "lost" in meditation. At worst, you will fall asleep and wake up when rested. You may, however, "preprogram" yourself by affirming beforehand that you will spend a set amount of time in trance. When you do finish, take your time coming back to ordinary reality. Breathe deeply and quickly, thank the powers that have protected you, and stretch. You may find it helpful to eat something afterward to complete the grounding.

Do not worry about whether or not your experience is "real." Nor should you worry about whether you are doing it "right," or progressing quickly enough. The point is to demonstrate that this ecstasy exists and is available whenever you have the will to seek it. Even in the early stages, you will probably find the exercise relaxing and pleasant. With practice, it may become much more.

Feasting with the Gods

Every culture has its own rituals for unifying the community and communing with its gods. In the Northern Way, one of the traditional practices for achieving both purposes is the communal feast, and more specifically, the *minnisveig* (memory-draught), derived, according to Grimm, from the old German for "man," leading to the later German, for "to remember," and *minion* "to love." "Minnis-öl," the memory-ale, was drunk to honor the dead, or to honor the gods.

In the sagas, minne is drunk at feasts, especially the great feasts which followed the sacrifices. The horn would be "signed"—hallowed by making a symbol over it, probably the sign of the Hammer—and raised high. Before drinking, the feaster might praise the hero being remembered, pray to the god, or make a vow. The custom has survived in the drinking of toasts at banquets, and to the honor of specific saints, especially Saints John and Gertrude, in German villages.

A libation seems to have been poured out on the ground or altar before drinking if the individual was going to drain the horn, or perhaps after the horn had made the rounds. Given the reported capacity of Norse drinkers, each one may have drained his own horn, although a communal cup is also reported. References in the sagas indicate that pairs of feasters might share one horn—a further illustration of GEBO's exchange. The cups or horns would be filled from a special sacred cauldron—the cauldrons in which Aegir brewed ale for the gods and the Gundestrop cauldron come to mind. The acquisition (or theft) of such cauldrons is a recurrent theme in the literature.

Men could drink the minne of friends or the gods at any time, but the setting for the more formal drinking was the sumbel (Old Norse, *sumbl*; Old English, *symbel*), the Old German equivalent of the Greek symposium, a formal feast. In particular, sumbel was celebrated at the great festivals, especially the spring and fall feasts, Yule, and Midsummer. Such feasts seem to have featured baked goods, including bread images molded in the shapes of the gods and brushed with butter, and the meat of the sacrifices.

References in the sagas indicate that the dedicated animal, sometimes with its horns gilded or adorned with a garland, was first solemnly led around the hall. Different beasts were preferred in various districts and periods, but the most sacred seems to have been the horse (particularly for Freyr). The eating of horseflesh was later suppressed in Europe with such intensity just because this totem animal was probably eaten only in a religious context. The boar was also offered to Freyr, and even now in Scandinavia marzipan images of boars are distributed at Yule. Oxen or bulls were also favored, especially black or white ones. There are indications that other animals, such as goats or lambs, were offered to other deities. The hare may have been eaten in the spring in honor of the goddess Ostara.

When the animal had been killed, its head and hide might be hanged from a sacred tree, while its blood was poured over the altar and into a bowl (blót-bollar). The celebrant used a whisk to sprinkle the temple and worshippers. Then the meat was cooked, usually by being boiled in another sacred cauldron. If the root word for *seidh* is indeed cognate with the English verb "to seethe," this sacrifice may have also featured divination. The best portion would be offered to the god, and the rest distributed to the feasters. The king, if present, was required to at least taste everything offered; offerings were made to the house-spirit as well.

This pattern is also familiar from Celtic history. For the Celts, as for the Germans, the greatest punishment was to be forbidden to participate in these feasts, a privilege that signified membership in the community as well as being part of its bonding. Individuals made offerings of flowers, fruit, milk, honey, or grain to house-sprites and local landspirits. Harvest customs included leaving part of the corn for the landspirits or the gods.

The Group Ritual

If working in a group, our ritual for GEBO and WUNJO starts on page 303. It is an abbreviated version of the minnisveig. A full-dress sumbel can involve several tables worth of meat and other dishes, honor most of the inhabitants of Asgard, and take all afternoon and evening. Even a full minne is likely to require several hours and a cask of mead. However, the form most common in the heathen community features a round in which each participant toasts one of the gods, a second in which ancestors or heroes are honored, and a third in which they toast whoever they will. Other variations might include a skaldic sumbel in which all the toasts are made in verse.

Chapter 6

HAGALAZ and NAUDHIZ

THIS AETT BEGINS WITH THE ICE EGG, the hailstone. This is a rune of potential and sometimes violent change. On the physical level, it is a rune of cold. NAUDHIZ, the rune with which we pair it for this chapter, is the source of need-fire, which can melt the ice, but tends to intensify whatever changes HAGALAZ has set in motion. HAGALAZ is a seed that can either nourish or destroy. Neither rune promotes tranquility. NAUDHIZ is the force of fate, which can bring opportunity or doom. How you experience these runes depends on how willing (and able) you are to face the facts of your life and make changes.

THE NINTH RUNE: ᚺ ᚾ ᚷ HAGALAZ

Pronunciation: "HA-ga-lahz"
Meaning: Hail

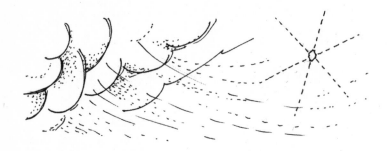

HAGALAZ hails Ice-seeds hither,
Harm is melted into healing.

The Ancient Meanings

ᚺ, the form of the rune used in the Elder and Anglo-Saxon futharks, is clearly derived from the Latin alphabet, whose sound it shares. In the Younger Futhark, however, the form ᚷ is different. It might be derived from the Greek X (Chi), an aspirated "kh" sound. Or it could come from the snowflake form found in many parts of the world, including on Pennsylvania Dutch barns, which often feature powerful protective hex (six) signs. It could also be interpreted as a bindrune formed by combining ISA with GEBO, or the upright and reversed forms of the protective rune ELHAZ.

The old Germanic, *Hagalaz*, the Old English *haegl*, and Old Norse *hagall* all mean the same thing—a hailstone. An old kenning for hail is an "ice egg," or a seed of ice, reflected in the rune poems. Here is the Anglo-Saxon:

> ᚺ *[hægl] byþ hwitust corna;*
> (Hail is the whitest of grain;)
> *(hwyrft hit of heofones lyfte,*
> (it is whirled from heaven's loft)
> *wealcaþ hit windes scura;*
> (tossed about by wind gusts,)
> *weorþeþ hit to wætere syðan.*
> (then melts into water.)

The Icelandic:
>   ✳*[hagall] er kaldakorn*
>   (Hail is cold grain)
>   *ok krapadrifa*
>   (and driving sleet)
>   *ok snaka sott.*
>   (and sickness of serpents.)

and the Norwegian:
>   ✳ *[hagall] er kaldastr korna:*
>   (Hail is the coldest of grains:)
>   *Kristr scóp hæimenn forna.*
>   (Christ created the primaeval world.)

This is clearly a traditional image—in the Old English poem "The Seafarer," "hail fell on the ground, coldest of grains" (Hamer 1970, ll. 32–33). However, in additional lines, interpretations differ. The Old English poem is largely descriptive, emphasizing the fact that the harsh hail can melt into water that nourishes the land. The Icelanders, as might be expected, seem more concerned with sleet than rain.

The sick serpents are something of an enigma, unless the poet is thinking of the stinging bite of sleet and hail. Hail might also be expected to cause considerable trauma to any serpent that came out of hibernation too soon! The Norwegian rune poem is the most intriguing. Thorsson suggests that "Christ" is a later substitution for a pagan Creator such as, "Hroptr," the Hidden One, or some other epithet for Odin. It is interesting that the creation of the world, whoever accomplished it, is believed to have involved ice. We have already encountered this myth in our discussion of URUZ, and will deal with it again when we come to ISA. In HAGALAZ we have the seed of ice; the primal crystal around which all the rest formed.

Modern Meanings

For Thorsson, HAGALAZ is the cosmic ice egg, the seed of Ymir, the stuff from which the world was made. Its form in the Younger Futhark represents the snowflake. It is fire and ice, cosmic harmony, the rune-mother that contains all other forms, evolution within a fixed framework. Osborn and Longland emphasize its significant contradictions and transformations, the cold and ice that contains harvest grain or the water of life.

Gundarsson presents an extremely interesting analysis of the crystalline structure of a hailstone, pointing out that its six-sided matrix is the same as that of a perfect quartz crystal. It is a "seed-pattern of shaping," a pattern with great power for the focusing and control of energy.

Aswynn believes that the first three runes of "Hagal's aett" are concerned with the Underworld, HAGALAZ in particular representing the goddess Hella and the realm that bears her name. In this interpretation, Hella is related to Holle, or Holda, the later Germanic Mother of Winter, who shakes out the snowflakes from her feather bed. As a rune of the Norns (northern goddesses equivalent to the Three Fates), HAGALAZ would belong to Urdh, the past. Aswynn also connects the word with *hachel*, the High German word for "witch," and the Old Dutch *haegtessa*. The powers of the Hag included weatherworking, and witches were believed to cause hailstorms.

The contradictions inherent in HAGALAZ are fascinating. Farmers in particular dread the hailstorm, which can flatten crops; yet hail is spoken of as a seed, which assumes greater significance when one remembers that according to Norse tradition, the world was originally solid ice, out of which the gods and the rest of creation emerged.

The later, snowflake form of this rune is perhaps more suggestive. The cold of *haegl* is dynamic—ice in the process of being changed to something else or ice preserving the pattern from which new life can come. The more mystical interpretations of this rune therefore seem to stress potentiality and birth. In this connection, the fact that this is the ninth rune in the Elder Futhark is interesting, since nine is the number of the waves of the sea who were Heimdall's mothers, and the number of nights Odin hung on the Tree in order to rebirth himself, and that Freyr had to wait to meet Gerd in the sacred barley field. A rune of Becoming, indeed. . . .

Is HAGALAZ a rune of Heimdall, father of humankind who was born from the (melted) waters of the sea, or of Hella, daughter of Loki and goddess of the Underworld? Like the hailstone, which can be a destructive missile or a drop of nourishing water, Hella herself has two faces, the cold face of death and the beautiful face of life. Descriptions of the Underworld portray it both as a place of cold and gloom and as a realm where life flourishes even when winter imprisons the upper world. The sacrificed cock thrown over its wall flies back revived. The Norse Underworld, Hel, is a place of eternal dank mists and bone-chilling cold, but it is also the Summerland. Death and rebirth are inextricably linked in Norse theology, and the pattern of HAGALAZ can show us the road to destruction or renewal.

Interpreting and Using HAGALAZ

Aswynn says that when used in magic, HAGALAZ causes disruption in preparation for change, or blight and destruction. But in its Younger form, identified as "heil" rather than "hail," it is also a powerful protection. Sibley sees it as a rune of disaster, unless it appears in conjunction with JERA, when its meaning is more likely to be that of a seed. It is a rune of cold and can be used in healing work to bring down a fever, though it should be balanced by some other rune, such as JERA, lest the chill be too extreme.

To Peterson, HAGALAZ indicates disruptive forces of nature, or predicts a setback due to events beyond your control. The querent needs to understand what is happening in order to take appropriate action and mitigate the consequences. Willis feels that the appearance of this rune means that one should live within the limitations of nature and accept events beyond human control (such as hailstorms). In a reading, it may mean a disruptive event, or a gamble, whose results will depend on accompanying runes.

In a reading, the rune often signals, "Watch out, change is coming!" However, despite its potential for chaos, HAGALAZ has considerable possibilities for new beginnings; it can be something that may change from harmful to helpful given time or a change in perceptions, the beginning of a creative effort, something that can be developed. The ice-seed is a matrix of transformation.

THE TENTH RUNE: ᚾ NAUDHIZ

Pronunciation: "NOWD-heez"
Meaning: Need

NAUDHIZ is Necessity,
Norn-rune forcing Fate from Need.

Ancient Meanings

NAUDHIZ, the "N" rune, is called in Old English *Nyd*, need or distress, and in Old Norse, *Naudhr*, whose meaning is the same, with an added implication of constraint. Its description in the Norwegian rune poem appears to continue the theme of the preceding rune, HAGALAZ:

> ᚾ *[Naudhr] gerer næpa koste:*
> (Need leaves little choice;)
> *nøktan kæir í froste.*
> (the naked man is chilled by frost.)

In the Icelandic poem the lack of choice is also apparent, this time in the social realm:

> ᚾ *[Naudh] er þyjar þrá*
> (Need is distress of thrall-woman)
> *ok þungr kostr*
> (and state of oppression)
> *ok vássamlig verk.*
> (and hard work.)

In the first Norse verse, the constraint implied by need is in man's inability to control his environment, especially if ill fortune has also deprived him of clothes. An evil fate imposes on some the distress of being made thralls.

The Anglo-Saxon rune poem is a bit more hopeful:

> ᚾ *[Nyd] byþ nearu on breostan;*
> (Need is nearest to the breast,)
> *weorþeþ hi peah oft nipa bearnum,*
> (yet often proves to children of men)
> *to helpe and to haele gehwaeþre,*
> (a source of help and healing, [or, omen of good])
> *gif hi his hlystaþ aeror.*
> (if they heed it betimes.)

While the Anglo-Saxon version does not deny the distressfulness of need, it suggests that its constraints have something to teach those who understand them. This is not the meek acceptance of sorrow taught by Christianity. Instead it counsels the sufferer to let himself be toughened by adversity.

Old Germanic poetry is weighted by awareness of the undependability of fortune. Even in the flush of prosperity, one is aware that things can change, and death waits for all. The wisdom of Hár counsels:

> Cattle die   and kinfolk die,
> You yourself will soon die too;
> But reputation   will never die
> For him who gets a good one.
>
> ("Hávamál": 77)

The poem continues with a catalog of things that cannot be trusted, from new ice to the troth of a king's son. The workings of wyrd are a staple of Anglo-Saxon poetry, but even at its most depressing, the wise man is counseled to endure with courage:

> Everything is full of hardship in the kingdom of earth; the decree of fate changes the world under the heavens. Here possessions are transient, here friends are transient, here man is transient, here woman is transient; all this firm-set earth becomes empty. . . . Good is he who holds his faith; nor shall a man ever show forth too quickly the sorrow of his breast, except he, the earl, first know how to work its cure bravely. (Hamer 1970, "The Wanderer")

The general conclusion is that no one can guarantee good fortune. Fate cannot be predicted—the only thing you can be sure of controlling when need constrains your actions is your own response to the challenge.

In the "Lay of Sigdrifa" we find another use for NAUDHIZ:

> Ale runes learn also,   that another man's wife
> May not betray your trust.
> On your beer horn scratch them   and the backs of your
>   hands,
> And NAUDHIZ on your nails.
>
> ("Sigdrifumál": 8)

Henry Adams Bellows (1969) interprets this as a charm to prevent the guest horn from being bespelled. Presumably Siegfried could have avoided a great deal of trouble if he had thought to scratch this rune into the horn filled for him by Queen Kriemhild. One might extend this into a general protection against being constrained by the will of others.

Modern Meanings

According to Thorsson, NAUDHIZ is the thesis and antithesis whose resistance to each other shapes the fate of the world. It is both trouble and deliverance. It is the friction that produces the needfire, a powerful rune for protection. The action implied by NAUDHIZ may be used to counter the effects of fate. Because of this connection, it is a rune of the Norns.

According to Wagner, Erda (Earth) bore Wotan (Odin) three daughters, the Norns, who dwell by the Well of Urdh (what has been), the sacred spring of fate. Whatever their origin, in the Eddas they are called Urdh, Verdandi (what is becoming), and Skuld (what shall be). One of their tasks is to preserve the Tree of Life by watering it from the spring and whitening its bark with clay; this keeps it growing, even while various creatures try to destroy it. The Norns seem to have fulfilled the same function as the Romano-Celtic Matronae, or the Parcae in Roman theology, with particular influence on the fates of the newborn, and sometimes three places were laid for them at the table. There are stories in which they give life-gifts like the good fairies (Ellis-Davidson 1964).

Aswynn identifies the rune specifically with the Norn Skuld, who rules the future, and whose name, according to her etymology, is related to the Dutch and German word *Schuld*, a debt. She makes an interesting connection between this and *weregild*—man-gold (or man-guilt), the fine paid in an attempt to compensate for a crime. Thus the concepts surrounding weregild are related to those surrounding the ideas of fate, or karma. Its realm is Niflheim, the land of chill fogs and shadows that is home to all the fears that imprison us.

The concept of Need in this rune seems to resemble the Greek concept of Ananke—Necessity, as discussed by James Hillman (1980). Its root involves concepts of constraint and narrowing—it is the factors in life that cannot be escaped, that define the kinds of action that can take place. The Greeks paired Time and Necessity as the two determiners of destiny. Ananke alone cannot be bribed. However, this constraint can have a creative function. Jungian thought speaks of the image that is its own necessity—that has a kind of inherent "rightness" that commands attention.

This suggests that one way to deal with Necessity is to use it to identify our own deepest needs and purposes, to find out who we really are. Those who succeed in life are those who have learned how to separate their lifework out from all the other possibilities, to focus their energies, and to work with the natural constraints and structures of the medium they choose. There can be no action without reaction, and without something to push against, one goes nowhere. The birthgifts of the Norns are those inner necessities that will give shape to our lives.

Gundarsson states that NAUDHIZ can be used to give strength to meet and overcome trials, to confront wyrd, to turn the bow-drill of Urdhr until fate is changed. NAUDHIZ can help one deal with stress, and summon up the adrenaline rush needed to confront disaster. It is a rune of the inner stress that can drive an individual to greatness or destroy him. In its negative aspects it can cause compulsive behavior and obsession.

Some of the images associated with the rune are the spindle and the fire drill which kindles the needfire. It can also be interpreted as a double sword stroke of protection.

Interpreting and Using NAUDHIZ

In a reading, the rune can indicate problems that weigh on the spirit, frustrations, blocks, but also constraints that can become helpful if properly used. The problem may be an opportunity for change and growth if properly approached. The need may also be for action.

Osborn and Longland call it a change rune, an omen of good, the necessity for transformation. Aswynn says that in a reading, the runes that follow NAUDHIZ indicate what is needed or required. According to Willis, it indicates delay, constraint, affliction, lack, chronic problems. There is a need for patience and endurance, and perhaps voluntary limitation of obligations, a learning situation. For Peterson, it is need, constraint, a stumbling block, a need for temperance.

Magically, Gundarsson feels that it is the rune of banishings and cleansing by fire, counterspells and sealing. In addition, it can be used to imbue other spells with the force of necessity, a runic equivalent of, "As I will so mote it be!" When doing rune reading or other divination, it should be drawn on the forehead or over the runes to strengthen their link with the forces of destiny.

HAGALAZ AND NAUDHIZ: STUDY AND EXPERIENCE

Melting the Ice

The most direct way to make contact with the forces of HAGALAZ would be to go for a walk in a hailstorm. Fortunately for farmers, hailstorms are not so frequent that you can count on one occurring while you are studying this rune. You can, however, spend some time remembering what it was like the last time you were in one—the clatter and rattle as the stones struck roof and sidewalk, the burning sting as they struck your skin, as if the frost giants were having a snowball fight (they play rough). A heavy hailstorm can flatten a field full of crops, and if the stones are large enough, injure animals.

If you have a hailstone available for examination, view it under a magnifying glass or microscope. Otherwise, look it up in an encyclopedia. Contemplating the six-fold structure of snowflakes might also be useful here. Despite their apparent destructiveness, hailstones are part of a larger pattern, and they are themselves microcosms of a pattern, the central and crossing planes that point to the six directions (four on the horizontal plane, up, and down), and according to some analyses, the axes along which the Nine Worlds of Yggdrasil are arranged (there will be more about this in our discussion of EIHWAZ). What is the pattern of your life? How do you relate to the energies of the six directions?

The Wheel of Change

These patterns can be explored through meditation and spellwork. Begin by drawing a diagram of the Younger form of HAGALAZ (✳) on a round piece of cardboard so that it looks like the spokes on a wheel. Place yourself at the center (by writing your name there, or even pasting a snapshot of yourself over the point of intersection). Label the top and bottom of the upright axis "Above" (Light) and "Below" (Darkness), and the other four points as the four elemental directions (North = Cold; East = Storm; South = Heat; West = Waves). Place the circle on a larger piece of cardboard, stick a pin through the center so that it can be spun, and test it until it moves easily.

Now make a list of six things in your life that you consider problems. These may be things that are stuck or things you are trying to stabilize. Boil them down to basic principles if you can. Place a word describing each problem on the base, outside one of the points of the Hagal-wheel (or you can do this one problem at a time, placing the word at the top).

Choose a time and place where you will be undisturbed, and take a few moments to focus and center. This may be easier if you work by candlelight. Then spin the circle three times, chanting:

> Around, around (I am) unbound,
> (or, "problem X" is unbound)
> In holy hour, by haegl's power!

Let go after the third spin, and see which problems each line of the rune is pointing to (or nearest). Use these conjunctions as a starting point for meditation. For instance, if you are having a problem finding work and the point that ends up closest is "West," you might consider whether the regular cycles of the waves and the tides offer any insights. Perhaps your employment problems are part of a repeating pattern in your life or your environment. In that case, you need to be aware of personal or seasonal cycles and catch them on the upswing. On the other hand, if the direction nearest was "Above," you might seek for clarity and information. If necessary, you can repeat the spinning process twice more for clarification.

Another way to use the wheel is as an autohypnotic device, in which you put your problem in the center and spin and chant (adding whatever other chants occur to you), while visualizing the forces of HAGALAZ breaking it up and reforming it. But be aware that the patterning of HAGALAZ tends to get the process of change off to a violent start.

Needful Knowledge

Change, however exciting, is not an end in itself. This is why HAGALAZ and NAUDHIZ make such an interesting pairing. Perhaps the first question should be, "What do you need to change?" It leads to others:

What do you need?
What do you need to do?
Who do you need?
Who needs you?

Whole systems of therapy are devoted to helping people analyze and meet their needs. Many of us suppress awareness of our needs or spend our energy pursuing things we actually don't need at all. Our bodies need good food, exercise, and rest. Our spirits need nourishment, exercise, and recuperation time as well. But a primary requirement that is often not addressed in contemporary counseling is the need to be needed by others. Our sense of self-worth should not depend on how others view our value, but there is a satisfaction in knowing that we are a productive part of the pattern of things. In analyzing our needs, we should take care to include those activities that are both satisfying and useful to others.

Studying NAUDHIZ provides an excellent opportunity to take stock of your life. List the things you need. List the changes that must occur if you are to get them. And while you are on the subject, look back at your life and try to understand the forces that put you where you are today. What fate, in terms of heredity and environment, was wished upon you at your birth. How has your background bound you? How have you transformed or transcended it?

Over the centuries, a great deal of energy has gone into arguing the question of fate versus free will. In some cultures, almost everything that happens is considered to be fated and people simply endure what life dishes out to them. Americans tend to assume that all problems can be solved given the appropriate technology. The harsh life of Northern Europe bred people who recognized that stories rarely have happy endings, and you should therefore put your energy into making a good fight of it, whatever the result might be. Success and prosperity were certainly desirable, but quality of life mattered more. Dame Bertha Phillpotts has suggested that

> The gods are mortal and subject to defeat not, surely, because the Northerns could not imagine immortality or permanent success, but because disaster is the final acid test of character. The valour of Odin and his peers, like the valour of human heroes, can only be proved by their fighting a losing battle, with defeat foreordained and foreknown. (Phillpotts 1928, p. 13)

The fact is that in the course of a long life everyone encounters some kind of trouble, whether it be illness or economic hardship or loss. If you yourself are spared, you will still have to deal with the problems of those you love, which can be even harder. As Dorothy Parker once said to William Randolph Hearst, "There are two billion people in this world, and the story of not one of them will have a happy ending."

This does not mean that you should not try to change things. The Norse hero never submits tamely; if his bowstring breaks in battle, he will seek to braid a new one from his wife's hair (and she may refuse). The sagas are full of stories of harrowing escapes and survival against odds.

To paraphrase the prayer used in the Twelve-Step Program, if you are to have any energy left for living, you must identify those things that you can change, accept the things about which you can do nothing—and learn how to tell the difference between them. Neither joy nor pain lasts forever. You may not "live happily ever after," but if you understand the necessity that drives you, it is possible to live triumphantly. Life will never be easy, but it can, at the deepest level, be satisfying, and like the lives and deaths of the characters in the sagas, an inspiration to those who follow.

Wyrd Sisters

Almost everyone has heard of the Three Fates of classical mythology. Their Germanic equivalents, the Norns, were popularized by Wagner in his Ring operas. However, in Norse literature, the Norns belong to an entire class of beings, usually personified as female, who influence the fates of humankind. Such beings also appear in Greek and Roman mythology, and probably have a common Indo-European origin. In practice, the distinctions between them are somewhat hazy, but essentially they fall into three groups—Norns, Disir, and Fylgjur.

The best known of the Norns are Urdh, Verdandi, and Skuld. These three watch over the well beside which the gods sit in council, and water the roots of Yggdrasil. Of them, the Vœlva says:

> From there come maidens   knowing much—
> From the well   that waits under the Tree—
> [Urdh hight one,   the other Verdhandi—
> scores they cut—   the third is Skuld]
> There they laid down laws,   there they chose lives
> For children they spoke örlög.
>
> ("Völuspá": 20)

Here they are represented as three maidens, like those to whom King Fridleif took his son to receive a blessing (Saxo 1979, VI, p. 181). They cast "scores," probably runes, to determine the fates of men. Later exposure to classical concepts of the three Parcae who spin out fate may have led to the adoption of that image, so that the term *örlög-thættir*, meaning "fate strand," was used for the threads the Norns spun at the birth of a child.

According to Grimm, "Urdhr" comes from the preterit plural of *verdha*, "to become." "Verdandi" comes from the present participle of the same verb, while "Skuld" is the past participle of *skula*, "shall," from which the future tense is formed. They therefore embody that which has come into being, that which is in the process of becoming, and that which shall be. In later references, the first is old, the second in her prime, and the third a maiden, but of the three it is only Urdh, or "Wyrd" who appears alone, the goddess of fate who carries off doomed men.

There are, however, other Norns, some descended from gods, others from elves, others from dwarves. As the High One tells Gangleri, "The good Norns who come from good stock shape good lives, but those who meet with misfortune owe it to the evil Norns" (Snorri, 1987, in "Gylfaginning," p. 44). This comment implies that particular Norns might be concerned with specific families. They may be related to the Matronae, the triple goddesses portrayed in Germano-Roman sculpture holding cornucopias or children. Inscriptions give them names like "Gabiae," meaning "richly giving." Bede tells us that they were honored on the night before Yule, still called Mother-Night by the descendants of the Vikings in the Shetland Isles. Frigg, of whom it is said in "Lokasenna" (Elder Edda: 29) "I ween that Frigg the fates knoweth, though she say it not herself," also seems to have some influence over the begetting of children, and might be considered their patroness.

As birth goddesses the functions of the Norns shade into those of the Disir, defined as goddesses or as female guardian spirits, perhaps the spirits of ancestresses, who watch over their descendants. In the Germanic, as in many other cultures, the honored ancestors could attain the status of demigods. In medieval times, the spirits of the dead were often sighted among the folk of faerie, and the good fairies who grant wishes at a christening in folklore are clearly descendants of the Norns and Disir of earlier times. Two other classes of protecting spirits, Fylgjur and Valkyries, will be discussed when we study ELHAZ.

On the farmsteads, sacrifice was offered to the Disir in the autumn, at the turning of the year, or in some parts of Norway, in February. In the sagas, the Disir often appear in dreams to warn of danger. When Disir, or "dream-women" come to Thorsteinn Siduhallsson to warn him he will be murdered and ask to whom they shall go after his day, he tells them to watch over his son. (Kelchner 1935, p. 134). In some cases, as in that of Hall of Sidha in Iceland as told in the *Flateyjarbók*, the Disir appear to have been particularly upset by the head of a family's prospective conversion to Christianity.

It should be noted here that in Germanic tradition male ancestors were also honored. The grave mounds of men of great deeds and powerful personality could become the focus of cult practice, in which offerings were made and the spirit of the ancestor was invoked for protection and fertility. Such spirits were given the title of "Alfar," and although they are not the nature spirits we think of when we hear the English equivalent, "elves," in British folklore, the spirits of the mighty dead do form one component of the host of faeries. The Alfar are particularly associated with the god Freyr, just as the Disir are with his twin, Freyja, and their worship, like all matters involving the cycle of death and fertility, appears to be derived from the cult of the Vanir.

However, it is the female ancestral spirits who are most concerned with the wyrd of those to whom they appear. The Old Norse term for the fate that they announce is *Ørlög*, defined as primal law, fate, weird, doom. Thorsson says that its literal meaning is "primal layers," and implies that one's fate is the result of the layering of actions that have taken place in the past.

When someone's luck runs out in the sagas, his friends often comment that an evil fate has been laid down for him by the Norns, or conclude that his Disir have departed from him. But what are these layers that create the fates of which we complain? There are the opportunities and limitations available in the environment into which we are born, and the historical forces that act upon men and nations. These, I think, are the gifts of the Norns. There are the factors we inherit—genetic tendencies to height or weight, health or illness, and talents or skills—the contribution of the Disir. And finally there is the influence of our own personal histories: habits, experiences, the consequences of choices that we ourselves have made. These may be personified by the fylgja, our guiding spirits, and the older we grow, the more they shape our lives.

The Measure of Fate

In the legends, the Norns (or Nornir in Old Norse) are sometimes portrayed spinning out the thread of life (or in Wagner, twining the rope that holds the fate of the world). In some traditions of Wicca, initiates are bound to the coven by "taking their measure," consecrating a cord that corresponds to certain body measurements. This cord is kept as magical link and a symbol of commitment. You can make such a measure for yourself as an affirmation of self-knowledge.

You will need a hank of red yarn—wool or cotton (any natural fiber)—or if you know how to spin, a spindle and some carded wool. Spend some time meditating on the concepts associated with NAUDHIZ, and then make a list of those factors, hereditary, psychological, and environmental (including the human as well as the natural setting in which you live) that compel or constrain you. What are the strands in the cord of your fate? What makes up the measure that binds you?

Consider each one carefully. Some compulsions you may wish to break, but be sure that you truly understand the function of each one in your life before getting rid of it. There are others that you may decide to keep once you have altered the way in which you deal with them.

When you have finished your preparations, set up your ritual space as usual, perhaps adding an altar to the Norns with three candles or a copy of Arthur Rackham's wonderful illustration from the libretto to Wagner's *Ring*. Say a prayer to the Norns before beginning, such as:

> Norns now I summon, need is upon me,
> To fathom well what fate has fashioned—
> What has been, what is being, and becoming.
> Be there truth in my seeing, truth in my saying,
> With fortune may my wyrd be woven
> With magic may I make my measure. . .

If you are working with yarn, measure out a strand your own height and a foot or so more for each "need" you have identified. If you are spinning, divide your wool into that number of clumps. Take a moment to name each one, using a little of your own spit to bind in the meaning. Then begin to spin the wool or braid together the strands of yarn. You may hum over your work or use this chant (written by Leigh Ann Hussey; music is included in the ritual for this rune on page 314).

> Spin, spindle, spin; to end is to begin.
> Spiral winds the wyrd yarn.
> Dying is a being born.
> Spin, spindle, spin.

As you work, contemplate the interweaving of all these elements in your life. Seek to understand, and by understanding, to master them. See this cord as nourishing, rather than constraining you, an umbilical between your future and your past. As you twine, you are binding your essence into a strong and integrated whole, and by doing so, weaving your own wyrd.

When you have finished, you should have a cord whose length is approximately your own height (if it is too long, knot off or double back the ends rather than cutting; if it is too short, you may have to undo part of it and twine or braid more loosely). Thank the Norns for their help, and put the completed cord in a safe place.

A measure so constructed will be closely connected to you and should be treated respectfully. If you ever cease to work with such things, bury, rather than destroy it. When doing spiritual work, you can wind it around your waist to intensify self-awareness. You will also find other uses, such as tying it around things you wish to bring into your life in magical workings.

Needfire

The first thing to note about making fire with a fire drill or bow is that it is not as easy as it looks in the movies (any sufficiently primitive technology requiring skill is indistinguishable from magic).

The basic principle involves creating friction between a piece of hardwood (the spindle, or drill) and soft wood (the fireboard) until the resulting powder becomes a glowing mass that will set the kindling you have gathered aflame. This can be done by turning the spindle swiftly between the palms of the hands, rolling down the shaft to keep pressure on the indentation in the fireboard, or by using a block with an indentation in it (the hand piece) to press down on the top of the spindle, while a small bow whose cord is wrapped around the spindle is drawn back and forth to turn it.

To make this work, the materials must be properly prepared, and you must practice. The *Boy Scout Handbook* recommends making the spindle about a foot long and three-fourths of an inch thick, trimming the shaft so that it is octagonal, and rounding one end and tapering the other. The fireboard should be about four inches wide, a foot long, and half an inch thick, made of some soft wood such as basswood, elm, willow, white cedar, aspen, or cottonwood. A V-shaped notch should be cut in the edge, touching a gouged indentation to hold the point of the spindle. The bow is a stiff branch about two and a half feet long, with a string of strong leather or stout cord. The tinder, shredded cedar bark, fine wood shavings, or some other quick-kindling material, is laid next to the notch in the fireboard so that the glowing sawdust will ignite it.

To drill, kneel on one knee and set your foot on the fireboard. Loop the bowstring around the spindle, place the tip of the spindle in the indentation in the fireboard and hold it down with the hand piece, steadying your arm against your knee. Now begin to saw the bow back and forth with gradually increasing pressure, turning the spindle. Keep this up until smoke is rising from the fireboard, and a glowing ember has formed in the notch. Flick the ember into the tinder and blow steadily into the flame.

An explanation of this process with diagrams can be found in the *Boy Scout Handbook* or many survival guides. I suggest constructing the equipment and beginning practice a month before you propose to use it in a ritual. I also suggest having consecrated matches available as a back up.

The Group Ritual

The HAGALAZ/NAUDHIZ group ritual can be found on page 311. Its theme is the need for change.

Chapter 7

ISA and JERA

LIKE HAGALAZ AND NAUDHIZ, ISA AND JERA are a pair in which a rigid force is countered by one that works for change. But this time, their energies are both more focused and less dangerous. Here, as always, we should guard against any tendency to interpret the pair dualistically. Although they balance each other, neither rune is "good" or "bad." Their value and impact depend on the context. To be frozen in a glacier is death, but if your life is falling apart around you, some of ISA's stillness could be very welcome!

THE ELEVENTH RUNE: | ISA

Pronunciation: "EE-sa"
Meaning: Ice

**ISA is the Ice, inertia,
Stasis, and serenity. . .**

The Ancient Meanings

In the Germanic languages, ISA appears to descend from the putative Indo-European *eis*, "ice," which is essentially the same word in English today. In southern lands ice was less of a problem, but the form of the rune would appear to have been adopted from the Greek and Roman alphabets, in which it has the same sound. Indeed, one might imagine this icicle sound and shape to have originated with the tribes who followed the melting glaciers northward.

The meaning of the rune, on the other hand, offers some interesting possibilities for discussion. The Anglo-Saxon rune poem offers the most encouraging interpretation:

> | *[Is] byþ nearu oferceald, ungemetum slidor*
> (Ice be overcold, unmeasurably slippery;)
> *glisnaþ glæshluttur gimmum gelicust*
> (glisteneth clear as glass, to gems likest;)
> *flor forste geworuht, fæger ansyne.*
> (a floor by frost wrought, fair to be seen.)

Here the picture is of an element whose very beauty makes it more perilous, with the hard clarity of crystal. Its qualities are all in the extreme—overcold, immeasurably slippery. Ice is dangerous, but "fair to be seen." One is reminded of certain images from folklore—the Castle of Glass in the

Otherworld where King Arthur seeks the Cauldron of Arianrhod; Snow White in her crystal coffin.

In the Norse and Icelandic poems, the images (as usual) are harsher. The Norwegian poem picks up the image of the slippery floor, but now it has become a bridge—bad enough when iced over, or worse still, an ice-bridge over a crevasse in a glacier, and even more treacherous when it is a blind man who must cross it. However, at least the bridge is a broad one, so what might be meant here is a kenning for the earth covered over by winter ice.

> | *[Is] kœllum brú brœiða;*
> (Ice we call the broad bridge;)
> *blindan tharf at lœiðha.*
> (The blind man must be led.)

The Icelandic poem paints a picture that is harsher still. Here, the ice is encasing natural features, specifically the waters that ought to be flowing. It covers the rivers as bark covers a tree trunk; the ice floes roof the tossing waves. Perhaps the ice-covered river is the "broad bridge" referred to above. For the Anglo-Saxons it was a floor, but farther north it rises higher, a roof for Ran's kingdom, and there are depths beneath it. Now it is not only the blind who must fear it, but all doomed men.

> | *[Iss] er arborkr*
> (Ice is bark of rivers)
> *ok unnarþak*
> (and roof of the wave)
> *ok feigra manna far.*
> (and destruction for doomed men.)

Images in "Hávamál" amplify the Old Norse attitude toward ice. In verse 90, women's love is likened to riding on ice with a young horse who has not been shod with cleated winter shoes. The surface is motionless, but those who are above can slide to destruction unless they go with great care. Ice is also included in the list of things that must not be trusted until they are done with:

> At evening praise the day,   a torch when burned,
> A sword when tested,   a maiden when married,
> Ice when you've crossed it,   ale when it's drunk.
>
> ("Hávamál": 81)

In the case of ISA, the following verse may be relevant:

> I ken a ninth (spell)   if I stand in need
> Of warding my ship on the waves,
> The wind I calm,   also the waves
> And lull to sleep the sea.
>
> ("Hávamál": 154)

However, if this is to be taken as a reference to the stilling of the sea by the cold, the image is considerably more positive than any of the others.

In general, the traditional rune poems interpret ISA as an element the Scandinavians knew only too well. Ice is hard and without motion. It constrains the movement of the waters, but those who try to walk on it may find themselves moving out of control. Its treachery is passive; it becomes dangerous when humans try to cross it, amplifying their own motions, or emotions, to destroy them. The people of the North had a healthy respect for the ice that yearly encased their land, but they did not let the dangers of the footing imprison them. The second lesson of the old verses is that with care—leading the blind man, shoeing the pony—even the most slippery ice may be successfully crossed.

Modern Meanings

Thorsson extrapolates from the physical characteristics of ice to portray a metaphysical situation in which ISA is the Primal Ice that was melted to reveal the world. It is antimatter, gravity, inertia, entropy—the inertia and stillness that attracts the active force of fire. Mythologically, it signifies the rime-thurses, the frost-giants, who are Thor's especial enemies. ISA is the center of the hailstone. It holds together ego awareness and provides a psychic bonding that can help an individual survive stress. When unbalanced, it can cause dullness and stupidity. ISA is the original point and line.

Gundarsson's interpretation follows similar lines. He calls ISA the elemental rune of Niflheim and gives it the qualities of solidity, contraction, stillness, calmness, and unchangeability. He suggests that the broad bridge is the bridge to the Underworld and is extremely low and easy to attain. But he warns against assuming that one's icy shielding is sufficient against all dangers. It can be used as a bridge, but if it breaks, one will fall into the turmoil of the waters below.

Aswynn waxes eloquent on the toughening effect that dealing with ice had on the Northern peoples; however, if it did have such an evolutionary function, the people whose development it probably most affected were our common

Cro-Magnon ancestors, who fled before the advancing glaciers or followed their retreat back northward across the land. Beyond that, it should be observed that extremes of climate, whether they be northern cold or desert heat, tend to have similar effects on human societies, limiting the size of social groups, but strengthening the ties within them. Certainly the Eskimos, who have lived more intimately with the ice than anyone, have a relatively peaceful and cooperative culture.

Aswynn identifies ISA with the Norn Verdandi, who rules the static realm of "what is," and with the goddess Rind, whose initial refusal to bear a son to Odin she equates with the frozen sterility of the world in winter.

Osborn and Longland interpret the Anglo-Saxon poem to mean that the rune represents that which is static, beautiful but useless. It is wealth that is not shared, an uncontrolled and intrusive aspect of Nature.

Like all other forces, Primal Ice can be good or evil depending on whether or not it is part of a balanced process. Action and inertia must exist in a state of balanced tension for inner or outer health. Absolute inertia and perpetual motion are the two primary forces governing the universe. In Norse mythology, the world began when the original ice was melted by the fires of Muspelheim (just as the inertia of Binah is activated by the vibration emanating from Chokmah in Kabbalistic doctrine), and the frozen edges of Niflheim continue to be melted by the boiling waters of Hvergelmir, lest another Ice Age recapture the earth.

ISA can represent the absolute inner stillness that is one goal of meditation, and as Thorsson points out, the ability to achieve that focus is necessary if one is to gather strength to follow a spiritual path. It becomes a problem only when the individual wants to remain in that state of rest and refuses to interact with the outer world (autism or catatonia!). This is the icy prison from which the princess Turandot must be released in Puccini's opera; the evil of C. S. Lewis's White Witch of Narnia, who has made a world in which it is "always winter and never Christmas!"

Interaction with ISA can occur at two levels. On the outer, its treacherous surface upsets the equilibrium of those who try to use it even though the ice itself never moves. In this sense, ISA can act as a shield that defends by letting the attacker's own energy defeat him. From inside, it is the ultimate integrity, the core of stillness to which the ego retreats to resist or rest. But if the personality is not balanced by forces that adjust and bend, this strength may become a prison, or, overstressed, shatter into glittering shards.

Interpreting and Using ISA

ISA may be uncomfortable, but it is one of the more significant and power-ful runes that can appear in a reading, and is of great use in magic.

Willis says that the appearance of ISA in a reading indicates that the progress of the matter under consideration will be "frozen" for the present, but may "defrost" later. It may signify something that at present is in abeyance. In some readings, the situation may have frozen beyond thawing.

Aswynn points out that on its own, ISA is inert, and simply preserves. It is the "I," the ego, the core of the personality, and she suggests that ISA is a good rune to use in focusing, concentrating the will, and protecting one's center.

ISA is indeed useful in magical shielding and protection. It can help to "cool a situation down," to negate disruptive or destructive energies, and can balance THURISAZ. It may indicate a personality pattern that is "frozen" in place and requires the balancing energy of KAUNAZ or SOWILO to change. In divination, it may indicate a frustrating situation with no change in sight.

Gundarsson calls ISA the antithesis of FEHU and says it can be used mag-ically to bind active forces, either of growth or of disintegration. Positively, it calms confusion or hysteria and numbs pain. In excess, it can cause bar-renness, paralyzing fear, insensibility, dullness, or obsession.

Peterson feels it indicates a "freezing-up" or cooling-off period in affairs, a barren period, after which a thaw will come. It can indicate coldness between people, emotional stiffness, or an inability to release emotions from within. It may indicate stagnation, or, more positively, a need to rest and retreat from activity in order to seek self-knowledge.

As suggested by Willis, the presence of ISA in a reading may indicate that a project, activity, or relationship is stuck, or losing momentum. If the reading is spiritual, it could indicate a need to balance the personality by invoking some active force, or possibly that the individual needs to seek inner stillness to balance too much action, depending on the context.

ISA can be the clarity of a cold anger that is so much more dangerous than fiery rage. Its strength is its hardness, but it is brittle, and in working to release a person or a situation from the grip of ISA, one should beware of the energy that will be released when the ice breaks. In addition to psy-chological cooling, ISA may also be used to invoke physical cold: in com-bination with HAGALAZ, to lower the body temperature and keep it there, in weather-magic to cool down a heat wave, and so on. But both these runes are extremely powerful, and should be used with caution. It would be best to include a rune of balance, such as JERA, in the working to keep the freezing process from extending beyond control.

THE TWELFTH RUNE: ⟨ ⟩ ᛃ JERA

Pronunciation: "YARE-a"
Meaning: Year

JERA'S Year-Wheel yields good harvest;
Right reward as seasons ripen.

The Ancient Meanings

The old Germanic JERA is the year, more specifically seen as the year's culmination, the season of harvest. In Old English, the word is *ger*, and in Norse, *ar*, both meaning "year." In Old Norse, the hard "yuh" sound of English is represented by *j*, while the *y* indicates a vowel sound ("i"). However, when writing runes in the Elder Futhark, ⟨ should be used to indicate the English or Old Norse "yuh," and the Anglo-Saxon rune *ger* (ᛄ) should be used for the same sound in modern or Old English, whereas the Younger Futhark *ar* rune (ᛃ) has the phonetic value of the letter *a* ("uh"), for which it should be used when writing in that rune set.

After the harshness of HAGALAZ, NAUDHIZ, and ISA, it is a relief to see the year wheel turn toward summer once more with JERA. Rightly is it called joyful, as in the Anglo-Saxon rune poem, when the earth bears fruit for all.

> ᛄ *[Ger] byþ gumena hiht, ðonne God Læteþ,*
> (Summer is called joyful, when God lets,)
> *halig heofones cyning, hrusan syllan*
> (holy heaven's king—shining fruits)
> *beorhte bleda beornum ond ðearfum.*
> (be born from earth for rich and poor.)

Old English leech books include many prayers and charms to be said when harvesting or using herbs. One of the most interesting is the often quoted "Æcer-bot," a ceremony for blessing the fields or protecting them against sorcery. The text is given in full in Godfrid Storms's *Anglo-Saxon Magic* (Storms 1975).

The first stage in the procedure consists of taking pieces of sod from the four sides of the field, anointing them with oil, honey, yeast, the milk of all the cattle on the land, and parts of most of the kinds of trees and herbs, and having them blessed by a priest. The farmer then faces east, lays the sods on four crosses made of quickbeam (rowan), and chants what is essentially a hymn to the sun. Next, the farmer turns three times sunwise (clockwise), lies upon the ground, and prays. Next, seeds from a beggar, incense, fennel, hallowed soap, and salt are placed on the plough, followed by the prayer below, which is the least Christianized of those preserved in the spell.

> *Erce, Erce, Erce, eorþan modor,*
> (Erce, Erce, Erce, mother of earth,)
> *geunne þe se alwalda, ecce drihten,*
> (may the all-ruling, everlasting drighten grant you)
> *æcera wexendra and wridendra,*
> (fields waxing and thriving,)
> *eacniendra and elniendra,*
> (flourishing and bountiful,)
> *sceafta scira herse-wælsima,*
> (bright shafts of millet-crops,)
> *and þæra bradan bere-wæstma,*
> (and the broad barley-crops,)
> *and þæra hwitan hwæte-wæstma,*
> (and the white wheat-crops,)
> *and ealra eorþan wæstma.*
> (and of all the crops of the earth.)
> *Geunne him ece drihten*
> (May the everlasting drighten grant him,)
> *and his halige þe on heofonum synt*
> (and his holy ones that in heaven are,)
> *þæt hys yrþ si gefritod wið ealra*
>   *feonda gehwæne,*
> (that his produce may from all foes be warded,)
> *and heo si geborgen wið ealra bealwa gehwylc*
> (and against every harm be secure)
> *þara lyblaca geond land sawen*
> (from witchcraft sown throughout the land.)
> *Nu ic bidde ðone waldened se ðe*
> (Now I pray the ruling one)
> *ðas woruld gesceop*

(who created this world)
þæt ne sy nan to þæs cwidol wif,
(that no woman may be so eloquent,)
ne to þæs cræftig man
(and no man so crafty)
þæt awendan ne mæge word þus gecwedene.
(that they can upset the words thus spoken.)

After this, the ploughman drives the first furrow, and a loaf kneaded with milk and holy water is laid in it with another prayer. The wheat-crops and barley-crops of the hymn are the shining fruits that the harvest of *ger* brings forth from Mother Earth.

The same meaning comes clearly from the Northern rune poems. The Icelandic poem states:

ᚼ *[ár] er gumna goði*
(Harvest is a blessing to men)
ok gott sumar
(and good summer)
ok algróinn akr.
(and fully ripe crops.)

But the Northern farmer knew better than to take anything for granted. The wisdom of the "Hávamál" tells us:

Acres sown too early,   trust not ever,
Nor too soon a son:
Weather wrecks the acres,   lack of wit, the son,
Each of them is a risk.

("Hávamál": 88)

The Norse poem begins with the same words as the Icelandic, and continues with a note of thanks to Frodhi, who was undoubtedly the "Lord" to whom the folk prayed for good harvests before the priests rewrote all their prayers. It is possible that Frodhi was the Danish name for the god called Ing by the Heardings and Freyr in Sweden.

ᚼ *[ár] er gumna góðe*
(Harvest is a blessing to men;)
get ek at ærr var Fróðe.
(I say that Frodhi was liberal.)

In Old Norse, *fródhr* means "wise." According to both Snorri and Saxo, this name was borne by an ancient king of Denmark, whose reign was a time of universal peace and unequalled prosperity. After he died he was carried around the land in a wagon (as the image of Freyr was later in Sweden) and finally laid in a burial mound.

Modern Meanings

Thorsson identifies JERA as a model of the cyclical pattern of universe (arising, becoming, passing) which expresses the blessings of the Norns in a different way. It is the yearly cycle of the sun, especially the summer half, when crops are sown, grown, and harvested. JERA represents the natural law of cause and effect (reward for right action) and governs both cosmic and physical fertility. It is the dynamic dyad and the omnipresent circumference.

For Aswynn, this is a rune of time, encompassing the powers of all three Norns. If one arranges the runes on a circular calendar, placing JERA in December, DAGAZ will appear at Midsummer. (On the other hand, if one begins the study of the runes in the winter, one comes to JERA at the height of the summer's growing season.) Like the cycle of the seasons, JERA manifests the principle of the eternal return.

Osborn and Longland focus on the application of the rune to farming. They interpret the rune's meaning as "season" and feel that it shows the complementary nature of ice and warmth in making the grain grow. Gundarsson reminds us that in the North, the year was divided into two complementary seasons, winter and summer. A good "year" is one in which all has been done according to the natural timetable to fulfill the cycle. Spiritually, this is a rune that governs the natural and harmonious unfolding of awareness. The growth of the spirit cannot be forced. Productive progress requires patience, planning, and continued care.

There seems to be a general agreement that JERA is the rune of transformation and balance, the expression of the cycle of the seasons in general, and from the Norse perspective, the balance between the primary forces of warmth and cold. This opposition, when balanced, provides the motion necessary so that things can change and grow. This rune is similar in both appearance and meaning to the yin-yang symbol, which expresses the relationship between active and passive forces. Psychologically and psychically, JERA shows us the necessity of recognizing the recurrent rhythms of our inner seasons. Spiritual development often progresses in a series of cycles, in which one keeps returning to areas already studied and skills one considered mastered with new understanding, rather than proceeding to enlightenment in a straight line.

The cold and stillness of winter are as essential to growth as the warmth and movement of summer. The sun's journey away is as important as her return. Too much heat can be as dangerous as too much cold, as in the "greenhouse effect," or for those of us who live in the American West, too much water can be as bad as a drought. Both physical and spiritual health are dependent on recognition of that relationship. In our work and lives, we need to know when to push and when to wait, how to "go with the flow" and work with the natural cycles and currents rather than opposing them. It teaches us that sometimes it is necessary to wait for things to achieve their natural fruition.

JERA can be seen as the spindle whorl, the circular weight that keeps the spindle turning in equilibrium, the balance and grounding for the spiral of Time itself. The rune is also a sign that although all things may pass, all things also return. The positive aspect of this is that nothing is ever lost forever—even the religion of the old gods! Reincarnation was one of the possibilities of the afterlife. The downside of this is that "what goes around comes around . . ." The evil that is done in one turn of the wheel will eventually come back to haunt those responsible—as the consequences of the damage that we have done to the earth are beginning to show up today. Perhaps JERA should be seen as a rune of both spiritual and physical ecology. Only when all elements are in balance, and in motion, can either a human being or the world survive.

Interpreting and Using JERA

JERA can be used to move energy through the body, to tune in to the flow of cosmic force in martial arts or in ritual. In healing work, it should be used to encourage natural bodily processes to move back into alignment. Its complementarity and energy can be used to energize a relationship. It is also one of the primary runes to use in gardening, inscribed on the backs of the plastic sticks that identify the plant or on the flowerpot, or sung over the plant to encourage the natural flow of growth energy.

Willis states that in a reading the rune may indicate the harvest season or that the querent will reap a reward for previous efforts. In general it is positive, though if the work involved was negative, the result will be also. Peterson says it can mean prosperity for a whole community, a good season. It is used in charms to invoke abundance. In the physical realm, JERA is most likely to indicate prosperity, reward for labor, and such. Spiritually, this rune should relate in some way to the need for movement and balance or to accept the natural cycle. Magically, it can be used to rebalance things that are out of alignment.

According to Aswynn, JERA is almost always encouraging in readings. It creates gentle changes, moving things faster when the lefthand angle is uppermost and slowing them when the angle on the left is lower. Gundarsson states that JERA should be used to effect purposes slowly and naturally, in accordance with the flow of wyrd, making slow and subtle changes when the time is right. It can help to manifest the forces of other runes.

JERA rules the creative process. In personal work, it should be used to guide the choice of times for rituals, especially initiations. It is used to develop spiritual potential, or conversely, to bring the negative layers of someone's wyrd to fruition. It should be used with care—speeding the growth process can encourage weeds as well as crops, and a spiral that leads upward can also turn down.

ISA AND JERA: STUDY AND EXPERIENCE

The Stillness of the Ice

ISA is the ice rune, carrying all the connotations that implies. To understand it, one must explore the implications for good or for ill of stillness, inertia, and rest. It is also, by extension, a rune of winter (for instance if ISA accompanies JERA in a rune reading about the weather). To understand it, one may meditate upon the function of winter in temperate climates, killing some, but also protecting and allowing the hidden seeds time to germinate and the soil time to rest. Seen from this perspective, ISA's stillness does not oppose JERA's cycle, but is rather a part of it.

Ice Rest

ISA can be used in meditation as a key to attaining this state of rest. One procedure is to lie down with spine and legs straight, arms by your sides. A North/South alignment is desirable. Decide how long you will spend in this meditation, then draw the rune ISA on your forehead. Regularize your breathing, counting four beats in, holding two, and four beats out, until you are focused. Then, limb by limb, relax each muscle group by contracting it and then allowing it to slacken completely.

It is best to start with the extremities, curling the toes and releasing them, then the muscles of calf and thigh. Work next on the fists and arms. Let awareness of the extremities fade as you proceed to contract and relax the muscles of your buttocks and belly, pectorals and shoulders, and finally scrunch up and then release the muscles of your face and scalp. This systematic procedure enables you to release tensions in muscles you may not have known were stiff. It is a useful way of beginning any meditation. However, if contracting muscles in this way causes them to cramp, substitute systematic stretching.

When your body is completely relaxed and inert, so that you can scarcely feel your limbs, begin to let the tensions in your mind and spirit go. One by one, identify the things that are worrying you, see them grow pale, or if you are more aurally oriented, let the words grow faint and fade away. One by one consider your concerns, your plans, your hopes and fears, and then, without approving or rejecting, simply let them go. Your object is to become still, doing nothing, desiring nothing, the primal line that shrinks to the primal point. Replace each image that appears with whiteness, emptiness, silence, purity, and rest.

When the time you have allotted for this meditation is over, begin to visualize warmth releasing your frozen limbs. One appropriate image is the warm tongue of the cow Audhumla, licking away the ice that imprisons you as mammalian mothers lick their newborn offspring to get the circulation going. If you begin with one hand, you can then use it to draw the JERA rune on your forehead, which will speed the process for the rest of you. Feel the ice melting and releasing you, warmth returning to your limbs, color returning to the world. Once more you may contract muscle groups, restoring sensory awareness. Memory of tasks and problems will also return, but at least you have had a moment of winter in which to rest and get ready to face them anew.

This meditation can be performed whenever necessary to relieve stress or calm frazzled nerves.

Harvest

The twelfth rune in the futhark, JERA, is pivotal in position, form, and function. It holds a middle position in its aett and in the futhark itself, and when the runes are drawn in a circle, provides the impetus to start the wheel turning back again. JERA also can be seen as continuing the work begun with HAGALAZ and NAUDHIZ, helping one to break out of old patterns and start new cycles, or to become more aware of the spiral of deeper cycles and patterns in one's life and the world.

One way to experience the energy of JERA is to work with growing things. Even growing a houseplant in a pot can be rewarding. Better still is planting a plot of ground. If you have had little luck with other plants, try a pot of herbs, whose aromatic leaves stimulate the senses and provide an almost immediate reward as a source of seasoning. Sweet herbs such as mints and lavender can be used to scent a healing bath, while for those who have only tried dried seasonings, the more familiar culinary herbs are a remarkable experience when used fresh in omelets or a salad.

The *Sunset Book of Growing Herbs* (available in many garden shops or nurseries) is a good primer for growing herbs, Michael Castleman's *The Healing Herbs* (1991) for using them, *Culpeper's Complete Herbal* (Meyerbooks 1990) for beginning to explore their traditional uses, Grieves's *A Modern Herbal*, for folklore, and the *Encyclopedia of Magical Herbs* (Cunningham 1991) for their magical symbolism.

Garden Magic

Among other things, JERA is a rune of garden magic. JERA and other appropriate runes, such as FEHU, URUZ, and INGWAZ, can be sung over the seeds and plants and inscribed on the backs of the plastic stakes on which the nursery prints the plant's name. Rune sounds can be combined in a Galdor-chant—"Fe-Ur-Ing-Jeraaaa . . ." or a spell like the following can be sung over the garden whenever you water.

> ᚠ   FE Fair be this field and flourish well, with
> ᚢ   UR Urgent force from up and under;
> ◇   ING Sing I now green things upspringing,
> ᚼ   JERA Year-wheel yield from hoar to harvest.

Offer your garden, or plant pot, as a shrine for the local landspirits. Invite them to come and live there, ask them to contribute energy to the plants and protect them from pests, and when things grow well, thank them. If you make food or drink offerings to the gods in indoor rituals, afterward you can set them out in the garden, where they will soon disappear. Milk poured into a depression in the earth or over a sacred stone set in the middle of the plot is also a suitable offering.

When you work with your plants, take some time to simply experience their energy and open yourself to awareness of the season—the intense energy of spring, the settled strength of summer growth, the mellow triumph of seed-time, and the peace of the fallow season.

The Germanic Calendar

The Germanic peoples divided the year into two seasons of twenty-six weeks each, winter and summer, counted in moons. In Old Norse the words for year and harvest are the same, and years might be counted as harvests. The word for a solar year was *sólargangr*, a course of the sun, beginning at Midsummer. Like the Celts and the Hebrews, they started their days at sunset.

Winter began between October 11 and 18 (possibly calculated as the first full moon after the autumnal equinox), with the festival called Winter Nights, at which offerings were made to the Alfar and/or the Disir. In Iceland, summer traditionally began on the Thursday between April 9 and 15 (again, possibly the first full moon after the spring equinox). This feast was called *Sumarmál*. This may have been the original date of the feast of Ostara. Eventually the Icelanders coped with the calendrical distortions of this system by intercalating four extra nights in the middle of the summer and an extra week every seven years.

A third major festival was Yule, celebrated around the Midwinter Solstice, or in the very far north, when the sun first returned to the sky after the Midwinter's darkness. In Iceland, Midsummer was the time for the Althing. Midsummer celebrations elsewhere depended on the locality; however, it remains a major holiday in Scandinavia today, with some customs, such as dancing the Maypole, that are celebrated earlier at lower latitudes.

In medieval Iceland, most of the official holidays were in the summer season. The Várthing (which may take its name from the goddes Vár, who hears oaths), or "Spring Thing," was held in each district at the end of the fourth week of the summer season to deal with local cases and prepare for the national assembly. The seventh week of summer was called *fardagar*, the moving days, in which tenancy and property were transferred. The date for the Althing was when ten weeks of summer had passed. At the nineteenth week, or eight weeks before summer's end, the *leith*, or "Autumn Thing," was held at the local level to deal with the summer's business and report on the Althing.

Month names varied according to era and locality. Some of the names are uncertain, and in Iceland, the summer months might simply be counted, rather than being named. Some of the winter moon names seem derived from ancient festivals and perhaps an old lunar calendar, while surviving summer names are related to activities. The names Midsummer and Jul (Yule) might have referred to the seasons surrounding the solstices rather than moons. For a more detailed discussion of Norse time concepts, see *Culture and History in Medieval Iceland* (Hastrup 1985).

Group Ritual

If you are working with a group and wish to perform the group ritual for ISA and JERA, it is on page 323. It explores the relationship between winter and summer as it develops out of the Old Norse Creation myth, in which the world came into being through the interaction of primal elements and forces.

Chapter 8

EIHWAZ and PERTHRO

LIKE MOST OF THE RUNES WE HAVE ALREADY STUDIED, the thirteenth and fourteenth runes in the futhark can be interpreted in a number of ways. However, when one looks at EIHWAZ and PERTHRO as a pair, the imagery that seems to dominate is that of the Tree and the Well. In this reading, EIHWAZ the Yew is identified with Yggdrasil, the Worldtree. Interpreting PERTHRO as the vessel of fate allows one to identify it with the wells at the roots of the Tree, which are the focus for so much archetypal imagery. Indeed, with these two runes we move into a world of primal meaning. For an interesting exploration of the relationship between these motifs, see *The Well and the Tree: A Study of Concepts of Cosmology and Time in Early Germanic Culture* (Bauschatz 1982).

Considered from this point of view, the god who dominates our consideration of EIHWAZ is he who was sacrificed on the Worldtree to obtain the runes, Odin. In the same way, PERTHRO may be seen as a rune of the goddess who seems to wait behind the Norns, she who is first among the Mothers who bless the newborn, Frigga.

THE THIRTEENTH RUNE: ᛇ ᛝ ᛉ EIHWAZ

Pronunciation: "AY-wahz"
Meaning: Yew Tree

EIHWAZ, yew of Yggdrasil,
Bow of Life and Death, worlds binding.

The Ancient Meanings

In all the rune poems this rune means "yew," either the living tree or the tree made into a bow. However, its placement in the rune row and its phonetic value differ. In the old Germanic (Elder) futhark, it is the thirteenth rune, and its sound comes from the vowel sound at the beginning of the name. Its position is the same in the Anglo-Saxon futhark, although the sound is closer to "*eo*." In the Younger Futhark, however, the rune is placed last (sixteenth), and appropriately enough, its sound is the final "r" of the nominative ending. There, it is drawn either as the reverse of ELHAZ ᛉ or as a kind of doubled version of the older form.

The Norse and Anglo-Saxon poems both describe the yew as a tree. In the Anglo-Saxon verses, the tree's rough exterior and deep roots are emphasized. Its strength is clearly protective; it burns well (or preserves a flame in its heart), giving joy to the home.

> ᛇ *[eoh] byþ utan unsmeþ treow,*
> (The yew outside is a rough-barked tree,)
> *heard hrusan fæst, hyrde fyres,*
> (but strong and firm, guard of fires,)
> *wyrtrumun underwreþyd, wyn on eþle.*
> (by deep roots upheld, joy to the home.)

The Norse poem focuses on the fact that it is evergreen, but also mentions its qualities as firewood:

> ᛦ *[yr] er vertrgrønstr víða;*
> ([yew] is the greenest of trees in winter;)
> *vant er, er brennr, at sviða.*
> (when it burns, it sputters.)

The Icelandic poem, on the other hand, shows us the wood already fashioned into a bow, presumably because the yew does not grow in Iceland and the only way in which people there would encounter it would be in the form of war gear. We see, therefore, a bow strung and ready for use, further described by the kenning, "giant of the arrow."

> ᛇ *er bendr bogi*
> ([yew] is bent bow)
> *ok brotgjarnt járn*
> (and brittle iron)
> *ok fífu fárbauti.*
> (and Farbauti (a giant) of the arrow.)

In "Grímnismál," Odin tells us that the dwelling of the god Ullr is located in Ydalir—the dale of the yew trees. According to Snorri, Ullr was the stepson of Thor and was a winter hunter—a god of the bow and snowshoes, who crossed the seas on a magic bone, possibly skates. In Skaldic verse the shield is called the "ship of Ullr." His name is found in many place names, often near others associated with the Vanir. Beyond this, we know little. His name seems to be cognate to a Gothic word meaning "glory" or "majesty," and it is possible that he was an early sky god who was assimilated into the Aesir as a deity of hunting. If so, there is a logical reason to consider the yew his sacred tree.

Modern Meanings

Thorsson identifies EIHWAZ with the Worldtree, Yggdrasil. According to his research, another name for the yew is the "needle-ash," and this is the kind of ash tree referred to when Yggdrasil is described in the Eddas. He points out that the yew, like Yggdrasil, is an evergreen, and the longest-lived of European trees. For this reason it was considered a symbol of eternal life and was often planted in graveyards, but for the same reason, it came to be considered a death tree as well. Symbolically, EIHWAZ is the world axis of Yggdrasil, which links opposing forces and provides a pathway between the worlds; it is an axis of transforming magical fire.

Aswynn's interpretation is similar. She identifies Yggdrasil with the human spine, conduit of Kundalini's fire, and like Thorsson sees it as a link between the worlds. Moving along it, one is in a state of transition or suspension, like Odin when he hung between earth and heaven, seeking the runes.

Gundarsson also interprets EIHWAZ as a rune of great mystical power, the force that links opposites and carries energy between them. The yew is a tree of life and death. Its poison can kill or facilitate initiation. The eternal spirit lies hidden within as the life of the tree is shielded by its rough bark, surviving the death of the body, to be reborn. The tree and the rune are therefore symbols of paradoxical opposites and the union between them.

Osborn and Longland focus on the paradox between the yew's rough exterior and its inner fire. They see the imagery in the Anglo-Saxon rune poem connecting Eoh with Wynn and Ethel. The paradox continues when one notes that though the tree is evergreen, its needles are poisonous, and its wood can make a bow that protects or kills. Willis, defining EIHWAZ as a bow, sees it as a defense against danger. The bowman has his sights on a clear target. Peterson sees in the yew resilient strength, ability to defect danger or difficulty.

The long life of the yew makes it a particularly apt choice for Yggdrasil the Eternal, as its association with graveyards makes it an appropriate candidate for the tree upon which Odin was hanged during his initiation to wisdom. Either way, the rune can stand for the Worldtree.

Yggdrasil serves a variety of purposes in Norse mythology, but some of its most interesting functions are in trance work. The Worldtree is used as a ladder by which to reach other "worlds" in shamanic visions all over the world, but especially in Siberia, which connects to the same circumpolar cultural complex that includes Scandinavia. Among the Araucani of Tierra del Fuego, the *machi* (shaman) ascends a tree trunk and drums and dances atop it to pray for power. Climbing trees or poles is found in initiation and healing rituals in locations as widely dispersed as Southeast Asia and the Caribbean.

This metaphor for astral travel would appear to come from an extremely archaic level of human consciousness. Tree symbolism may be the origin of the tripod from which the Delphic oracle prophesied and is almost certainly the inspiration behind the *seidhhjallr*, the high seat in which the Norse Völva sits to prophesy. Among some Siberian tribes, the cosmic tree connected heaven, earth, and the Underworld, or extended through seven or nine heavens. The idea of a Tree of Worlds is also familiar to students of Kabbalah. Clearly, the cosmic tree functions as a pathway between planes of consciousness. Exactly how those planes (or worlds) are arranged and what they contain depends on the system in question. (For further information in this area, see Mircea Eliade's *Shamanism*.)

Trees in general seem to play a significant role in European mythology. Both the early Celts and Germans worshipped in sacred groves. Some species of trees were sacred to specific gods. In the Mediterranean the oak belonged to Jupiter; in the North, to Thor, but in practice, any particularly ancient and impressive tree might become an object of veneration. Sacrifices and offerings were hung from the branches; the decorated Maypole and the Christmas tree are both survivals of this custom. To this day, pieces of cloth are tied to the branches of the trees around sacred wells in rural districts of the British Isles as offerings.

In practice, almost any tree can serve as a symbol of Yggdrasil. A tree is literally a link between earth and sky. Its roots draw up moisture and nutrients from the earth, while its leaves use the energy of the sun to transform them. Through the leaves carbon dioxide is absorbed from the air, and oxygen is returned to it. A tree is constantly moving energy up and down, and this power can be sensed if one is in the proper state of consciousness. Embracing a tree trunk, or meditating with one's back against it, allows one to experience some of the power of Yggdrasil.

Interpreting and Using EIHWAZ

EIHWAZ can be a rune of paradox, or of the connections between opposites. Depending on the context, it could indicate spiritual ascent or exploration, or a movement from one state or situation to another. It might indicate an apparently difficult or dangerous problem that can be turned to advantage, or the need to look at the connections between things—the roots of the matter, or the outcome.

Willis believes the rune means that an apparently bad situation will reverse itself or turn favorable; a hindrance or minor catastrophe will do no harm. Aswynn points out the usefulness of EIHWAZ as a "backbone" for bindrunes. She recommends visualizing the rune along your spine and moving its energy up and down to link your unconscious with your higher consciousness so that you are aware of both simultaneously. Gundarsson suggests making gand (magic) wands and staves out of yew, perhaps because spells projected through this wood will fly as strongly as if shot from a bow. It can be used to send messages between the worlds, to ward those who travel to other realms, and as a shield in magical duels. In readings, I most often find that it refers to making connections.

In healing, EIHWAZ can be used for back problems, to strengthen or straighten the spine. If one chooses a favorite tree to represent Yggdrasil, inscribe it with the rune. Drink offerings can be poured out at its roots, and prayers and food offerings can be tied to the branches.

THE FOURTEENTH RUNE ᛈ PERTHRO

Pronunciation: "PER-thro"
Meaning: Lot, Cup, Game Piece

**PERTHRO pours its play from rune cup,
chance or change for man or child.**

The Ancient Meanings

The "P" rune does not appear in the Younger Futhark, where BERKANO serves for both "*b*" and "*p*" sounds, when the latter are necessary. In one late Danish futhark (King Waldemar's, thirteenth century) it is written as ᛒ or ᚴ.

However, in Old Norse *P* rarely appears. The Northern and Southern Indo-European languages seem to have used either *B* or *P* respectively. Ulfilas's Gothic dictionary has only seven words beginning with *P*, very few are found in the Anglo-Saxon poems, and most Old Norse words beginning with *P* are loan words from other languages.

The rune name is given in old Germanic as PERTHRO, interpreted as "a device for casting lots," and the shape of the rune is often interpreted as that of a dice cup. Lots can be cast for gaming or divination. Tacitus describes what would appear to be an early method of casting the runes.

> No people are more addicted to divination by omens and lots. . . . They cut a twig from a fruit-tree, and divide it into small pieces, which, distinguished by certain marks, are thrown promiscuously upon a white garment. Then the priest of the canton, if the occasion be public; if private, the master of the family; after an invocation of the gods, with his eyes lifted up to heaven, thrice takes out each piece, and, as they come up, interprets their signification according to the marks fixed upon them. (*Germania*: 10)

Elsewhere Tacitus indicates that gambling was a major recreation (or perhaps addiction) among the German tribes:

> They play at dice, when sober, as a serious business: and that with such a desperate venture of pain or loss, that, when everything else is gone, they set their liberties and persons on the last throw. The loser goes into voluntary servitude. . . . (*Germania*: 24)

This attitude toward games of chance seems to be characteristic of warrior cultures. Practices that sound almost identical are described among the North American Indians.

This rune, given the name PEORTH, is included in the Anglo-Saxon rune poem, in which it is usually translated as "chess piece."

> ᚴ *[Peorð] byþ symble plega and hlehter*
> (The chess/gaming piece means play and laughter)
> *wlancum [on middum], ðar wigan sittaþ*
> (where in the middle, the warriors sit)
> *on beorsele bliþe ætsomne.*
> (in beerhall blithely together.)

At least in the earlier period, the game referred to is probably not chess but a Northern board game called in Old Norse *hnefa-tafl* (variant, *hneftafl*), sometimes translated as "draughts," or "tables," a game that reflects the strategies of Iron Age warfare as chess does that of the feudal age. A modern version of this has been published as "Swords and Shields." A somewhat less complex version of the game was played in Ireland as *fidchel*.

A gaming piece in Old Norse is *töfl*. Pieces were white and red, or sometimes made of precious metal. All pieces moved like the rook in modern chess and captured by surrounding the opponent. The outer pieces attacked and the inner defended the king, whose goal was to escape from the center of the board. Sometimes dice were used to determine the number of squares a piece could move. Playing such board games was a favorite occupation on long winter evenings around the fire, and they are often mentioned in the sagas.

This is presumably the game referred to in the verses from the "Völuspá":

> Playing hneftafl in the garth   they (the gods) were right joyful,
> Nor did they lack gold
> Until there came three maidens from the thurses—
> Much was their might—from Jotunheim.
>
> There, afterward,   the most wonderful
> Golden tafl-pieces   in the grass they will find,
> The ones that in elder days   the kindred had owned.
>
> ("Völuspá": 8, 61)

The Anglo-Saxon poem gives us an image of warriors taking their ease in the hall with a board game, a friendly and intellectual combat suitable for fighters, yet without bloodshed (although, as with the dicing, it might lead to economic disaster). It is a typical pursuit of peace. This is undoubtedly why in "Völuspá" the playing of the board game becomes the symbol of the Golden Age of the Aesir at the beginning of the world, and of the restoration of Divine Order at the end of the poem.

In the earlier verse, the idyllic mood of the first two lines is broken by the arrival of the three thurs-maidens. Hollander and other translators interpret this as a reference to the Norns. Although Snorri tells us that all of the races have their Norns, I believe this is the only indication that "the" Norns— Urdh, Verdandi, and Skuld—are of jotun kin. On the other hand, almost every character in the Edda who is not specifically identified as a Van or Ás seems to be an etin of some kind, so perhaps we should not be surprised. What this tells us is that the Norns are sprung from the world's primal powers. Their arrival on the scene signals the shift from the first phase of creation, in which the world was made and named, to the second, in which life was given to humankind, the Aesir and the Vanir warred and became allies, and the sequence of events that will eventually lead to Ragnarók began. Fate and Chance have entered the world.

Of course the casting of lots or the playing of a game (or flipping a coin) has long been seen as a means by which fate can manifest, so it is perhaps to be expected that the gods' gaming should lead to the arrival of the Norns. However, the Norns are concerned not only with fate in general, but with the fate awarded to each being at its birth. These verses, therefore, lead us to a possible secondary meaning for the rune, which has to do with birth. Wardle and some other writers on the subject have identified PERTHRO with the old German root word for childbearing (*ga-burdh-iz*). He believes that the *wigan* and *beorsele* of the Anglo-Saxon rune poem should be *wifan* and *beorthsele*, "wives" and "birth hall." This interpretation is not necessarily supported by philology—why would there be a need for the *P* rune at all, if *P* and *B* were interchangeable? But the symbolism is sufficiently intriguing to be worth further exploration.

Some interesting verses in "Svipsdagmál" illuminate the connection between childbirth and the Worldtree that shelters the Norns. In order to gain access to his beloved, Svipdag must trade riddles with the mysterious Fjolsvith, who is presented here as an etin, although the name is elsewhere given as an epithet of Odin. He has already asked for the name of the ash that spreads its branches over the land. Fjolsvith names it Mimameith—Mimir's Pole, or Tree (the tree over Mimir's well, i.e., Yggdrasil). When the hero asks what becomes of the tree's fruit, he is told:

> From the tree the berries   shall be borne to the fire,
> For women in extremity [literally, "hysterical"];
> Then out will come   what was hidden within,
> Such power among men   has the bane [or "the one who
>   metes out fate"].
>
> ("Svipsdagmál": 16)

The meaning of the final word in the original version, "mjötudr," is obscure, and in translations is sometimes assumed to mean the tree itself. Although most parts of the yew tree are poisonous, the flesh (but *not* the seed) of the berries can be eaten. However they may contain some substance that stimulates uterine contractions in childbirth, thus being both "divine" in operation and a bane. One thinks also of the verse in Sigdrifa's song. Perhaps the help runes referred to include PERTHRO:

Help-runes you must know,   if you would aid
Children to come forth from women;
Cut them on the palms [of your hands]   and clasp her
   wrists,
And ask help from the Disir.

("Sigdrifumál": 9)

In the ancient literature, the Norns, the Well, and the Tree are linked in the imagery of fate, which is manifested in the playing of a game, the casting of lots, or of the runes themselves to determine the fate both of grown men and of the newly born.

Modern Meanings

For Thorsson, PERTHRO is a rune of the mysteries of fate, the power of the Norns that decides the outcome of runic divinations. It governs the laws of cause and effect (horizontal plane), and of synchronicity (vertical). PERTHRO is at once the well and the cup in which the runes are tossed. It is the power of becoming, consistency and change.

Gundarsson describes the rune more specifically as one of divination and points out that among the ancient Germans the same method was used to cast both the dice and the runes. Both allowed wyrd to become manifest. Dicing reveals personal fate, while rune casting reveals that fate in the context of the wyrd of the world. He sees PERTHRO as a rune of Mimir, the "embodiment of the self-awareness of the cosmos," rather than of Urdh, essentially a passive source. Understanding it allows one to work with fate.

Aswynn also identifies the rune as Mimir's Well, but for her it is the Womb of Space as well. She sees them both as images for the repository of ancestral memory, the Akashic Records, or the Collective Unconscious. She identifies PERTHRO as "the" rune of fate, and of Frigg as goddess of childbirth and the power behind the Norns.

However, there are other interpretations. Osborn and Longland translate the Anglo-Saxon word as "tune," indicating good cheer, recreation, etc. Peterson feels the rune means something unknown, unrevealed, hidden; a mystery, like the unborn child, that will be revealed in due time. He points out that the old name "Perdhra" could mean "fruit tree" (Oxenstierna 1965) and offers *peru*, "pear" as a translation, since the pear is a womb-shaped fruit.

PERTHRO is one of several runes in the Elder Futhark whose ambiguity is a source of both frustration and opportunity. There is not enough evidence for the "real," original meaning of the rune to be established. Since the ancient authorities are inconclusive, one must seek illumination in the insights of more recent writers regarding its significance—and from one's own intuition. The way to understand PERTHRO is literally through the meditation on the rune itself—the rune provides the key to its own meaning.

All interpretation must begin with the verses in the Anglo-Saxon rune poem, linking image to image in Northern literature. The meanings that emerge center around the lots cast for a newborn child, and incorporate elements of play, chance, and destiny, particularly within a social context.

As a dice cup or a gaming piece, PERTHRO refers to games whose outcome can be taken as symbolic or significant. Like NAUDHIZ, it seems to refer to the workings of wyrd, but where the former may indicate the working out of a terrible purpose, PERTHRO has a much more cheerful aspect. It may involve the fates, but it is not to be taken too seriously (even if this involves the kind of grim humor favored by the Vikings at "moments of exceptional interest"). The warriors who diced in the hall went into battle laughing.

In Norse tradition, Loki is the trickster, but Odin is notorious for tricking those who try to evade their fates. What matters does not seem to be what one's fate is so much as how one meets it, and the ideal is to respond with courage and good humor to whatever comes along. Odin certainly detests a coward, and presumably the Norns are also likely to respond more favorably to those who accept their answer cheerfully.

At a deeper level, however, I believe that PERTHRO can be interpreted as the rune of the Runes themselves. In the "Völuspá," the gaming of the gods and the first appearance of the Norns is immediately followed by the creation of humanity. PERTHRO is the womb/well into which Yggdrasil drops its berries to stimulate the birth of destiny. One might even say that the berries are the runes, fallen from the tree and taken up from the well, uniting male and female archetypes of creation. From the Well/PERTHRO, the runes, and the pattern of destiny they express, are born. PERTHRO is the cauldron of transformation, which is portrayed on the Gundestrop cauldron (a silver cauldron decorated with images of gods and humans, probably made by Transylvanian craftsmen for a Migration Period king in what is now Denmark) into which the slain warriors are plunged so that they may be born anew.

On the human level, PERTHRO is a rune of the Disir, the Norns in their aspect as giver of fate to the men. Frigg, who knows all fates but tells none, is the greatest of the Matronae, the divine mothers who bless the newborn. She is the power behind the Norns, as Freyja Vanadis is first among the Disir. Though it is nowhere given in the literature, one might award to Frigg the epithet of Asa-dis, mother goddess of the Aesir. She was invoked by laboring women, who went to the birthbed as men to the battlefield, risking their own lives so that life might go on. PERTHRO may also therefore be seen as a rune of the women's mysteries of the North.

With this rune especially, there is no single "right" interpretation. But though PERTHRO may be hard to define, as a focus for meditation it is exceptionally fertile.

Interpreting and Using PERTHRO

The appearance of PERTHRO in a reading is an omen that one should explore the implications of the operation of fate, or of chance in the context of the reading. The appearance of PERTHRO could mean that forces already set in motion are working themselves out, or that an unexpected or apparently random factor is going to intervene. On a psychological level, it could involve needing to deal with uncertainty, or being willing to take risks, or even a need to lighten up and play. In business, it could mean risk, or something unexpected, good or bad. In terms of personal development, PERTHRO may refer to those opportunities and constraints with which one was "fated" at birth—factors determined by heredity and the environment into which one was born.

According to Willis and Aswynn, in readings it indicates disclosure of something previously hidden, unexpected luck, a good guess. Aswynn finds it may indicate information that the querent is not meant (or not yet ready) to know. Gundarsson believes that PERTHRO can be used to intensify or speed up the action of wyrd. He finds it useful as a rune of meditation, to recover hidden knowledge about the runes, and to learn how to use the runes in the modern world.

Upended, PERTHRO is useful in bindrunes to "pour out" other runes into manifestation; upright, to contain them. In healing, it can be drawn over the womb, open end downward, to get a blocked menstrual flow going smoothly. It is drawn with the opening downward to open the womb for birth, upward during pregnancy to prevent miscarriage.

PERTHRO AND EHWAZ: STUDY AND EXPERIENCE

Roots

EIHWAZ may best be experienced as a rune of the Worldtree, encountered both in its physical manifestations and as a cosmic mandala. A first step in understanding it could be to develop a relationship with a living tree, preferably an evergreen, though you can work with any species that is accessible and attracts you. Hallow it to the work you are doing by drawing the EIHWAZ rune on its bark with charged water, your own blood, mead or beer. You may also want to pour out a libation at the roots of the tree.

A tree is literally a link between earth and heaven. Its roots draw moisture and nutrients from the earth, while its leaves use the energy of the sun to transform them. Through the leaves carbon dioxide is absorbed from the air and oxygen is returned. In addition to nutrients, the tree is constantly moving energy between the soil and the sky.

To connect with this energy, sit on the ground or a backless seat with your backbone against the tree. Find a position in which as much of your body as possible touches the trunk, and relax against it. Then, ground yourself by allowing your awareness to sink downward through your body and into the earth, focusing on the points at which you are in contact with the earth and the tree. Seek to follow the roots of the tree as they spread through the ground, anchoring it, and you. When your awareness is firmly rooted, begin to move it upward again through the tree trunk and your backbone, which has now become part of the tree. Continue moving your awareness upward until it spreads into the branches and you sense the free movement of energy in the sky. Then send your consciousness downward again.

Practice manipulating the movement of consciousness with the aid of the tree until you can sense the flow of energy in yourself and in the tree trunk. Allow yourself to participate in the tree's interaction with wind and water and soil. Learning to track the flow of life in the tree will make it easier for you to sense the movement of power in your own body and can assist you in raising energy through the chakra system up the spine. When you finish meditating in this manner, be sure to thank the tree.

Working with a real tree will help you to internalize its physical structure, which can then serve as a map for trance journeying. Germanic cosmology is built around the concept of Nine Worlds arranged in or around Yggdrasil. To these worlds, the rune EIHWAZ is the key.

Rebirthing

Experiencing PERTHRO requires one to work with concepts of (re)birth, fate, and chance. Playing any game involving the casting of dice prepares the mind to deal with concepts of change and chance. The old game of *Hnefatafl* (also the Lappish *Tablut*, Welsh *Tawlbwrdd* and Irish *Brandubh* or *Fidchel*), on the other hand, is a test of strategic thinking, requiring one to visualize in all four directions. A version of brandubh called "Swords and Shields" is published by Milton Bradley.

The pattern of these games differs from modern chess in a number of ways. Though there is less variation in the way the pieces can move, the fact that they are oriented to the center requires a major shift from dualistic to multidimensional thinking. The Norse version is a more complicated form of the Celtic game, but the structure of both reflects essential social and cosmological concepts of the relationship of the parts to the center, of the inner garth and outer garth (Utgard), where outlaws roamed. The grid was a symbol of universal order, with a post or stone (also representing the king) at its center. For an interesting analysis of these concepts, see Nigel Pennick's *Games of the Gods*.

In *Heidhrek's Saga*, King Heidhrek is involved in a riddling contest with an old man who can only be Odin. One of the questions is "Who are the maids that fight about their unarmed lord, the dark all day defending and the fair slaying?" It is interesting to find the pieces, elsewhere called "soldiers," here referred to as maids, recalling Valkyries or the companies of dark and bright Disir who threaten or protect in prophetic dreams, foretelling the fate of the dreamer. Thus, contemplation of the tafl-pieces contained in PERTHRO leads us back to a consideration of wyrd, and its influence on our lives.

In our study of NAUDHIZ we encountered the concept of wyrd as necessity. In looking at PERTHRO, we can focus specifically on the fate laid out at birth—the gifts of heredity and environment that shape our lives.

This is a time to analyze one's own inheritance, following, where possible, the maternal line. What physical characteristics have you derived from your ancestors? What other gifts, in the form of family traditions or traits of character, were part of your inheritance?

The characters of your parents might be considered part of your environment. For good or for ill, the personalities of your family, and the resources and limitations of the home and town and region in which you grew up, have determined the way you grew. Childhood memories have an insidious power, and our mothers often have power to reduce even those who are otherwise completely in control to a state of incoherent exasperation. Only when you understand and accept the influence of the forces that formed you will you be able to compensate for or fight them and exercise some control over your own spiritual and psychological evolution.

No matter how unsympathetic one's immediate relatives may seem, following the line of descent back far enough should bring you to a generation whose ideas are more in harmony with your own. Try making an altar to the Mothers, with pictures of female relatives, women of power, women from earlier times, or goddesses, especially Frigga. Offer candles and flowers and milk in a bowl (which is poured out onto the ground the next day) and ask for blessings and luck to follow you.

A special ritual to the Mothers can be performed when a child is born. The Disir should be honored at whatever ceremony is used for naming (even if the child is being given a Christian baptism you can bless it in the name of all its grandmothers). If the naming is pagan, an altar and offerings for the Disir can be set up, as the good fairies were invited to christenings in medieval fairy tales. Cast runes for the newborn by drawing three for the wyrd of inheritance, three for the influence of the environment, and three for the luck the future will bring.

If you are working with the stadhyr positions, notice how closely the stance prescribed for PERTHRO, silly though it may seem, resembles the squatting position assumed by women giving birth in many traditional cultures. If you try it, take particular notice of how the energy moves through your body. In this stance, even men may feel a contraction in the gut reminiscent of birth pangs.

The Nine Worlds

> Nine worlds I know, the nine homes
> Of the glorious world-tree the ground beneath.
>
> ("Völuspá": 2)

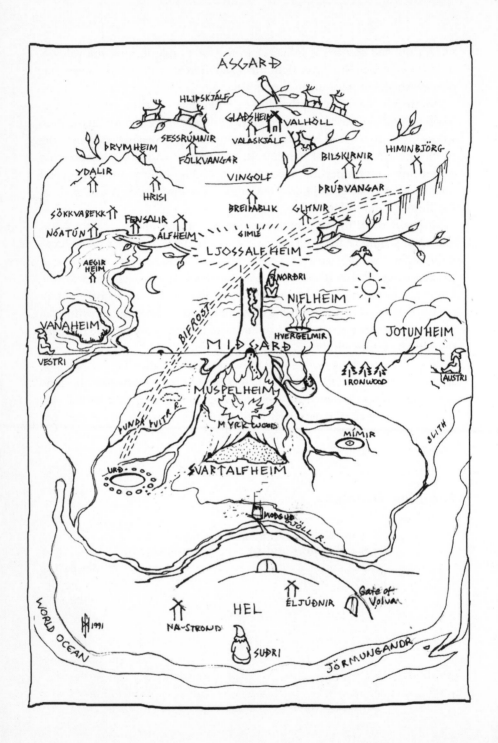

The Nine Worlds or "homes" referred to by the seeress are usually held to be Asgard, Ljósalfheim, Midgard, Svartalfheim, and Hel, Niflheim, Jotunheim, Muspelheim, and Vanaheim. To explore Yggdrasil, one begins with Midgard—Middle Earth—the "real" world—the reality in which you and I and this book all have our being. But no travel agency will sell you a ticket to Midgard. You may travel east of the sun and west of the moon and never find the place where the Worldtree grows. To reach it, one must find the center of Middle Earth, which is located "within." To worry about whether the worlds and the Tree are located in another dimension or in your head is fruitless. I prefer to visualize the way to the Otherworld as leading off at right angles to all the dimensions we know. We seek that road by going within, but once there, the direction in which we follow it is "away" into nonordinary reality.

The Nine Worlds are located in the universe of the shaman. Although each culture maps this alternate reality it its own way, the journey to reach it is made in much the same way. Each of the "Worlds" deserves its own chapter, and every traveler who explores the worlds sees them somewhat differently; however, the information preserved in the Eddas provides us with a common starting point. A number of attempts have been made to diagram the positions of the Nine Worlds. The directions and relationships I use are based on a combination of common sense and analysis of the material in the Eddas and are similar to the system proposed by Thorsson in *Futhark*.

Midgard

Midgard is the world of Man and Nature. As its name suggests, it is located neither at the top nor the bottom of creation, but in the midst of it. Those who dwell here are neither high nor low, but partake of the natures of all realms. Midgard strongly resembles the world of waking reality, seen with the eyes of a seer, or a child, so that everything has meaning. The other creatures one meets here are both their natural selves and something more. The farther one penetrates towards its center, the more magical Middle Earth becomes, until one comes to the Worldtree itself, the axis of all realities.

Here we encounter a paradox. The Tree grows in the center of the world, and yet all worlds are contained within the Tree. One encounters the same problem in vision or dreaming, in which the protagonist has the subjective experience of moving freely through a world that, physically, exists only within the neurons of the brain. Midgard, therefore, has all the natural features and inhabitants of the world we know, and yet it is a "middle ground" where we can interact with beings from another reality.

Snorri's description suggests that all the worlds, including Midgard, lie beneath the roots of the Worldtree, but I have found it most useful to visualize Midgard as a plane intersecting the Tree at its base, where the three great roots plunge downward, thus placing it midway between the upper and lower worlds.

Niflheim

Of Niflheim ("Mist-home") we know that it is located to the north of the Tree, and lower than Midgard. *Nifl* means "mist," or "fog" (the Old German is *nibel*, related to the Latin *nebula*). These mists may result from the original meeting of primal ice and fire. Within Niflheim may be found the Well Hvergelmir, "the Seething," the source of all rivers, including the Gjöll ("the roaring"), which flows eventually past Hel. The name "Niflhel" (Mist-underworld), which is sometimes confused with it, seems to refer to a particularly depressing sector of Hella's realm. Symbolically, Niflheim may be seen as the direction of the mist-shrouded primal ice out of which the world was formed by interaction with the forces of fire, a realm of frozen and static existence that yet holds the potential to bubble into life.

Muspelheim

Muspelheim is the abode of fire. It would seem to be located to the south, since it is from that direction that Surt and the men of Muspel will ride at Ragnarók. We are told nothing more about them, but presumably they are a division of the Jötun-kind, and as destructive as fire. Another etin associated with fire is Löge (not the same as Loki), who seems to represent a more benign elemental aspect of fire. The brightness of Muspel's fires lights the air in parts of the Underworld, so parts of it at least may be imagined as lying below the plane of Midgard. Symbolically, it may be considered as a realm of violence and burning passion.

If Niflheim occupies the north and Muspelheim the south, it seems logical to place Jotunheim and Vanaheim to the east and west, respectively, occupying a plane somewhat higher than Midgard, adjoining the Upper World of Asgard and the Ljósalfar.

Jotunheim

Jotunheim is the homeland of the Jotnar. The roots of its moist mountains are visible from the road to the Underworld, but the peaks on which the cliff giants dwell are presumably close enough to Asgard to require the vigilance of Heimdall. References in the Eddas and in folklore indicate that it is a large and varied region, mostly mountainous, populated by numerous Jotnar whose halls and fields are much like those of men and gods, but on a gigantic scale. As indicated in our discussion of THURISAZ, the etin-kind seem to personify primal natural forces found in a number of pantheons as the elder generation of the gods. Symbolically, Jotunheim may be viewed as the home of primal and often chaotic forces that can be both disruptive and benign.

Vanaheim

The original home of the Vanir, Vanaheim, may be most usefully placed in the west. The Vanir are strongly associated with the fertility of the seas as well as that of land, and I tend to picture it as an island in the western ocean, like that of Nerthus or Nehalennia. It is presumably inhabited by those Vanir who were not sent as hostages to Asgard, though no details are given. In that sense it might serve as a locus for the pantheons of Earth religions that predated the Aesir. Symbolically, it can be seen as a source of fertility and harmony with the cycles of earth and sea.

If Niflheim and Muspelheim are the sources for fire and ice, the primal forces of creation, Jotunheim and Vanaheim may be seen as the homes of those spiritual forces that preceded the Aesir and were retained as part of the Germanic spiritual ecology. Their connection with the plane of Midgard indicates the continuing relationship of those forces to the physical, "outer" world in which we live, as well as to the inner realms of nonordinary reality.

Ljósalfheim

Immediately above and below the plane of Midgard, modern tradition places the worlds of the Light and Dark Alfar. To some extent these worlds are a literary construct, established to bring the number of named worlds up to nine, for the material that has survived in the Eddas tells us nothing about them. However, they are conceptually useful.

Ljósalfheim is the world of the Light, or Fair Alfar. Although their home is not named, there are references to such beings in the Eddas. The Alfar are named with the Aesir as recipients of sacrifice, and the abode of Freyr in Asgard is called Alfheim. Snorri tells us that the Light Elves, "fairer than the sun to look upon" live there (1987, "Gylfaginning": 17, p. 19). More interesting still is the hall called Gimlé ("Lee of Flame," or "Fire Roof"), located in the south of Asgard or in a third heaven above it. After Ragnarók, Gimlé will be the home of the spirits of good and righteous men, but now it is inhabited only by the Fair Elves.

Svartalfheim

If Ljósalfheim is inhabited by bright elves, Svartalfheim is presumably the abode of their opposites, the Dark Elves, who according to Snorri "live down in the earth and are unlike the others in appearance and much more so in character." The Dark Elves have been identified with the dwarves, who are said to be earth dwellers, although in the myths, dwarves seem to dwell throughout the worlds. References in the sagas make it clear that at times offerings were made at grave mounds to the spirits of ancestors who were then addressed as Alfar. It is therefore more likely that the Dark Elves who live in the earth are to be associated with grave mounds.

In *The Road to Hel*, Ellis-Davidson demonstrates that at times notable men became objects of cult worship after their deaths, and that this worship was often performed at their grave mounds. Such spirits were called álfar, and their cult seems to have been closely associated with that of the Vanir. This would explain why the name Alfheim is given to the hall of Freyr. Only later did they become confused with landspirits and nature elementals. The distinction between bright and dark elves may be a late development, influenced by Christian light/dark dualism and value judgments regarding "above" and "below." It must be remembered that in some references, all the worlds (including Asgard) are located beneath the roots of the Tree. The homes of the Alfar could therefore be seen as the abodes of ancestral spirits, their brightness depending on whether they are hostile or benign.

Thorsson offers a psychologically, if not academically, satisfying solution to this problem by identifying Ljósalfheim as the realm of intellect, a focus for spiritual patterning, devic forces, or platonic archetypes. Svartalfheim, on the other hand, is presented as the locus of the personal unconscious. The shades that inhabit it are the shadows of one's personal past acting on the psyche.

Hel

Highest and lowest on the Tree are the worlds of Asgard and Hel. If a case can be made for Alfheim as a home of ancestral spirits, such an identification is even more probable for the realm of Hella.

Despite the fact that its name has been transferred to the Christian place of punishment, in Norse mythology, Hel is not necessarily evil. The Underworld is simply the abode of the dead, both good and bad, and parts of it at least seem to be as attractive as the Celtic Summer Land.

Hel is surrounded by a wall with at least one gate in it. Greenery grows there even when there is winter in the world, and a slain rooster thrown over its wall will rise up crowing on the other side. Inside, we know that Hella's hall, Eljudhnir, was decked out with shields and provisioned with mead and beer to receive the god, Baldr. (For the full story, see "Gylfaginning": 49 in the Younger Edda.) There is also another hall, however, called Na-strond (Corpse-strand), a thoroughly unpleasant place walled with serpents and awash in their venom where the evil dead go. Near the eastern gate of Hel one may find the grave mound of the Völva, whom Odin summoned to interpret the dream of Baldr. Deeper still, the serpent Nidhögg gnaws forever at the roots of the Tree.

Hel may be interpreted as the depths of the collective unconscious. Like Odin we seek its darkness in search of wisdom. It is a state of being in which the seer has easy access to visionary knowledge, but should be sought only by the experienced and resolute, and with trained guidance, not because it is frightening (although deeply buried terrors may be encountered there), but because its peace is so seductive.

Asgard

Concerning Asgard we know a great deal more. In the "Gylfaginning," the High One gives Gylfi a verbal tour of the homes of the gods. Each of the major deities has his or her hall, suitably splendid, and some have their own regions as well.

Other creatures dwell at the top of the Tree—an eagle sits on its topmost branches, and a squirrel called Ratatosk runs up and down the trunk carrying insults between the eagle and Nidhögg. Four harts gnaw the green shoots from the branches, and in Valhöll, the hart (or elk) Eikthyrnir browses, and from his horns flow the waters that fill the well of Hvergelmir. Here, the Tree is called Læradh (the Shelterer). The she-goat Heidhrun also feeds on its buds and from her teats comes the endless supply of mead for Odin's heroes.

Asgard is the home of the gods, and it is here that one journeys to meet and work with them. It is the state of being in which one can experience the spiritual reality of divine forces.

The Three Wells

If the study of EIHWAZ provides an opportunity for learning about Yggdrasil and the Nine Worlds, PERTHRO leads one to consider the three wells that lie at the roots of the Tree. They may be considered aspects of a single Well, as there is a single Tree. However, there are significant differences in their natures and functions.

Best known of the three is the Well of Urdh. It is located beneath the root closest to the river called the Thunderflood, which rushes down from

Asgard. Beside it are the judgment seats of the gods. Its water is exceptionally clear and with it the Norns water (and whiten) the roots of the Tree, to give it the strength to resist the gnawing of the serpent Nidhögg. It is sometimes called the Well of Wyrd (the Old English form of Urdh), or the Well of Fate. As Urdh is the Norn of that which has become, it is beside her well that the gods make judgments based on the actions of the past.

The second well is that of Mimir, said to be located in the direction of Jotunheim. One name for the Tree is Hoddmímir—the Treasure of Mimir. Another is Mimameith, which may mean something like "the Pole of Mimir." The name Mimir may be related to "memory," but it also seems to have implications of wisdom and inspiration. In one story he is one of the Aesir, given as a hostage to the Vanir and killed by them. His head was preserved by Odin and gave him counsel. In other versions he is the dwarf (or perhaps the Jotun) who guards the well and took Odin's eye as the price for a drink from it. There the eye remains, and may be considered the means by which the god "sees" the intuitive, inspired, side of things.

Since the name given the Tree when it drops the fruit that brings forth that which is hidden, whether it be a child or wisdom, is Mimameith, perhaps it is the Well of Mimir into which the fruit falls. The result is birth, the act of becoming, or creation.

The third Well, Hvergelmir, is to be found in Niflheim. Despite Niflheim's association with clammy, clinging mists and primal ice, *Hver* means "cauldron" and was used to describe natural hot springs in Iceland. Certainly Hvergelmir is vigorous, since it is the source of the world's rivers. It receives its waters from the hart Eikthyrnir, who is nourished by the Tree. We have, therefore, a cycle in which water moves from the wells to the Tree, through the hart and back into the well again. The past is constantly being transformed into the future in Hvergelmir.

Together, the three wells and the tree express the cyclical relationship between death and birth that is so basic to Germanic cosmology. The Worldtree is constantly being destroyed and as consistently renewed. After all has been destroyed at Ragnarók, the life hidden in the leaves of the Tree will emerge to repopulate the world.

The Group Ritual

If you are working with a group, the ritual for EIHWAZ and PERTHRO can be found on page 332. The theme of the ritual is the relationship between self-sacrifice and self-knowledge, between death and birth, as seen in the relationship between the Tree and the Well.

Chapter 9

ELHAZ and SOWILO

LIKE THE PREVIOUS PAIR, ELHAZ AND SOWILO contrast a power associated with the depths with one that shines down from the heights. The energy of ELHAZ comes from the Underworld, or the unconscious—that place "below" or "within" that is our doorway to the inner realms. The power of SOWILO, on the other hand, is solar and heavenly, and floods down from "above." To contact ELHAZ, one must first seek stillness, while the force of SOWILO impels to action. But a major function of each is protection, which can require either defense or attack. Used together, they are complementary.

A second point of relationship between the two runes is that of guidance. One way to invoke the protection of ELHAZ is through the action of a guardian spirit who can serve as a guide and teacher as well as a protector. In the rune poems, the sun is hailed as the way-shower—our point of reference and guide through the natural world. In their own ways, each rune can provide you with illumination and enlightenment.

THE FIFTEENTH RUNE: Y ELHAZ

Pronunciation: "EL-hazh"
Meaning: Elk

ELHAZ, ELK is sharp tined sedge,
Totem power provides protection.

The Ancient Meanings

The "Zh" rune is the sound of the nominative case ending in the old Germanic languages. Later this sound evolved into the terminal *r* of names such as Freyr, and the rune, reversed, appears as *yr*, "the yew bow," at the end of the Younger Futhark, which does not include the *z* sound at all. Upright, this rune shape was used in the Younger rune row for *m* (see MANNAZ).

The Old Germanic rune name ELHAZ can be read as "elk" (*Alcis alcis*, the European elk, in America called the moose). The word *Alcis* also occurs in a passage in Tacitus (*Germania*: 43) in which it could refer either to the sacred grove itself or to the divinity or twin divinities (similar in function to the Gemini) worshipped there. Grimm favors the "sanctuary" interpretation and cites a number of instances in which Old Germanic *ala* (Gothic *alhs*) is used to mean "temple," or "sanctuary" (Grimm 1967, I, p. 67). Interestingly enough, there is some evidence for the connection of a pair of warrior twins with the sun cult (Gelling 1969, p. 176ff) Yet another possible interpretation is *Algiz*, or "swan."

The Anglo-Saxon rune name *Eolh-secg* is translated as "elk sedge," by Winsell. "Eelgrass" has also been suggested. Wardle interprets it as *ealhes ecg*, meaning "holy-place edge" (or "sacred sword"). Thorsson tries to reconcile these two meanings by suggesting that eelgrass is in fact a kenning for a sword. On the other hand, Beryl Mercer and Sid Birchby have translated *Eolh* as "heal-pebble"—amber—and equate it with the protection of Brisingamen, a lovely interpretation, but one that unfortunately does not seem to fit too well into the rune poem.

> ᛉ *[Eolh secg] eard hæfꞇ oftust on fenne*
> (Elk-sedge [or eelgrass] is found mostly in fens,)
> *wexeð on wature, wundaπ grimme,*
> (waxes in water, wounds grimly,)
> *blode breneð beorna gehwylcne*
> (with blood burns whatever warrior)
> *ðe him ænigne onfeng gedeþ.*
> (that goes to grasp it.)

The Anglo-Saxon poem, which is the only one to include this rune, clearly describes a marsh plant whose edges inflict the same kind of sting as a paper cut. Presumably the question of whether this is protective or harmful would depend on whether you are grasping the sedge or hiding behind it.

The protective force of ELHAZ was incorporated in traditional bindrunes and sigils, especially the figure called the "Helm of Aegir" or the "Helm of Terror," consisting of an eight-fold cross terminated with ELHAZ, as shown. It appears all the way from Iron Age carvings to Icelandic grimoires. In the *Volsungasaga*, it is identified as the helm used by Fafnir to transform himself, which Wagner translated into the tarnhelm (helm of invisibility).

Modern Meanings

Thorsson describes ELHAZ as a sign of protection. He identifies the horned elk with the harts that feed on the Worldtree. The rune could also represent the solar stag, a yew bow, or even the Divine Twins. If one interprets the word as *Algiz*, the "swan" (or Valkyrie swan-may), the rune could stand for the link between man and his fylgja, or spirit guide, which may take an animal form. In his reading, the protection of ELHAZ comes from one's relationship with a personal divinity (in function rather like the Roman genius) or spirit guardian. The rune can be represented by the fingers splayed in the sign of warding.

Peterson, working from the word "elk," traces the rune's meaning back to Old European hunt magic. Osborn and Longland, looking at the Anglo-Saxon poem, point out that eelgrass is dangerous, but that knowledge of one's environment allows one to operate safely and ward off dangers. Wardle reads the Old Germanic word as *Akiz*, from the Gothic word for axe, and derives the rune shape from the double-bladed axe used in Bronze Age ritual. In his reading, the rune name in the Anglo-Saxon poem should be *ealhes ecg*, meaning "holy edge" or "Sword of the Halidom."

Aswynn reads the rune-names as *Algiz* or *Eolh*, and believes that its use as a termination makes it primarily magical in function rather than serving as a sound rune like the others. She suggests that the Divine Twins were originally a Vanic pair such as Freyr and Freyja. For her, the upright and reversed forms of the rune are feminine and masculine. When these two forms are combined in a bindrune, they represent marriage. She also points out that drawn sideways, the rune shape is called a "crow's foot" and links it to the raven symbolism of Valkyries. She agrees with other writers, however, in seeing this rune as a force for connection and protection.

Gundarsson's discussion seeks to integrate the rune shape's meanings in Elder and Younger Futharks by stating that both elk (*Elhaz*) and man (*Madhr*) refer to the incarnation of the spirit in human form. He sees its three "arms" as representing the three elements (air, fire, and water) that comprise the Bifrost bridge, emphasizing the rune's function as a connection. As a protective force, it is a fiery energy that repels all that is unclean, warding and making holy at the same time.

To avoid confusion, it might be easier to simply title this rune "Protection," since this is the one thing on which most commentators appear to agree. A second concept that seems to have won general agreement is that it can help link the natural and divine worlds. The magical protection of ELHAZ is gained by through the integration of matter and spirit. Its hallowing effect is not imposed from without but manifested from within.

No act of ancient man could make a holy place out of a forest grove, which is by its very nature sacred. The magic was in opening oneself to awareness of the divinity that manifested through it. This was how the Norse who colonized Iceland, having neither ruins nor legend to guide them, identified the sacred places of their new home, and this is how those who seek to recover the ancient traditions in new lands must do it today.

As others have pointed out, the posture of standing with arms upraised, identified by Grimm as the one used by the Germanic peoples (and many others) for prayer, is the shape of ELHAZ.

The connections of this rune to "man" and "yew" are intriguing, but in the Elder Futhark, both meanings are amply covered by other runes. I find it more useful to explore the implications of interpreting the word ELHAZ as Alcis, the great elk of the primeval forests. The role of the elk or stag is almost obscured in the later mythology; however, the beasts themselves remain as part of the ecology of Yggdrasil. Four harts, which eat the shoots of Yggdrasil, bear the names of dwarves. Another horned beast, Eikthyrnir, also feeds on the Tree. From its horns flow the waters that fill the Well Hvergelmir, from which come all the rivers in the Nine Worlds. The antlers that adorned the eaves of Heorot, Hrothgar's hall, suggest a surviving belief in their protecting power.

A number of interesting possibilities arise if the rune's shape is seen as that of an antler, for since the time of the Paleolithic hunters, the connection between human, animal, and spirit has been symbolized by horns. The splayed antlers of the rune are the horns of power borne by the shaman on the Gundestrop cauldron (note that in Celtic art antlered goddesses are found as well). Antlered figures are found in Bronze Age Scandinavian rock carvings.

The Horned One is Lord of the Animals, whose physical forms provide nourishment for the body, and whose spirits protect and inspire. The Horned God survived as a deity through the Middle Ages and has been retained in contemporary Wicca as the major image of Divinity in masculine form. Gundarsson comments that Freyr seems to be the Germanic deity most likely to have fulfilled the functions characterized in Celtic religion by the Horned God as Lord of the Animals, although there is no direct evidence demonstrating this. The sign of the horns is still made by European peasants for protection against evil.

The image of the horned god is a masculine symbol for the Divine incarnate in the natural world. A feminine symbol common in European mythology is the swan-may, which relates to a second possible meaning for the rune—Algiz, the swan. The horned beast stands at the top of Yggdrasil, but we are told that two swans swim in the Well of Urdh at its roots. It seems paradoxical to find the terrestrial beast at the top of the Tree and the birds beneath it, but the water in which they swim probably comes ultimately from the horns of Eikthyrnir. In a sense, therefore, the elk and the swan are two faces of the same thing.

In Celtic legend, swans may be male or female, but in Germanic tales the magic swan is usually a maiden. Valkyries in particular, like the one whose swan dress Volund the Smith stole in order to catch her, may travel about in this form. These tales belong to the class of "animal-wife" stories that originate in shamanic cultures, in which the animal power willingly or through the compulsion of the shaman lives with him, protects him, and grants him power.

The Northern version of this belief appears to have survived in the concept of the fylgja, whose English cognate is "fetch," a personal or family spirit that (according to Thorsson) could appear as a geometric shape, as an animal, or as a female (all the fylgjas described in the sagas belong to men, so we can only speculate on the form in which the fetch of a woman might appear).

This view of ELHAZ opens up some interesting possibilities. If the rune is seen as a means by which a human can manifest spiritual energy, or a link between the worlds, perhaps one way to enable this to happen is by working with totem animals or allies. The ancients believed that such spirits had an independent existence. We may consider them a projection of the spirit, or a personification of qualities that complement the characteristics of the conscious personality. Such an ally becomes more powerful as it is worked with and has many functions in magical practice, from strengthening the spirit to protection in danger, or providing guidance in visionary journeying.

Interpreting the rune as sharp sedge grass, or even as *alhs*, the sacred grove, changes the image, but retains something of the meaning. As sedge, it is remarkable for its ability to wound the warrior who grasps it. But one can move even through sharp sedges if one goes gently, allowing them to bend. Whether animal or vegetable, the power of ELHAZ cannot be forced. The dangers of the sacred grove are less apparent, although there are passages in Tacitus that suggest that it was only by sufferance that men were allowed to enter it standing. The point to remember, however, is that the grove is also a temple made by Nature, not by Man.

In Finnish legend, Lemminkainen is set to search for the Elk of Hiisi and the Swan of Tuonela. In the course of his adventures, he is cut to pieces by eelgrass and must be sewn back together by his mother before he can return to the world of men. This remarkable juxtaposition in a Northern legend suggests that the images associated with ELHAZ are connected at some level

modern scholarship does not understand. The energy of this rune is ultimately protective, but it is a power that depends on integrating our humanity with the divinity manifest in the natural world. Its magic is as great in the
heavens as in the Underworld. To invoke it, we have only to root ourselves
in the earth and lift our arms to the skies.

Interpreting and Using ELHAZ

The appearance of this rune in a reading almost certainly means protection
for the querent, possibly by means of drawing on natural powers or allowing
previously suppressed aspects of the personality to operate. Willis says it
indicates a beneficent new influence, willing sacrifice, the exchange of lesser
for greater good. The querent will be protected (or at least warned). For
Peterson, the appearance of this rune indicates "luck in the hunt," the successful outcome to a quest, success through striving, or rewarded effort.

Thorsson sees ELHAZ as a two-edged rune, dangerous to the untrained.
The forces with which it puts one in contact must be identified with, not
"grasped." The rune can also be used to turn back an attack so that it wounds
the attacker. For Gundarsson, the major use of the rune is in warding and
hallowing. It can act powerfully to cleanse the energies. It is especially powerful against ghosts and beings of the lower worlds.

ELHAZ is one of the most generally useful of runes in practical magic.
Combined with other runes in a bindrune, it invokes their force for protection. With ANSUZ, it wards a computer, with RAIDHO, protects luggage.
Used alone, it can be drawn on door and windowsills to protect a house or
on the hood of an automobile. It is drawn on the forehead when one is going
into danger and projected outward to create a circle of protection. The Elk
rune is used to protect or hallow in situations in which Wiccan traditions
would use the pentagram. Note that the reversed form of the rune is the
same as the circled peace symbol, and is likely to be confused with it by the
casual observer. It can therefore be displayed without arousing comment and
is easy to find in the form of jewelry.

THE SIXTEENTH RUNE: ⟨ ᛋ SOWILO

Pronunciation: "So-WEE-lo"
Meaning: Sun

SOWILO sets the sun wheel soaring;
Guiding light by land or sea.

Ancient Meanings

In form the *S* rune is one of the most straightforward in the rune row, its shape being essentially the same in the Latin and modern alphabets as in the futhark. Its name is equally apparent—it is the Sun. Exploring the significance of the Sun itself for ancient peoples, however, leads the student on an interesting journey.

In the Anglo-Saxon rune poem, the moving sun guides the journeying sailor and with its brightness gives him hope and direction.

> ᛋ *[sigel] semannum symble biþ on hihte,*
> (Sun to seamen is a hope on high)
> *ðonne hi hine feriaþ ofer fisces beþ,*
> (when they ferry over the fishes' bath)
> *oþ hi brimhengest bringeþ to lande.*
> (until the sea-horse brings them to land.)

If SIGEL is a seaman's journey rune, it would fulfill the requirements for the rune described by Sigdrifa:

> Sea-runes cut   if you want to ward
> The sail-horses on the sea:
> You shall put them on the prow   and write them on the
>   rudder,
> Burn them into the oars:

However high the breakers   and dark the waves,
You will still come safe home from the sea.

("Sigdrifumál": 10)

The Icelandic poem focuses on the sun's ability to destroy the ice, on land or at sea. Here the sun is seen as a golden shield, defending against the cold.

ᛋ *[Sol] er skyja skholdr*
(Sun is shield of the sky)
ok skinandi roðull
(and shining ray)
ok isa aldrtregi.
(and destroyer of the ice.)

The image of the shield recalls the lines in "Grimnísmál":

Svalin he is hight   who stands before the sun,
A shield for the shining goddess,
Bergs and brine   I know would burn
If he fell from there.

("Grímnismál": 38)

The Norwegian rune poem agrees with the others regarding the rune's meaning, but links the sight of the sun with respect for the holy cycles of life in nature, and for mankind.

ᛋ *[Sol] er landa ljóme;*
(Sun is the light of the lands;)
lúti ek helgum dóme.
(I bow to heaven's doom.)

The verb here, *lúta*, means "to lout down," to bow, as when Thomas the Rhymer met the Queen of Faerie and "louted down upon one knee." One form of prayer may have involved standing with upraised arms in the form of the ELHAZ rune, but Ibn Fadlan describes the Rus traders as prostrating themselves before the images of their gods. Apparently, at times the Germanic peoples also bowed down in adoration, especially, it would appear, in honoring the sun.

There are a number of references, mostly poetic, to the sun in Norse literature. In the "Alvismál" (15–16) the dwarf Alvis (All-wise), tells Thor that the sun is called Sól by men, Sunna by gods, Dwalin's playmate or bane by dwarves, Eygló (Ever-glow) by the Jotun, Fagra Hvél (Fair Wheel) by the

Alfar, and Alskír (All-shine) by the Aesir's sons.

According to Snorri, basing this part of his commentary on "Grímnísmál" stanzas 37–39, Sunna, the daughter of Mundilfári, was placed in the sky to drive the horses Arvak (Early-wakener) and Alsvith (All-strong). Their heat is cooled by a bellows, called Iron-cool (or coal), and a shield, Svalin (Cooler), goes before. The sun moves swiftly, because she is hunted by the wolf Sköll until she reaches the sheltering grove at nightfall. Presumably eclipses occur when he catches up with her. Indeed, at Ragnarók, the wolf Fenris is fated to do so, but before this happens, the sun, there called Elfbeam, will have borne a daughter, "no less lovely than herself," who will light the new world.

Modern Meanings

For Thorsson this rune means the sun and its light, the solar wheel, the wheels of the solar wagon and the sun disk itself. This force is the lightning bolt that links heaven and earth and guides the vitki through the paths of Yggdrasil. It can also be seen as the whirling wheels of energy that are the chakras, linked by the Tree. SOWILO is the will to victory. It is the illuminating beacon that guides the seeker across the sea of consciousness, a rune of the serpent mysteries of the North and a link between light and darkness. Similarly, Willis sees it as the light that vanquishes evil.

Osborn and Longland interpret SIGEL as the sail that drives the ship referred to in the rune poem, or the jewel (quartz) that allows the navigator to perceive the position of the hidden sun. The sun is a guiding beacon indicating good weather and a safe journey. For Peterson, it is the life force, consciousness and wholeness, or the power to calm the stormy sea.

Aswynn emphasizes the fact that the sun in Norse myth is feminine, and suggests that in Northern Europe (as perhaps in Japan) the welcome heat and light of the sun were seen as nurturing and therefore feminine. She defines the difference between SOWILO and RAIDHO as being the difference between the sun disk and the chariot that bears it—between that which controls (SOWILO), and that which is controlled. For her, SOWILO is definitely a rune of the higher self, which directs the process of individuation; it provides spiritual guidance. She also connects SOWILO with the lightning stroke of Thor, with the myth of Baldr, and with Odin's remaining eye (the eye in Mimir's well representing the moon).

Gundarsson's discussion of SOWILO focuses on this rune as a source of invincibility and triumph, the rune of the will, here defined as the force that leads the vitki through death and darkness. Doubled in a sun wheel, it is a shield; alone, it is a thunderbolt sword, powerful both in attack and defense. SOWILO's will, however, is primarily active and transformative, giving victory over the self. As with other forces, will is neutral, its spiritual value depending on the ethical principles that define its goals.

Most commentators seem to agree that SOWILO is a rune of illumination and movement, whether it is interpreted as the sun rolling across the sky-road or guiding the ship across the sea. The shape of the rune in the Elder Futhark suggests the lightning, which is commonly held to strike from clouds to earth, as in the lightning flash that flares down the Tree in Kabbalah. Actually, in nature, electrical forces attract lightning up from earth to a cloud, like kundalini rising up the spine. So if the rune is interpreted in natural terms, the movement of SOWILO is the result of a mutual attraction between the forces of earth and heaven, of the human spirit and the Divine.

In *The Chariot of the Sun* (1969), Peter Gelling and Hilda R. Ellis-Davidson analyze evidence for a Bronze Age Scandinavian solar cult. Early petroglyphs show the sun disk being carried by a ship, drawn by horses, or as part of a male figure (either as its body, or representing a shield). In some carvings, male or female figures are leaping over a sun symbol, presumably to acquire its energy. In at least one, a male figure of this type with an erect phallus is facing a female figure in a Great Marriage symbol. From this, Gelling and Ellis-Davidson deduce Bronze Age worship of a sun god.

Nonetheless, in later Norse mythology the sun is personified as female, as she is even more prominently in the Baltic lands. I would suggest that in the North the sun was not originally anthropomorphized as a deity at all, but rather worshipped without personification. This would accord more closely with the general tendency of Norse myth, in which the Aesir and Vanir have personalities and functions, but are not (with the possible exception of Thor) gods of natural forces. In the mythology, it is the relatively undifferentiated Jotnar who are associated with the primal forces of nature, and allegories of natural events do not appear.

I suspect that Snorri's genealogy of Sunna is a late addition, in the style of classical mythology. Although some have read the story of Baldr as a myth of the winter decline of the sun, this view may be inspired by the fixation of nineteenth-century folklorists on solar mythology. If the Baldr story is an allegory of the fading midwinter sun, it is more likely, if allegorical, to be a vegetation myth, influenced by Mediterranean motifs of the dying god. Early mythologists began with the assumption that myths are invented to explain natural phenomena; however, this may itself be a myth of Western civilization. An analysis of Native American and other "primitive" mythology yields many stories of culture heroes and creation—a multitude of legends about how things got the way they are now—but relatively few nature allegories. Perhaps people who are still close to the powers of nature feel less need to "explain" them.

On the other hand I believe that a case can be made for the continuation of a sun cult, in the sense that respect and reverence were still offered to its power, into the early medieval period. In the second part of *Chariot of the Sun*, Gelling and Ellis-Davidson demonstrate the continued popularity of sun symbols in ornament. Bronze Age carvings of sun disks feature four or six crossed spokes, concentric circles, or occasionally a spiral. Iron Age ornaments favor the whirling or straight-armed *fylfot* cross (swastika), sometimes combined with serpentine forms or in association with ships or horses. It should be noted that the swastika symbol, whirling both left and right, is found in cultures all over the world. It is particularly popular as a luck sign in Hindu art. Several forms of swastika were used in Nazi symbolism, but it is the widdershins-whirling straight-armed form that was most associated with them.

The references from Norse literature cited above refer to the practice of saluting the rising sun, and several Anglo-Saxon charms direct the user to face sunward, move deasil, or place magical items in the light of the sun. Rites to strengthen the sun survived in Northern folk custom, including rolling a cartwheel covered in burning straw down hill at midsummer and throwing flaming disks of wood into the air. Rolling the wheel into a river or pool was especially fortunate, possibly representing the sun's disappearance into the sea.

Setting up a blazing tar barrel on a pole and carrying it around the town was a Midwinter ceremony in northern Scotland (replaced in the Up-helly-a festivities in the nineteenth century by the burning of a mock Viking ship!). Sir James Frazer (1959) demonstrates that sunfires were kindled to promote good weather and ward off disease, hail, thunder, and other disasters. Some of these customs require the participation of paired youths, and twinned figures with horns or horned helmets are found in conjunction with sun symbols on artifacts like the Gallehus horn (Gelling and Ellis-Davidson 1969, p. 176).

Interpreting and Using SOWILO

In a reading, SOWILO indicates illumination, clarification, the appearance of a guiding principle, change or development after a period of stagnation. It is a beacon of hope for those who strive. The sun rune means strength, energy, life force, success or luck, honor and achievement. It is also the light of truth and enlightened consciousness. It may indicate health or a need for rest to restore it. It can be interpreted as a journey rune, especially a journey over water (in conjunction with RAIDHO and LAGUZ), or even a sailor. Its illumination may arrive through the help of a teacher. In conjunction with ISA, it may mean that the will has been blocked. In excess its force leads to willfulness, arrogance, cruelty, and isolation, the clearest example being its use as the symbol of the SS by the Nazis.

Magically, SOWILO provides guidance in journeying, and can be inscribed on luggage for protection along with RAIDHO and ELHAZ. Invoking it helps one find the right path, both physically and spiritually. It "throws light" upon a situation (think of the cartoon image of the lit light bulb). SOWILO's active force can be used to break up inertia; it counters the immobilizing force of ISA, strengthens the will, and helps one to gain access to inner guidance, and thus is a good rune for fighting depression or a slump.

As a rune of the will to victory, it can be used to kindle and maintain the energy needed to carry creative projects through to completion. Used in conjunction with JERA, it strengthens natural growth and healing processes, and can help plants use the sun's energy.

Gundarsson states that SOWILO and the swastika can be used to understand the currents of power that flow deasil through the heavens and widdershins through the earth. The symbol of the swastika is associated with Thor's hammer and can be used for hallowing. SOWILO activates and vitalizes, strengthening leadership and charisma. It can be used to great effect in chakra meditations.

ELHAZ AND SOWILO: STUDY AND EXPERIENCE

The Protection of the Horns

Whether it is interpreted as an elk, a swan, a protective circle of sharp-edged sedges, the hero twins, or Freyr and Freyja, ELHAZ is a rune of protection. Its power can be swiftly invoked to ward off any danger by making the sign of the antlers with the thumb, forefinger, and little finger extended and the other fingers curled, and it can be inscribed on luggage, wallets, cars and houses, or anything else you want to protect. It radiates outward and increases in force in response to the intensity of the danger.

The ELHAZ stadhyr, standing with feet together and arms upraised, is one of the ancient positions of prayer. To raise ELHAZ energy, ground and center while standing, or bend and place your palms on the earth, reaching deeply for power. When you have a strong sense of the energy, slowly stand with hands at your sides and draw the power upward. As it fills you, lift your arms, extend them at an angle, and project the energy out through the crown of your head and the tips of your fingers in offering, or bring your arms downward again so that the energy forms a protective sphere. While doing this, meditate on your guardian spirit.

The first part of the balancing exercise in the ritual can be taped and played to help you internalize the procedure. With practice, this can be done swiftly to reinforce your shielding against hostile or intrusive emotions or psychic energy, or you can learn to accomplish this through visualization, standing without moving your arms. Protection is intensified by drawing the rune with a fingernail on your forehead, chest, or the palms of your hands.

Guardian Spirits and Spirit Journeying

Spirit journeying is both safer and easier if one works with a guide or ally. The fylgja, or fetch, is an Old Norse term for a personal guardian spirit. A fetch in the shape of a human, an animal, or a crescent goes before its owner, but if he is fey, it comes after him. *Fylgja* is also from a verb, meaning "to follow" (Old English, *folgjan*), and is used in the sense of backing up or siding with someone, hanging around, belonging. According to Thorsson, the fylgja is "a numinous being attached to every individual, which is the repository of all past actions and which accordingly affects the person's life; the personal divinity. Visualized as a contrasexual entity, an animal, or an abstract shape." (Thorsson 1989, p. 119).

When working in a Norse context, I prefer to refer to the spirit guide as a fylgja if it appears in human form. If you want to keep the gender consistent, you could use the term "fylgju-kona" for a female spirit, and "fylgju-madhr" for a male.

One's fylgja is always around, although it can ordinarily be seen only by those with the "sight" or in emergencies. All of the references in the sagas are to female fylgjur attached to men. It is not clear whether the spirit always takes the form of the opposite sex to its owner (like the Jungian animus or anima), or whether the fylgja is simply a personal form of the matrilineal spirit guardian.

In some of the Eddic poems, the protecting role of the fylgja is taken by a Valkyrie, who is a human or supernatural woman skilled in battle magic who becomes the protector and lover of the hero. Some of these stories share the motif of the "spirit-wife," who can assume beast shape by putting on an animal skin. For Valkyries, the most common shape is that of a swan. Such spirit-spouses are also common in the lore of Siberian shamanism.

The terms *norn*, *dis*, and *fylgja* are sometimes used interchangeably in the sagas. Probably their meaning varied from district to district, or from individual to individual. Definitions vary among modern writers as well. As you develop your own views, you should examine Thorsson's definitions (in *Futhark*), and those of Gundarsson in *Teutonic Magic*.

Another term which seems to be part of this continuum is *hamingja*, which can mean "luck, fortune," "life force," or "a guardian spirit," which is often used interchangeably with fylgja.

In "Vafþrúðnismál," stanza 49, the hamingjur are Jotun maidens, possibly to be identified with the Norns. The term's root—hamr or "skin/shape—" supports an interpretation that identifies it more closely as an aspect of the individual to whom it belongs. In the sagas, a person's luck is sometimes transferable—permanently from a man to his heir, or temporarily from a king to his follower. The hamingja may take the form of the individual him/herself, or it may appear in the shape of an animal.

The hamr is the animal form taken by a practitioner of seidh for astral journeying. Old Norse literature is rich in stories of shapeshifting and vocabulary derived from the hamr root. Some of the shapes cited in the literature include bear, wolf, swan, seal, mare, and hare, but it can be almost any kind of creature. Odin can change into a serpent or an eagle and is served by wolves and ravens and the eight-legged horse, Sleipnir. Freyja can take the form of a falcon or a pig, and possibly a mare (the latter are two of her epithets). The beasts who draw the chariots of the other gods may be their totems.

Someone who changes form easily is *hamrammr*—"shapestrong"; a journey taken in another shape is *hamfarir*; *hamask* means to fall into a state of animal fury; *hamslauss* to be out of one's shape; and *hambleytha* is the act of leaping out of one's skin. One is reminded of the Navajo term, "skinwalker" for a witch who takes wolf form. For simplicity's sake, I favor referring to a spirit guide who appears in animal form as the hamingja and the shape that an experienced seidh practitioner uses for astral travel as the hamr.

The guided meditations included in the rituals for the runes are a form of spirit journeying. As you become more familiar with the practice, you may want to try making such trips on your own. Following the instructions for reaching the Tree with which each meditation begins (if necessary, read them onto a tape, leave ten or fifteen minutes blank space, and then read the instructions to return), travel to the Tree, and then move out in whatever direction you would like to explore. This will be much easier if you have the assistance of a fylgja or hamingja, whom you can simply ask to take you where you need to go. Remember to retrace your steps when you return.

The meditation for ELHAZ/SOWILO offers you an opportunity to make contact with a such a guide/guardian. This figure will become more concrete and useful if you repeat the meditation to the point where you encounter your guide and spend the rest of the time getting to know each other. You should ask what to call your guide, and whether she/he/it is willing to continue to work with you. You may also ask how you should honor her, and if she has any advice for you. Michael Harner's book, *The Way of the Shaman*, offers a well-tested and practical system for learning how to work in this way.

These encounters should be repeated until the guide can be clearly visualized and heard and easily invoked, and at regular intervals thereafter. You may want to set up a spirit altar with pictures of your fylgja or hamingja that you contemplate when beginning your meditations. In shamanic practice it is common to collect images of one's spirit helper; teeth, bones, or fur (if the species is not endangered); jewelry, or other such items, and to paint the image on one's magical gear.

Like any other friendship, in order to flourish, the relationship with a totem or spirit guide needs cultivation. Many people who work in this way develop strong and continuing relationships with clearly defined figures. Others may find that their guide appears in different forms for different journeys or may develop a large circle of "invisible friends." Shamanic guides simplify and speed journeying, are often sources of illuminating and useful information and advice, and can get you out of trouble quickly if you encounter anything disturbing while journeying.

Sun Worship

SOWILO can be experienced on a number of levels. The first and most obvious one is that of the sun, a power of both physical and metaphysical importance to Northern European peoples. As indicated in the discussion of the rune, honoring the sun seems to have been a common practice in Germanic culture. This would seem to have been done especially in the morning and is a very positive way to start the day. Taking note of the progress of the sun puts one in harmony with the cycle of the day.

In medieval Iceland, time was counted not in hours but by day-marks, that is, by noting the position of the sun with regard to particular features in the landscape. The day was divided into eight three-hour periods (like the canonical services of a medieval monastery). Obviously this method of telling time worked best for those who were permanent residents of a particular place and had lived there long enough to note the position of the sun at different times of the year.

Knowledge of time was identified with knowledge of the place—time and space were two aspects of the same thing. Identifying the day-marks for your own environment and using them to tell time can be very interesting psychologically, especially if each observation is accompanied by a prayer. Doing so aligns your personal time with that of nature.

One way to work with the energy of SOWILO is through the second half of the balancing exercise in the ritual, either following the ELHAZ exercise, or separately. In either case, begin in a standing position, with arms upraised. If you have been sending energy outward in offering, now turn your palms upward to receive the power of the sun. Turn your face to the sun as well, and through closed eyelids, sense its radiance. Take a few moments to experience the sun's illumination, drawing its power into your body with every breath. Then, slowly bring your arms to your sides, bend at the knees to assume the SOWILO stadhyr position, and after a moment, touch the ground to pass on any excess energy to the earth in offering.

Symbolically, all clockwise motions put one in harmony with the energy of the sun. Clockwise circle dancing is found in a number of traditions (as well as in European folk dancing). It raises positive energy (or invokes fair weather) by aligning the dancers with the Coriolis force of the Northern Hemisphere and the movement of the sun, which appears to move from east to west each day, and from south to north between Midwinter and Midsummer, and north to south during the other half of the year. Actually, of course, it is Earth's orbit that is changing. In the same way, we work magic not by compelling spiritual forces to obey us, but by altering our relationship to the world.

Sun mandalas are among the world's most ubiquitous religious symbols. Circles of all kinds surrounding crosses, spokes, swastikas, and concentric rings are found in all cultures, and are everywhere used as signs of luck, prosperity, and power. The spokes of the sun wheel are the seasons of the year. In the North, lack of sun is more likely to be a problem than lack of rain, and in arctic regions, the long winter nights make the return of the sun a psychological event of considerable magnitude. It is not surprising, therefore, that the sun should also become a symbol of illumination, guidance, and protection.

Victory

The root of the Anglo-Saxon name for this rune, SIGEL, is *Sig*, the Germanic word for victory. The root was extremely popular as an element in personal names and appears often in spells and invocations. The Valkyrie Sig-drifa (victory bringer), awakened by Sig-frid (victory/freedom), greets the powers of day and night in what appears to be a traditional prayer, and prays that those present will have victory. The Anglo-Saxon journey charm adapted for the ritual invokes "sig" power for every aspect of existence.

It is unfortunate that all the words surviving in English that could be used to translate *sig* have Latin roots, for it would seem that in the original languages, *sig* may have had connotations that are not present in words like "triumph" and "victory." Certainly those meanings are included, but the ancient usage seems to carry a sense that might be rendered better as "success" in whatever one is attempting. If SOWILO/SIGEL is a rune of the will, part of its meaning is the affirmation that what one has willed is that which will be, very much in the sense that "As we will so mote it be" is used in Wiccan traditions.

SOWILO can be used as a rune of victory, not necessarily in the sense of conquest or "power over," but very much as an enabler of "power to." It is therefore extremely useful in prayers for empowering oneself or another, or to give a driving affirmative force to a bindrune or spell. SOWILO can be used to dispel mental or physical lethargy. It gives quick energy and the will to solve problems. As a journey rune it helps the traveler (or his luggage) to get to the right destination. It enlightens and illuminates.

The Group Ritual

If working with a group, the ritual for ELHAZ and SOWILO can be found on page 341. It focuses on the theme of protection, which is common to both runes. The earth-power of ELHAZ and the sky-power of SOWILO work together so that protection may be given and received.

Chapter 10

TIWAZ and BERKANO

THE RUNES THAT BEGIN TYR'S AETT can be seen as masculine and feminine. Viewed together, the Irminsul—the tree of TYR, another name for TIWAZ— and the birch tree, BERKANO, show how a similar force can function in very different ways in different environments. The Tree of Tyr is set up in the center of the assembly, indeed, it is the center, the axis around which the social structure takes form. The birch tree remains connected to the earth, even when it is planted in the garth. While the Irminsul points to the sky, the birch is rooted in the depths, maintaining its connection with the source of life.

And yet both have a radiance that marks them as holy. The name *Tiwaz* reflects the blinding brightness of heaven. Tyr is the first of the *reginn*, the shining, mighty powers. But the birch tree is also a shaft of light in the shadows of the forest, a white maiden that stands at the edge of the snows. She may be interpreted as a symbol of Frigg, the queenly goddess who bestows the gift of sovereignty.

THE SEVENTEENTH RUNE: ↑ TIWAZ

Pronunciation: "TEE-wahz"
Meaning: Tyr

TIWAZ is the rune of Tyr:
Victorious victim, enjoining Justice.

Ancient Meanings

The sound of the rune TIWAZ, or TYR, is that of the letter *T*, which it resembles, and its form was presumably derived from the letter in the Greek and Roman alphabets. As a god, Tiwaz is etymologically descended from the Indo-European Dyaus, or Diewos, which developed into the Latin *divus*, and the Sanskrit *deva*, both meaning a god, as well as the god names Zeus, Jupiter (Dyeu-pater), and Diana. In the Teutonic languages, the relationship is seen most clearly in an early form, *Teiwa* (inscribed on a second-century helmet found in Austria). The root word seems to have meant "bright," or "shining," a term used in many languages to describe the gods.

TIWAZ/TYR is one of the two runes named after a deity, and mastering its meaning requires us to understand the god whose name it bears. However, the character of Tyr himself is not nearly as straightforward as it might appear. In the Anglo-Saxon rune poem, for instance, his warlike characteristics are not mentioned at all.

↑ *[Tir] biþ tacna sum, healdeð trywa wel*
(Tir is a guiding star, well keeps faith)
with æþelingas; a biþ on færylde
(with princes; it is on course)
ofer nihta genipu, nefre swiceþ.
(over the mists of night, never failing.)

The identity of this star has been much debated. One possibility would be Mars, which is often quite visible. But Mars rises and sets at odd times. A guiding star needs to be more dependable. From the context, the star of Tir is more likely to be the polestar. A myth that may refer to this is the story of how Thor threw the frozen toe of the Jotun Aurvandil into the heavens so that it became a star. In "Hymiskvidha," Tyr's father is said to be the Jotun Hymir. In "Skáldskarpamál," Hymir is one of three Jotnar associated with the sea. Beryl Mercer has suggested that Aurvandil (Old English, Orwendil) should also be listed as an ancestor of Tyr. The Anglo-Saxon rune poem, therefore, may be referring to Tyr's ancient function as a sky god, whose ancestral star guided mariners across the sea.

The men of the Viking period, however, remembered Tyr for other reasons.

↑ *[Tyr]er einhendr ass*
(Tyr is the one-handed As)
ok ulfs leifar
(and leavings of the wolf)
ok hofa hilmir.
(and king of temples.)

The Icelandic rune poem quoted above refers to the myth of Tyr binding the Fenris wolf and having his hand bit off in the process, which is virtually the only story about Tyr that has survived. However, Tyr is also called the lord of temples. Just as the word *ás* meant not only one of the Aesir, but specifically "the" god, Odin, the word *tyr* (retaining or recovering its original Indo-European meaning) could be used as a kenning for a god. Odin is "Sig-Tyr," the god of victory; the "wagon-Tyr" is Thor.

The Norwegian rune poem essentially repeats the first line of the Icelandic one. In the second line, we have the blacksmith blowing on his bellows, presumably to forge swords and spears for war.

↑ *[Tyr] er æniendr ása;*
(Tiw is the one-handed member of the Aesir;)
opt værðr smiðr at blása.
(often has the smith to blow.)

Snorri supports the warlike definition of Tyr in his description of the gods.

> There is a god called Tyr. He is the boldest and most courageous, and
> has power over victory in battle: it is good for brave men to invoke him.
> He who surpasses others and does not waver is called "Tyr-valiant." He
> is also so well-informed that a very knowledgeable man is called Tyr-
> wise. (1987, "Gylfaginning": 25).

These are the qualities upon which Sigdrifa is relying when she advises Sigurd:

> Cut Victory-runes   if you want to win
> And engrave them on your sword-hilt—
> On the blade-guards some,   and some on the plates,
> And call on Tyr twice.
>
> ("Sigdrifumál": 6)

And indeed, the Tyr rune has been found scratched on spears in Germany
and England. In the early period, he may have been worshipped by the tribes
under a variety of names, including Teiwa, Saxnot, and Hermin. The Vikings
also thought of Tyr as a war god, and yet in the sagas, it is Odin to whom
men sacrifice for victory in battle, and Thor who is invoked as the great
defender. What then was the function of Tyr?

The Romans identified Tyr with their war god, Mars, and a Romano-
German inscription refers to him as Mars Thingsus—Tyr of the Althing. A
reading of the sagas shows that much of the work of the Althing was devoted
to dealing with blood feuds. If the problem could not be solved by negotiation,
the final remedy was the holmgang, a strictly supervised judicial combat. The
use of single combat to decide issues is well-supported in the older literature.
It becomes clear, therefore, that Tyr's role in fighting was to make sure that the
battle served divine justice.

Modern Meanings

Thorsson defines Tyr as a sky god who is specifically associated with justice
as decided by war and judicial combat. He is the self-sacrificing sovereign
who rules cosmic order, precise and careful. The rune TYR is also identified
with the Irminsul, the tree of Mars, which separates earth and heaven.
Osborn and Longland interpret Tir as the polestar, which is a dependable
guide for mariners. Wardle cites Reuter's identification of Tir with the star
at the midpoint of the heavens and concludes that it marks the point where
the Irminsul, a symbol of the world axis whose equal arms could be considered to resemble the rune, meets the sky.

According to Widukind's tenth-century chronicle, the Irminsul was a sacred pole set up by the Saxons in honor of Mars, called by the Saxons, Hermin, to celebrate their victory over the Thuringians. Thirty years later, Charlemagne destroyed it. A ninth-century chronicle described Irminsul as "the column of the universe, upholding all things" (Ellis-Davidson 1964, p. 196).

The god whom the Latin writers identify with the Roman Mars is Tyr, and his connection with the Irminsul supports the theory that he was the original sky god and lord of the Worldtree (note that the Tyr rune is also part of the astrological symbol for Mars). Gundarsson agrees and interprets the one-ended form of the rune as separating earth and heaven, reflecting Tyr's unipolar and single-minded character (in contrast to Odin's flexibility).

The TYR rune resembles a spear even more than it does a tree and was in fact sometimes inscribed on spearheads. However, by the Viking period, the spear had become firmly associated with Odin, whose spear Gungnir sanctified the slain. Possibly the scepter-spear is yet another symbol taken over by the Odin cult from that of Tyr. Ellis-Davidson states that there are no one-handed spearmen among the Bronze Age rock carvings of Scandinavia; however, there are numerous representations of spears (also axes and swords), and several godlike figures holding them.

The identification between spear and sovereignty was known in the ancient Mediterranean. According to Pausanias, Hephaistos made a scepter for Zeus that was called *doru*, "spear." In Rome, the Imperator began a military campaign by touching a sacred spear and crying, "Mars, awake!" A more manageable form of the spear is the wand. According to Pennick, the "kings" on some decks of old French playing cards carry a scepter or rod on the end of which is a hand.

Interpreting and Using TIWAZ

In a reading, this rune can indicate a legal problem, a situation in which one must fight for one's rights, in which one must seek justice. The querent needs to pay stern attention to duty and serve a higher truth, through self-sacrifice if necessary. The rune can provide moral strength and will to succeed. Willis states that the TIWAZ rune can be used to obtain victory in any matter in which there is competition. It indicates strength of will, determination to win, and the possibility of conflict. For Peterson it means victory in legal, political, or physical combat or disputation, and for Thorsson, justice and victory won by self-sacrifice.

Aswynn sees this as the rune of the spiritual warrior, governing conflict and confrontation, and stimulating the courage and energy needed to come through difficult situations. It is most useful in legal matters when combined in a bindrune with RAIDHO. According to Gundarsson, it helps one to develop courage, strength, and honor and makes one aware of one's duty. It binds woe-working forces and promotes order. Negatively it indicates rigidity, prejudice, and loss of perspective.

TIWAZ can be extremely useful in magical work in the personal and social realms. It is helpful in focusing one's energy and directing it single-mindedly to achieve a given purpose, especially one involving self-discipline. It can be used to bolster courage and determination in difficult situations. It is a rune of victory, especially in situations involving law, but since Tyr is a god of absolute justice, if you invoke him, be sure that you are right, for he will do justice, not necessarily see that you win. (If you need mercy, you would do better to call on Thor or Forseti, who resolves conflicts.) Given this understanding, inscribe the rune on legal papers. If you are feeling combative when you are called for jury duty, visualize a spear drawing the rune across the courtroom (wouldn't it be interesting to see a judicial system based on justice instead of compromise?) or perhaps TIWAZ and THURISAZ. TIWAZ can be drawn on your right hand and THURISAZ on your left for balanced protection.

TIWAZ can also be used in workings that address situations of international tension, once more assuming that you are willing to pray for the "right" side, not necessarily your side, to win. Tyr Wolf-binder can be invoked in any situation in which violence must be used to counter greater violence, especially war. It is a rune to be inscribed, along with SOWILO, on the weapons of modern as well as ancient warriors, while ELHAZ and THURISAZ are drawn on other gear for protection.

THE EIGHTEENTH RUNE: ᛒ BERKANO

Pronunciation: "BER-kah-no"
Meaning: Birch Tree

BERKANO, Birchtree, Bride and Mother,
Brings us Earthpower for rebirthing.

Ancient Meanings

BERKANO is essentially the same in form and sound as the letter *B* in the Greek and Latin alphabets, although it is used for words whose roots would begin with an *f* in the Mediterranean languages. The Norse name for the rune, *bjarkan*, seems to derive from an archaic name for the birch tree, being much closer to the Old Germanic form than it is to the Icelandic *björk* or to the Old English *beorc*. The name of the birch tree may derive from the putative Indo-European root *bherek*, meaning "bright," or "shining," so that birch, *betula alba*, signified "the white tree."

Beorc definitely seems to mean "birch," even though Osborn and Longland cite a gloss on the Anglo-Saxon rune poem giving its meaning as *populus*—poplar, and feel that the verses are far more descriptive of the English black poplar tree.

> ᛒ *[Beorc] byþ bleda leas, bereþ efne swa ðeah*
> (Poplar/Birch bears no fruit, bears without seed)
> *tanas butan tudder, biþ on telbum slitig,*
> (suckers, for from its leaves it's generated,)
> *heah on helme hrysted fægere,*
> (splendid are its branches, gloriously adorned)
> *geloden leafum, lyfte getenge.*
> (its lofty crown, lifting to the sky.)

The birch tree, on the other hand, reproduces by seed. It will, however, grow up from shoots if it is cut back. In any case, there is no such problem with the Northern verses. In the Icelandic poem—

> ᛒ *[Bjarkan] er laufgat lim*
> (Birch is leafy branch)
> *ok litit tre*
> (and little tree)
> *ok ungsamligr viðr.*
> (and youthful wood.)

The Norwegian poem is more intriguing.

> ᛒ *[Bjarkan] er laufgrønstr líma;*
> (Birch is the greenest-leaved of branches;)
> *Loki bar flærða tíma.*
> (Loki was lucky in his deception.)

The meaning of the first line is clear enough, but what deception of Loki's involved a birch tree? Like many kennings, this one remains obscure. One would like to believe, however, that one of the verses in the "Sigdrifumál" refers to BERKANO. Certainly the smooth fair bark of the birch seems ideal for writing runes.

> Branch-runes you must learn   if you want to heal
> And know how to treat wounds.
> Cut them on the bark   of forest trees
> Whose branches bend eastward.
>
> ("Sigdrifumál": 11)

Modern Meanings

Osborn and Longland are at variance with almost everyone else in identifying the *Beorc* of the Anglo-Saxon rune poem as the black poplar, which in the north reproduces by suckers, not seeds, and stands tall against the sky. In their interpretation it represents continuous growth and is an example of the masculine principle.

Thorsson, on the other hand, calls it a rune of the Earth Mother in both her bright (Nerthus) and dark (Hella) aspects. Its dual shape suggests a pregnant belly and breasts. According to him, BERKANO reveals the mystery of the perpetual cycle of birth, death, and rebirth from the womb of the goddess. She rules over rites of passage.

Gundarsson concurs, identifying the rune with Nerthus, whose functions were divided between Hella and Freyja in the North, and retained by Holda in Germany. BERKANO "is the rune of the earth who receives the sacrifice/seed and holds it within herself, guarding and nourishing it until the time has come for it to return to the worlds outside again" (Gundarsson 1990, p. 129). It especially rules the birth processes of spring, and can also be considered a rune of the Disir.

Aswynn ascribes the rune to Berchta (Perchta), as does Wardle. She states that Berchta guards mothers and children, and it is to her garden in the Underworld that the spirits of infants go. She may be an aspect of Frigga, but abandoned children are in her especial care. Wardle describes the rune as the shining May Queen, and her birch the May tree. He interprets the rune shape as an image of the open womb, making BERKANO the sequel to the birthgiving of PERTHRO as the *b* sound is related to the *p*.

Actually, maypoles may be made out of any tall, straight, tree; however, in Scandinavia it is a custom to cut birch twigs in April or May and bring them inside to bud in the warmth of the house. Planting a birch tree in the yard of a house is traditional in Sweden, and lads carry birch twigs in procession on May Day to celebrate the return of vegetation. Birch trees are also brought into Scandinavian churches at Midsummer. Aswynn tells us that in the May folk rites of Holland, birch branches are used to whip women for fertility, and a bunch of birch twigs is tied to the door of the newly married. On the other hand, at Christmas the shoes of naughty children may be filled with birch switches instead of presents.

If we can assume that BERKANO is a birch tree rather than a poplar, the rune may be interpreted as a symbol of the tree goddess found in many cultures, female and motherly, source of nourishment and protection. This figure is archetypal, transcending the goddess-personae to which different peoples have ascribed it.

The Canaanite mother goddess, Asherah, was represented by a carved tree trunk. Indian villages have sacred trees to whose nymphs they make offerings; dryads are common in the Mediterranean. Some peoples believe that trees are inhabited by the souls of their ancestors. Often, particular sacred trees were believed to grant women safe delivery in childbirth. Tree spirits are common in European folklore, and the birch tree is a logical home for the white maidens who haunt Germanic legend.

In the early Germanic period, god and goddess images were made from tree trunks or branches whose natural form suggested the deity, with a little carving to suggest sexual characteristics. The birch tree in particular is maidenly in form, but motherly in function; both tree and rune express the essential paradox of birth, death, and transformation that is at the heart of women's mysteries.

My preference is to see it as a rune of Frigga, as the most motherly, as well as the most queenly, of the Northern goddesses.

The birch is primarily a tree of cold climates and high altitudes. It must have been one of the first trees to return after the ice age, and is still one of the few trees that grows in Siberia, where it serves as world-axis and road to the otherworlds in shamanic ceremonies, to the heavens when upright, and to the Underworld when planted upside down. It has been sacred in Northern Europe for a long time. Its branches are used for switching to improve the circulation as part of the sauna ritual. Aswynn says that the Lapps used to erect a northward-leaning birch pole with a nail in the top to indicate the polestar for ceremonies.

A good case can be made for BERKANO as a healing rune. According to Jeanne Rose's herbal, birch oil, which smells something like oil of wintergreen, can be used as an antiseptic or a stimulating rub for sore muscles. A decoction of the leaves acts as a diuretic, dissolves kidney stone, and can be gargled for a sore mouth and canker sores. Birch-leaf tea calms the nerves and induces sleep. Aswynn says that in Holland a liquid made from its leaves is rubbed on the scalp for baldness, and that it is a rejuvenator.

Interpreting and Using BERKANO

BERKANO is a rune that one might expect to turn up at significant life passages. It seems to indicate birth and becoming, rootedness, the feminine. Gundarsson calls it a rune of "bringing into being," the first protection given a child at birth, the first of the layers of fate to be laid down for the child's life. It is useful in all female fertility magic and women's mysteries. It hides the workings of other runes until their action is ready to be revealed and is a rune of hidden transformation and growth. Aswynn says it is a useful healing rune for women's troubles and menstrual problems and has great protective power, especially for girls.

According to Willis, it is a rune of birth on the physical plane, nourishment, the relationship of mother and child, the female principle and domestic matters in general. It suggests success for new enterprises or something beginning. Peterson feels it indicates healing, recovery, regeneration, new growth from old roots (because new shoots grow from the stump of a felled birch). Birch has some of the same pain-relieving and febrifugal qualities as willow. It may also point to a need for collection and conservation of energy, nurturance, and shelter.

TIWAZ AND BERKANO: STUDY AND EXPERIENCE

The Hand of Tyr

Tyr, who at first glance may seem one of the more obscure of the Aesir, upon closer examination becomes a figure of intriguing possibilities.

The sovereign sky god, the Worldtree, and the hand form a complex of symbols that seems to go back to an extremely early time. Gelling and Ellis-Davidson's discussion of the hand symbol in *The Chariot of the Sun* adds some interesting evidence. Single handprints are often found in connection with Bronze Age Scandinavian rock carvings of the sun disk. The one-handed Irish god, Nuadu was ritually deposed when his hand was cut off in battle and only after he was given a new hand of silver could he reign once more. The hand, whether represented by a palm print, an armed fist (the Red Hand of Ulster), or a hand at the end of a scepter, seems to have been a symbol of regal authority. In addition to the Ulstermen, a number of Scottish clans have legends in which a chieftain cuts off his hand and throws it onto a piece of land to claim sovereignty. The hand is also, of course, a symbol of law, and shaking on bargain still constitutes a legal agreement.

Pennick's chapter on "The Royal Centre, Fairs and Sacred Boards" in *Games of the Gods* (1989), provides some evidence that may illuminate these relationships. Medieval fairs were laid out on a grid based on the same principles that governed both Germanic and Celtic concepts of spatial organization, with four (sometimes subdivided) sectors surrounding a sacred center, which was the place of the king. This center was marked by a pole (representing the sacred tree often planted at the center of a town, and surviving in the maypole, which still stands in the central square of many German villages) at whose top was placed a glove.

When this pole was raised, the fair was open, and the law of the fair took effect within its borders. The cry, "The Glove is up!" opens California's Renaissance Pleasure Faire to this day. In her discussion of the significance of attaching Grendel's hand to the eaves of Heorot, Ellis-Davidson remarks that it may recall "an earlier tradition of a great hand which once symbolized the power of a deity" (1988, p. 159). It seems to me very likely that this was precisely the case, and that the glove on its pole at the center of the medieval fairs was in effect the hand of Tyr at the top of the Worldtree. For more background on these concepts, see Hastrup's *Culture and History in Medieval Iceland*; *Celtic Heritage*, by Alwin and Brinley Rees; and Pennick's *Games of the Gods*.

Tyr's association with the realm of sovereignty lead one to re-examine the relationship between war and justice. Georges Dumézil (1973) proposes a tripartite model of Indo-European mythology in which Tyr's functions parallel those of the Roman Dius Fides or the Indo-Iranian Mitra rather than Ares/Mars, as a god whose primary concerns involve cosmic and worldly order and social contracts. The Anglo-Saxon Rune Poem's intimations that the Tyr-star keeps faith with princes may support this. However, in the surviving mythology Tyr does not go to war. Rather than seeing him as a battle god, he should be viewed as a god of law, especially as determined by judicial combat. The holmgang, or formal duel, was distinguished from other kinds of fighting in that it was subject to strict rules and took place in a formally delineated enclosure.

In the later period, the functions of the ancient Indo-European sky god seem to have been divided, Thor inheriting his thunder and responsibility for fatherly protection, Odin, his spear of sovereignty, and Tyr, his concern with maintaining the law of earth and heaven. This law was primarily expressed in the institution of the Althing.

The Althing was the setting for both verbal and physical trials. However, Germanic legal procedures were not necessarily intended to achieve abstract justice, but rather to stop a fight—what Dumézil calls "a pessimistic view of the law." Hence even murder could be paid for with were-gild, or feuds settled on the field of honor. Tyr's loss of his hand in a fraudulent guarantee may result from this attitude, since it was an eminently practical (although a painful and basically dishonorable) solution to the problem of controlling the wolf's appetite.

The fact that Tyr's role in the binding of Fenris could not be transferred to another god underlines its importance. Gundarsson believes that Tyr was the chief actor in the binding of Fenris because the wolf is the embodiment of the forces of chaos, and therefore the god of law's chief enemy. However, the relationship between wolf and war god may be even more complex. Snorri tells us "The gods brought up the wolf at home, and only Tyr had the courage to go up to it and bring it food" (1987, "Gylfaginning": 34).

Thus, the wolf takes his hand into its mouth in pledge that the fetter will not bind it not only because Tyr is presumably the most honorable of the Aesir, but because it is Tyr who has cared for it. In helping to bind Fenris, Tyr not only breaks an oath but betrays a trust. He and the wolf are linked by more than his hand. Tyr's role has become almost parental, and he and Fenris therefore become the polarized aspects of a single archetype.

It is possible that this story reflects a devolution from TIWAZ's original function as supreme sky god and guarantor of true justice, and that Odin's expansion from responsibility for magic and shamanic functions (a much more flexible and uncontrolled mode of action) into sovereignty screwed up the system. However, Tyr's sacrifice can also be seen as a higher law in conflict with a lower one, or two kinds of power achieving equilibrium. As Odin sacrificed self to self and gave his eye to gain true vision, so the uncontrolled violence of war (the wolf) is bound by cosmic justice (the god). Functionally, the mutilations of Tyr and Odin are parallel.

Spiritual Warriors

There has been a polarization of violence/nonviolence in our society. It takes major brainwashing to turn people into soldiers, yet unpremeditated and domestic violence is even more likely to occur when people are not accustomed to dealing with this energy. Banning guns and other weapons may cut down on accidents, but it does not prevent people from attacking each other with frying pans and kitchen knives. It is hypocritical to pretend that we are nonviolent because we do not personally kill things. Even people who find it hard to step on a spider have no qualms about eating a hamburger. Unless we have the physiology to survive on a vegetarian diet, we live by the deaths of other beings, and even vegetarians must kill plants to survive.

Aggression presents a special problem in neo-paganism, a religion dedicated on the whole to living in a state of love and harmony with all Earth's
children and deriving its identity in part from a reaction against the competition, violence, and greed we see in the dominant culture. In their effort to
reject the values of the patriarchy, pagan men in particular may attempt to
suppress aggressive impulses to the point where they suppress a great deal of
their own vitality. The stag has horns so that he can battle with other stags,
not to kill, but to demonstrate his virility. Any man who wears the antlers of
the Horned One in ritual is denying part of the god if he does not come to
terms with this energy.

Of course, the ability to fight is not limited to men. Jung says a woman
who acts aggressively is haunted by her animus, but in fact the ability of the
female to defend her young is as much a survival trait as the ability of her
mate to defend his family. Certainly in the sagas, the females are as deadly as
the males, especially when they do not have the outlet of physical violence.
The Valkyrie is the embodiment of battle fury.

The capacity for violence is a survival trait bred into humankind, a powerful
natural drive. The modern, technological world gives us few positive outlets
for this energy, and yet the pressures of our lives are constantly causing our
bodies to send us hormonal messages to fight or flee. Suppressing those
impulses exacts its own toll, yet if we give way to them, we lose the ability to
function within society. In ancient Germanic culture, one response to this
problem was the status of *berserkr*, a warrior who gave way to his fighting fury
within the context of battle. Berserkrs who were overcome by it at other times,
like Kveldúlf ("Evening Wolf"), Bialfi's son, were a distinct liability around
the homestead and often became outlaws.

The Viking world offered regular opportunities to exercise (or exorcise)
violent impulses in warfare. In the modern world, we must find other ways
to deal with them, not by denial or suppression, but by transforming and dis-
ciplining their energy. In our fight to do this, we have as patron and role
model the god Tyr, the god of war who is himself the means by which violence is bound.

Binding the Wolf

The connection between the wolf and the god of war is extremely ancient.
Even in a just war, the real winners are the wolves and the ravens. On the
other hand, the wolf can have a positive connotation. In Latin myth, it is a
she-wolf who nurtures Romulus and Remus, the twin sons of Mars.
European mythology recognizes the relationship between wolves and men in

the use of the word "wolf" or "wolf's head" for an outlaw, and the legend of the werewolf, a skin-changer who turns into a wolf when the moon is full. Wolves, along with bears, were the shapes most often used by berserkr warriors. Interestingly enough, in Navajo folklore "wolf" is a name for a worker of evil magic.

In reality, wolves are no more greedy or ferocious than any other wild animal, but their intelligence, endurance, and pack organization make them a formidable predator. It is quite possible that early humans learned some techniques for group hunting by observing wolves. North American wolves rarely if ever attack humans, but the evidence that European wolves attack anything available (including humans) in starving times is more convincing. Perhaps it is the very similarities between wolves and humans that contribute to the terror they inspire in European legend. We fear the wolf outside because we are too aware of the power of the wolf within.

The story of Tyr is inextricably bound up with that of the wolf Fenris, who represents unbridled violence and greed. The best summary of the myth of Tyr and Fenris can be found in Snorri Sturluson (1987, "Gylfaginning": 34).

One of Tyr's functions is to bind the wolf whether he appears as unbridled destructive fury in nature or the force that impels nations to make war, corporations to rape the environment, or individuals to battle themselves. The individual work for the TIWAZ rune involves learning to deal with both the energy of the warrior and the forces that energy is meant to control.

The original material for "Binding the Wolf Within" below was written by James Graham. This is a very powerful inner exercise, which can be taped and done individually, visualizing the ribbon, or tying it to your own hand.

MEDITATION: BINDING THE WOLF WITHIN

> Where men make war, Fenris walks the world;
> But in the hallows of each human heart,
> the wolf lies waiting.
> To keep him from Midgard
> It is there you must bind him.
> To bind him, you must understand him;
> to find him, you must seek within.
> Sink down now, still mind and body. . . .
> Sink into your own darkness
> where the wolf is dwelling . . .
> What part of you is Fenris?
> Where lives the fear that destroys you?
> What force stands between you
> and your true will?

Seek for that power that devours your happiness,
the part of yourself you hate,
the thing you long to change,
seek for your inner enemy. . . .
This is the wolf that you will meet.
But how will you face it?
Sign yourself three times with the rune of Tiwaz.
Let all anxiety melt away,
allow the power of the rune to fill you
with strength, daring,
and the fortitude to do what must be done.
Within you lies darkness; this is the Wolf's lair—
Call it out of the shadow, give it shape,
name it Fenris.
Let the image steady in your mind.
All others shudder before it—only you can face it.
For a long time now you have been feeding it;
You and this beast know each other very well.

The wolf has come—
Look upon each other with unflinching eyes.
You have seen this wolf in every conflict
you ever faced—
it was at your throat when you wished to speak
and feared to,
it left you wounded and bleeding
when you most needed your will and vitality.
Boldly face its soul-piercing stare,
its sharp and bloody teeth,
its huge and eternal hunger. . . .
But feed it no more fear.
Remember the triple rune that is on you
and breathe deeply, evenly,
conserving your strength.
Now invoke the Tyr within yourself;
call upon your sovereign soul.
Call out the name of Tiwaz
and summon him down from the skies,
from the forest of his Mysteries,
from the Law Rock of the Althing . . .

He comes, a column of light,
the flare of a swordblade,
single of purpose and will as he is single of hand—

He, who knows the beast best of all
yet does not fear it, greets you by name
His eyes pierce more sharply
than those of the wolf—
he sees the rune you bear,
his gaze grows gentler.
But he does not draw his sword.
The Justice Lord draws from his sword belt a rope.
He tethers one end to the great neck of Fenris;
You offer him your wrist—
With the other end of the rope he binds it;
your fingers close. . . .

The god speaks—
"You shall not kill each other—
that is the first agreement by which I bind you.
Death breeds more death,
the spiral may be stopped
only by understanding your enemy.
Speak to the wolf that it may hear you;
listen to the wolf, hear what it says.
Understand that understanding binds you,
and all the bonds made between you
must be maintained."

He holds up the handless wrist of his right arm
in warning—
"Do not sever that which ties you together!"
Tyr stands aside, waiting, as witness.
Now you must speak to the wolf,
ask why it has harmed you, negotiate,
agree on compensations.
What does the wolf want?
What are you prepared to give?
With every agreement that binds you both,
wind the ribbon around your wrist once more.
How many times have you bound yourself?
What agreements have you made?
Remember them!
These are the bonds by which the wolf within
is bound.
Though the ribbons disappear,
this fetter will remain.
Tug on the ribbon now

let its touch bind you back
into awareness of the world. . . .

These are the bonds that hold you
though the ribbons disappear,
this fetter will remain.
To remember, you have only to sign yourself
with the rune of Tyr
and wind the ribbon
around your wrist once more. . . .

Use the power of TIWAZ to strengthen self-discipline, fast, exercise, or tackle tasks you have put off. Other activities include playing hnefatafl, paying special attention to the spatial relationships and the place of the king, and working with concepts of justice in general.

The best fictional treatment of the concepts surrounding Tyr I have found is a story called "The Hand of Tyr," by Paul Edwin Zimmer, which appeared in the anthology *Greyhaven*, edited by Marion Zimmer Bradley. Dick Francis's novel, *Whip Hand*, whose protagonist has only one hand, is a remarkable portrayal of the relationship between fear and courage. For more information on hnefatafl and sacred space, see Nigel Pennick, *Games of the Gods*. For an illuminating discussion of the natural history and human folklore of wolves, read *Of Wolves and Men*, by Barry Lopez.

The Spirit of the Tree

BERKANO is the third of the tree runes in the old Germanic futhark, the others being, of course, "thorn" and "yew." The Anglo-Saxon rune list adds ᚪ *ác*, the oak tree, and ᚫ, for *æsc*, the ash. The thorn is distinctly dangerous, and the yew tree somewhat sinister. But the birch, despite its capacity to endure the most harsh conditions, is a more friendly, domestic tree, graceful and filled with healing virtue.

I have dealt with trees as objects of worship in the discussion of the rune, and in the chapter on EIHWAZ. The association of trees with goddesses extends to mythology in the form of southern dryads and the Scandinavian *iarnvidjur* (woodswives), or *skogsrå*, the woods-roes.

These spirits appear as fair young women, whose true nature may be told from the fact that in back they are hollow or appear to have bark instead of skin. Folktales of such beings seem to be variants on the motif of the "fairy lover." In one story a man is exhausted by going out every night to sleep with his mistress and must be saved by his friends. However, in other stories, a hunter who pleases a woods-sprite is rewarded with game. There is even a tale about a charcoal burner who lived with a woods-roe as her husband and had three children by her.

German folklore is enriched by a whole forest full of *wood-minne, bilwisse* (well-knowing), *wood-schrats* (who according to Grimm received cult worship), *holzweibel* (holt-wives), and moss maidens. Though sometimes masculine forms were seen, they appear to have mostly been female. In England, the Anglo-Saxons lumped the whole crew together as *wuduælfen*. An interesting British custom is attached to the cutting of live elder wood, in which the woodcutter must say:

> Owd Gal, give me of thy wood,
> as Oi will give some of moine,
> when I graw inter a tree.

> (Briggs 1976, p. 316)

One wonders if this prayer has some connection with the folk belief that trees may sometimes become home to the souls of ancestors, a concept which may survive today in the request made by some to have their ashes buried under a tree.

Perhaps the best-known presentation of tree spirits in modern times is J.R.R. Tolkien's portrayal of the Ents in *The Lord of the Rings*. There are as many kinds of Ents as there are species of tree. Their culture is characterized by a view of time that thinks in seasons rather than days and decades rather than years. In *The Lord of the Rings*, the male Ents live in the wild forest, while the females, who favored fruit-bearing and domesticated trees, went away long ago and have been lost.

Surely the Swedish birch tree, planted securely in the farmyard where it can watch over the family, is the kind of tree an Entwife would choose.

Living with the Landvaettir

Tree spirits are only one species of what Scandinavians call "The Invisible," the myriad beings who in British folklore populate Faerie. By the end of the Middle Ages, their population had grown to include the spirits of the dead and a variety of devolved deities, as well as sprites associated with human activities. They were classed according to function, and so in addition to forest spirits, one found spirits of hills and crags, water wights, mer-folk, and the duergar who lived under the earth. More homely wights included the spirits of hearth and garth, of mine and mill.

A generic term for the spirits of nature is *landvaettir*—land wights. Their essence seems to be the concentrations of energy associated with regions, and groups or individual living things. Human perceptions, unable to deal with pure energy fields, personify and perceive them in physical form, human, animal, or plant.

Landvaettir may act as the guardians of a region. As we learned in the discussion of THURISAZ, Iceland was guarded by beings who appeared in the forms of a giant, a great bird, a dragon, and a bull. Native American tribes identify their own regional figures. According to Chippewa tradition, for instance, the north is guarded by a white buffalo, the east by an eagle, the south by a coyote, and the west by a black bear. The elemental archangels who guard the directions in Western ceremonial magic serve the same purpose. States and countries have their own totems, preserved in heraldry and in customs such as the naming of a "state bird, animal, tree, and so on." For the United States, the totem is the eagle that sat at the top of the Iroquois Worldtree, and for Russia, a bear.

We can invite the Norse gods to join us wherever we may go, just as the Angles, Saxons, Jutes, and the rest did when they migrated to Britain and the Icelanders did when they colonized their new land. But if we are to worship as they did, we also need to make contact with the spirits native to the land in which we live. In places like Britain and Scandinavia, thousands of years of continuous habitation have identified the sacred places. Stone menhirs mark the ley lines; grave mounds show where ancestral spirits lie. The aboriginal inhabitants of the United States left fewer marks upon the land. Still, anthropology and local folklore can give you a start wherever you may be.

In California, for instance, Native American folklore tells us that Grizzly and Coyote are important spirits, but each region within the state has its own guardians. Where Indian legends are unavailable, you can make contact with the spirits in the same way the Icelanders did, exploring the area and opening yourself to its spiritual power. If you did not visit the wilderness to talk to the Jotnar when you were studying THURISAZ, you might want to try it now, focusing this time on the lesser wights of forest and hills.

This work can be done on a very personal level as well. A number of years ago a group of people living at Findhorn in Scotland discovered that they could communicate with the spirits of the plants they were growing, learning when to water, when to harvest, and the like. The plant kingdom, responding to this attention, rewarded them with vegetables of unusual quality and size. At Findhorn they called the plant spirits with whom they were communicating devas. They could as well be called garden wights. The Swedes plant birch trees in their front yards, but the spirit of any tree that grows in your yard can be a powerful guardian.

Review the material on magical gardening from the discussion of JERA. If you started gardening at that time, your plants should be well established by now. Take some time to talk to them and to listen to what they have to say. Talk to your tree. Create a shrine in your garden (or in a flowerpot, if you are doing houseplants!) and make offerings to the landspirits there. Even a cement "garden gnome" from a nursery can serve as a useful image of a land wight. If an appropriate statue is unavailable, a stone or a stout length of branch driven into the ground will do just as well. You can make a ring of smaller stones around it—let your imagination be your guide.

Sauna Rite

One of the major uses of the birch in Scandinavia is in the sauna, a practice most familiar from Finland but known in some form throughout the North. The ceremonial sweat seems to be a circumpolar custom. The ancient Irish had sweat houses, and the Icelanders sweated over natural vents of volcanic steam. Originally the sauna took place in the dwelling, and the stones were heated in the central hearth, but at an early period folk began to build separate sauna houses. The traditional Finnish sauna house was used for many other purposes, including an infirmary and birth hall. One of Finland's legendary heroes was born in a sauna.

The association with healing extends to the powers of the sauna itself, which cleanses the mind as well as the body, and produces a state of detachment and clarity. According to H. J. Viherjuúri,

> The ancient Finns believed, like many other primitive peoples, that fire came from heaven and was sacred. The fireplace and the piles of stones were altars. The sauna was a place for the worship of the dead, who were supposed to return gladly, even after death, to so pleasant a place. Sometimes the sauna was heated with choice firewood, and then all the diseases and evils of the body were driven out by means of various rites and magic spells. Even unhappy love affairs could be settled by the sauna. Some people believed that the throwing of water over the stones was a form of sacrificial ceremony. The Finnish word löyly, meaning "the steam which rises from the stones," originally signified spirit, or even life. The word corresponding to löyly, in languages related to Finnish is lil, meaning "soul." "In the sauna one must conduct oneself as one would in church," according to an old Finnish saying. It was forbidden to make a noise or to whistle, or to speak indecently in a sauna, because all evil influences had been driven out. (Viherjuuri 1965, pp. 17–18)

As in the Native American sweat lodge, the heat comes from stones that have been heated in a fire of birch, spruce, or pine, although the sauna is a permanent building that includes the hearth or stove that heats the stones. The scent of birch is inextricably associated with the true sauna experience.

The human body can tolerate much higher temperatures when the heat is dry. The dry air starts perspiration, which is increased when water is thrown on the stones, but the excess moisture is immediately absorbed by the wooden walls.

The correct procedure for taking a sauna is as follows:

1. Spend some time (twenty minutes) lying prone at 140°F first to let entire body sweat.

2. Sprinkle water on stones with whisk or dipper ("one cup for each man and one for the sauna," but this much may not be necessary in a well-heated stove); aim for 175°F and 10 percent humidity, those who find it too hot can move lower on platform.

3. Make whisks from silver or curly birch in early summer; dried whisks must be soaked briefly in warm water, placed on stones and turned several times. They can be resoaked if necessary, but should not be too wet. A birch whisk will last two saunas if used by only one person. Start at top of the body and work down; the soles of feet should be well whisked. Whisking activates blood circulation in the capillaries.

4. Wash in a separate room or in sauna with soap and cloth, or soapy water lathered up by whisk and applied with whisk to loosen dirt and dead skin.

5. Rinse with warm water, clean all soap off of the sauna too.

6. Cool the body by plunging into snow, an icy lake, or very cold water. Some people then go back to the sauna to sweat and whisk some more after this cooling.

7. Allow the body to cool off naturally in air until a leaf will fall off the skin. Do not dress until the body is at normal temperature.

8. Rest silently for fifteen to twenty minutes; then eat and drink.

The folklore of the sauna clearly indicates that the practice originally had spiritual significance, probably focused by some kind of ritual. The Romans at an early period of their history buried their dead beneath the family hearth. If this is an ancient European custom, it might explain the Finnish belief in the attraction of the sauna for the spirits of the dead. This association would be especially telling in an underground sauna, in which the experience would be a return to the grave mound as a womb in which to commune with the ancestors and be renewed and reborn. Although we do not know exactly how the sauna was used in pre-Christian times, I suggest the following procedure:

1. Enter in silence, reverently, and offer your first prayer to the stones and the fire. Draw the runes KENAZ (ᚲ) and NAUDHIZ (ᚾ) over the stones, and pray to Hoenir, the god who gave spirit to humankind upon their creation, for understanding.

2. Draw the rune LAGUZ ᚱ over the bucket of water, and when you splash the stones, inscribe ANSUZ ᚠ in the steam and pray to Odin to breathe in önd, the breath of the spirit, with the steam.

3. Draw the BERKANO ᛒ rune over the birch whisk, and pray to Lodhurr, who gave sense and circulation to the body, while whisking yourself.

4. Afterward, you may use ISA ᛁ to help yourself cool off.

You may also call a rune ring around yourself in the sauna. While sweating, you might want to pray to the Jotnar Jordh and Loki, spirits of earth and fire; Aegir and the spirits of water; the Alfar; and Birchmother during the first round. Pray to the gods if you try a second round. When you sauna, you are voluntarily subjecting yourself to the purifying heat of KENAZ. Give yourself to it, allow the fire to melt all uncleanliness or dis-ease from mind or body, which will flow out of you as LAGUZ.

Depending on your experience and endurance, you may find it useful to divide the experience into "rounds." Decide on what you want to accomplish with this purification, and divide your goal into three or four stages—e.g., getting rid of physical stress or pain, outmoded ideas, emotional trauma, spiritual confusion. Or use the heat to move yourself through the three states of matter: solid, liquid, and gaseous (the realms of Earth, Water, and Mist of Norse cosmology).

If you cannot use a private sauna, rent time in a commercial sauna at a gym or hotel. If it is a large one, share the rental with a few like-minded friends and hold your own ceremony. The runes do not have to be chanted aloud. If you are sharing the sauna with strangers, intone and visualize them silently.

The Group Ritual

If you are working with a group, the ritual for TIWAZ and BERKANO is on page 353. In this ritual, you will make the journey from Utgard to the Assembly—from the wilderness of chaos and alienation to the safety and order of the community.

Chapter 11

EHWAZ and MANNAZ

WITH THE SECOND PAIR OF RUNES IN TYR'S AETT, our focus shifts to humanity. We consider what it means to be human, recognizing that individuality is the result of innumerable compromises and connections between the self and the other, whether that other is outside oneself or within. EHWAZ and MANNAZ enable us to explore ourselves as individuals, in relation to other humans and as children of the gods.

THE NINETEENTH RUNE: ᛗ EHWAZ

Pronunciation: "EH-wahz"
Meaning: Horse

EHWAZ, Eoh, extending energy,
The holy Horse links god and human.

The Ancient Meanings

EHWAZ is the Horse rune. Its use for the "*e*" sound is characteristic of the old Germanic languages, although in later Icelandic it migrated to a long "*a*" sound, which is probably why the rune does not appear in the Younger Futhark.

The Anglo-Saxon rune poem associates the horse with the aristocracy, prosperity, and mobility.

> ᛗ *[Eoh] byþ for eorlum æþelinga wyn*
> (Horse is a joy to princes in presence of earls,)
> *hors hofum wlanc, ðær him hæleþ ymbe*
> (Horse in pride of its hooves,)
> *welege on wicgum wrixlaþ spræce*
> (when rich men, mounted, bandy words,)
> *and biþ unstyllym æfre frofur.*
> (and is to the restless ever a comfort.)

Notwithstanding its determinedly secular interpretation in the Anglo-Saxon poem, the horse was one of the primary sacred animals of the Indo-European peoples. The "white horses" carved into the chalk hills of Britain, if not created by the Anglo-Saxons, were certainly maintained by them. Tacitus reports (*Germania*: 10) that white horses yoked to a sacred chariot were observed for purposes of divination. Other examples of the use of horses, especially white ones, in divination are cited by Grimm (1966, II: p. 2). Grimm also cites numerous examples of the use of a horse's head to frighten away evil in German and Livonian folk culture.

In Scandinavia, horses were specifically associated with Freyr and the cult of the Vanir, and sacred horses, which were never ridden, were kept at sanctuaries such as Thrandheim in Norway. Stallions called *Freyfaxi*, "mane of Freyr" are featured in two of the sagas. The horses of the god were, however, sometimes sacrificed, and horseflesh was probably forbidden for human food in medieval Europe just because eating it had been part of the worship of Freyr. It is possible that the stallion fights described in the sagas were originally a kind of divinatory rite as well. *Seidhkonas*, or seeresses (and in medieval folklore, witches), were believed to take the shapes of mares at night to roam abroad.

Another reference to horses is an odd episode from *Flateyjarbok*, which tells how the woman of the farmstead preserved the phallus of a horse with leeks, wrapped it in linen, and brought it out as an object of worship. The power of the horse to control fertility was invoked by Egil Skallagrimsson when he set a horse's head upon a stake (the *neidhstong*) and carved it with a runespell to frighten the landspirits away until King Erik and Queen Gunnhild should be driven from Norway.

Horses are also associated with Odin, the only one of the Aesir who typically rides rather than driving a wagon, although supernatural horses draw the chariots of the sun. His eight-legged horse, Sleipnir, is, however, somewhat unusual, being the offspring of Loki in mare form by the Jotun stallion Svadhilfari and able to gallop between the worlds. The horse is also appropriate to Odin as a god of the dead; *jódis* (dis of the horse) is a byname for Hella. A descendant of Sleipnir, Grani, is given to the hero Sigurd in the *Volsungasaga*.

Modern Meanings

Thorsson explains the meaning of EHWAZ as symbiosis between partners—man/horse, man/woman, for example—or opposites working together harmoniously toward a single goal. The horse is Sleipnir, the vehicle for the psychic journey, or the fylgja or the twin horses or the twin hero-gods. Osborn and Longland call EHWAZ the vehicle of transcendence that increases physical power; the body, which is the vehicle for the soul. Aswynn views it as the persona or vehicle that forms a link between one's emotional attitudes and the external world. She sees it as a rune of partnership, cooperation, and adjustment. It represents the etheric body, the vehicle for astral journeying.

For Gundarsson, EHWAZ is the vehicle of communication between the worlds, a rune of the fylgja, or beast-fetch, the totem animal of the vitki (wizard). Since the horse is sacred both to Odin and to Freyr, it can symbolize the joining of mystical inspiration and earthly prosperity. One might see it as a rune of the alliance between the Aesir and Vanir. It governs the harmonious union of dualities, whether of equals, as in joint kingship, friendship, and marriage, or guidance, as in the relationship of man/horse or god/man.

The domestication of the horse led to a significant extension of man's ability to travel for hunting or herding, to move objects, and to make war. In such situations, the bond between horse and rider can become intense (some of Francis's descriptions of steeplechase riding convey a sense of almost mystical union). The psychological impact seems to have been a virtual expansion of consciousness, and the horse swiftly acquired immense spiritual and symbolic significance. The horse sacrifice was a major ritual from Ireland to Siberia; the beast could represent sovereignty, the tribe, the solar light, or simply the most valued possession the people had. The white horses carved into the chalk hillsides of Britain were equally sacred to Celt and Saxon.

A case can be made for connecting the horse cult with the equally ancient Indo-European cult of the Divine Twins. In Hindu mythology the Asvins were sons of the sky or the sun, whose parents took the forms of horses to conceive them. They are the physicians of the gods and may appear with horse heads or in a golden chariot drawn by horses. In the Greek and Roman pantheon, Castor and Pollux, the hero-twins and sons of Zeus called the Dioscuri, are often portrayed on horseback.

Stories of brother or twin heroes are common in the genealogies of the Germanic royal families, the most suggestive, from this point of view, being the Anglo-Saxon Hengest and Horsa (Stallion and Horse). According to Tacitus, the Naharvali, a tribe on the North Sea, worshipped twin gods called the Alcis, "revered under the character of young men and brothers" (*Germania*: 43), whose attributes were the same as those of Castor and Pollux. Ellis-Davidson mentions the find of an urn from the La Tène period in the same region showing men on horseback connected by a crossbeam, which is similar to the Spartan symbol for the Dioscuri (1964, p. 169).

Although the twin gods seem to be mainly associated with fertility, healing, and youthful skill in warfare, their duality may also have sexual implications. Tacitus tell us that the priest of the Alcis presided over the ancient rites conducted in the sacred grove "dressed in women's apparel." Interestingly enough, although "by Castor and Pollux" was a common Roman oath, women swore simply "by Castor." One wonders whether this indicates the survival of an Indo-European tradition in which the power of the horse was invoked for fertility by women.

The horse may also represent the psychic or spiritual energy of individual or tribe, an energy that can carry one to the realm of the gods. In Siberia, the drum is the "horse" of the shaman. In the Afro-diasporic traditions (Voudoun, Umbanda, Santeria, etc.), the worshipper who is possessed by a deity is referred to as a "horse" and the deity his "rider." Glosecki (1989) suggests that this metaphor may have been used for possessory experience in Germanic culture as well.

The relationship between horse and rider is significantly empowering—together, they are able to do things that neither would accomplish alone. However, the effectiveness of the relationship depends on the wisdom of the rider and the willingness of the one who is ridden. Its success requires cooperation and harmony.

A sense of transcendence through the equal union of opposites may also occur in sexual union. It has been suggested that the twins were originally not identical, but one of the brother-sister pairs (such as Freyr and Freyja in the shapes of a stallion and a mare), common in early mythology. If so, nothing of the sort survived in the mythologies in which the twins retained a major role. Another possibility is that the transsexual aspect of the worship of the Alcis (like the transsexuality of the shaman) symbolized the union between masculine and feminine aspects of the psyche and the ability to move between the worlds.

EHWAZ would seem, therefore, to represent extension of strength through union and spiritual or physical energy, operating in both the physical and spiritual realms. In the physical world, it may be considered a rune of Freyr, the Divine Stallion. Freyr's blessing is invoked for cooperation for peaceful purposes, political and social unions, and fertility as a result of sexual union. Sacred kingship and physical power are also implied. In the spiritual realm, EHWAZ can also be seen as a rune of Odin as master of trance magic, which facilitates union and cooperation with the spiritual worlds, the gods, and spiritual forces within and without, a rune of protection for spiritual journeying.

Interpreting and Using EHWAZ

Depending on the context, the meanings of this rune in a reading can include change and movement—travel or development either spiritually or physically, or an increase in capacity in either the physical or spiritual realms as a result of cooperation with another. It may also indicate the possibility or the need to change a situation through changing one's relationship to it, or to others involved in it. It can be used as a protective rune in workings involving trance or altered consciousness.

Thorsson states that it stands for connection, loyalty, and the principle of teamwork, especially in tandem, a dynamic harmony with the other that accepts differences, present or new partnerships. Willis feels that in addition to change, especially involving movement or travel, it may mean one is on the right track, and success is imminent, or that assistance from someone sensible and reliable is on the way.

Peterson associates it with physical or astral travel, precognition. Aswynn feels that in divinations, the rune refers to relationships with a mother or other older female, the instinctual drives, or the female libido. Negatively it can indicate loss or the breakup of a relationship.

She also suggests combining ELHAZ and EHWAZ in a bindrune to hunt a wandering spirit or to invoke Wodan as the wild hunter. Gundarsson recommends its use for fertility, especially magical, as an aid to sympathetic magic, bringing power under the guidance of wisdom, for building a rapport with any vehicle of motion (living or mechanical), and for physical or astral travel. It can be used to deal with thought forms and other extensions of one's power.

THE TWENTIETH RUNE: ᛗ ᛦ MANNAZ

Pronunciation: "MAN-naz"
Meaning: Man

In MANNAZ every man is master;
All Rig's children are relations.

Ancient Meanings

In Old English, the name for this rune is *mann*—meaning "man," "human."
In the Old Norse it is *madhr* (or *mannr*)—which though masculine, means
"human" as opposed to supernatural beings such as Jotnar, in the same way
as the English have used "man" or "mankind."

In Anglo-Saxon, males might be called "weapmen" (weapon-men), and
females, "weavemen" or "wifmen" (weaving men) respectively. In Icelandic,
a female human could be *kvenn-madhr*, while a male is *karl-madhr*.
Interestingly enough, "man," with one *n*, is an ancient neuter word for a
human, derived from the Old High German and in Old Norse found only in
the old laws and poetry. In Old Norse, *mann* with two *n*'s is a masculine
noun, which is used to form two pages of compound words in the Icelandic
dictionary. In the Younger Futhark its form evolved from the crossed *M*
shown above, to an intermediate closed form ᛉ ,which apparently lost its top
to take a form identical with the older rune for ELHAZ ᛦ.

The interpretation of this rune (and of the human condition) in the Anglo-
Saxon rune poem would appear to have been heavily Christianized. Although
it begins in a traditional way by emphasizing the importance of kindred and
cheerfulness (and the form of the rune itself could be seen as a doubling of the
rune *wynn*, "joy"), the writer of the poem is swift to point out the hopeless-
ness of depending on human help. The moaning about the will of the Lord
and the "wretched flesh" that follows foreshadows a multitude of medieval
writings adjuring poor sinners to place no faith in the world or the body.

As Osborn and Longland observe, the verse expresses the transitory
nature of human life, from heedless joy to dust—a depressing view of the
human condition, in which all fates eventually end badly. This Anglo-Saxon
attitude toward doom is a descent from the earlier Germanic pessimism,
which, however gloomy, at least enabled one to derive a certain satisfaction
in fighting shoulder-to-shoulder to the finish against overwhelming odds.

> ᛗ *[Mann] byþ on myþe his magan leof:*
> (The mirthful man is dear to kinsmen,)
> *sceal þeah anra gehwylc oðrum swican,*
> (yet every man must fail his fellow)
> *forðam drihten wyle dome sine*
> (since the will of the Lord dooms)
> *þæt earme flæsc eorþan betæcan.*
> (that the frail flesh to earth be taken.)

The Old Norse verses present a more robust picture. As in the Anglo-Saxon,
in both the Icelandic and Norwegian poems the flesh may return to earth,

but in the process the dust is "augmented," added to, or perhaps even enno-
bled. One is reminded of Hamlet's soliloquy on the progress of the dust of
Caesar through the guts of a beggar. The Norwegian poem continues with a
puzzling reference to the hawk's claw for which I have found no adequate
explanation. One wonders if the line might refer to the bird-track shape of
the rune in the Younger Futhark, or as Gundarsson suggests, to the hawk as
a messenger between the worlds. A friend of mine who is a falconer has also
observed that the strike of the hawk's claw means death.

> ᛉ *[Maðhr] er moldar auki;*
> (Man is an augmentation of the dust;)
> *mikil er græip á hauki.*
> (great is the claw of the hawk.)

In the Icelandic poem, man not only augments the dust, but adorns the ship.
This gives the whole stanza a far more cheerful perspective. Here, the first
verse is, "Man, or [other humans] are the joy or comfort of men."

> ᛉ [Maðr] er manns gaman
> (Man is the joy of man)
> *ok moldar auki*
> (and augmentation of the dust)
> *ok skipa skreytir.*
> (and adorner of ships.)

The same words conclude stanza 47 of the "Hávamál":

> When I was young   I travelled alone,
> And wandered off the marked way;
> Rich I thought myself   when another I found,
> Humans are man's comfort.

In the Old Norse view, humans are defined not only by the fact that they are
made from the dust of the earth and will return to it, but by the things they
do (such as braving the seas in ships) and by the joy they take in comradeship
and community. The individual's character and courage were important, but
much of one's worth was defined by one's place in the community. This could
be earned, as when a man distinguished himself as a member of a great lord's
war band, or be born to, if one belonged to or advanced the interests of one's
aett, or kindred. A man with neither kin nor comrades was an outsider, sus-
pected of being an outlaw or wolf's head. In a harsh environment, cooperation is essential to survival.

Modern Meanings

For Thorsson, the rune MANNAZ is the human archetype, the rune of Heimdall, father of mankind, that identifies humanity as progeny of the gods (an inherited rather than contractual relationship with the gods). It is man as a manifestation of the Divine, the expression of fulfillment of human potential: intelligence, reason, memory, tradition. In addition, he sees it as the archetypal androgyne. It is the rune of Máni, the moon, the synthesis of intuition and rationality, transformation and essence.

Gundarsson provides a thought-provoking analysis of theRíg myth and its relationship to Celtic and other analogues. He points out that the heir to Ríg's name and sovereignty is not his son Earl (the hereditary nobility), but the youngest of Earl's sons, Kon, who masters runelore ("Rígsthula": 46). Although Kon, like his brothers, is a warrior, it is knowledge—his intelligence—that enables him to win kingship. From this, Gundarsson reads MANNAZ as the rune of the rational mind, in which the powers of the right and left sides of the brain, or thought (Huginn) and memory (Muninn, Mimir), interact.

Aswynn also discusses the "Rígsthula" story, and sees Heimdall as the equivalent of the legendary Mannus, although in the poem he is the progenitor of classes of society rather than tribes. From the rune's similarity in form to EHWAZ, she reasons that MANNAZ is a rune of the "hug," or fetch, as man is the highest animal, in which mind rules instinct (as the spirit rules the shape in which one performs trance journeying).

The identification of the "M" rune with the moon suggests all sorts of additional associations—the man in the moon; the relationship between the moon and fertility—moon cycles in woman and man; spiritual inheritance and access to the collective unconscious. All of these are very similar to the concepts associated with the sphere of Yesod in Kabbalah, which governs physical fertility and access to the astral realm of images. Heimdall is identified in the mythology with Ríg, the "Father of Mankind," who begot the progenitors of the three classes of humankind: rulers, farmers, and servants (the jarl, the carl, and the thrall), and is the special champion of Freyja, who rules the fertility of nature.

Tacitus (in *Germania*: 2) tells us that the ancient Germans believed themselves descended from a god called Tuisto (whose name has been speculatively related to *Teutates*, the Celtic god name from the same root that gives us the Celtic *tuath* "tribe"—and the Germanic *Teuton*. In Tacitus, the tribes are further descended from Tuisto's son Mannus, from whose three sons were descended the Ingaevones (on the North Coast), the Herminones (in the center), and the Istaevones (elsewhere, perhaps the east?).

According to Grimm, the Saxons traced their descent from Ingvingvar (Ingvio or Yngvi, who is also found in Danish and Swedish king lists), the Franks from the Iscaevones and Iscio, and the Thuringians from Hermundurus (Istio or Irmin, as in the Irminsul). Tacitus tells us that the other tribes believed themselves descended from other sons of Mannus in the same way. A study of ethnography makes clear that the most common self-identification for tribal groups is a word that means "the People," or "Men." In many cases, the names by which they have become known to history are those given them by their neighbors (as in "Navajo"). It is not surprising, therefore, to find the Teutonic tribes identifying themselves as the children of an eponymous "Mannus." We are all the children of the original human ancestor.

In studying MANNAZ, we confront the question of what it means to be human. The idea that humans should depend upon and take joy in each other expressed in the Norse rune poem and "Hávamál" is a concept that has appeared regularly in English literature, especially in *Hamlet*, in which Shakespeare, taking the story of Amlethus, son of Orvendil, told in Saxo's history of the Danes, seems to have absorbed much of the old Germanic ethos (Malone 1964). One of Hamlet's chief concerns is the meaning of humanity. His inability to rejoice in either man or nature are symptomatic of his dis-ease and disharmony.

> What a piece of work is man! How noble in reason! How infinite in faculty! In form and moving how express and admirable! In action how like an angel! In apprehension how like a god! The beauty of the world! The paragon of animals! And yet, to me, what is this quintessence of dust? Man delights not me, no nor woman neither. (Shakespeare, *Hamlet*, 2.2.315–321)

Although Shakespeare may have read Saxo, it is unlikely that he could have known the rune poems; however, he has managed to capture their spirit. Mankind is both divine and animal, distinguished by his powers of intellect and memory, but the essence of human nature is the ability to relate to the rest of humankind.

Interpreting and Using MANNAZ

Depending on its position and associations in a reading, this rune might indicate either the positive or negative aspects of the human condition. It seems to raise questions of identity and function—what it means to be human, and how one fulfills one's potential, as well as how one relates to human society and what one's purpose and function in life should be. In a reading on a spiritual question, it might indicate a need to tap into the powers of the collective unconscious, to draw on race memory for creative solutions and a way of revisioning the world.

Thorsson feels that the rune indicates self-realization, the fulfillment of human potential, acceptance of the human condition. Gundarsson says that MANNAZ is useful in mental work, for strengthening intelligence and memory, and for psychic awakening. It can also be used, with OTHALA, to claim one's inheritance as a human being, especially in cooperation with others on the same path. In magic, it is the rune of the vitki, the integrated and disciplined mind. Its danger is pride, if one thinks that one has been set apart from the rest of humanity.

Aswynn finds that in readings, the rune refers to people in general, their nature depending on the other runes involved. Inverted, it can mean an enemy, or occasionally a male homosexual. It relates to legal affairs and situations involving mutual cooperation. It aids in intellectual effort, especially in conjunction with ANSUZ, RAIDHO, and EHWAZ. For Willis, it is a rune of interdependence, responsibility, cooperation, and social relationship. It indicates people in service occupations, or a need to get outside help. It can also contribute to clear and creative thought and the power of creative visualization. To Peterson, however, it represents the self, humanity, human frailty or untrustworthiness, and distrust.

EHWAZ AND MANNAZ: STUDY AND EXPERIENCE

The Holy Horse

The Horse Rune expresses the mystery of the relationship between freedom and control. The horse was the first domesticated creature to significantly extend human range and power. In the discussion of the rune itself, we have seem something of what it meant to the ancients. What is its significance for us today?

Even more than the book, the film of *The Black Stallion* captures the essential mystique of man's relationship with the horse. In reality horses are large, strong, and often rather stupid creatures, but in the film the superb photography transforms the relationship between the boy and the horse into a metaphor of transcendence. The Stallion is a creature of incomparable grace and power who willingly submits to partnership with the boy, physically a much smaller and weaker creature, because together they can achieve what is not possible for either alone. The boy gives the horse purpose; the horse gives his rider power. One sees a similar relationship, and a similar beauty, in Gandalf's horse Shadowfax in the film of *The Two Towers*. Those who have been privileged to watch a performance of *Cavalia*, the wonderful French-Canadian show featuring Liberty Horses and dressage, know just how magical the connection can be.

Laura Hillenbrand expresses the nature of this partnership most eloquently in her book *Seabiscuit*.

> Man is preoccupied with freedom yet laden with handicaps. The breadth of his activity and experience is narrowed by the limitations of his relatively weak, sluggish body. The racehorse, by virtue of his awesome physical gifts, freed the jockey from himself. When a horse and a jockey flew over the track together, there were moments in which the man's mind wedded itself to the animal's body to form something greater than the sum of both parts. The horse partook of the jockey's cunning; the jockey partook of the horse's supreme power. For the jockey, the saddle was a place of unparalleled exhilaration, of transcendence. (Hillenbrand 2001, p. 80)

Horses are not the only animals that have this relationship to man. The shepherd and his dog, the mahout and his elephant all work in close companionship. Today, some may find the same sense of extension of capacity through interaction with a fine car, a fighter airplane, or a computer. But the horse is the first and perhaps the most beautiful of man's servants, and the exhilaration of its speed provides a sense of transcending boundaries to achieve ecstasy. It is not surprising that the horse, and its cousins the Pegasus and Unicorn, are still such a staple of fantasy.

Humans are the only creatures who so consistently extend their grasp through this kind of intimate interaction. To manage a horse requires more than the skill needed to use an inanimate tool (though when working with computers, one sometimes wonders). The horse has a will of its own and must be understood. The rider may be smarter, but unless the horse is willing to cooperate, he will go nowhere. Mastering the horse therefore requires more than strength and skill; it needs understanding.

Ergi

The nature of the relationship between rider and ridden has led to its frequent use as a sexual metaphor. In the ideal sexual act, both participants experience a sense of augmented energy. As they move together, they can achieve an ecstasy possible to neither alone. One partner penetrates the other, but is that penetration an act of mastery or of surrender? Is the one who receives submitting, or a conqueror? The truth is that in their interaction, they are both.

This is the paradox, and this is why sexual metaphors in turn are so often used for the relationship between human and god.

An obscure term found in Norse literature, *ergi*, may illuminate this mystery. It appears to have two mutually contradictory meanings—it is used as a sexual insult and in reference to certain kinds of magic. For instance, the passage in which Snorri describes Odin's shamanic skills (learned, presumably from Freyja) ends with the memorable words:

> But the use of this magic is accompanied by so great a degree of effemination (ergi) that men were of the opinion that they could not give themselves up to it without shame, so that it was to the priestesses that it was taught. (trans. 1990, *Ynglingasaga*: 7)

As an insult, it is apparently an accusation that the male being insulted takes the female role in intercourse. I would suggest that the receptivity implied can also be spiritual.

Most religious traditions recognize a sexual element in spiritual ecstasy. Erotic metaphors permeate mystical poetry, and Tantrism has developed a sexual yoga as one means of union with the Divine. Psychic work can stimulate all of the energy centers of the body, including the sexual, and feelings of arousal are not uncommon in trance. However, I believe that the metaphor refers primarily to a more profound penetration of the human spirit by the Divine. As C. S. Lewis has said, "We are all feminine in relation to God."

The cross-dressing common in shamanic traditions may express this relationship as well as liminality. The priest of Alcis, "*ornatus mulieribus*," may have dressed as a woman as a part of his role as servant of the horse-taming twins. According to Saxo, the festival of Freyr (to whom horses were sacred) at Uppsala featured effeminate gestures, mimes performing on a stage, and the "unmanly clatter of bells" (1979, vi, p. 185). Clattering ornaments are a traditional part of shamanic costume, and so is cross-dressing.

The spiritual skill that above all identifies the shaman is the ability to go into trance and journey through the Otherworld at will. Although the shaman is an active participant in the process, trance work of any kind requires the ability to let go, to relinquish conscious control. This might well be enough to explain why individuals who are concerned with power and control would find it threatening. The paradox is that in the world of the spirits, power and control can only be attained by first relinquishing them.

Spirit Steeds

The medieval Church and those influenced by it justly feared anything that smacked of shamanism because in trance work one interacts with a variety of spiritual beings that have nothing to do with Christianity.

Shamanic experience is rich in imagery of riding. The drum is the "horse" of the shaman; there are horse heads on some shamanic staffs. But more important, the shaman journeys with the help of spirits that usually appear in animal form. The ally will guide or carry the trancer where he or she wishes to go, give advice and counsel, and assist in finding information for the shaman or others. The two become partners in their work in the inner worlds.

The other type of trance work for which the metaphor of horse and rider is often used is of course god-possession. Like many other aspects of religious behavior, the question of whether possession is a spiritual experience or a psychological pathology depends on the effects and the context. Although god-possession was not common in the Viking age, there are indications that in an earlier period the Germanic peoples, like most other cultures, included it in their religious practice.

For such an experience to be productive, it must be a willing partnership. Whether full trance or a simple inner awareness of the presence of the deity is involved, there is an interchange. For the human partner, experiencing a deity brings a heightened awareness, fullness of life, knowledge, energy, and ecstasy. But what do the gods gain from this companionship?

Mythology is full of stories in which the gods quarrel over offerings. These have been interpreted as the naive tales of people who know no better than to ascribe human greed to their deities. I would suggest that what the gods are getting out of the offerings we make to them, and the worship and meditations in which we invite them into our lives, is a different way of experiencing the physical world. Power and glory they may have, but they do not have flesh or a human mind. We are not their slaves, but their partners in a productive interaction, like the mating of lovers, or the union of horse and rider.

Riding the Spirit Road

If you began work with a totem or ally during your study of ELHAZ, the connection should be well-established by now. If you feel comfortable in this relationship, perhaps now is the time to make contact with one of the gods. Prepare by rereading Snorri's account of the Aesir and Vanir in the Poetic

Edda, or Ellis-Davidson's descriptions, but try to retain an open mind regarding which deity you will see.

Ready your place of working as usual and make sure you will not be disturbed. To help you journey you may drum for yourself or use one of the tapes of shamanic drumming made by the Foundation for Shamanic Studies. Or you may find that listening to Wagner or meditation music will help you get where you want to go.

The format of the meditations should be quite familiar to you by now. Use it to journey to the Worldtree, and summon your ally. This time, your request is to be guided to meet the god or goddess whom you need most right now (or who, perhaps, needs you). The journey may take you to Asgard or one of the other worlds; you may encounter your deity on the plain of Midgard; or in a landscape for which you have no name.

Do not be surprised at the form in which your deity may appear. You may see many figures—focus on the one who appears most often, or who insists on approaching you. Ask the being's name, and look or ask for distinguishing characteristics by which you may identify her/him. Find out what kind of worship/offerings the deity desires and what sort of help he or she is offering you.

When you return, look up the god you met and find out as much as possible about her or him. For many of the Norse deities we have little more than a name, but what you learn in vision should be consistent with what is known, or at least should not contradict it. The UPG ("unsupported personal gnosis"—that is, information that comes to us in our own visions) is *a* truth. It can deepen our relationship with the god/desses, but should not be treated as *the* truth. In subsequent meditations you can ask for more information. Set up an altar as directed, and insofar as practical, fulfill the requests of the god (you can point out that if the deity wants something expensive, he or she ought to provide the money).

Note that a deity who has not been worshipped for a long time may be unfamiliar with the conditions of modern life and begin with unreasonable requirements. Do not hesitate to explain and negotiate. You are not expected to beggar yourself, only to give such honor as you can. If you work with your deity regularly, communication will become more sophisticated.

This may seem a rather odd way to talk about divine beings; it is based on my own experience. We cannot know for certain what the gods are—only that they are alive and well and eager to communicate. My current theory is that although they originate in the divine wisdom that is beyond all personification, the personae under which we perceive them are formed by human cultures and limited by their perceptions. The more we work to bring the old gods into contemporary human consciousness, the more they will transcend it.

The Family of Man

Everybody wants to know where they came from, as a first step to understanding who and what they are, and thus all peoples develop some myth to account for the origins of humankind. In Norse literature there are two tales that tell the story. The first is the account of how the gods gave life to the first human pair, Ask and Embla. The second, the story of Ríg, deals with the origins of the classes of society.

The Gifts of the Gods

The story of Ask and Embla is told in the "Völuspá" as follows:

> Then from among   the holy people,
> Three Aesir, kind and mighty, fared homeward.
> They found on the shore,   having little might,
> Ask and Embla,   lacking orlög.
>
> Önd (breath) they had not   Odh (consciousness) they ha
>   not,
> Neither being nor movement;   nor good looks.
> Odin gave them önd,   Hoenir gave them odh,
> Life gave Lodhurr   and good looks.
>
> ("Völuspá": 17–18)

The three great gods are Odin and two companions, whom the scholars describe rather helplessly as "hypostases of Odin." Hoenir appears several times in the legends. He is one of the twelve who sit in the judgment seats of the gods. He was with Loki and Odin when they killed Andvari and took his hoard, and was one of the hostages sent to the Vanir. It is prophesied that after Ragnarók he will act as priest for the next generation of gods. Of Lódhur we know nothing else at all.

The names *Ask* and *Embla* are usually translated as "Ash" and "Elm." In other words, instead of being modeled from the dust of the ground, the Germanic progenitors (male and female simultaneously) were created from trees. Humanity not only originates from trees, but when the new world is formed after Ragnarók, it is among the leaves of the Tree of Life that Lif and Lifthrasir, progenitors of the new race of humans, will be found. From earth came their substance, but what makes them human—"fated"—are the gifts of the gods. What exactly are the gifts that effect this transformation?

The gifts of Lódhur are, in Old Norse, *lá*, *læti*, and *litr*. *Lá* is variously translated as "life" or "vital spark." *Læti* is "movement," or "manner," and *litr* is "health" or "looks"—the "being, bearing, and blooming hue" of

Hollander's translation. Lódhur gave, therefore, those things that identify the physical body and enable it to function efficiently. He is the protector of the *lich*, or *lyke*, the physical shape in which we walk the world.

The gift of Odin is *önd*, literally "breath," whose metaphoric meaning, as in so many other languages, is "spirit" or "soul." This concept is one of the most pervasive in religion. The winds are the breath of earth, and planetary life depends on our atmosphere. Inspiration is the drawing of the first breath that signals the beginning of a life; expiration is the rattle of breath at its end. Respiration enables the body to metabolize. Breathing is the act that animates the body, the dynamic, invisible, transforming power that signifies the transition between two states of being, the link between the physical and spiritual worlds. It is perhaps to be expected that this should be the gift of the god who walks between the worlds.

Hoenir's gift is *ódhr*, translated variously as "sense," "mind," "wit," and the faculty of speech. There is an adjective with the same spelling meaning "frantic," "vehement," "furious," or "eager." But this concept is more complex than that would imply. Dr. Martin Schwartz (1992, April) of the University of California has traced the etymology of *ódhr* and its older cognate, *wodh*, back to their Indo-European roots and demonstrated their relationship to concepts having to do with intellect.

However, no single modern English word can encompass all its implications. In the older languages, mental activity is not the coldly logical process developed by Western civilization. Rather, the words associated with it have implications of excitement and motion, the initiation of action, like the dance of electrons. One imagines Einstein's feelings as the theory of relativity unfolded in his consciousness, or Odin's experience as he took up the runes. In Old Germanic theology, thinking is an act of ecstasy.

What does this tell us about the nature of humanity? A human being participates in the three states of being. As physical beings we are solid matter; by breathing we are constantly transforming matter, participants in the catalytic process that animates the planet; and we are spiritual beings who can share the creative ecstasy of the gods.

The Kin of Ríg

The origins of human society are the subject of the "Rígsthula," the story of Ríg. In early king lists, Odin and Freyr are the most popular progenitors; however, the beginning of "Völuspá" refers to "Heimdall's children," and it is thought that this may have inspired the poet of "Rígsthula" to identify Ríg, whose name is cognate to the old Celtic *rix*, the Latin *rex*, and the Germanic *reiks* or *rik* with Heimdall. However, some authors continue to identify him as Odin, and indeed his actions do fit the Wanderer's personality.

The poem presents certain problems for the citizen of a democracy, since it seems to propose a divine origin for an ethnically based, stratified society. As Ríg goes walking through the world, he visits three couples: Great-Grandfather and Great-Grandmother, Grandfather and Grandmother, and Father and Mother. Each couple is engaged in actions characteristic of their classes, or perhaps of stages of human development; servants, free farmers, or nobility respectively. Ríg sleeps between man and wife, and nine months after each visit, the woman bears a son. The sons are Thrall, who marries Drudge; Carl, who marries Daughter-in-Law; and Earl, who marries Erna, the Efficient. All have children whose names indicate their roles.

The activities of Ríg's children and grandchildren imply that they are content with their lot and desire no other. However, a look at Germanic history shows that there were, in fact, opportunities for social mobility. Even in Iceland, where great store was placed on bloodlines and family connections, freed thralls could work their way up in the world. In the poem, it is the youngest of the last group of sons, Kon ("Noble Descendant"), who learns runecraft and rivals Ríg himself, gaining the name and wisdom of a king. It must also be noted that although inequalities did exist, the three "classes" lived in an integrated society. The differences in status were much greater than the differences in lifestyle. The "Rígsthula" is about class, but it is also about community.

"Rígsthula" requires us to examine our assumptions regarding the relationship between heredity, environment, and free will in determining the role we will play in the human family.

Who Are You?

Studying MANNAZ provides a good opportunity to consider what it means to be human. It is a rune of self-knowledge and acceptance. Identify all the things that make you a unique individual. List, as well, the things with which you are less satisfied. If you are working with a partner or group, share lists, and accept them for each other. If you are working alone, seek Heimdall in meditation, tell him what they are, and ask him to transform them. Give to your partner a list with the following questions, or record them onto a tape, allowing time for you to answer:

Who are you?
What is your name?
What do you look like?

What do you like about your appearance?
What don't you like about your appearance?
Are you your body?
What are you really good at?
What are you bad at?
Are you an introvert or an extrovert?
What does your spirit look like?
What is your totem or fetch?
If you were an animal, what would you be?
What is the earliest thing you remember?
What is the best thing you remember?
What is the worst thing you remember?
What do you dream?
Are you ruled by your body, your mind, or your emotions?
In what state of consciousness do you spend most of your time?
What is the best idea you ever had?
What really turns you on?
What is your name?
Who are you?

The Group Ritual

If working with a group, the EHWAZ/MANNAZ ritual is on page 361. It builds on the creation story and the story of Ríg to provide a context for communicating and connecting with your deep self, with your community, and with the gods.

Chapter 12

LAGUZ and INGWAZ

IN LAGUZ AND INGWAZ WE HAVE THE PAIRING of a god rune whose powers are manifested in the social (as well as the natural) realm with a nature
rune that has strong associations with the goddess. LAGUZ is a rune of the
waters, and although the sea in Northern mythology is the home of both
masculine and feminine powers, continental waters in both Celtic and
Germanic myth tend to be feminine. Like the goddess Nerthus, whose home
is surrounded by water, the origins of the god Yngvi/INGWAZ are in the Low
Countries along the North Sea. Both are associated with the cycle of birth

and death; both are keys to the mystery behind the fertility of the land and the people who depend on it.

THE TWENTY-FIRST RUNE: ᛚ LAGUZ

Pronunciation: "LAH-gooz"
Meaning: Lake, Leek

From LAGUZ' Lake life ever-flowing
Wells from Mother-depths of darkness.

Ancient Meanings

The LAGUZ rune represents the "L" sound, its form most probably derived from a reversal of the equivalent letter in the Greek and Roman alphabets. Its meaning is essentially water—a lake or a river, given as *Logr* in Old Norse, and *Lagu* in Old English. As a pun or by association, the old Germanic *Laguz* leads us to *Laukaz*, the leek, as well.

In the Anglo-Saxon rune poem, LAGU is the wild ocean over which the Angles and Saxons ventured to reach Britain. These are the verses of a landsman, terrified by the ungovernable waves of the sea.

> ᛚ *[Lagu] byþ leodum langsum geþuht,*
> (The sea seems interminable to people)
> *gif hi sculun neþan on nacan tealtum*
> (if they shall venture on rolling ship)
> *and hi saeyþa swyþe bregaþ*
> (and the waves of the sea terrify them, and)
> *and se brimhengest bridles ne gymeð*
> (the sea-stallion heeds not its bridle.)

Similar sentiments are expressed in Anglo-Saxon poetry, as when in the "Wanderer" the protagonist defines his exile as being forced to fare over winter's icy waves, and sees, instead of his lord's hall, "the yellow waves, the seabirds bathing, stretching out their wings, while snow and hail and frost fall all together" (Hamer 1970, ll.46–48). "Care is renewed for him who must continually send his weary spirit over the icy waves" (ll.55–57). In the "Seafarer," the lonely hardships of seafaring are described with even greater vigor and detail, nonetheless, "the heart's desires incite now me that I should go on towering seas, among the salt-waves play . . . to see the lands of strangers far away" (ll.33–38). For some, the waters were not only a place of wretchedness, but a road to adventure.

Certainly this was true for the Vikings, for whom the sea was the hunting ground not only of the fisherman, but of the warrior. Perhaps for this reason, the Icelandic poem takes things more calmly. Here, the streams and geysers are commonplace, and the sea is represented by a kenning.

> ᛚ *[Lœgr] er vellanda vatn*
> (Water is welling stream)
> *ok viðr ketill*
> (and broad kettle [or geyser])
> *ok glommunga grund.*
> (and land of the fish.)

The Norwegian verses begin with nature, but finish with an ambiguous reference to golden treasure.

> ᛚ *[Lœgr] er,*
> (Water is where)
> *er fœlr ór fjalle foss,*
> (a cascade falls from a mountain-side)
> *en gull ero nosser.*
> (but ornaments are made of gold.)

One cannot help thinking of the votive hoards that were cast by both Celts and Germans into sacred pools. Treasures continued to be associated with water in legend. One of the most notable was the hoard of Andvari, who took the form of a pike to guard the gold hidden beneath his waterfall. This treasure included a magic ring that eventually came into the hands of the Nibelungs (the Burgundians), and the curse he had laid upon it doomed them. In the end the hero Hagen returned the treasure to the waters by throwing it into the Rhine. Various versions of the story appear in the *Volsungasaga*, the *Nibelungenlied*, and of course Wagner's *Ring* cycle.

If one extends the meaning of the rune to include the leek, another series of meanings are added. Sigdrifa's advice to Sigurd includes the instructions:

> Thou shalt bless the draught
> And danger escape
> And cast a leek in the cup;
> For so I know
> Thou shalt never see
> Thy mead with evil mixed.

("Sigdrifumál": 9)

Grimm collected a number of expressions featuring leeks in *Teutonic Mythology*. In Old Norse, boiling wound leeks means forging swords; the leek is said to be used in divination, and to drive evil spirits away. A leek hung up in the house wards off misfortune (Grimm 1966, IV: p. 1682). The hero Helgi Hundingsbane is given a leek by his father when he is born, presumably to confer strength and bravery.

There is some evidence that leeks played a part in the cult of the Vanir. In the *Flateyjarbók* (see the reference in the discussion of EHWAZ), the stallion's phallus is preserved by being surrounded by leeks and wrapped up in linen. This may be because the leek is a strong-smelling plant with long, pliant leaves. However, a bone-handled scraper found in the mid-fourth-century grave of a woman in southwest Norway bore the inscription "linalaukr," or "linen and leek," the final sounds being represented by a bindrune and followed by a reversed FEHU, as follows:

ᛚᛁᚾᚨᛚᚨᚢᚲ ᚥ (Antonsen 1975).

It seems reasonable to speculate that the knife had ritual uses and the woman who owned it was a priestess. Freyja in some of her aspects is associated with the production of linen, and leeks, as indicated above, could preserve magically as well as physically. "Linalaukr" could well have been part of a magical invocation.

Modern Meanings

For Thorsson, LAGUZ represents the basic energy and secret source of organic life: primal potential, initiation into life, and passage across the waters through death. It is the unknown, a manifestation in Midgard from other realms. Osborn and Longland, working from the Old English, state that Water is a powerful, unpredictable, and dangerous element that cannot be governed by human agencies, a ship out of control.

Gundarsson's interpretation is more naturalistic. For him, the rune signifies primal water, the rivers of yeast and venom that flow from Hvergelmir, and the water that flows from the sacred wells. There is some ambivalence toward an element that brings prosperity or destruction. Life-giving running water is contrasted with stagnant, poisonous water. LAGUZ is the rune by which life is brought forth into the light. As the leek, it is a protection against danger, especially that which comes in drink. It is a rune of transition between life and death.

Aswynn describes LAGUZ as a feminine rune, associated with Nerthus and/or Njordr. She suggests that Nerthus is the mother of Tuisto and ancestress of Mannaz and Ingvio. Aswynn also feels that the use of "lauka" in spells may be a metaphor for sorcery, and the leek, the herb that is boiled in the seidh cauldron. Thus, water in this connection may mean astral substance. It is a transmitting agency that can be used to influence others, especially in dream states. Willis has a similar interpretation, seeing LAGUZ as a woman, feminine energy, the moon cycle, or amniotic fluid. Peterson, on the other hand, sees the leek as a phallic symbol, and LAGUZ as the male principle.

LAGUZ can be interpreted as a rune of the goddess Nerthus, whose temple was on an island in the ocean, and one of whose symbols may have been a ship (leading to her identification with Isis of the ships by Roman writers). A Mother Goddess called Nehallenia had a shrine on an island off the Dutch coast, and she seems to have been invoked for safe passage across the ocean. Teutonic religion features a consistent association of ideas linking ships, water, fertility, and the life cycle. It is important to remember that in early Northern Europe, territorial goddesses were associated with watersheds and had their shrines at the headwaters of rivers or in sacred springs.

The waters, underground and on the surface, can be interpreted as the blood of the goddess of the planet, as the earth is Her body. According to some theories, water systems may be the carriers of ley-line energy. The goose or duck was both a traditional shamanic steed and a Celtic symbol of the territorial watershed goddess. Perhaps because northern peoples were familiar with water as both a liquid and a solid, the distinction between earth and water was less important. "Moist Mother Earth" a pagan Russian epithet for the earth-goddess, is an example of how these ideas might be connected.

Contemporary interpretations of this rune seem to focus on a variety of concepts associated with water and the feminine. Even the Anglo-Saxon warning of danger is simply a description of what can happen if one tries to constrain powerful natural forces. The meanings proposed recall the archetypes associated with the sephiroth of Binah and Yesod in Kabbalah. The definition given by Willis in particular depends heavily on Yesod associations, with its emphasis on the moon and the astral. Thorsson's interpretation relates more to the Binah energies, the sea of space or the primordial soup from which all manifestation is born. It should be pointed out, however, that in Norse myth, the moon is masculine, and Aegir, whose great cauldrons brew ale for the gods, is the elemental deity of the deep sea, as his wife Ran is its destructive power. Life is cradled in the waters of the womb, but a fountain of fluid carries the sperm to its destination. The shape of LAGUZ is somewhat phallic, and the rune can be interpreted as the upwelling seminal power of the male as well as the receptive and conceptual energy of the female.

Interpreting and Using LAGUZ

In divination, LAGUZ may indicate a woman or a feminine influence, new life or creativity welling up from the depths of the unconscious, or a need to become more flexible or to learn to understand and move with the currents of life, possibly transitions. Willis says it governs the powers of conception and birth. Matters pertaining to the psychic or the unconscious, contact with the spiritual (astral) realm, the realm of the imagination. It can indicate a need to go with the flow, or promise that sympathetic help is coming.

According to Peterson, the leek is a healing herb, a balm, psychic or physical protection, a neutralizer of poisons, an aid to intuition. The rune can be inscribed on tools used for these purposes. Gundarsson says LAGUZ can be used to set other runes to work in secret.

LAGUZ is one of the most useful of the runes in spellcraft. It has a powerful effect on the female reproductive cycle, especially menstruation. Drawing it emerging from an upended PERTHRO on the womb can help to relieve menstrual cramps and get the flow started, or stimulate contractions in childbirth. It is probably one of the "help runes" drawn on the palms of midwives. For the same reason, pregnant women should use care in dealing with this rune. Combining it with FEHU and applying it to both partners should aid in conception.

Intone LAGUZ and draw the rune on the brow to dissolve writer's block or dispel a sense of constraint and sterility. Combine it with URUZ to increase its power. The rune can also be used with URUZ and THURISAZ in rain magic. Be careful to specify how much water is desired.

Include the leek with other protective herbs in wreaths or dried nosegays hung in the house. The herb is also used in Vanir rites and Norse women's mysteries. It is not recommended as an addition to mead, but a stalk can be used as a blót teine to sprinkle the folk in blessing or to stir mead while being brewed, or any other magical potion. Cream of leek soup is a fine dish for Norse celebrations.

THE TWENTY-SECOND RUNE: ◇ ᛜ INGWAZ

Pronunciation: "ING-wahz"
Meaning: Ing, Yngvi

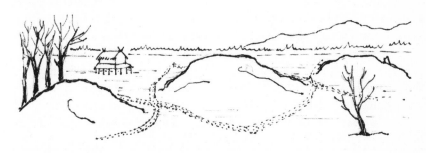

**INGWAZ wanders the world in his wagon,
And dying, leaves life in the land.**

Ancient Meanings

The "Ng" rune is found only in the Old Germanic and Anglo-Saxon futharks. Like TIWAZ, it has a god name. In this case, the Anglo-Saxon rune poem is one of the main sources of information on the deity. The poem tells us that

> ᛜ *[Ing] wæs ærest mid East-Denum*
> (Ing was first among the East-Danes)
> *gesewen secgun, oþ he siðan est*
> (seen by men, till he to the east)
> *ofer wæg gewat; wæn æfter ran;*
> (over waves went, his wain after ran,)
> *ðus Heardingas ðone hæle nemdun.*
> (thus the Heardings named the hero.)

According to some historians, the Heardings may be identified with the Asdings, the royal dynasty of the Vandals. The part of the tribe who migrated southward carried the name throughout Europe, while the Wendels retained it in Sweden, where the royal dynasty were known as Ynglings, whose history is given by Snorri Sturluson in the *Ynglingasaga*. However, the god's origins seem to lie on the Continent, on the North German coastal plain where he may be identified with the Inguio, son of Mannus, son of Tuisto, from whom were descended the Ingævones. Yngvi or Inguio figures in the king lists as an ancestor of many of the royal families of the Old English kingdoms as well as Sweden, and by the time of the *Volsungasaga*, "Yngling" was used as an honorific.

Any Germanic king worth singing about could trace his ancestry back to some god or other, so we may assume that the Ing worshipped by the East-Danes was divine. His nature can be deduced by the reference to the wagon in the poem, and even more by the customs of the Swedish royal house as reported in *Ynglingasaga*. The cart in particular marks Yngvi as one of the Vanir, for the practice of carrying an image of the deity about in a wagon is reported by Tacitus on the Continent with the earth goddess Nerthus, and later in Sweden (in the "Tale of Ogmund Bash," included in John McKinnell's translation of *Vigaglums saga*), when the passenger is Freyr.

Ing, like Scyld and Frodhi, may have been a local name of the god of herd and harvest who eventually subsumed all of his aspects under the title "Freyr," meaning "Lord." The reference to a journey over the sea links Ing in particular with Scyld, who is given as the ancestor of Danes in *Beowulf*. According to the story, the child Scyld the Scefing (Shield son of Sheaf) was brought over the sea in a ship filled with treasure, reigned long and prosperously, and when he died, was given a ship burial and sent back over the sea as he had come.

Various Old English accounts give other versions of the same story, in which the child arrives with a sheaf of wheat. William of Malmesbury reports how a group of monks proved their right to a piece of property by floating down the river a shield on which were set a sheaf of wheat and a candle. As Ellis-Davidson points out, "a series of traditions has gone into medieval times bringing together a divine child, a sheaf of corn, and a vessel moving by supernatural power." (1964, p. 105).

Modern Meanings

Thorsson tells us that Ing is the seed energy needed for gestation to result in plenty. It signifies the cycle of withdrawal, transformation, and return; something working in the unconscious, a storehouse of potential energy that must undergo a gestation period in order to gain strength. Ing was the Old Germanic fertility god, the consort of the earth mother, who gives up his power to her to be released in the spring.

Gundarsson elaborates on this interpretation, calling Ing the male counterpart to Berkano, the sacrificed consort whose seed brings fertility to man and nature. Ing unites man with earth and the nature-wisdom of the Vanir. Its shape (the Old Germanic form) may represent the seed or the castrated male, who gives up his male identity (at least for a time) to cross gender lines in search of shamanic wisdom. It is a rune by which power is stored, and it converts active to potential power. To Willis, the form of the rune suggests the scrotum, the seed bag.

According to Aswynn, Yngvi as a title of Freyr, meaning "son of," and "Land of Yng" may be the spiritual meaning of the name "England." She feels that the Anglo-Saxon form ᚼ is a female fertility symbol, whereas the Old Germanic alternative, ◇, is the male form. If the Anglo-Saxon form is duplicated end to end, it looks like a DNA chain. Yng may be a rune of genetic inheritance and reincarnation, by which the *hamingja*, life force, was passed to a chosen heir.

Osborn and Longland derive from the Old English poem an interpretation of Ing as the god in the wagon whose passage calms the waves, or releases the creative powers of the psyche. It is the power to fecundate the imagination and transform the universe. Ing may also represent a beacon or firebrand (kept in the inglenook of the fireplace), or the constellation Bootes (Ursa Major is the god's wagon).

Although INGWAZ is clearly associated with a god, he is a deity about whom we have no myths, only a few references to folk practice. On the other hand, the information we do have makes it apparent that Ing is the deity in his aspect of grain god, the seed that is planted, flourishes, and is cut down so that it may go into the earth and be reborn. The harvest may be made into bread or beer and be renewed in the bodies of humankind. Another version of the same myth is found in the songs about John Barleycorn. Frodi the fruitful, a legendary Danish king whose name was also applied to the god, received offerings at his grave mound. In times of famine, the Yngling kings of Sweden were expected to lay down their lives in sacrifice to restore fertility to the land.

Symbols associated with the cult of the fertility god (and goddess) include both the ship and the wagon, since in the North food came from both the land and the sea. In an agricultural cycle, birth and death are part of a necessary sequence. The ship carries the spirit of the god through the waters of the underworld/womb so that he may be born again. The cult of the grain god is closely associated with that of the ancestors. The belief seems to have been that the dead continued to live within the mound.

Even when cremation was practiced, grave goods, sometimes including wagons, were buried with the ashes. Burial in a ship, or surrounded by the outline of a boat in stones, provided the deceased with transport across the dark sea. Offerings continued to be made at the mounds of particularly notable men, who acquired the status of "elves," or demigods. In this context, the fact that the god Freyr lives in "Alfheim" acquires new significance.

INGWAZ is a rune of birth and death, of fertility that is part of the natural cycle. Its two forms can support a number of interpretations. The closed, diamond shape of the Old Germanic rune can be seen as the male or female seed, the scrotum or the ovaries. The interlaced Anglo-Saxon form inevitably recalls the position in which Hindu gods and goddesses are so often portrayed, completing and balancing their powers through sexual union. A Hindu symbol much like the rune represents the union of Shiva and Shakti (the male and female principles). Ing may be a god, but to function, he must interact with a goddess. He is the child who is born from the womb of the sea; he is the lover whose embrace makes Mother Earth grow fruitful; and he is the sacrifice who goes back into the sea or the mound to renew the land.

Interpreting and Using INGWAZ

INGWAZ represents creative power, especially in its masculine form, transition to a new stage in a cycle, an ending that leads to a new beginning, transformation, possibly sacrifice for a positive purpose, and fertility. As such, it is closely related to FEHU and JERA and is one of the runes that can be used in gardening. In addition, it is a rune of power for brewing, especially of beer.

Willis says INGWAZ indicates completion, a transition, or a new beginning, a successful conclusion to a project, or relief from anxiety about it. Peterson feels it indicates peace and bounty in the external world, sensuality, serenity, and love. Aswynn states that the seed form can be used as a magic circle or to contain other runic energies. INGWAZ can be seen as a progression of the JERA and KENAZ energies.

Obviously INGWAZ is a rune of sexuality, particularly useful for enhancing male energy so long as the individuals concerned understand that its power requires giving as well as getting, or begetting. For the rune to function properly, partners or forces must interact in equality. In meditation, it can be a key to understanding the spiritual significance of the life cycle, to understanding and dealing with death as part of life.

LAGUZ AND INGWAZ: STUDY AND EXPERIENCE

Waterworld

The relationship between earth and water in early Europe is hard to understand for folk raised in an environment in which roofs do not leak, streams run through cement culverts, and mighty rivers are dammed. Only occasionally does a great storm release the waters and remind people what the word "floodplain" means. For our Northern European ancestors, the situation was considerably different.

According to some scholars, the runes evolved along the North Sea, a region of marsh and meadow where at times the land seems about to dissolve into the sea. In Iceland and Sweden the lakes are many, and in Norway, where the country is mountainous, fjords cut deeply into the land. It is easy to understand, given such an environment, why folk should have been constantly aware of the relationship between land and water. Like our own bodies, the earth is permeated and nourished by life-giving fluid. It is not surprising that early European peoples defined regions as watersheds and made offerings at the sources of rivers. Votive treasure was cast into lakes. Along the seacoast, low lying offshore islands were set aside as goddess shrines.

The role of water as source of life is easy to understand. Water never dies—even when it disappears, it is only changing its state from liquid to vapor. It is drawn up to the clouds whence it will fall once more as life-giving rain. Sea and stream are alive with fish, and still water, even stagnant, seethes with a yeasty soup of living things. Unborn mammals are cradled in the waters of the womb. Living things must drink more often than they require food. Water therefore has powerful magic in all things having to do with fertility, health, and renewal.

Studying LAGUZ provides a good opportunity to examine your relationship with this element. If it rains, go for a walk—without an umbrella. Spend some time near a lake or pond, or by the sea. Visit an aquarium, investigate the watershed from which your water comes. Drink at least one glass of water each day, and as you do so, sign it with the ᛚ rune and spend a few moments thinking about its source.

This is also an excellent time to explore the craft of brewing and to make herbal teas and infusions. Chant appropriate runes over the pot as it bubbles—sing the spells into the brew.

The Waters of LAGUZ are a source of healing and transformation, one key to women's mysteries. Tacitus tells us that the shrine of the fertility goddess was on an island. Once she had made her circuit through the land, her image was ceremonially bathed before being returned to its home. This reminds one of the cult of the Greek Hera, whose statue was taken once a year to the sea or a sacred spring to be bathed in order to renew her youth and virginity. Likewise, the Navajo Changing Woman goes into the sunset (and, presumably, the Western Ocean) to be transformed from old woman to young girl.

Healing Baths

In LAGUZ, the static force of ISA has been set in motion by the transformative power of HAGALAZ. Now the waters flow freely and can be used to perform a rite of renewal. The format is similar to the strengthening bath you took when you were working with URUZ, but the focus is different.

If you have access to a hot tub, by all means use it; however, this work can be performed equally well in a bathtub. Since you are using your bathroom as a temple of the waters, your first task will be to clean it thoroughly. When you have done so, create an altar where you will be able to see it while lying in the bathtub. You will need a blue or green candle or votive glass and a holder for incense (something aromatic, rather than sweet, such as pine). You may also want to add appropriate pictures, such as a photocopy of the plate on the Gundestrop cauldron that shows the warrior being put into the cauldron of renewal; or pictures of lakes or the sea; of sea-goddesses or mer-folk, or the like. A tape recorder and an environmental tape of water sounds at least a half hour long would also be useful.

At night, when you can be sure you will not be disturbed, begin your ritual. First you may want to claim the room as sacred space by carrying the lit candle around it, or turning clockwise with outstretched hands intoning "Laaa-guz . . . ." As hot water runs into the tub, consecrate it by inscribing the rune ᛚ over the water. Charge the water with crystalline bath salts or a pinch of sea salt. If your salts are not scented, pour a little of some pungent oil, such as oil of rosemary, into the bathwater.

Now light the candle and incense and turn out the lights. Turn on the recorded water music. Before getting into the tub, take a moment to affirm your purpose in this ritual with words such as:

> **Lake of life where I shall lie,**
> **Waters of the womb awaken.**
> **All ill dissolve, all evil banish.**
> **Let LAGUZ every limb renew.**

Then draw the rune up from your belly across your chest.

Lie down in the tub and, limb by limb, relax your body. Regularize your breathing. As you listen to the tape, allow images to form in your imagination. See yourself suspended in a lake, or a cauldron, or even the depths of the ocean. As the warm water relaxes you, visualize all stress and strain and pain dissolving out of your body. If your troubles are of the heart or spirit, let them wash away as well. Let even the flesh itself dissolve away. And then, held in the life-giving embrace of the waters, feel your body forming once more around your bones. Allow those images that will speak to your deepest concerns to come to you. The ending of the tape and/or the cooling of the water will be your signal to return to ordinary consciousness.

When you emerge, like the tree trunks Ask and Embla cast up on the shore, reclaim your protections by invoking awareness from Hoenir, breath from Odin, and movement, health, and appearance from Lodhur. Drain out the water, declaring that with it goes all the stress you dissolved away. Dry off with a clean towel. Affirm yourself renewed and restored.

This procedure can be repeated as needed, for instance when recovering from an illness, at the end of the menstrual period, or after a particularly stressful week. LAGUZ can also be combined with other runes for specific purposes—for instance with ELHAZ, focusing on the images of the elk, the sedge grass and the swan in their dark pool, for magical protection; with URUZ for health and strength; or with FEHU and INGWAZ for fertility.

God of Peace and Plenty

Inguio, or Yngvi, according to the mythic genealogy of the Germanic peoples as recorded by Tacitus, was one of the sons of Mannus, son of Tuisto, whom we encountered during the discussion of MANNAZ. Ing appears as an ancestor or name element in the royal lines of Sweden and the Anglian kings of Bernicia.

Snorri traces the Swedish royal line from Njordh and his son Freyr, and says that "Frey was known by a second name Yngvi; that name was used long after in his race as a name of great worth, and his kinsmen were afterwards called Ynglings" (*Ynglingasaga*: 10). He further recounts how after Yngvi-Frey's death he was said to be still alive in his mound, and offerings were made to him there. When men realized that the good seasons continued even though Frey was dead, they left him in the mound rather than cremating him, "called him god of the earth, and ever after sacrificed to him, most of all for good seasons and peace."

Snorri also mentions the Danish king Peace-Frode, a name that is attached to three kings in Saxo's *Gesta Danorum*. The last of these, a great bringer of peace and giver of laws, is the subject of Book V of his history. Interestingly enough, Frodhi's death, like that of Yngvi, is concealed from the people. Before being placed in his mound, his body is carried about in a cart, blessing the countryside. Since one of Freyr's titles is *inn fródhi*, "the fruitful," it seems likely that the two figures are functionally the same. Drawing on the rune poem, Ellis-Davidson (1964) speculates that the worship of the god of peace and plenty was carried by the Vandals from South Sweden to Denmark and the Low Countries.

As indicated in the discussion of the rune itself, Yngvi is a figure associated with the fertility of the land. Furthermore, this peace and fertility are not destroyed by death of the body—indeed, death may be an essential part of the cycle. This should surprise no one who has observed the cycles of nature, in which death and burial—of the decaying body or of the seed—is a prerequisite for the fertility of the coming season.

In *The Road to Hel* (1943), Ellis-Davidson shows that the Germanic peoples practiced both burial and cremation at various times and places. Cremation seems to have released the spirit to join Odin or one of the other gods in Asgard. Dying "into the hill" and being buried in a mound ensured a continuation of life in the Underworld in which the power of the deceased could still bless his or her descendants. The latter practice is clearly associated with the cult of Yngvi, the Divine Ancestor.

The cult of Yngvi seems to be the Northern version of the worship of the vegetation god that was preserved in folk practice through the Middle Ages in the mummer's plays and songs about figures like John Barleycorn, who is not cut down in his prime, but when he is a bearded old man. Yngvi offers a role model for a life lived well and productively, and a death that is only a transformation.

Yngvi is a role model for a male life cycle that is not focused on (though it may at times include) war. Many an Yngling king wore a boar-crested helm into battle, but his courage and ferocity were generally directed not toward conquest, but to defense and protection. To be productive, a land requires peace so that men can till the soil and good seasons. Temporal power can keep war from ravaging the fields. But it requires spiritual power to gain the favor of the elements so that rain and sun will bless them. The real test of a king was not whether he won battles, but whether he made the crops grow. It is this power that the male focuses and transmits, and that the female awakens so that she can receive it once more.

Meditating on INGWAZ can have powerful effects for both men and women. For men, it can be a key to men's mysteries, through participation in a mythic cycle that begins with the emergence of Sceaf from the sea, continues through a radiant youth to union with the queen/goddess in the Divine Marriage, begetting offspring and defending them, governing well, and finally death and transformation into an ancestor. Obviously not every man will literally or physically do all of these things, but they are all powerful as metaphors. For a woman, meditating on this cycle can lead to a new understanding of her relationship to the masculine.

Invoking the Ancestors

If ancient practice is to be believed, we can live so as to bless those who follow us, whether or not they are our physical descendants. While we still walk this earth, we can invoke our own spiritual and physical ancestors to bless us with their wisdom and power. Ancestor worship is found in many parts of the world, especially among agricultural peoples. It is a continuing tradition in China and Africa. In Catholic countries, the "Day of the Dead," in which families picnic at their relatives' gravesites, fulfills the same function.

For us, "ancestors" can include not only those of our physical forebears who are not likely to turn in their graves at the thought of being honored in a heathen ceremony, but those whom we consider our spiritual ancestors. For instance, I always invoke Sigrid the Proud, who would have been quite happy to let King Olaf, who was courting her, keep his Christianity if he had also allowed her to worship the old gods and said so in a classic statement of religious tolerance.

Among the Germanic peoples, the traditional time to honor the ancestors was at the Fall Feast, celebrated around the time of the first full moon after the fall equinox. This seems to have been the Germanic equivalent of the Celtic Samhain, which also both honored the dead and began the new year. In some areas both Alfar and Disir were worshipped at this time; in others, the Disir had their own feast in February. The celebration can be set up as a full feast, with food as well as drink, or observed simply by passing the memory ale. Suggestions for both are included in the discussion of GEBO and WUNJO.

In addition to toasting the ancestors, you can honor them by setting up an ancestor altar with pictures and candles on a low table, or if you can keep it safe from animals and small children, under a table or in a box on the floor. One arrangement is to have a multilevel altar in which the images of the gods are on top of the table and the ancestors below. If you have a yard, another option would be to carve the names of your "ancestors" on a piece of wood and pile over it a mound of earth or a heap of stones.

Whatever your arrangements, when you celebrate a *blót* to the ancestors, and whenever you feel the need of strength and guidance, light candles, and lay flowers and food offerings on the altar/mound. Call on the ancestors by name, praise their virtues, and ask them for what you need for the coming year. Take a few moments to experience your connection with the earth and with the cycle of death and renewal.

The Group Ritual

If working with a group, the group ritual, which starts on page 371, honors Yngvi/Frodhi/Sceaf as the harvest-god who comes out of and returns to the sea, and Nerthus, or Erda, as the goddess of the earth and the waters..

Chapter 13

DAGAZ and OTHALA

WITH DAGAZ AND OTHALA WE COME TO THE END of Tyr's aett, and the end of the futhark itself. If you are working with a group, this is also the meeting at which you complete the journey begun over a year ago. This way may at times have seemed long and weary. Indeed, we have covered a vast territory—for the nine worlds are encompassed by the symbols of the runes. And yet, at the end of the journey, we find the runes that signify the dawning of a new day over the place that we now know to be the country of the heart, and the comrades who in spirit are our kin.

THE TWENTY-THIRD RUNE: ᛗ DAGAZ

Pronunciation: "DAH-gahz"
Meaning: Day

Dagaz is a bright day's dawning,
Life and growth and light for all.

Ancient Meanings

The word for "day" is essentially the same in all the Germanic languages, being "daeg" in Old English, "dag" in Swedish and Danish, "dagr" in Old Norse, and "Tag" in German. Even the Latin word, "dies" is related. However, for a long time there were a number of options regarding how the several related dental sounds should be spelled. In Old Germanic and Anglo-Saxon runes, the hard "d" sound (as in **d**ay) and the soft (as in **th**e) were both spelled with d; the hard "t" (as in **T**yr) by t; and the soft (as in **th**orn) by þ. According to Richard Cleasby and Gulbrand Vigfusson, the Old Germanic rune appears to be formed by placing two Latin Ds back to back, necessary because the single D had evolved into þ. The inventors of the Younger Futhark used t for both *d* and *t*. When Old English and Old Norse are written in Latin letters, þ/Þ and ð/Ð, are used (sometimes dh appears as an attempt to transliterate the latter).

Fortunately, the meaning of the rune is more straightforward than its form. The Anglo-Saxon rune poem presents a rosy picture of the effect of daylight.

> ᛗ *[Dæg] byþ drihtnes sond, deore mannum,*
> (Day is God's sending, dear to men)
> *maere metodes leoht, myrgþ and tohih*
> (the great lord's light means mirth and happiness)
> *eadgum and earmum, eallum-brice.*
> (to rich and poor, useful to all.)

In Old English poetry, the light of day, youth, and warmth are regularly contrasted with cold, age, and darkness, understandable in the North, where the psychological impact of the dwindling days of winter can be severe. In Old Norse, Day is personified as the son of Night (a giantess) by a mysterious figure called Delling ("shining-one"), who is said to be of the family of the gods. This arrangement may perhaps reflect the fact that the Norse time unit, the *solarhringar*, begins with night (just as the Jewish day begins at sunset and the European holidays of Halloween and Christmas still begin on the eve) and is divided into two parts: sunset/sunrise and sunrise/sunset. The night thus gives birth to the day. Then, says Snorri:

> All-father took Night and her son, Day, and gave them two horses and two chariots and put them up in the sky, so that they should ride round the world every twenty-four hours. . . . Day's horse is called Skinfaxi, and the whole earth is illuminated by his mane (1987, "Gylfaginning": 10).

In "Vafþrúðnismál" we get a more poetic version.

> Tell me, Gagnrath ["Gain-Counsellor"]   since you wish
>   from the floor
> To test your might,
> What is that horse called   that above us draws
> The day over humankind?
>
> Skinfaxi ["shining mane"] he's called   who draws the dawn
> Each day over humankind.
> Best of horses   seems he to the Götlanders,
> Brilliant that mane shines.
>
> > ("Vafþrúðnismál": 11–12)

Day and Night were often honored together. When Sigdrifa (another name for Brunhild) is awakened by Sigurd from her enchanted sleep, her first act is to salute the day in the prayer that according to Hollander begins as "Hail to thee, Day, hail Day's sons; hail Night and daughter of Night;" ("Sigdrifumál": 2–3) which appears in many of our rituals in this book.

Day is also seen as a unit of time, divided by "day-marks" determined by the position of the sun in relation to local landmarks. In "Hávamál" (80) it is included among the things that can only be trusted when ended—"at evening praise the day . . . ." In other expressions, its significance seems to be an extension of that accorded the sun.

In some futharks, DAGAZ appears as the final rune. The symbolism of ending with an awakening is very attractive; however, it is equally effective to let the rising sun show us that we have come home.

Modern Meanings

Osborn and Longland, following the Anglo-Saxon tradition, see DAGAZ as
the light of strength and comfort that comes from the Creator, the sun.
Thorsson states that DAGAZ is the rune of daylight, especially at dawn or
twilight, and of awakening. It expresses those moments when the light is
especially noticeable because it is just coming into being, or is about to disappear. It is the "mystical moment" of paradox and liminality, in which right-
and left-brain thinking mesh to form a third state that encompasses both and
brings inspiration—bipolar creativity. DAGAZ is the light of consciousness
given by the gods to mankind. Its appearance indicates the dawn of hope and
happiness, sometimes in unexpected places.

Gundarsson provides an illuminating analysis of the story of Day's conception given in Snorri, seeing it as a myth of synthesis and transcendence.
He goes on to analyze DAGAZ as a completion of the exchange of energies
that takes place in GEBO, and the moment of union with the Valkyrie
achieved in ELHAZ. He sees the rune as an emblem of mystical illumination
in which for one blinding moment the seeker is one with the universe. For
him, it is therefore chiefly a rune of meditation leading to transformation.

Aswynn feels that it can indicate either the dawning or noon. She sees it
as a rune of Time, the counterpart of JERA. For her, DAGAZ expresses cat-
aclysmic change, in which energy, having reached a point of saturation, is
converted into its opposite. It can represent the end of one phase and the
next one's beginning. It catalyzes change without altering its own nature. She
associates the rune, in various ways, with Loki, Surt (as destructive fire), and
Heimdall, the guardian of the threshold of Asgard. It is the synthesis and
transmuter of polarities. For Aswynn, DAGAZ is a rune of Midsummer. She
links it to the death of Baldr.

I would rather identify JERA as a rune of the summer harvest, and
DAGAZ with the Midwinter rebirth of the sun, an approach that would be
more consistent with the fact that the "day" begins with its eve, as winter
begins the year. This would also be more supportive of her reference to the
DAGAZ symbols carved by some later Viking visitor at the entrance to the
Neolithic grave-temple at Newgrange in Ireland, where the light of
Midwinter's dawning strikes down the passage to the center of the mound.

Thorsson's ascription of liminality to this rune may derive from its bipolar shape, in which the two identical halves are balanced. It can equally be
interpreted as a combination of GEBO and KENAZ. The shape also suggests a Möbius strip or the figure 8 of eternity. DAGAZ is an expression of
the delicate balance of diverse forces exhibited by the shaman who walks at

once in both worlds, at home in both, bound by neither. The ability to simultaneously integrate internal and external perceptions is required for shamanic operations. The change in consciousness resulting from the synthesis of those perceptions may be identified with the "shamanic heat," the moment of illumination that is part of the shaman's initiation.

However, the Anglo-Saxon poem and the name of the rune itself offer a less complicated interpretation: DAGAZ is the bright light of day that cheers mankind after night's darkness and that reveals and clarifies. In qualities and functions it is strongly related to SOWILO. Given the cosmological background, this dawning is the inevitable conclusion to the darkness. As such, DAGAZ can refer either to a clarification of physical affairs or spiritual enlightenment.

If one is experimenting with the stadhyr, the stance for DAGAZ would be the "Osiris" position, in which one stands with arms crossed upon the breast and fingers touching the shoulders, an appropriate connection, given that Osiris is the god of rebirth into eternity.

Interpreting and Using DAGAZ

Most interpretations of this rune are positive—in a reading the appearance of DAGAZ indicates that good things are coming! If life has been difficult, it says there is light at the end of the tunnel. As a seasonal indicator it refers to the coming of spring. Willis feels that it indicates increase and growth in any area, depending on associated runes. This may mean slow and measured progress rather than sudden success, but the eventual result may be a dramatic change. Adopt a sunny attitude and persevere. Peterson calls it a rune of the present moment, a turning point, a signal to seize the opportunity.

In magical work, DAGAZ is the moment of sunrise or sunset. It can be used to begin or complete a working. It can potentiate the power of other runes for transformation, signify or contribute to new beginnings or a successful conclusion.

Aswynn finds DAGAZ particularly useful in transforming consciousness by linking the activity of left and right brain by drawing the rune from one eye to the other so that the lines cross over the "third eye" in the center of the forehead. In magic, she uses it to designate the area outside time and space, "between the worlds." This quality makes it useful as a way to cause things or people to become effectively invisible.

In fact, there is some external evidence for the existence of this "third eye." Researchers using a brain scanner at Princeton University have identified the point behind the middle of the forehead where the two lobes of the brain join as a site that "plays a crucial role in what other people are thinking and feeling" (Zimmer 2004, p. 63).

THE TWENTY-FOURTH RUNE: ᛟ OTHALA

Pronunciation: "OH-tha-la"
Meaning: Ancestral Property

**OTHALA is holy heart-home
for clan and kin of mind and body.**

Ancient Meanings

The "o" sound in the Old Germanic futhark is represented by OTHALA, whose form may be derived from the Greek Omega Ω . It appears with the same form in the Anglo-Saxon futhark as ETHEL, meaning homeland or property. However, in the Younger Futhark the "o" sound was represented by *u* or *au*. Later, the Anglo-Saxon *ós*, derived from *As* (a god) appears to have been borrowed by the Norse as *óss*.

In Old Norse, the cognate word to *ethel* is *ódhal*, which has a variety of meanings. The oldest perhaps is "noble," like the Anglo-Saxon *æthel*, an atheling, or noble. By derivation, this extended to property held in allodial tenure in unbroken succession from father to son for three generations, or for thirty years, or that which through some other legal provision had become inalienable to the family. The status of odal lands was much like that of entailed property in English law.

The Anglo-Saxon rune poem makes the nature of an odal estate clear.

> ᛟ *[Eþel] byþ oferleof aeghwylcum men,*
> (An estate is very dear to every man)
> *gif he mot ðaer rihtes and gerysena on*
> (if he may there rightly and peacefully)

brucan on bolde bleadum oftast.
(enjoy in the hall frequent harvest.)

Although OTHALA does not appear in the Norse rune poems, the Viking period attitude toward land is made clear in the literature. "Hávamál" in particular is full of pithy sayings on the subject, viz:

> Your own farm is better   though it be small,
> To everyone his own home is a hall.
> Though two goats you have   and a thatched roof,
> That's better than begging.

("Hávamál": 36)

Modern Meanings

To Thorsson, OTHALA is the clan stronghold, the sacred enclosure, the spiritual heritage or inalienable inherited qualities of a clan or family, transmitted by the fylgja. In totality, these qualities comprise the *kynfylgja* (kin-fetch). The rune governs wise management of resources and the prosperity of the family. It is a rune of kinship.

This is also a rune of Odin, symbolizing the distinction between the protected and orderly world of kin and community and the open, alien world into which the runewise go to obtain knowledge. OTHALA is a state of balance between order and chaos, with the community safely enclosed; it is the inside, or self, as distinct from externals, the immediate social group, the spiritual homeland. It indicates stable prosperity and well-being as well as growth, although one must always be vigilant to preserve custom and order. Its appearance in a reading may indicate a new home, or productive interaction with outsiders. Its opposite, or perversion, is totalitarianism and slavery.

Gundarsson develops the concept of OTHALA as boundary between innangarth and utangarth. That which is *in* the garth is not only inherited territory, but kinship, social position, law, and custom. Complex laws governed the means by which kindred were recognized, and the odal group could be increased through various kinds of exchange. An outlaw was literally an outlier, who lived outside the boundaries of the community.

Gundarsson also provides a further discussion of the kin-fylgja who embodies the family's "might" attached to its chief or most notable member. Upon his death, she transfers her protection to his most worthy descendant (a process illustrated by the incident in *Viga-Glum's Saga* in which a gigantic armed woman appears to Glum, who recognizes her as the guardian spirit of his grandfather Vigfus). Gundarsson states that this inheritance may include not only the genetic material inherited from one's physical ancestors, but the spiritual legacy of one's previous lives. As the final rune of the futhark, OTH-ALA "contains" the power of all the other runes, our mystical heritage.

Aswynn sees OTHALA as a combination of GEBO and INGWAZ and calls it "the gift of Ing." She sees the inheritance involved as genetic at the magical level. In ancient tradition, this meant the blood that was shed to take and to defend a territory. The land was secured for future generations by living on it and dying for it. This also refers to the mystery of the sacrificed king whose blood may be shed to renew the land. A corollary is the need to choose marriage-partners carefully, for their blood and beliefs will become part of the future relationship between the family and the land.

The Odal rune represents the virtue of loyalty toward one's family, village, and country. Osborn and Longland note that in Anglo-Saxon law, odal land was inherited or freehold, as opposed to land held by feudal tenure. *Ethel* is "home," the place where man harvests his experience through reflection and contemplation and increases his creativity.

The Odal rune incorporates a number of extremely powerful concepts. The symbol of the sacred enclosure, whether physical or psychic, can be very useful. Whether or not one owns property, one can claim a sacred space in vision that will be an inalienable refuge. This rune relates to the human need both for personal space and for a community to which to belong.

A concept often discussed in relation to OTHALA is the idea that spiritual affinities may be genetically determined. The Nazis misused it in their dogmas of the "Folk" and attempts to use Teutonic religion to promote racial purity. These days, it is easy to see the dangers in that kind of exclusive thinking. However, one might use the same argument with those Amerindians who object to European "theft" of Native American religion. The inheritance rune can refer to physical (genetic), cultural, or spiritual (karmic?) legacies. Does everyone who is descended from a given ethnic group automatically understand its culture and religion? What about people with no blood relationship who seem to have an instinctive flair for the ways of another culture? This is the kind of problem for which the doctrine of reincarnation offers a possible solution. There are more than one kind of "roots."

As a rune of kinship, interpreting OTHALA first requires that the family or community in question be defined. Many who are alienated from their blood relations find a new family in their religious or other affinity group. This is particularly common among those who change their religion. Rather than physical inheritance, OTHALA may indicate connection with an ethnic group-soul. An odal kin group can be formed deliberately by a group that creates a cultural or religious community and joins its energies to develop a group-soul (fylgja) to maintain it. OTHALA is the rune that governs and empowers the attempts of such a group to recover the Old Religion.

OTHALA also covers our relationship to the environment—not only family property, but also the region in which we live. Here, even though we follow a Northern European spiritual path, we who live in North America, must look to the Native American tribes who are our elder brothers in this land for guidance in understanding its spiritual ecology. Although some writers prefer to reverse the position of this rune and DAGAZ, the reference to harvest in the Anglo-Saxon rune poem makes OTHALA a good rune to put at the end of the second half of the futhark to balance JERA.

Our inheritance includes the physical environment—the land upon whose health the survival of the kin group depends. Including the land and its creatures within one's psychological kin group necessarily leads to a change in one's relationship to it. Those who enter a Native American sweat lodge honor "All my relations," as they go in. Kinship can be defined by race, culture, or environment. OTHALA involves all three.

May we treat all creatures as our kindred, so that the land we love will become our inheritance.

Interpreting and Using OTHALA

In a reading, this rune may refer to an individual's family (whether physical or spiritual) and place in his community. It may indicate living conditions—finding a house or congenial roommates, for example. It could also refer to finding an affinity group or establishing a relationship to the land. Willis identifies its meaning as a building or land, a person's house or family home, an inheritance or legacy, inherited psychological or physical traits, work. Peterson says it means inheritance, the ancestral homeland, retreat, or inner nature or essence.

Gundarsson says that OTHALA can be used to strengthen family ties and to recover the family cultural inheritance. It helps one to access wisdom and power from all parts of one's heritage, including past lives. In a reading, it may mean contact with the homeland of one's physical or spiritual ancestors. It can help with the acquisition of possessions and immobile property, such as land, and protect what you own. It also acts on matters of legal inheritance. It defines the place of working of the other runes.

Use OTHALA in all workings involving the protection or strengthening of home and family. In a bindrune with ELHAZ it wards the threshold. With MANNAZ it strengthens the community. With FEHU or JERA, it brings prosperity. With ANSUZ and DAGAZ, it can stimulate the rediscovery of ancient lore and ritual, and open our eyes to our spiritual heritage.

DAGAZ AND OTHALA: STUDY AND EXPERIENCE

Daybreak

DAGAZ is a rune whose shape is itself a mystery. It appears as the stylized blades of a double-axe, or perhaps as the butterfly of transformation. Rounded, it is the mathematical figure eight of eternity, a Möbius strip, or the physicist's symbol of a "strange attractor."

In use, it is the most gentle of the three fiery runes (the others being KENAZ and SOWILO). Its energy contributes to gradual, rather than dramatic, healing, focus, centering, and understanding. It is a rune to release tensions and burdens and to lift the spirits, a rune of dynamic stability.

Awakening

One of the meanings of DAGAZ is surely that of spiritual awakening, a concept that has received a certain amount of attention in New Age circles. It seems to mean what in Christian circles would be called a conversion experience, but of course it is not limited to any single theology. In more general terms, it is a sometimes sudden and sometimes gradual growth in awareness of the spiritual world.

Such a phenomenon is perhaps more dramatic in our secular society, in which large numbers of people are agnostics or atheist. But even in traditional cultures in which no one ever consciously doubts the existence of the gods, many may go through life observing only the form of religion. We all believe in the existence of the Queen of England and the President of the United States, but the nature of that belief is very different for those who have actually met them.

In a spiritual awakening, the dawning of changed consciousness shows one clearly things that were only tales or shadows before. It is not only the fact, but the quality of belief that changes, as if a lost sense had been regained.

One example of such a process in a pagan culture is the making of a shaman. Often the "call" is signaled by a traumatic event, such as a dangerous illness. But it may also be the culmination of a sequence of dreams or other disturbances. Recognizing the nature of these experiences and learning how to deal with them is the only alternative to going crazy. At least in a traditional setting there is a cultural context within which to place such phenomena. In modern Western civilization anyone who starts seeing auras or hearing gods talk to him is likely to be considered crazy indeed.

Nonetheless, if you persist in your study of the runes and practice the exercises described in books like this one, you are likely to find your consciousness changing. "Psychic" experience is not uncommon—synchronicity, clairvoyance or -audience, significant dreams, and vivid "lucid dreaming," or trance. You may indeed have been drawn to these studies because you have already had experiences that others would consider "odd."

You are probably not going crazy. But common sense and discipline will be necessary if you are to integrate your new awareness into your life in a productive way. Spiritual experience is real—it is also highly subjective, and can easily devolve into self-delusion. Magic is an art, not a science, with all the strengths and weaknesses that comparison implies.

Some guidelines include the following:

- Remember that spiritual experience does not automatically confer spiritual worth—that will depend on how you use it.

- The insights that result from trance and vision may be as valid as those arrived at by logic or research, but are not necessarily superior—they are different, and should be validated by other information wherever possible.

- The truth you see, even with the eyes of the spirit, is not necessarily the same as that seen by others, even those on the same spiritual path.

- Take your physical condition into consideration when interpreting information gained psychically—blood sugar highs and lows, lack of sleep, your mooncycle, or biorhythmic fluctuations can all contribute to negative experiences (or give you a misleading "high").

- Evaluate all insights in the light of common sense—spiritual insight should not make you blind!

Ostara

The coming of DAGAZ is celebrated at each of the festivals between Yule and Midsummer that honor the strengthening of the light. But the feast, and the goddess, that this rune signifies above all is Ostara. According to the Venerable Bede, Eostre (Anglo-Saxon), also called Ostara, is the goddess whose feast was held in Eostremonath and in English gave her name to the Christian holiday celebrated during April, Easter.

We have little information about this goddess and her worship; however, some things can be deduced from etymology and context. The root word for her name means "resplendent," or "shining," and was therefore given to the

East, from which comes the shining light of the dawn. She can be pictured as a radiant maiden dressed in white. It is probable that the egg and rabbit (or hare) symbolism still associated with Eastertide is inherited from her festival. In the North the hare was a sacred animal, surrounded with taboos and possibly eaten only at this festival.

The power of Ostara and the dawning can be invoked at the Spring Feast in April, or on any day at the dawning, as a ritual of renewal. Make a list of things that have shadowed your life and that you wish to get rid of. Before the sun rises, wash yourself and put on clean clothing (white, if possible). Then go outside to a place where you will be able to see the sun rise. Lay wood and kindling for a fire (or charcoal in a hibachi or cast iron pot), and have ready some sweet herbs or lumps of resin incense (frankincense or myrrh). Bring a flask of milk and some bread or cakes as well.

As the sun rises, face it with arms crossed upon your breast in the ancient posture of respect, which is also the stadhyr for DAGAZ. As soon as it has cleared the horizon, say the prayer to Day et al. from the "Sigdrifumál," which is included in the group ritual for this chapter on page 384.

Then light your fire and sprinkle the herbs or incense upon it. Honor the goddess with a prayer like the following, adjusted as necessary for your needs and the season.

> Hail OSTARA, eastward arising,
> Laughing goddess, Lady of Light—
> To dawn dominion over darkness
> Thy glory has granted, gracious goddess,
> Winter's wrath by winds of warmth
> The radiant maiden's might has melted;
> [Everywhere green plants are growing,
> Flowers flourish, beasts are bearing,
> Milk and all that men have need of
> The frozen earth now freely offers.]
> Highest and holiest goddess, hear us/me.
> Let thy light's illumination
> Banish sorrow, bear us/me blessings,
> Grant success, and a good season
> To those/he/she who seek/s thee here
> this springtide/dawning!

Take your list of things to be banished and drop it on the flames. As it burns, visualize each item as a scene in which the light grows until the light is all you can see. You may add some words to banish each problem "as the darkness is destroyed by the Day!"

When the fire has burned down and the sun is high, scatter the ashes on clean earth and pour the milk over them, add the cakes and cover them with soil. Give thanks to the gods and the powers of nature, and go in and have a good breakfast. Eggs would be appropriate, or perhaps pancakes!

Innangarth

At several points during these discussions we have encountered the concept of "Utgard," the wilderness outside the walls. Now it is time to consider the sacred ground that lies within. "Garth," "gard," and "guard" come from the same root—the area protected by a boundary. Even the shape of OTHALA seems to reinforce this concept, being at once an enclosure and an opening. It is essentially the same as the Egyptian cartouche container and, like a cartouche, can be used in a bindrune to "contain" or shelter other runes. The walls of the garth are a barrier between the sacred contents and the outside world.

The same root gives us "gird," the verb that describes the act of establishing that protection, which can be as great as a walled castle, or limited to the space surrounding a traveler, as in the Anglo-Saxon charm (number sixteen in Storms's *Anglo-Saxon Magic*) which begins: "*Ic me on thisse gyrde beluce and on Godes held bebeode . . .*" and can be loosely translated, "With this rod I gird me round; by —— [insert deity of your choice] protection I am bound."

In religious terms, "innangarth" means the *temenos*, the temple precincts, the circle of stones. But before the stone circles were erected, or even the henges of wood that preceded them, the sacred space was the circle of firelight—the hearth that was the center of the home.

It is near the fire pits in the outer caves where the Cro-Magnon clans made their homes that the "Venus" figurines, the first representations of the Divine in human form, have been found. Though the shamans later penetrated into the womb of the earth to paint their hunting spells on the walls of the caverns, the family hearth remained a center of worship. In many cultures, the hearth was the shrine of the ancestors.

Although in the later period separate "godhouses" were built in Scandinavia to hold the images of the gods and make offerings (a good thing, too, since the procedure involved splattering the blood of the sacrificed animals around the room), the long fire pit in the center of the hall was the focus for all the activities of life, including domestic ritual. The fireplace or stove—the source of food and warmth, is the center of the home to this day, but contemporary culture has forgotten that the home is also holy.

The gods can be feasted out of doors, but the setting most often associated with the sumbel is the hall. Both Aesir and Vanir appreciate being welcomed into our homes. On a more domestic level, however, one can make offerings to the house spirit, known as a *nisse* in Norway and Denmark and a *tomte* in Sweden. This being is the equivalent of the English "brownie," the Latin *penate*, or the Dutch *holdergeest*. In Old High German we find the term *inguomo* or *ingeside*, the guardian of the interior. German house spirits often have red hair and beards, while Norwegian nissen wear gray. All wear red caps.

Traditionally, the tomte lives in a rock near the hearth in Scandinavian homes. If you do not have a fireplace, you can place the rock next to your stove. The size and shape of the rock are up to you, but it should be big enough so that it won't get lost when you are sweeping! A clean boulder the size of a small melon will usually do.

Clean the area where the rock will be placed, and if it is by the fireplace, lay a new fire. In the evening, when the family is gathered, place the rock by the fireplace or stove. Put flowers around it. Set a paper cup of milk, beer, or whisky beside the rock, and with it a paper plate of cookies or bannock (do not, however, refer to these offerings aloud). Say something like:

> Brownie, to this house be welcome!
> In this house let there be good cheer,
> A welcome for friend and stranger,
> Mirth and music, cleanliness and good order.
> In this house let there be food and drink in plenty,
> In this house let there be prosperity,
> Harmony and health, love and luck for all.
> Honored one, for thy help we thank thee.

Light the fire and throw aromatic herbs upon it. Try to visualize the house spirit as the fire burns (if you are using a stove, turn on a burner to boil water for tea!). Leave the offerings out overnight and burn whatever is left in the morning. Make small offerings to the brownie whenever you have a family feast (Thanksgiving, birthdays, etc.), when you need his help to make the gremlins return a lost object, and when preparing for heavy housecleaning.

Clan and Kin

The early Germanic peoples had no concept of race, and not until well into the Viking period (under strong pressure from kings who wished to impose Continental style feudal monarchies) did the idea of a "nation" have much meaning. During the migrations period there was some sense of what it meant to be a tribe or a people, though even this was variable as subgroups split off and formed new alliances. A "people" was effectively comprised of those who marched together as a migratory army, created not by common descent but by common interests.

What was and continued to be important was the kin group—the clan and the extended family. In ancient times, however, the modern model of the nuclear family would have been barely comprehensible. The most successful unit for survival was a large household, usually including a multigenerational family as well as thralls, freedmen, houseguests (who might stay for a winter or more), and depending on the status and interests of the master of the house, warriors. This group worked together, and together performed the ceremonies that honored and propitiated the local landspirits and family ancestors. The clan, or kindred (*kuni* in Gothic), was a "community of descent," a looser grouping of families descended from a common ancestor.

Marriage, as indicated in the discussion of GEBO, was a social and economic alliance between two such families, affecting everyone within the kin group because it involved them in a complex network of loyalties and obligations. For each individual, the crucial grouping, beyond the people he or she was actually living with, was the aett—not, in this case, referring to the runes, but to the eight degrees of kinship.

In Iceland, a cognatic lineage consisted of an ancestral couple and their descendants and those to whom you were linked by marriage. A stock was all your ancestors, and a kindred all your relations within a significant degree. Your kinsmen were those you could count on for certain kinds of help. Originally the aett, or kin group, may have consisted of those who held land in common. The term "coming into aett" was used for the affiliation of illegitimate children. For a fuller discussion of the complexities, see Hastrup's *Culture and History in Medieval Iceland* (1985).

The degree of relationship determined rights of inheritance and the share of weregild to be paid or received. In the family of a reiks, it might determine who was eligible for election as the new chieftain.

Alliances within a tribe were mutable, but loyalty to the immediate kin group was absolute—unfortunately it was usually demonstrated by the continuation of blood feuds, sometimes for several generations, thus providing us with the plotlines for most of the Icelandic sagas. However, there was a second type of relationship that could be as enduring—the loyalty of a sworn warrior to his lord. Anglo-Saxon literature, in particular, is full of examples of house-carls who refuse to desert their earl in a doomed battle, even when their plight is the result of his misjudgment.

Although modern groupings of people who worship the old Germanic gods are unlikely to share a common family or even ethnic descent, they can become linked through shared loyalty. As Herwig Wolfram points out, "Whoever acknowledges the tribal tradition, either by being born into it or by being 'admitted' to it, is part of the gens and as such a member of a community of 'descent through tradition'" (1988, p. 6).

It is this "descent through tradition" that can determine who are our spiritual kin even if we, like the migrating Germanic tribes, must develop that tradition as we go along. Tom Johnson has suggested that it must have been possible for outsiders to be initiated into the "family religion" so that the offerings might be made by other members of the household when the men of the family were away. Any group of people that worships together functions as a family unit, formed for spiritual rather than economic survival.

In the heathen traditions that have developed during the past twenty years, some groups have called themselves hearths or kindreds. So long as group members recognize that their community is one of choice and adoption, not necessarily of heredity, both these terms seem appropriate to me.

The Group Ritual

If you are working with a group, the ritual for this chapter will be found on page 383. Its purpose is to experientially explore the meaning of the concepts behind DAGAZ and OTHALA.

Chapter 14

BRINGING BACK
THE RUNES

YOU HAVE NOW "TAKEN UP" all twenty-four runes of the Elder Futhark, and you have begun to understand them. To *master* them will be the work of a lifetime, or more. There is a sense in which even Odin is not their master, for as the world changes, the meaning of the runes changes as well, and he is always taking them up, crying out in anguish and wonder, as new insights and interconnections appear. To continue your study, you must teach others, and you must use the runes, always use them, for only thus will they continue to reveal their secrets. This is why it has taken me almost twenty years to prepare this book. Each time I thought it was ready I discovered new elements to include. Even now, it must be considered a work in progress, as I continue to find new meaning. "One rune leads on to another rune" indeed!

Meditation on the runes can bring great inspiration, but the runes reveal their secrets most powerfully through interaction with the solid realities of the world. In this final chapter, therefore, I offer some suggestions for using the runes in divination, and two rituals for "graduating" to the journeyman stage of taking up the runes.

DIVINATION

The "Hávamál" asks,

> Do you know how to engrave,   do you know how to read
>   them?
> Do you know how to stain,   do you know how to prove
>   them?

("Hávamál": 144)

The word translated here as "engrave" is *rist*. The verb given as "read" comes from the same root as the medieval English *rede*, or "counsel." So the second question asks whether you know how to interpret, or get advice, from the runes. The third verb seems to be related to a term meaning "to get," which I take to mean the process of making the engraved rune-sign easier to see by coloring it in. The fourth skill, "to prove," is given in the sense of proving a theorem— checking out your interpretation to see if it works or is true. Thus, these lines provide a pretty good summary of the process of divining with the runes.

Just how the ancient Germans and Vikings used the runes for divining is not known for certain. Indeed, Yves Kodratoff (2003) points out that there is far more reference to the use of the runes for other purposes, such as healing, in the lore. However, various references seem to suggest that the runes were cast in some manner, and this is the way in which they are used most often today. If the runes were used in divination, they were probably on staves (slips of wood halved to create a flat side on which to carve the runes) about six inches long, rather than on disks or chips.

The ancient Germans appear to have drawn three runes from a group cast onto the ground to get their answer and cast the runes no more than once in a day. Sibley has recreated a method used in rural Scandinavia, in which rune sticks (of the Younger Futhark) are cast one aett at a time on a white cloth. Meaning is determined by noting which rune staves lie together, and by observing the runic patterns created by the fall of the sticks themselves. However, this technique requires considerable practice, both in casting and interpreting. A simpler method is the contemporary one in which rune disks are laid out in a significant pattern (inspired, no doubt, by the method used for reading tarot).

Three-Rune Divination

In a rune cast, meaning is derived from the relationship between the rune drawn, its position in the pattern, and the nature of the question.

The simplest method is to draw three runes from a bag or rune cup and interpret their relationship. For instance, if you were seeking guidance in getting a new car and the three runes you drew were: ᚺ, ᛟ, and ᚲ, you might conclude that you would suddenly discover a vehicle or help in finding it close to home and that you should check the engine especially carefully.

A "Runic Roundtable" is an interesting and instructive event for a moot or festival. Someone in the group asks a question and draws three runes, and the group discusses possible meanings. Here are three spreads drawn in response to questions at a moot in California.

In the first, the asker questioned whether he should change jobs. The three runes drawn were:

ᛈ ᛞ ᛃ

PERTHRO tells us that it's a gamble—anything could happen. But DAGAZ and JERA indicate that the change will open up new perspectives, ending an old cycle and leading to a new one. Conclusion—go for it!

In another question, the asker wondered about the future of "a large-scale spiritual project." The runes were:

ᚠ ᚢ ᛟ

In the discussion, the group concluded that the idea was very creative, and a great deal of energy was becoming available to implement it. The result would contribute to or result in a home and heritage. Only after we had come to this conclusion did the asker tell us that the project was to create a homestead for heathen families. We agreed that the effort was likely to be successful.

A third questioner asked about the outcome of a custody battle over the asker's grandchild. The runes were:

ᚢ ᛁ ᛋ

Interpreted in the context of the question, we decided that URUZ meant that a lot of energy had been expended in regard to the situation. The presence of ISA suggested that the asker needed to stay put, to provide a core of stillness and stability. It could also mean that the situation would not change. However, drawing SOWILO to complete the spread probably meant a victory for the asker. The asker said that currently she had custody of the child, and we decided that the runes were saying that she would keep the child, at least through the summer.

Unlike Hebrew lot casting, in which the fact that the letters are all consonants means that any collection of lots is likely to spell a word, rune casts are not usually explicit. But occasionally they can be extremely clear. At one point I was struggling with arrangements to go to Iceland for a festival and asked the runes whether I would get there. The answer was:

ᚱ ᛁ ᛃ

I looked at the runes and burst out laughing. Clearly they were saying, "RAIDHO, you will travel to ISA, Iceland, at JERA, midsummer." And indeed things did work out and I had a wonderful time.

The Past/Present/Future Layout

A more detailed version of the three-rune divination is the past/present/future layout, in which three runes are drawn for each time period. Given the question about buying a new car, a spread of:

past: ᚠ ᛉ ᚺ
present: ᛚ ᚾ ᛏ
future: ᛗ ᛋ ᚾ

might be interpreted to mean that in the past there was money for a good car but the vehicle grew old and at last suddenly collapsed. In the present it is necessary to go back to first principles—a productive relationship between masculine and feminine forces, working within legal requirements. In the future, a way to find a new car will appear; you will follow the right road to success in a way that will meet your need.

These runes can also be interpreted down as well as across. In this spread, wealth comes from the left side of the equation, which will also locate the new car. The right side represents the one who drove the old car to its ending, but also the one who will push the transaction through to completion. The sudden end of the old car has led to the need to find the *right* new car.

The Elemental Layout

Another rune spread that can be useful is the elemental layout. In this arrangement, the central rune stands for the querent and/or the core of the problem, while the other runes are placed in the positions of the four directions/elements and interpreted in the light of their meanings. For instance, if your question had to do with a romantic relationship, a layout might be interpreted as follows:

(North)
ᚠ
(West)ᛋ   ᛗ   ᛞ(East)
ᛟ
(South)

Central to the situation is a need for connection. In the North, position of stability and earth, we find FEHU, the rune of sexual potency—this suggests that the attraction in the relationship is a stabilizing factor and will continue. In the South, home of passion, we find OTHALA, indicating that passion will tend to keep the relationship focused in the home. In the East, source of communication, DAGAZ suggests that the connection will lead to new insights and awakenings, while the West, associated with cycles and tides, shows the sun rune SOWILO setting at the end of its triumphant course. All in all, this layout indicates an extremely positive and supportive relationship.

The Nine Worlds Layout

Finally, for questions having to do with one's spiritual progress, I like to use the Nine Worlds layout, in which runes are set out in the same arrangement as the worlds on the Worldtree. The first rune drawn is set in the middle, as indicated in the diagram below.

8. Asgard
6. Ljósalfheim
4. Vanaheim   2. Niflheim
1. Midgard
3. Muspelheim   5. Jotunheim
7. Svartalfheim
9. Hel

This is the position of Midgard—Middle Earth—the world of humankind, and indicates the situation or state of mind of the person asking the question or his/her status in relation to the problem. The second rune goes in the "north" in Niflheim. It suggests factors that may either be causing lack of progress—stasis—if negative, or more positively, elements that are stable. The third rune, in the "south," is for Muspelheim, the world of the fire giants. It will indicate the passions or strong motivations, that are affecting the question for good or ill. Fourth, we draw a rune for Vanaheim, home of the Vanir who work with the cycles of nature. Here we find emotions, tides and cycles, and factors that may affect productivity. Once more these factors may indicate positive patterns, or being stuck in a loop. The fifth rune is for Jotunheim, the world of the elemental powers. The Jotnar, or giants, represent extremely strong and often chaotic energies. Their power can destroy, or break up a situation and bring change.

The next rune chosen, the sixth, can be placed in Ljósalfheim, the realm of the Light Elves. Although these elves, or Alfar, can include the spirits of the dead, those who dwell in this "world" seem to be of a higher order, perhaps spirits who have not yet incarnated, or those who have passed beyond the need to come again. Their world seems to be one of archetypal patterns, and in a reading, it is here we look for motifs or themes affecting the outcome. The seventh rune, on the other hand, is for the patterns imposed by the personal unconscious, in Svartalfheim, world of the Dark Alfar. Following Thorsson's interpretation of this "world," these are the "shadows" cast by old traumas and memories. In order to deal with them, we must face and understand them. For the eighth rune we move to the top of the Tree, where the gods dwell in Asgard. The rune drawn for this position indicates which deity or god-energy is interested in the question or governing the outcome. Finally, a rune is drawn for Hel, the Underworld, the home of the ancestors. This gives us the chthonic aspects of the situation, those relating to the social or cultural background or the collective unconscious. If the answer is still unclear, I may draw a tenth rune "for the Well of Wyrd," to see what the Norns have to say.

As an example, if the question was whether or not the asker should seek further formal spiritual training, a Nine Worlds layout might be read thusly:

8. Asgard—|
6. Ljósalfheim— ↑
4. Vanaheim— <   2. Niflheim— ↾
1. Midgard—X
3. Muspelheim—ϟ   5. Jotunheim— ⇂
7. Svartalfheim— ß
9. Hel— ⟨⟩

In Midgard, the center of the situation and the "home" of the querent, we find the rune GEBO, the gift, which is also the rune of exchange. This suggests that the querent is already involved in a situation of spiritual give-and-take and tends to pass on whatever he or she receives. In Niflheim, the home of stasis and/or stability, we find a rune of flux, LAGUZ, indicating that the situation is changing. In Muspelheim, home of passion, stands SOWILO, the rune of the sun, which suggests that the course to which passion impels the querent will be victorious. Jotunheim, from which blows the winds of change or chaos, hosts EIHWAZ, the rune of the Worldtree and its connections, indicating that there is a pattern even in the wild energy that sometimes appears. In Vanaheim, the torch of KENAZ shows us that the home fires are still burning, and so long as the querent touches base regularly he or she will be okay.

The appearance of TIWAZ in Ljósalfheim suggest that a certain formality in the intellectual and structural aspect of the training would be desirable. BERKANO in Svartalfheim, however, indicates that personal factors having to do with the mother may affect the querent's ability to profit from training. In Asgard, home of the gods, we find ISA, indicating that they are a source of stability, an underlying foundation of belief that does not change. In Hel, home of the ancestors, we find JERA, indicating a recognition of the cyclical patterns underlying human religious practices. The time has come to return to the ways of our ancestors. Training that helps the querent to do this will be useful.

Traditionally, the runes are cast or laid out on a white linen cloth. Until you have memorized the layout patterns, you may want to arrange them on a piece of paper with the positions marked on it. Runes can be drawn from a bag or shaken in a covered cup before being drawn. Putting two runes together enables one to focus their meaning. In the same way, a rune can be interpreted in the context of its position. It is always wise to invoke the blessing of Odin and the Norns before reading the runes, with a prayer such as:

> I ask here the aid of Odin, All-father,
> Tree-Rider, reveal thy runes—
> Let me read truly.
> From Urdh's well understanding
> Let me draw, and wisdom utter.
> Hail all ye Aesir, and Asynjur, help me—
> Bestowers of blessings
> From these words breed good fortune.

Practice and Learn

Other rune layouts include the year-wheel, in which a primary rune is drawn for each month and a secondary rune added to aid in interpreting it. It is advisable to write down the rune drawn for each month and return it to the rune cup before drawing for the next, to allow the maximum number of options.

As you meditate on the runes, you will find their meanings become more clear to you. Practice by drawing pairs of runes at random and speculating on how they might mutually illuminate each other. When reading for another person, state the meaning of the position it will fill: "The first rune is for Midgard, center of the situation," or "Now draw one for Asgard, to see what the gods say," and so forth. You will find that the combination of question, rune, and position narrows down the meanings so that they can be stated with some confidence. However, there will be times when a conclusion that makes no sense to you will nonetheless mean something to the person with the question.

RUNESPELLS

In addition to communication and meditation, runes can be used in spells. Runespells are referred to in a number of places in the Eddas, most notably in stanzas of the "Hávamál" and in the "Lay of Sigdrifa," when the Valkyrie counsels Sigfrid. Runes are cited for use in battle, healing, childbirth, travel, weather, seduction, wisdom, eloquence, and the like.

In most cases, unfortunately, the catalogues seem to be a rune master's boast, and anyone with the skill to use them is expected to know which runes are intended. In the old days, rune masters taught them to their students. Today, we must ask Odin himself to teach us, and open ourselves to receive this knowledge through study and meditation. The following list of applications of runes for different purposes should be considered advisory rather than prescriptive. Choice should always be governed by the situation, and often, when your energy is engaged, you may find yourself inspired to use a rune that reason might not have suggested, but that turns out to be surprisingly appropriate.

Sample Applications

Binding/stopping: |

Unbinding/starting: N ⟨ Γ

Protection: ϒ Þ

Success: ϟ

Healing: ⟨

    To bring down fever: N |

    Stanch blood or knit bone: | ⌐

    Strengthening: ⋔ ϟ

    Circulation: Γ ⟨

Bless drink, protect from poison: Γ ϒ

Childbirth: ⟨ Þ ⋔ ϟ

Baby blessing: ϟ ϝ Þ Γ Þ

Sexual attraction: ϝ ◇ Þ Þ

Sexual fidelity: | ⊗ M

Prosperity: ϝ ⟨ ◇ ⋔ ✕

Justice, legal success: ↑ ϟ ϒ

Speech/communication: ϝ

    To ease: Γ

    To bind: |

Learning/wisdom: ϝ ϟ ⋈

Fire: ⟨

    To stop: |

    To start: ✝ ϟ

To calm strife: | Γ Þ ◇

To counter hexes: N ϒ

Warding

Many of the early inscriptions that have survived were scratched on objects to protect them. Bindrunes or inscriptions make good car charms or luggage tags, as indicated above. Another way in which such inscriptions can be used is to protect your home. The general public is only vaguely aware of the existence of runes and has no backlog of prejudice against them, so if you choose to paint runes of protection on your house, they will probably be considered ornamental! Chanting a rune ring can create a circle of protection from the inside, turning as you chant and projecting the runes outward (this is the most feasible method for use in apartments), or from the outside, chanting and inscribing each rune with consecrated water or oil as you move around the building.

A more elaborate approach is to create bindrunes of protection and paint them on the walls or on a plaque that is attached to the building. The first rune, as in any protection spell, is ELHAZ. Others that might be added could include TIWAZ of the polestar to watch over you in the north, FEHU to invoke the protection of the Vanir in the west, THURISAZ, to get Thor's help in the east, and SOWILO, for the protective blessing of Sunna in the south. Contain each bindrune within a JERA or an OTHALA. The generic bindrune for house protection is OTHALA plus ELHAZ.

Runic inscriptions can also be mounted above your doors. For example, you might adapt a charm inscribed on an ancient helmet: "I am called (Name): the one wise to danger: I give good luck." (Name) *haitia: farauisa: gibu auja.*

(Your name in runes)

᛬ᚾᚨᛏᛁᚠ᛬ᚠᚠᚱᚨᚾ᛬ᛋᚠ᛬ᚷᛁᛒᚾᚨᚾ᛬ᚲᚠ

You can also comb through the Eddas for suitable inscriptions. The "Hávamál" is a good place to look, although unless your home situation is extremely tense I would not recommend stanza 1. Better is stanza 37: "Your own place is better, though it be small." This is the Viking equivalent of "there's no place like home," which could be written out in runes in English as:

ᚲᚢᚱ᛬ᚲᚢᚠᛋ᛬ᛁᛋ᛬ᛒᛖᛏᛏᛗᚱ᛬ᛏᚾᚷ᛬ᛁᛏ᛬ᛒᛖᛋᛈᚨᛚ

Or, if you want to be more succinct, in Old Norse: *"Bú es betra, thót litit sé"* is, in the Younger Futhark:

ᛒᚢ᛬ᛁᚴ᛬ᛒᛁᛏᚱᚠ᛬ᛏᚠᛏ᛬ᚾᛏᛁᛏ᛬ᚼᛁᚠ

Once you begin to think along these lines, other applications will occur to you—a bindrune of KENAZ and ELHAZ above the stove or fireplace, for instance, THURISAZ and SOWILO by the fuse box, LAGUZ and ELHAZ where you are worried about the plumbing, and so on.

The Group Ritual

If working with a group, you have reached the point of graduation. The graduation ritual starts on page 393. The rite can be adapted for individual work. The runic initiation that follows it is intended for one individual at a time and requires a much higher level of commitment from the initiate and from his or her friends. In any case, take this opportunity to write, or complete, a rune poem of your own.

> Into the deep I gazed—
> I took up the runes,   took them up, screaming,
> Then fell back again.

("Hávamál": 139)

A visit to any New Age bookstore will reveal dozens of books promising spiritual enlightenment through one system or another.

An individual epiphany, though it may well result from this study, is not the purpose of taking up the runes. Odin himself, having got them, did not then ascend to the heavens to escape from the Wheel of Karma. Nor did he keep them for personal self-stimulation. Having won the runes, we are told, he gave them away—some to gods, some to elves or dwarves, and some to mortal men.

I counsel you who have completed this book to do the same. If you simply close the book and put it away, congratulating yourself on your accomplishment, the runes that now shine so brightly in your awareness will wither like faerie gold and whirl away on the wind. The only way to hold on to the runes is to give them away. Continue to study and meditate, but above all, *use* them—in divination or healing, warding or blessing. Thus, they will become part of your life, and life will continue to teach you what they mean.

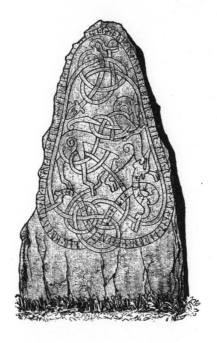

Part Two

The Rituals

INTRODUCTION

There are many ways of learning and many kinds of knowledge. By reading and thinking about the runes, we understand them with our minds. By seeking out activities that manifest their energies, we integrate them into our lives. But it is through meditation and ritual that we internalize them and incorporate them into our souls. Those who study the runes in all three ways will never forget their meaning.

As you work through this book you will probably do some of the solo rituals for each rune. However, anyone who has ever worked with a kindred, a ceremonial lodge, or a coven knows that the impact of ritual is intensified when it combines the energies of a number of people. If you have the good fortune to be studying the runes with others, you will find that doing the folllowing rituals will be a powerful aid to your assimilation of the runes. Even if you are working alone, you will benefit from reading through them and doing the meditations.

All of the rituals have the same basic structure. The group begins by chanting the entire futhark, visualizing the runes as a shimmering circle of bright shapes surrounding the ritual area. This creates a warded and focused space for the work that follows. Next come invocations to whichever gods and goddesses are appropriate. These are followed by the "work" of the ritual, which may include offerings, prayers, spells, dramatized myths, or other actions intended to manifest the meaning of the runes. These acts prepare the mind for the guided meditation in which the message reaches deeper levels of consciousness. As you approach each ritual you may be tempted to read the meditation ahead of time. If you are doing the work with a group, it is better to wait until the ritual. When the meditation is finished and everyone is grounded, all powers that have been invoked are thanked, and the rune ring is taken down. Ritual work uses energy, so it is highly desirable to have food available or to go out for a bite afterward. Be very sure that everyone is grounded before they have to drive home.

You will notice that some of the rituals incorporate quotations from the Elder Edda that are translated more freely than they are elsewhere. You may prefer to substitute a version from another translation, such as Hollander's. Where I have included material written by participants in my classes, authors are indicated in the text.

Chapter 1

TAKING UP THE RUNES:
A Ritual Journey

THE RITUAL FOR THIS FIRST MEETING is a pathworking, or guided meditation, for a journey to the Worldtree to encounter the runes. To help participants focus, the pathworking takes place within the context of a protected circle. The various parts of the ritual can be divided among participants. The Meditation should be read by someone with a strong, pleasant voice, slowly and with expression.

You will also find it helpful to draw each of the runes in bright red on a large card or half a piece of typing paper. When you call the rune circle, hold up each card in turn, or tape them in a circle around the room so that people will see them as they turn.

Except for the rune cards, no tools or props are actually necessary to perform the ritual, but you will find that it helps everyone to focus if you use a knife or a runewand or staff to draw the runes in the air as you call them. An altar provides a focus for the action. It need not be elaborate. Cover a small table or box with a plain cloth, or a cloth upon which you have embroidered or painted the runes around the edge or in a circle. Upon this, set a pair of candles and the stacked rune cards.

In order to focus attention and move people into the proper psychic state, it is useful to begin with some kind of blessing for the sacred space. Those who are coming to the study of the runes from another pagan tradition will probably feel more comfortable if they cast a circle and honor the quarters. Those who are already practicing heathens may begin with the hammer rite, or in whatever manner is familiar. You can, if you choose, add such an opening to the rune circle specified in the text.

Viking religion was practiced outdoors in sacred groves or holy places, in the family hall, or in permanent temples and shrines. They did, however, have procedures for self-warding and for claiming or sanctifying a piece of ground.

When a place is a part of nature or permanently devoted to the gods, or the ritual being performed is an accepted part of your culture, it is not necessary to establish sacred space before working—you don't need to cast a circle before opening the presents on Christmas morning. However, when we are trying to recover the spirituality of our ancestors, we need all the help we can get to make the psychological transition from our ordinary lives. This is especially true when we hold meetings in cluttered living rooms. If you are experienced in ritual work, you may devise your own opening and closing procedures or use the Hammer Rite given by Edred Thorsson in *Futhark*.

My current preference, however, is to begin rune rituals by having the entire group call the rune ring—intoning and drawing each rune in the air as one turns in a circle. By the end of the meetings, everyone should have memorized the futhark and be able to call the rune ring from memory.

ESTABLISHING SACRED SPACE

Participants stand in a circle, facing the altar. The leader faces north and begins to intone the runes, inscribing each rune in the air as it is chanted and turning to the right, so that by the time the whole futhark has been called everyone has turned in a complete circle. In later rituals, the entire group will call the rune ring in unison, or you may choose to sing the "Futhark Song" given below.

ᚠ FEHU	ᚺ HAGALAZ	ᛏ TIWAZ
ᚢ URUZ	ᚾ NAUDHIZ	ᛒ BERKANO
ᚦ THURISAZ	ᛁ ISA	ᛗ EHWAZ
ᚨ ANSUZ	ᛃ JERA	ᛗ MANNAZ
ᚱ RAIDHO	ᛇ EIHWAZ	ᛚ LAGUZ
ᚲ KENAZ	ᛈ PERTHRO	◇ INGWAZ
ᚷ GEBO	ᛉ ELHAZ	ᛞ DAGAZ
ᚹ WUNJO	ᛋ SOWILO	ᛟ OTHALA

Now that we have called the runes, let us sing them into power with the "Futhark Song," by Jennifer Tifft.

INVOCATIONS

A different speaker invokes the blessing of the gods with Sigdrifa's prayer.

> "Hail to thee Day, and Day's bright boy,
> Hail to the Night and her daughter's joy.
> With eyes that bless us may you see
> And grant to those here, victory.
> The goddesses and gods we call
> And holy earth, who gives to all—
> Give us here wise words and weal,
> And in this life, the hands that heal!"

("Sigdrifumál": 2, freely translated)

A second speaker may offer this prayer or create something in a similar vein:

> Odin, High One, here we hail thee—
> Riddle-master, Tree-rider, Rede-lord, come.
> Word-smith, craft us wit and will
> To walk thy way, to win thy wisdom.
> Goodly mede of galdr grant us,
> Let sound and shape and sense speak clear.
> Runelore let us learn, Allfather—
> Rune might's mysteries reveal!

MEDITATION

At this point, all lights are dimmed or extinguished. Instruct all participants to arrange themselves comfortably. The person reading the meditation will need a votive or a mini-flashlight to see the text. If desired, the meditation may be accompanied by the steady beat of a drum at medium tempo. In reading, emphasize the capitalized names of the runes. Afterward, allow time for everyone to return to normal consciousness. Then the rest of the lights may be turned on.

> You are at ease, still and silent,
> Centered upon the earth.
> Breathe in . . . and out . . . in . . . and out . . .
> (4 beats in, hold 2, 4 beats out, hold 2)
> Let the cares of the world of men be gone.
> You are relaxed, at peace, you sit in safety.
> Safely you will fare forward, safely you will return,
> You will remember all you need to know.

As you relax, feel the solid earth supporting you.
Let your awareness sink downward, inward,
Deep into earth's core . . . now draw it up again.
Fill yourself with its power. . . .

Move out of your body now.
See a place that you know well.
Look at the ground; is it grass or stones?
Feel the texture, hear the sounds around.
As you gaze, you see the beginnings of a path.
Follow it away from the fields you know,
Through bushes that become a woodland,
Woods that turn to forest,
Forest that grows thicker, darker,
Till you are walking through a tunnel made of trees.

When at last the forest thins,
Before you is a clearing.
In its center grows the greatest of all trees,
So vast you cannot see around it,
So tall it pierces the sky.

Three great roots plunge through the soil.
Beneath the nearest, a passage opens.
You pass within and find a dim, featureless light
That shows you the way.
From the north to the east you fare,
Spiraling downward,
And from the east to the south again.
As you turn westward,
A cool mist swirls around you, veils of mist,
Moist and soothing,
Drawing a curtain to separate you from the world.

You float in the mist,
And hear nearby the roaring of a mighty river,
Water that rushes over rocks and rapids,
Booms as it falls; mist swirls, and you see
The Thunderflood's fury, and in the depths flashing
A fish—swift flickering reflection of sunlight.
The mist drifts and eddies. Turning, you follow
And glimpse, white with rime,

The roots of the Worldtree.
A well lies beneath them, mirror-dark in the shadows.
Deep is that well, from which the Norns drink daily,
And weave the world's wyrd at the base of the Tree.
The Tree rises high from its roots in the depths,
The bark is all slabbed and twisted,
Easy to climb for the one who has need.
Is this the root or the trunk of the Tree?
Are you in the depths or the heights?
Distance and direction have no meaning here.
Above, the wood is worn and use-smoothed;
See there the spot where for nine nights, alone,
The High One hung between the worlds.

Would you seek the runes?
Ask a blessing of Odin before ascending.
Then, moving carefully, clamber upward.
Let its branches embrace your body. . . .
Sink back, oh seeker, upon the Tree,
Hanging between earth and heaven,
Sense the abyss that opens below you,
The immensity above, the roots and the branches,
The nine worlds and the spine of spirit
That links them. . . .

Wind whispers past you, ravens wing round,
Croaking their wisdom, they perch in the Tree.
Suspended, your own stillness deepens;
Your body is bound but your spirit flies freely.
Summon now the sacred runes!
Let the symbols soar before you—
Runes you will find and rightly read,
Of wondrous weight, of mighty magic,
Which by the wisest god are given;
As each is named, you must see it,
Accept it,
Make it your own!

FEHU, in cattle and fertile fields
Freyr finds wealth for friends unfailing;
URUZ, aurochs, urges earthward
Spirit strength to shape creation;
THURISAZ, the Thorn of Thor

Force that frees, or fights a foe;
ANSUZ, OS, is Odin's Wisdom,
Intellect in ecstasy;
Upon RAIDHO the road is ridden,
To work and world around together;
KENAZ kens creation's fire,
Its torch transforms the hearth and hall;
GEBO unites the gift and giver,
In equal exchange of energy;
WUNJO wins Wishfather's blessing,
Joy joins folk in family freedom;
HAGALAZ hails ice-seeds hither
Harm is melted into healing;
NAUDHIZ is Necessity,
Norn-rune forcing fate from need;
ISA is the Ice, inertia,
Stasis and serenity;
JERA's year-wheel yields good harvest
Right reward as seasons ripen;
EIHWAZ, Yew of Yggdrasil,
Bow of life and death, worlds binding;
PERTHRO pours its play from rune-cup
Chance and change for man or child;
ELHAZ, Elk sharp-tined or eel-sedge
Totem power provides protection;
SOWILO sets the sun wheel soaring,
Guiding light by land or sea;
TIWAZ is the rune of Tyr
Victorious victim enjoining justice;
BERKANO, Birchtree, Bride and Mother,
Brings up earth power for rebirthing;
EHWAZ, Eos, extending energy,
The holy horse links land and people;
In MANNAZ every man is master,
All Ríg's children are relations;
From LAGUZ's Lake life everflowing
Wells from mother-depths of darkness;
INGWAZ wanders the world in his wagon
And dying, leaves life in the land;
DAGAZ is a bright Day's dawning,
Life and growth and light for all;
OTHALA is the holy heart-Home,
For clan and kin of mind and body.

Be still and think on the things you've learned:
"These runes you know   that queens ken not,
Nor any human's child . . .
Needed by men's sons
No use to an etin's son.
Hail to whoever speaks them,   hail to whoever knows them
Good those who grab them,
Hale those who heed them!"

(adapted from "Hávamál": 146, 164)

The runes you have won will remain with you.
Now you must recall awareness,
Over your limbs regain control.
Carefully from the Tree climb downward—
The bark of the trunk is all slabbed and twisted.
Easily you will descend
Until midst tangled roots you're standing
Beside the well where wait the Norns.
Offer your gratitude to Odin. . . .

Now the mists are rising, gray cloud engulfs you,
Cool cloud caresses, root and pool are hidden.
Turn and make your way upward,
From the west to the south,
From the south to the east and north once more.
You emerge from beneath the arching root
And see the Tree rising above you.
There before you is the path by which you came.
Follow it. Go back through the tunnel of trees.
Come out into the light again.
Look ahead—there is the place that you know.

Sit down, feel the weight of your flesh,
The solid ground below.
Sink down into your body.
Remember what you have learned.
Now breathe in and out, in and out again.

(Read more quickly from here.)
Sigh and stretch. Open your eyes.
You are in the sacred enclosure once more.
You step onto solid earth. Steady you stand now.

> All here is darkness. Sit down and center—
> Breathe in and out . . . in and out again . . .
> The mists now fade; mortal sight wakens,
> Welcome rune-wielders, to the world returning.

RETURNING TO THE WORLD

Those who greeted the gods should now thank them.

> Our thanks to you gods, thanks to the goddesses,
> Thanks be to Earth that givest to all!
> Thanks to Odin Allfather, Runemaster,
> Who hast granted us this gift of wisdom!

Open Circle

Starting facing north and turning to the left, visualize the rune ring fading and sinking into the ground.

Celebration and Grounding

After the ritual you should allow time for everyone to shift back to mundane consciousness before returning home. The best way to do this is to provide some food and drink, which should be available after every meeting, and let people socialize. Appropriate foods include Scandinavian crackers or hearty breads, cheese, apples, apple cider, and if desired, beer or mead.

Be aware that response to trancework varies. During the meditation, some people will simply feel as if they have been listening to a story. Others may apparently fall asleep. They will awaken naturally, and will have a subconscious memory of what they heard. A few people may have difficulty returning to normal consciousness. Ground them with salt, water, and food. If necessary, you may have to take them through the meditation again privately to pick up any soul pieces they might have left along the way.

Chapter 2

FEHU / URUZ:
A Ritual for Abundance

THE PURPOSE OF THIS RITUAL is to manifest abundance and prosperity, the gifts of the Vanir. For this ritual you will need a cloth, gold candles, cards on which ᚠ and ᚢ have been drawn, and pictures of the deities. Everyone should have a deposit slip from his or her checkbook, or a piece of play money. You will also need a pen with gold ink, a chalice or drinking horn, a pitcher of milk, a platter with bread or cake, and a dish of chocolate coins covered in gold foil. The prayers can be spoken by the leader or divided up among the group. If possible, Freyr should be invoked by a woman and Freyja by a man.

ESTABLISHING SACRED SPACE

Participants stand in a circle, facing the altar. The leader faces north and begins to intone the runes, inscribing each rune in the air as it is chanted and turning to the right, so that by the time the whole futhark has been called everyone has turned in a complete circle. In later rituals, the entire group will call the rune ring in unison.

ᚠ FEHU	ᚺ HAGALAZ	↑ TIWAZ
ᚢ URUZ	ᚾ NAUDHIZ	ᛒ BERKANO
ᚦ THURISAZ	I ISA	ᛗ EHWAZ
ᚨ ANSUZ	ᛃ JERA	ᛉ MANNAZ
ᚱ RAIDHO	ᛇ EIHWAZ	ᚱ LAGUZ
ᚲ KENAZ	ᛈ PERTHRO	◇ INGWAZ
✕ GEBO	ᛉ ELHAZ	ᛗ DAGAZ
ᚹ WUNJO	ᛋ SOWILO	ᚷ OTHALA

INVOCATIONS

Gods and Goddesses

"Hail to thee Day, and Day's bright boy,
Hail to the Night and her daughter's joy.
With eyes that bless us may you see
And grant to those here, victory.
The goddesses and gods we call
And holy earth, who gives to all—
Give us here wise words and weal,
And in this life, the hands that heal!"

("Sigdrifumál": 2, freely translated)

Invocation to Freyr

(Light gold candle.)
Hail, lord Freyr! All hail to the great god,
Helper of humankind, hail!
Father of the fertile field, fairest of fighters,
Bestow thy blessings now.
Thou art the offspring of Njordh and of Nerthus.
In Alfheim all adore thee.
Thy glory has melted the heart of the maiden—
We hail thee, Husband of Gerd!
Frodhi the fruitful, fill now our meadows
With crowds of calves and cows;
Sceaf of the Scyldings, soon let us gather
gladly your golden grain;
As Ingvi we will hail thee, ever returning,
In thy wagon we worship thee still.
The bright boar, Gullinbursti, bears thee to bless us,
Sun-bright splendor of life—
Strong as a stallion, thy phallus fulfills us,
Lord and lover, let us live anew!

Invocation to Freyja

(Light gold candle.)
"Hail Freyja! All hail to the goddess,
Highest and holiest, hail!
Brisingamen's bearer, Bride of the Vanir,
We boldly bespeak thee here.
Gefion the giver, gold-bright goddess,
Grant us thy favor now.
There where thou sittest in splendid Sessrumnir;
Linen-clothed Lady of Love.
As Syr we salute thee, Hildisvini's rider,
Boar-Ottar's savior art thou.
Gullveig the golden, fast bound in the flames,
Reforged thee thy fate in the fire.
Mardoll of the waters, mighty thy beauty,
Mistress of gods and men;
Mare of the Vanir, as Gondul dost thou gallop,
Bearing kings from the battlefield.
Lady of life, light dost thou kindle—
Goddess, show us thy glory!"

(from *Brisingamen*, adapted)

OFFERINGS

Our Lord and our Lady, loudly we call you,
Fertile Freyr and Freyja, brother and bride.
Luck-bringers, lustily giving Earth goodness,
Hear us as we hail you, hither to help us!
Grateful, our gifts to the givers we offer—
Sacrifice to source returning,
Blessings rebounding!

(Collect deposit slips and play money and place before altar.)

We give to you now the growing gold of Nerthus;
(Offer bread.)
The milk of Audhumla, nourisher of men;
(Offer milk.)
The bright tears of Freyja, bringing folk blessing.
(Offer chocolate coins.)
Accept now our offerings, Lord and Lady of Life!

PRAYER FOR PLENTY

Oh ye who multiply all manifestation,
We pray to you for plenty—
Not in greed or aggression,
Nor by depriving any other of life or livelihood,
But by the natural, positive, and productive
Turning of the wheel of JERA,
That we may have food and fire and fellowship,
And appreciate your bounty!

Each of you, be still now,
And let the gods see in your hearts
The things that you need . . .

*(Silent prayer in which each one asks gods for what is needed,
while the priest or priestess blesses the deposit slips or play
money by inscribing a bindrune of prosperity upon each with the
gold pen.)*

LITANY OF PROSPERITY

(Leader): Lord of Luck, bless us with the best of fortune—

(All): May Fortune's favor swiftly find us!
(Leader): Goddess of gold, grant us abundance—
(All): May Fortune's favor swiftly find us!
(Leader): May income spring up like sprouts in a cornfield—
(All): May Fortune's favor swiftly find us!
(Leader): Let our hands flow with gold, while gold does not
  bind us—
(All): May Fortune's favor swiftly find us!
(Leader): Help us to do our work without distraction—
(All): May Fortune's favor swiftly find us!
(Leader): Give us the health to work without tiring—
(All): May Fortune's favor swiftly find us!
(Leader): Give us the inspiration to do work men will value—
(All): May Fortune's favor swiftly find us!
(Leader): Let us find work that we enjoy doing—
(All): May Fortune's favor swiftly find us!
(Leader): Let us find a multitude of sources of income—
(All): May Fortune's favor swiftly find us!
(Leader): Let us be generous and share our wealth with others—
(All): May Fortune's favor swiftly find us!
(Others may add their own requests here.)
(Leader): Freyr and Freyja, grant us thy favor—
(All): May Fortune's favor swiftly find us!

MEDITATION

At this point, all lights are extinguished except for the candles on the altar.
Instruct all participants to arrange themselves comfortably. The person reading the meditation will need a votive or a mini-flashlight to see the text. Near
the end, someone redistributes the deposit slips or play money back to their
owners, so that when they open their eyes, the slips are there.

Read slowly, allowing time for visualizations to build. At end of meditation, allow a little time for people to recover; then turn lights on.

You are at ease, still and silent,
Centered upon the earth.
Breathe in . . . and out . . . in . . . and out . . .
(4 beats in, hold 2, 4 beats out, hold 2)
Let the cares of the world of men be gone.
You are relaxed, at peace, you sit in safety.
Safely you will fare forward, safely you will return.
You will remember all you need to know.

As you relax, feel the solid earth supporting you.
Let your awareness sink downward, inward,
Deep into earth's core . . . now draw it up again.
Fill yourself with its power. . . .

Move out of your body now.
See a place that you know well.
Look at the ground; is it grass or stones?
Feel the texture, hear the sounds around.
As you gaze, you see the beginnings of a path.
Follow it away from the fields you know,
Through bushes that become a woodland,
Woods that turn to forest,
Forest that grows thicker, darker,
Till you are walking through a tunnel made of trees.

When at last the forest thins,
Before you is a clearing.
In its center grows the greatest of all trees,
So vast you cannot see around it,
So tall it pierces the sky.
Walk around it . . . from its base wind many paths.
The path that draws you leads westward. . . .

Move forward through wild heathland,
Where winter-browned bracken clings to the slopes,
And prickly tangles of gorse choke the paths.
Frozen mud crunches beneath your feet.
The world is dead with cold, and very still.
The land falls away into dim distances,
A flat landscape broken
By occasional clumps of struggling trees.
Here, even the brambles must fight to live.
The sky is dim, and you shiver in an icy wind.
You pause on a rise, striving to see your way.
You are looking for the land of promise.
You are seeking the place
That will provide what you need.
You are searching for the source of abundance,
But in the land before you mist is all that you can see.
Or perhaps it is dust, for it seems to be moving—
Clouds of dust billow outward
As something approaches.

The earth trembles, a deep bellow
Echoes the moan of the wind.
Now you see tossing horns and massive shoulders.
It is only one beast, but it is monstrous—
The aurochs, the wild bull of ancient days.

Look around you—there is no place to run to.
And this thing is between you and all that you desire.
Its mighty legs churn the earth.
For a moment you cannot see it—
But in those dark clouds you glimpse shapes.
Strange they are, and yet all too familiar.
These are the things that keep you from prospering.
Look at them. . . .
See what forms they assume. . . .
Give them names. . . .

(Allow a few moments for everyone to visualize those things that
impede them from achieving prosperity.)

Then, once more, the aurochs is charging toward you.
Hooves make a thunder on the barren earth.
The sharp horns lower as the beast comes on.
You cannot run.
You must draw from the beast itself
The strength to meet it.
Only you can transform the things that oppose you.
As the horns point toward you,
Force flares out from them.
Open your arms. Embrace that wild energy.
Let the fire of the aurochs's rolling eye set you aflame!

And now it is upon you! Reach!
Grasp the hard curve of the horns, grip fast!
Sensation shocks through you.
Flip with the force of the charge—
You are flying, up, up, higher, higher. . . .
You land in a patch of thick green grass.
Turn. The great cow shape is still there,
But now the horns point downward.
The beast is licking the frozen soil.
It is no bull that stands before you now.
The great cow's udder swings heavily as she moves.

Each motion releases a white stream of milk.
As the milk touches the ground,
Earth grows green once more.
Across the barren landscape, rivers are flowing,
Trees bud, and shrubs burst into flower
Where the milk of Audhumla soaks into the soil.
Everywhere the mists are lifting—
Remember the obstacles that held you.
Now see each of them transformed.
You have found the land of the Vanir.
What takes shape before you
Is the clear manifestation
Of everything you need.

(Allow time to visualize prosperity in manifestation.)

Look well.
Remember.
Believe.

The path you follow curves.
You see the great Tree once more.
You have been walking around it.
There before you is the path by which you came.
Follow it. Go back through the tunnel of trees.
Come out into the light again.
Look ahead—there is the place that you know.

Sit down, feel the weight of your flesh,
The solid ground below.
Sink down into your body.
Remember what you have learned.
Sit down and center—
Breathe in and out . . . in and out again . . .
(Read more quickly from here.)
Sigh and stretch. Open your eyes.
You are in the sacred enclosure once more.
Welcome rune-wielders, to the world returning.
You are in the sacred enclosure once more.

THE GIFTS OF THE GODS

(Leader): Behold what is before you!
Now is the moment of manifestation!
Now the wild magic gives life to us and to the land!
Behold how the gods give good gifts to their lovers—
 receive the blessing of prosperity!

The fruitful field is filled with a golden harvest.
Behold the seed of Freyr, may it satisfy your hunger!
(Bless bread ◇ and pass around.)

The cow of creation has milk enough for many.
Behold the gift of Freyja, may it quench your thirst!
(Bless milk, ᚺ pour into horn, and pass around.)

The givers of all good things grant us prosperity.
Take the gold of the gods, and use it wisely!
(Bless "coins" ᚠ and pass around.)

(All): Lord and Lady, in this hour
You have blessed us with your power:
As we receive, so shall we give;
As we have shared your love, we live!

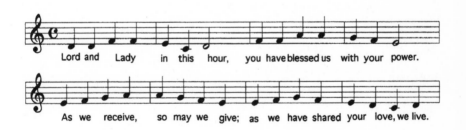

Lord and Lady in this hour, you have blessed us with your power.
As we receive, so may we give; as we have shared your love, we live.

RETURNING TO THE WORLD

Thank the Gods

> Our thanks to you gods, thanks to the goddesses,
> Thanks be to Earth that givest to all!
> Our thanks to Freyr and Freyja for all their gifts,
> Past, present and future.
> Let us carry the blessing of the Lord and the Lady
> Into the world!

Open Circle

Starting facing north and turning to the left, visualize the rune ring fading and sinking into the ground.

Chapter 3

THURISAZ / ANSUZ: Thurs Spells

THE PURPOSE OF THIS RITUAL is to use the magical craft of ANSUZ to control the energy of THURISAZ, specifically in the area of weatherworking, whether you need more rain or less. Use this ritual as an example. Identify a force that is out of balance, and follow the pattern and procedures used here. If the weather in your region is currently perfect, find out what forces are making this so and reinforce them. If, however, there is a problem, personify it as a Jotun and use the spell skills of ANSUZ to battle it. This may include a free-association incantation and a pathworking as given here, or other actions. Alternatives for flood or drought are included in the ritual script.

Feel free to adapt the weather spell and the relevant parts of the pathworking to meet your own needs. Write a new section in which you visualize the gods acting upon the weather in whatever way is appropriate for your region at the time you are doing the ritual.

For this ritual, you will need a cloth (preferably white or blue) for the altar, a votive light or candle for each god, incense, cards on which ANSUZ and THURISAZ have been drawn, and pictures of Thor and Odin. You will also need a platter or basket of bread, a chalice or horn of mead or cider, and if you are invoking rain, a bowl of rainwater. Also useful are a staff or hammer (a five-pound mallet type with a shortened handle, not a carpenter's hammer), and a drum.

Remember that your weatherworking *must* be appropriate to your climate. You will be working with serious energy here, and you do *not* want to unbalance a situation further. If you have not studied the meteorological situation sufficiently to know what you are doing, you will be better off simply asking the gods to give you the "right weather for the season." For more information on the ethics and techniques of weatherworking, see Inanna Arthen's article, "Theory and Practice of Weatherworking" in the 1989 Spring/Summer edition of *Fireheart*.

At the end of the discussion, or during the potluck that follows the ritual, remind everyone that the runes that will be studied next month are RAID-HO and KENAZ. They should prepare by reading the material in the next chapter and follow up as many of the suggestions for further reading and experience as they can. Each person will need to bring a candle in a votive glass to class for the next ritual.

ESTABLISHING SACRED SPACE

Participants stand in a circle, facing the north. Intone the runes, inscribing each rune in the air as it is chanted and turning to the right, so that by the time the whole futhark has been called everyone has turned in a complete circle. The leader may also swing a hammer clockwise above the heads of the participants as a blessing.

ᚠ FEHU	ᚺ HAGALAZ	↑ TIWAZ
ᚢ URUZ	ᚾ NAUDHIZ	ᛒ BERKANO
ᚦ THURISAZ	ᛁ ISA	ᛗ EHWAZ
ᚨ ANSUZ	ᚴ JERA	ᛙ MANNAZ
ᚱ RAIDHO	ᛇ EIHWAZ	ᛚ LAGUZ
ᚲ KENAZ	ᚴ PERTHRO	◇ INGWAZ
✕ GEBO	ᛦ ELHAZ	ᛪ DAGAZ
ᚹ WUNJO	ᛋ SOWILO	ᚯ OTHALA

Elemental Jotnar

Primal Powers, we pray protection—
Kári (COW-ree), we call you, wind of wisdom,
Löge (LOW-geh), now listen, lord of flame,
Ocean-lord, Aegir (EYE-yeer), open your cauldrons,
Ancient Ymir (EE-meer), Earthly essence,
Watch and ward us at our working!

INVOCATIONS

Thor

Redbeard, firebeard, bringer of lightning,
Life-giving stormlord, lover of feasting,
Father of freedom, fighter most doughty,
Donar, defender, dearly we need thee.
Hear us, hero, hasten to help us.
Gifts thy great goats gallop to bring.
Prosper thy people: pour on earth plenty,
Rain in abundance, right for the season!

Odin

High-flying Huginn, hear us now:
Muninn, rememberer, meaning-giver.
Roving ravens, race to aid us:
Wise forever, forgetting never,
Black birds bring us wisdom's words.
Odin, All-father, Önd you have given.

Mind and meaning may we master.
Warden of words and wit and wisdom,
Sacred song and spell inspire us.

WORKING

Spell Casting

(Leader): Hear the words of the High One:
"Then I became fertile   and grew in wisdom,
And waxed and did well:
One word to another   word led on,
One work to another work.

("Hávamál": 141)

I know a third spell   if I should need
To bind my enemies.
I blunt the blades   of those who attack me,
No weapon they have can bite.

("Hávamál": 148)

I know a fourth spell   if men would bind
Bonds upon my limbs,
So well I sing   that I go free,
Fetters fall from my feet,   handcuffs from my wrists."

("Hávamál": 149)

Sing we storms, the spell we utter.
Break the bonds that brought the drought!
*(At this point a signal will be given to the first person to the right
of the celebrants; he or she will read the first of the lines in the
sequence. Moving widdershins about the circle, each person
reads the next line after the person on his or her left has finished
reading. If you don't have enough people, start around the room
again.)*

Version A: To Bring Rain

(by Paul Edwin Zimmer)

(1st Person): Rain . . .
(All): Rain . . . Rain . . .
(Leader turns rain stick, etc.)

(2nd Person): Oh, the rain . . .
(All): Rain . . . Rain . . .
(3rd Person): Wet, cool rain . . .
(All): Rain . . . Rain . . .
(4th Person): Heavy, wet rain . . .
(All): Rain . . . Rain . . .
(5th Person): Sweet rain falling . . .
(All): Rain . . . Rain . . .
(6th Person): Rain falling down . . .
(All): Rain . . . Rain . . .
(7th Person): Rain water falling . . .
(All): Rain . . . Rain . . .
(8th Person): Heavy rain falling down . . .
(All): Rain . . . Rain . . .
(9th Person): Cool, wet rain falling down . . .
(All): Rain . . . Rain . . .
(10th Person): All the rain, heavy rain falling down . . .
(All): Rain . . . Rain . . .
(11th Person): Wet, cool, abundant, the rain falls down . . .
(All): Rain . . . Rain . . .
(12th Person): In sleek, wet sheets the rain falls down . . .
(All): Rain . . . Rain . . .
(13th Person): To the thirsty land, wet, cool rain falls down,
   quenching, cleansing, healing . . .
(All): Rain . . . Rain . . .
(Leader): The rain falls down, to wet the thirsty land.
Open our hearts, that we may understand
The giver, the gift, the storm winds wild.
Come ride rain clouds, Thor, earth's child!
Thunderer come, we call your name!
Our word and will are now the same!
We dance the sacred dance and drum.
Thunder! Thunder! Thunder, come!
(All join hands and dance widdershins, continuing to chant,
"Thunder, Thunder, Thunder, come!")

Version B: To Stop Floods

(by Hilary Ayer)

(Leader): Sing we surcease now,
Spelling the sun to shine.
Balance we bring now, sun with rain.
Let the earth dry not, neither let the earth rot.
Sow for the folk the seed-safe ground.

(At this point a signal will be given to the first person to the right of the celebrants. Moving deasil about the circle, the group calls, and each speaker responds with his line.)

(All): Oh Rain
(1st Person): Fall moderate and timely.
(All): Oh Streams
(2nd Person): Flow ordered in your banks.
(All): Oh Sun.
(3rd Person): Entice our earth to flowering.
(All): Oh Earth
(4th Person): From wet grief refrain.
(All): Oh Thor
(5th Person): Hold thy thunder harmless.
(All): Oh Thor
(6th Person): Let the plowman sow.
(All): Oh Thor
(7th Person): Father of the feasting.
(All): Oh Thor
(8th Person): Fecund earth to flourish,
(All): Oh Thor
(9th Person): Plenty forth to furnish.
(All): Oh Thor
(10th Person): Redbeard, hold thy lightnings.
(All): Oh Thor
(11th Person): Journeyman's companion.
(All): Oh Thor
(12th Person): Batter him no more.
(All): Oh Thor
(13th Person): Light rain to the watersheds.
(All): Oh Thor
(14th Person): Smile at Sunna's coming.
(All): Oh Thor
(15th Person): Bless the land that blooms.
(All): Oh Thor
(16th Person): Set the balance springing.
(All): Oh Thor
(17th Person): Grieve not growth of grain.
(All): Oh Thor
(18th Person): Smile and circle feasting horn.
(All): Oh Thor
(19th Person): Bid thy thunders stay.
(Leader): The sun shines bright to bless the land.

Open our hearts to understand
The giver, the gift, the storm winds wild.
Set floods to flight, great Thor, Earth's child!

MEDITATION

All lights are extinguished except for the candles on the altar. Instruct all participants to arrange themselves comfortably. The person reading the meditation will need a votive or a mini-flashlight to see the text. Read slowly, and allow time for recovery when done.

You are at ease, still and silent,
centered upon the earth.
Breathe in . . . and out . . . in . . . and out . . .
(4 beats in, hold 2, 4 beats out, hold 2)
Let the cares of the world of men be gone.
You are relaxed, at peace, you sit in safety.
Safely you will fare forward, safely you will return,
You will remember all you need to know.

As you relax, feel the solid earth supporting you.
Let your awareness sink downward, inward,
Deep into earth's core . . . now draw it up again.
Fill yourself with its power. . . .

Move out of your body now.
See a place that you know well.
Look at the ground; is it grass or stones?
Feel the texture, hear the sounds around.
As you gaze, you see the beginnings of a path.
Follow it away from the fields you know,
Through bushes that become a woodland,
Woods that turn to forest,
Forest that grows thicker, darker,
Till you go through a tunnel of trunks and branches.

When at last the forest thins,
Before you is a clearing.
In its center grows the greatest of all trees,
So vast you cannot see around it,
So tall it pierces the sky.
Walk around it . . . from its base wind many paths.

The path that draws you leads westward. . . .
(Version A: To Bring Rain)
(Look at this land, this wasteland.
This brown land, baked dry by the heat,
A low lake, with a little water
But much mud.)
(OR Version B: To Stop Floods)
(Look at this land, this wasteland.
Waterlogged hillsides break loose in landslides;
Undercut cliffs collapse,
Muddy waters ruin houses and drown the fields.)

(Continue for both versions.)
Look at the land. What lurks here?
Something unseen shimmers in the air.
West of the wasteland, winds whirl over the sea.
Feel beneath your feet, forces moving.
All around you, empty country
Is filled with forces, felt but not seen.

Now the quest begins. Concentrate:
Hold in your heart the Rune ANSUZ.
Imagine ANSUZ, its image against the sky,
Branches slanting down. See in the blue
Two black dots. They dart in the sky,
Flying on fleet wings to meet you.
Two black-feathered birds, bigger now, nearer—
Nearing, now, night-black they come.
Two black ravens, rapidly
Circling around you,
Flying at your face, flying at your eyes.

Before you can blink, the ravens fly in—
Into your eyes, into your mind—
Weaving patterns of wisdom within your mind.
All things you know . . . all things you remember. . . .
Now see with new eyes: know you can see
Patterns rightly with raven-pierced eyes.
What will you do with your newfound power?
Close one eye now; see with single vision—
Now you know how. New insights fill you.

Look again at the land around you.
See now its secrets. Southward fire-giants lurk.
Strong stone-giants stir beneath the ground.
ANSUZ shows a shape in the shimmer of the sea . . .
Wind thurs, a weather thurs, wildly whirling.
(Version A: To Bring Rain)
(Thirsty this waste where the wind thurs whirls,
Deasil winding, the winds whip northward.
Storm clouds are carried toward the polestar,
Arch away from the coast, bring blizzards to midlands,
A wind thurs, a weather thurs, wildly whirling,
Bearing the blessed rain away from the land.)
(OR Version B: To Stop Floods)
(Sodden this waste where the wind thurs whirls.
A warm current, unwise child,
Loops north along the coast,
Warm air rises, winds whirl widdershins,
Weighted with moisture, eastward they spin—
A wind thurs, a weather thurs, wildly whirling,
Dumping storm-mead to drench the land.)

(Continue for both versions.)
What will you do with your newfound power?
Muninn, the raven of memory remembers
The rune that masters the might of the thurs.
The rune THURISAZ—remember THURISAZ. . . .
Now breathe in breath and power:

Remember Redbeard, the raven asks?
Thor, the Thunderer, thurs-destroyer?
Muninn shows the mighty maker of storms.
Imagine him above you. Asa-Thor!
The great God-form grows above you,
Widdershins or deasil whirling, white with cloud.
Now breathe out moisture, breathe out power.
Fill the God-form with breath and power.
Energy flows from you, filling the God-form.
Grow now, fill the God-form, feel the God-form.
Now gaze through the God's eyes.
Gaze on the weather.

Huginn says, hold out your hand
Grip with the God's hand—grasp the lightning!

Huginn says the hammer holds the power.
Your hand now holds the hammer.
Energy flows, electric, alive with force—

(Version A: To Bring Rain)
(Feel its power crackle, pulling the clouds.
Reach out with the rune, reach out with the hammer.
Reach north, grasp the wind from the north;
Reach south, seize the high wind from the south.
Call the clouds, complete the circuit.
Above the land, blending together,
Two Jet Streams join in a giant THURISAZ.
The Son of Earth rides through the air!
Fire flashes, and water pours!

As you, weather-wise, are yourself again,
Watching pouring water wet the dry grass.
Red-bearded Thor rides the rain-filled clouds,
Thundering over the thirsty land,
Throwing bright lightning.

A horn sounds on high, horsemen in the air,
One-eyed Odin and the Einheriar,
Gallop over gray-black ghostly stormclouds.
Odin and Asa-Thor act together.
You know now your power to help the land.)

(OR Version B: To Stop Floods)
(Spin its power sunwise, into the sea,
THURISAZ . . . thrust that warm current
Back southward,
Down and then westward, along the equator.
Draw down from the north the cold sea waters;
Send El Niño back where he belongs.

The Son of Earth rides through the air!
Fire flashes, and dry winds blow!

As you, weather-wise, are yourself again,
Watching the skies clear and blaze with blue.
Red-bearded Thor banishes the rain-filled clouds,
Thundering over the sodden land,
Throwing bright lightning.

A horn sounds on high, horsemen in the air
Shatter with sharp hooves the gray-black stormclouds,
As one-eyed Odin and the Einheriar
Stride through the sky.
Odin and Asa-Thor act together,
And you act with them.
You know now your power to help the land.)

(Continue for both versions.)
Ahead you see the shining path
Curving around the mighty Tree.
There before you is the way by which you came.
Follow it. Go back through the tunnel of trees.
Come out into the light again.
Look ahead—there is the place that you know.

Sit down, feel the weight of your flesh,
The solid ground below.
Sink down into your body.
Remember what you have learned.
Now breathe in and out, in and out again.
(Read more quickly from here.)
Sigh and stretch. Open your eyes.
You are in the sacred enclosure once more.

THE GIFTS OF THE GODS

Both blessings by Paul Edwin Zimmer.

(Bless mead.)
Invoking the aid of Odin our father
And Bragi the bard-god, the brew of dwarves,
Poetry we pour, the potent drink.
Quaff now this cup of Kvasir's blood,
Remember the roving Rider of Yggdrasil
Stole the stuff to bestow on men.
The gallows-god in Gunnlod's bed
Won the wondrous wine of bards,
And in form of feather flew with the gift,
The magical mead, that men might sing!
Give thanks for the gift to Gauta-Tyr,
And raise now the praise of the Raven-god!
(Pass mead around.)

ᚦ *(Bless bread.)*
The corn is Thor's sister; the rain god must care
For his kin in the cornfield as he flies through the air—
Pour forth, Thor, thy storms,
Let Earth give birth once more!
Let the sweet seed breed in the soil,
Greedily drinking the sinking rain,
Flooding in mud like blood,
Slowly flowing to grow
Full-breasted food for the brood of her nest,
Pour forth thy storms, Thor; cover the Earth,
That our ever young Mother once more may give birth
(Pass bread around.)

RETURNING TO THE WORLD

Thank Gods and Goddesses

Praise to the gods, praise to the goddesses,
Grace be to Earth that givest to all!
Thanks offer Thor, and honor to Odin,
The word and will that ward the world!

Let us now thank the Powers
Which have protected us:

Elementals

Ymir whose body has upheld us,
Aegir, opener of ocean,
Löge, lord of fiery light,
Kári, carrying winds of wisdom,
Jotnar, primal powers protecting,
Be blessed, bright ones, in your domains.

Open Circle

Starting facing north and turning to the left, visualize the rune ring fading
and sinking into the ground. The leader may carry a hammer widdershins
around room, followed by participants.

Chapter 4

RAIDHO / KENAZ:
The Fire Faring

FOR THIS RITE, YOU WILL NEED AN IMAGE of the earth goddess in some kind
of wagon. A Venus of Ullendorf-style image can be modeled in clay or Sculpi
and carried in a toy wagon with a candle; you can carve a stylized head and
pubic triangle onto a piece of wood in the style of Bronze Age images found
in Danish bogs; or you might settle for photocopying a picture of the goddess
and attaching it upright on a flat piece of cardboard with stylized wheels.

You will also need a votive light for everyone in the group if people have not brought their own. The leader should have a drum. The most appropriate food and drink are bread and beer, and pine- or evergreen-scented incense should be burned.

ESTABLISHING SACRED SPACE

Participants stand in a circle, facing the north. Intone the runes, inscribing each rune in the air as it is chanted and turning to the right, so that by the time the whole futhark has been called everyone has turned in a complete circle.

ᚠ FEHU	ᚺ HAGALAZ	↑ TIWAZ
ᚾ URUZ	ᚾ NAUDHIZ	ᛒ BERKANO
ᚦ THURISAZ	ᛁ ISA	ᛗ EHWAZ
ᚨ ANSUZ	ᛃ JERA	ᛗ MANNAZ
ᚱ RAIDHO	ᛇ EIHWAZ	ᛚ LAGUZ
ᚲ KENAZ	ᛕ PERTHRO	◇ INGWAZ
ᚷ GEBO	ᛉ ELHAZ	ᛞ DAGAZ
ᚹ WUNJO	ᛋ SOWILO	ᛟ OTHALA

INVOCATION

"Hail to thee Day, and Day's bright boy,
Hail to the Night and her daughter's joy.
With eyes that bless us may you see
And grant to those here, victory.
The goddesses and gods we call
And holy earth, who gives to all—
Give us here wise words and weal,
And in this life, the hands that heal!"

("Sigdrifumál": 2, freely translated)

MEDITATION

Turn off all lights except what is needed to see the meditation. Read slowly, allowing time for visualizations to build.

You are at ease, still and silent,
Centered upon the earth.
Breathe in . . . and out . . . in . . . and out . . .
(4 beats in, hold 2, 4 beats out, hold 2)
Let the cares of the world of men be gone.
You are relaxed, at peace, you sit in safety.

Safely you will fare forward, safely you will return.
You will remember all you need to know.

As you relax, feel the solid earth supporting you.
Let your awareness sink downward, inward,
Deep into earth's core . . . now draw it up again.
Fill yourself with its power. . . .

Upon the earth you are seated,
In a room in (your state and city),
In the (decade) of the twenty-first century.
You came here in a vehicle.
The food in your belly came from a store;
The cloth you wear was woven in a factory.
You live in a vast city full of people you do not know.
Clocks and calendars define your days.
Harsh lights hurt your eyes.
You wince at the clatter of machines.

But it is time to make a journey now.
Where we go, no car can carry you.
You must summon a steed of the spirit
To ride the road we follow now.
Center yourself,
Let all other images fade;
Call the one who will carry you
From age to age, between the worlds. . . .

Out of the darkness appears
The one that will bear you.
Mount, look about until you see a road,
Glimmering in the darkness.
Follow it.

The electric lights of the city grow fewer.
Pass scattered streetlamps,
Then gaslights' softer glow.
Hooves strike cobblestones with a hollow ring.
You hear the clatter of other horses
Before and behind, on the streets around you,
But mist hides them.
Is this your goal?
This place is still too crowded,
Full of the stink of people and coal fires.
Fare onward.

Now folk move through the streets with lanterns.
In windows you see candelabras of silver.
Streets grow muddy. Houses are fewer.
Candles glimmer through uneven glass.
Wood smoke scents the air
As you move through a town,
But the surrounding countryside
Is dark beneath starlight.
Through farmstead doors
You see great hearths' red glow.
Rushlights gutter on tables.
The road is rutted by wooden wheels.
Is this your goal?
These folk huddle together, afraid of the darkness,
Afraid to speak their minds.

Ever greater and darker grows the landscape.
Homes are smaller, fewer;
The path narrower, rougher.
Little lights glitter bravely in the night.
Easy to get lost here.
In the distance another horse whinnies;
You see the shadows of other riders.
Do they know where they're going?
Are they on the same road?
You urge your mount toward them,
But they disappear.
You must continue on alone.
What are you seeking?
What is your true path and where does it lead?
Move onward, ever onward, seeking your own way.

A chill wind ruffles your clothes,
Bringing scents of woods and sea.
You ride in a wilderness of evergreens,
Striving to see through shadows,
Shivering at a wolf's long howl.
And then, at last, light glows between tree trunks.
The path widens; ahead are houses
Stoutly built of logs.
In the open space between them burns a bonfire.
Lights flicker in the forest.
From every direction, folk are coming.
Torch flame streams upward upon the cold air.

At last you can clearly see your fellow wanderers.
No longer are you alone.
You hear hoofbeats and the creaking of wagons.
Dark shapes of carts and riders
Are emerging from among the trees.

Only you are light-less.
Pause, reach out to the nearest tree,
Ask for a branch, that you too may have fire.
The wood comes free in your hand,
Rough-barked, the end a knot sticky with pitch.
The sharp scent fills the air.
Faster, you move forward.
Now folk are all around you.
They wear homespun, furs, and leather—
Their appearance is strange, but you know them.
The houses are rough, the forest wild,
But the place feels like home.
Is this where the road has been leading you?
Something still is missing—

(Drumbeat begins.)

A distant drumbeat grows ever louder. . . .
In the forest firelight is glowing;
Around the bonfire people gather.
Down the road from the north come flaming torches;
Sounds of rejoicing clearly carry.
On the highroad hoofbeats rattle;
Wagon wheels rumble, folk cry welcome!
Rush forward with the others
As the cart comes out of the darkness.
The goddess is in it, the world she has circled—
She is the turning earth and the wheel
And the trees and the flame.

(Light quarter candles, candle on cart, other candles around room.)

To this moment, to this place,
Your road has brought you.
Sink down into your body now and open your eyes.
This is earth's heart, where we welcome Nerthus,
The sacred center where past and present are one.

VISIT OF THE GODS

With royal rider round the circle
Rolls the sun wheel's sacred wagon!
Our Mother makes her way to meet us,
With fire and feasting make Her welcome!

(All): We ride the road to reach the center,
Between the worlds we wind the way,
Gather the kindred to light the torches
Kinsmen kindle the fire today!

(The drum continues to keep rhythm for chanting as the cart is carried around. As the cart reaches each one, the leader lights his/her votive from the candle with a taper.)

(Leader): Child of Earth, receive the holy fire!

The wagon is carried around the circle and replaced in front of the altar. The following song may also be sung here, or during the feast.

Festal Day

(All): 1. Oh the holy gods are coming
For their high festal day;
Merry meeting, joyful greeting
As their cart wends this way!
And the people are all singing
As the torches blaze high;
What rejoicing they are voicing
To the earth and the sky!
(Solo): The fertile land lies waiting
For the sun and the rain;
The empty heart is hoping
To find love once again!

2. Now the gods a gift of gladness
With their bounty bestow,
Fortune finding, and unbinding
Teach each seed how to grow!
And the sun and moon together
Join the stars in their play;
Light is blazing, all amazing
'Til the world learns the way!

The holy fire of life is lit
Inside every heart;
And it will burn within us
Though the gods may depart!

Oh the holy gods are coming for their high festal day, merry meeting, joyful greeting, as the gods wend this way! And the peo- ple are all sing -ing, as the torches blaze high; what re - joi - cing they are voi - cing to the earth and the sky! The fer - tile land lies waiting for the sun and the rain; the empty heart is hoping to find love once a-gain! (instrumental accent)

FIRE MAGIC

What is the knowledge you have need of?
What is the bane that you would burn?
In flickering fire find now the image—
Focus on the flame . . . let the torch transform it!

(All gaze into their candle flames and summon the image of the thing to be illuminated or changed. Drum beats steadily.)

FEAST

By many roads we have traveled to reach this place.
But we are all children of one mother.
Let us rejoice in the kinship she has kindled!
Behold the blessed beer,
(Bless beer. ᚲ*)*
The spirit of life,
Whose fire enlivens the hearts of humankind.
Behold the holy harvest, *(Bless bread.* ᚠ*)*
The bread of life,
Whose fuel warms the bodies of humankind.

RETURNING TO THE PRESENT DAY

It is time now for us to return to the world
From which we came.
Close your eyes.
See in your mind's eye the bonfire in the forest.
Now remember the villages and farmsteads,
The cities lit by candles,
Streetlamps, gaslights . . . and finally,
The electric lights of the present day.
Thank the steed that has carried you.
Sit down, feel the weight of your flesh,
The solid ground below.
You are in (city and state)
In the twenty-first century.
Sink down into your body.
Remember what you have learned.
Now breathe in and out, in and out again.
(Read more quickly from here.)
Sigh and stretch. Open your eyes.
You are in our hall once more.

Thank the Powers

Now let us thank the Powers
That have protected us—
Aesir, Asynjur, receive our honor.

Open Circle

*Starting facing north and turning to the left, visualize the rune
ring fading and sinking into the ground.*

Chapter 5

GEBO / WUNJO: The Gift of Joy

THIS RITE IS BASED ON THE MINNISVEIG. The version here retains the basic pattern of sharing the horn, but only a few of the gods (those with whom your study of the first eight runes has already made you familiar) are honored. If you have more time, others can be added, with invocations in the style given here. Rounds can also be drunk in honor of ancient heroes and departed friends.

The procedure for a sumbel is essentially a very simple one. After the space has been hallowed by calling the rune ring, the meditation sets the scene. Participants then fill their plates, and the invocations begin, starting with Mother Earth.

The usual drink provided is mead or beer; however, actual alcohol does not seem to be essential for the ritual—I have experienced remarkable effects in a minnisveig in which all we drank was Martinelli's Sparkling Cider. The horn that has been hallowed to the gods acquires its own charge of energy, and the resulting "high" is quite distinct from the usual effects of booze. Gundarsson reports that with the proper spells, spring water will do as well!

As the horn comes to each person, he or she may add a new prayer, invocation, or vow, or simply bless the horn and lift it in honor of the god before drinking. While the horn is going around, everyone else is silent. Take this opportunity to open your awareness to the power being honored. Visualize the deity. As the horn goes around, carry on your own conversation with him or her in your heart. At a certain point in the proceedings (different for each person), you may experience a change in consciousness, and taste the joy of being in the presence of the gods. This may not happen the first time you try this. The more you learn about the gods you are invoking the better it works, and the faster you can focus on the task at hand.

In this version of the rite, Heimdall is invoked after Mother Earth as Guardian of the Way. His welcome is followed by an invocation to Freyr and Freyja. After the first prayer, embrace the person on your left and on your right, seeing them as images of the god or goddess of love and life force. Put some energy into the exchange. At this point also the wagon or basket full of gifts is carried around, and each one takes something. The gifts do not have to be expensive, but they should be appropriate—a votive candle in a glass, for instance, or a cloth or leather bag suitable for holding runes.

The next invocation is to Thor, as giver of strength and "good" weather. Bring in his vital energy, and after the horn goes by, exchange the grip of strength with your neighbor, right arm clasping right arm, and left arm the left so that they cross. Stand for a moment, braced and solid, feeling the god's power. The final invocation in this sequence is to Odin, giver of ecstasy. As the horn goes around, think about the gifts that he has given—spirit, the mead of inspiration, the runes. After the horn, the leader of the group should carry around a bowl with the runes in it. Each person draws a rune as Odin's gift. If necessary, read ahead in the book to interpret the rune.

If you have time, other deities can be added. Otherwise, finish by thanking all the deities and powers invoked for their presence, and opening the circle. It is advisable to have additional food available for grounding afterward.

When a full-scale feast is planned, one may set up separate altars for the gods around the room, usually consisting of a piece of cloth, a votive candle, an image or picture if available, and a small glass and plate on which to place offerings. People eat as the horns go around, and take bits of food to the appropriate altars as they feel inspired. In a really large group, it may be better for each one to raise his own horn in toast as the invocation is offered, adding his own prayers simultaneously or silently before drinking, and spending a few moments in contemplation. Invocations to fifteen or so gods with a group of as many people can take a long time.

To perform the rite, you will need at least one large goblet or drinking horn. Large cow horns, which can be made into drinking horns by sanding and, if the interior is still rough, lining the inside with melted paraffin, can be purchased at Tandy Leather stores. Finished drinking horns are often available at events of the Society for Creative Anachronism. Sources for horns may also be found online.

To fill the horn, you will want the equivalent of a bottle of beer (or two-thirds of a bottle of wine) for each round. The exact amount depends on the number of people (if the goblet is small, you may have to refill halfway around) and the size of the horn. Three bottles of Martinelli's, for instance, will serve a dozen people invoking seven gods. Gifts may be carried in a child's wagon covered with a cloth, or in a big basket. It will be easier to draw the runes from a bowl or cup than from a bag.

ESTABLISHING SACRED SPACE

Participants stand in a circle, facing the north. Intone the runes, inscribing each rune in the air as it is chanted and turning to the right, so that by the time the whole futhark has been called everyone has turned in a complete circle.

ᚠ FEHU	ᚺ HAGALAZ	↑ TIWAZ
ᚢ URUZ	ᚾ NAUDHIZ	ᛒ BERKANO
ᚦ THURISAZ	I ISA	ᛗ EHWAZ
ᚠ ANSUZ	ᚴ JERA	ᛗ MANNAZ
ᚱ RAIDHO	ᛇ EIHWAZ	ᚱ LAGUZ
ᚲ KENAZ	ᛈ PERTHRO	◇ INGWAZ
✕ GEBO	ᛉ ELHAZ	ᛞ DAGAZ
ᚹ WUNJO	ᛋ SOWILO	ᛉ OTHALA

MEDITATION

The meditation is read at the beginning of the ritual to establish the mood and context for the sumbel.

Sink down upon the strong support
Of Earth, our Mother.
Secure upon her breast,
Breathe in . . . and out . . . in . . . and out . . .

She is solid and secure, but you are alone here.
Look around you; you are lost,
And the land is barren and strange.
From the corners of your eyes,
You see menacing shapes.
You ready yourself to face them—
Alone and lonely.
Bare is brotherless back. But who will aid you?

Another human form appears. Who is it?
A friend? A lover?
It is a companion you can trust.
The strange shapes recoil.
You have never been so glad
To see anyone in your life.
You want to express your gladness,
But what gift can you give your companion?

Do you have anything?
Reach into your heart for the proper gift.
Stretch out your hand now, and as you do so,
Your companion reaches toward you.
Your arms cross, and there is a gift for you.
What is it?
Something you know only now that you needed!
A gift of freedom freely given!
These crossed lines link your lives;
These lines link lovers.
These are links of love and loyalty.
You go on together. The half-glimpsed foes flee.
Together you may win wealth,
Wander through the winter's wonder.

The lines that link you lead on to a high hall
Blazing with light and warmth.
You win your way there to the warm hearth,
To the place of wealth and wine and welcome.
Warm heart, know well, here are others linked by WUNJO.

Sink back into yourself now, and open your eyes.
Breathe in and out and in and out again.
Let that hall become this hall,
And those inner allies, one with this company.
(Turn to feasting table.)
Brothers, behold the bounds of being.
Sisters, see the sacred center.
As Aegir ale brewed for the Aesir,
As Hár bore magic mead to Midgard,
These gifts we give back to the holy gods.

(Inscribe GEBO rune ✕ over food and drink, then invite all participants to fill their plates and take their seats again. They may eat between invocations, while the horn is going around.)

SUMBEL

After each invocation, the horn is passed around. Each person adds an appropriate prayer, expressing gratitude for gifts received, and if so inspired, pledging offerings, or simply lifting the horn in salute. When the horn returns to the invoker, he or she pours out the remainder into the offering bowl. If time allows, additional gods and goddesses may be honored as well.

To Earth

Erce, Erce, Erce, Eorthan Modir,
Rooted, we reach for ancient wisdom;
Strength we draw from sacred soil.
Nerthus, now our need is near us,
Honor we offer—a holy harvest.
Bring forth in beauty, Bride and Mother—
Goodly gifts for the kin of Ríg,
Mother Earth, we hail thee!

(Make offering to hearth, send bread and salt around circle.)

To Heimdall

Odin's offspring by Aegir's daughters,
Royal Ríg, we hold thee dear.
Come to bless your children's children.
Heimdall, hearken to us here!

*(Heimdall may be invoked as Guardian of the Gate who opens the
way to the gods, as Defender of Freyja, as Watcher of the Gods
who sees and hears all, as son of the nine waves, as the Ram, and
especially as Father of Humankind.)*

To Freyr and Freyja

Lord and Lady, loudly we call you,
Fertile Freyr and Freyja, brother and bride.
Luck-bringers, lustily giving Earth goodness,
Hear us as we hail you, hither to help us!
Grateful, our gifts to the givers we offer—
Wunjo's wonder we exchange.
In man and maid we make you welcome.
Join us in Joy, fair Lord and Lady!

*(Invoke Freyja as Lady of Love, luck, prosperity, etc., and Gefion
the Giver; Freyr, as Lord of Love, luck, fertility, and commerce,
Giver of Peace and good seasons. Embrace the Lord and Lady on
your left and right. Take a gift as the wagon rolls around the
circle.)*

To Thor

Redbeard, firebeard, bringer of Lightning,
Life-giving stormlord, lover of feasting,
Father of freedom, fighter most doughty,
Donar, defender, dearly we need thee.
Hear us now, hero, hasten to help us.
Gifts thy great goats gallop to bring.
Prosper thy people: pour on earth plenty,
Rain as is needed, right for the season!

*(Invoke Thor as protector against danger, giver of physical
strength, and bringer of rain and sunshine. Ask for enough rain.
After the horn goes by, clasp crossed arms with the next person in
an exchange of strength.)*

To Frigga

Frigga, fair one, fate all-knowing,
Bright is thy beauty as the white birch tree.
Wyrd the Norns spin, wisely weaving,
Queen over Asgard, in thy arms Allfather lies.
Twelve mighty maidens circle about thee,
Torches bright around a hearthfire,
Rivers flowing from a well:
Radiant lady, ram-cart riding,
Bless the mother and the maiden,
The new-born babe, the blood of women.
Mother of Mysteries, make us wise!

(Invoke Frigga as All-mother, queen of the gods, source of wisdom and love, guardian of the home, sacred center from whom we draw serenity.)

To Odin

Odin, Oski, Wotan, Wunjo!
Of all that lives, the truest lover,
Sender of Önd, thyself once offered,
Greatest of gifts and greatest giver,
Now open Othroerir's ecstasy:
Rider of Yggdrasil, Runes releasing,
Bragi's brew on bards bestowing,
To thy delight let us drink deeply—
All-father, to our feast be welcome!

(Invoke Odin as Giver of the Runes, of the Poetic Mead, and of Ecstasy. Call him Oski, Fulfiller of Desire, and Wunsch—Wishlord. Pass the rune cup around after the horn, and let each one draw a rune for the next person in the circle. After the horn has gone completely around, allow a few moments of silent contemplation in which to savor the bliss of the presence of the gods.)

RETURNING TO THE WORLD

Thank Gods, Directions

The food is finished, horns are emptied.
The time comes for our feast's conclusion.
Hail to you, Aesir, Hail Asynjur,
All whom we welcomed here with gladness,

(Name all the gods who have been invoked at the sumbel.)

We thank you now for bestowing blessings.

Open Circle

Starting facing north and turning to the left, visualize the rune ring fading and sinking into the ground.

Chapter 6

HAGALAZ / NAUDHIZ: Needfire

THIS RITUAL DRAMATIZES THE EXPERIENCE of cold and heat and the lighting of the needfire, followed by a meeting with the three Norns. To perform
the complete ritual as written, you will need the following:

- Fire drill (bow, spindle, fireboard, hand piece, sawdust, dry wood, shavings, kindling), matches
- Fireplace or hibachi and wood for a fire
- Candle
- Cauldron or metal pot draped in cloth
- A piece of dry ice
- Bottle of water
- A clean fireplace poker
- Drum
- White ice cream or sherbet
- Mulled cider, spices
- Paper cups, bowls, spoons
- Runes, rune bowl

The rune bowl should be set on the altar, which might be decorated with three stones to represent the Norns, a quartz crystal for HAGALAZ, and a spindle (of the kind used in spinning wool) for NAUDHIZ. Set chairs for the Norns behind it.

Select a firemaker and someone to assist him or her, a drummer (if not the leader), and three women to represent the Norns. The leader's role can also be divided between a priest and a priestess. With fewer participants, you may decide to scale down the ceremony. For instance, you can skip the needfire and dry ice (although when carried off successfully, they are extremely effective), and begin the ritual with the words "Fire thaws freeze" while the leader carries a candle around the circle. A single priestess could give the blessing of all three Norns, though it is more effective with three people.

Participants should get as cold as possible before starting the ritual (open windows, take off coats, etc.). While the ice cubes are being passed around, the firemaker gets ready to use the drill. Ideally, he or she will succeed in lighting a fire with it, but this is a difficult operation and cannot be allowed to hold up the ritual. The firemaker and the leader should agree beforehand how long to spend trying for a flame. If the fire is not lit in ten or fifteen minutes, the assistant should unobtrusively strike a match to help things along (perhaps a paper match inscribed with ᚾ!).

ESTABLISHING SACRED SPACE

Participants stand in a circle, facing the north. Intone the runes, inscribing each rune in the air as it is chanted and turning to the right, so that by the time the whole futhark has been called everyone has turned in a complete circle.

ᚠ FEHU	ᚺ HAGALAZ	ᛏ TIWAZ
ᚢ URUZ	ᚾ NAUDHIZ	ᛒ BERKANO
ᚦ THURISAZ	ᛁ ISA	ᛖ EHWAZ
ᚨ ANSUZ	ᛃ JERA	ᛗ MANNAZ
ᚱ RAIDHO	ᛇ EIHWAZ	ᛚ LAGUZ
ᚲ KENAZ	ᛈ PERTHRO	ᛜ INGWAZ
ᚷ GEBO	ᛉ ELHAZ	ᛞ DAGAZ
ᚹ WUNJO	ᛋ SOWILO	ᛟ OTHALA

MAKING NEEDFIRE

(The following was provided by Leigh Ann Hussey.)
>Storm wind sets us all a-shiver.
>Ice-seeds strike cold through our bones. —

>(Pass ice cubes in a metal bowl around the circle; each one holds a cube or feels the bottom of the bowl until he or she feels cold. Intone "Ha-ga-laz. . . .")

>Feel the frigid ice enfolding . . .
>Where shall we find a fire to free us?

>(The firemaker begins sawing with bow and drill; the drummer starts a slow beat, which gradually quickens, climaxing after about ten minutes or when the fire is lit. If necessary, use a match!)

>NAUDHIZ, NAUDHIZ, now we need thee!
>Needfire force the way to freedom!

>(While firemaker is working, all sing the following chant.)
>Spin, spindle, spin; to end is to begin.
>Spiral winds the wyrd yarn,
>Dying is being born.
>Spin, spindle, spin . . .

Spin, spindle, spin, to end is to begin,

Spiral winds the wyrd yarn, dying is a being born.

(After ten minutes or as fire is being lit in the hearth or hibachi, all may simply chant, NAUDHIZ, NAUDHIZ, etc.! The firemaker lights a candle from the flame and carries it to the cauldron as the leader pours water over the dry ice to create a fog, OR you can carry the candle and a lump of ice or quartz crystal around the room.)

Fire thaws freeze; ice fixes flame,
Waxed the world in this wise.
Fixing and flowing all things form;
So work we this world from the worlds.
(The firemaker carries the candle around circle. Then all put on cloaks, jackets, etc. to warm up.)

MEDITATION

Read the meditation slowly, allowing time for visualizations to build.

Now we are met and our sanctuary hallowed,
So let us seek the realms within.

You are at ease, still and silent,
Centered upon the earth.
Breathe in . . . and out . . . in . . . and out . . .
(4 beats in, hold 2, 4 beats out, hold 2)
Let the cares of the world of men be gone.
You are relaxed, at peace, you sit in safety.
Safely you will fare forward, safely you will return.
You will remember all you need to know.

As you relax, feel the solid earth supporting you.
Let your awareness sink downward, inward,
Deep into earth's core . . . now draw it up again.
Fill yourself with its power. . . .

Move out of your body now.
See a place that you know well.
Look at the ground; is it grass or stones?
Feel the texture, hear the sounds around.
As you gaze, you see the beginnings of a path.
Follow it away from the fields you know,
Through bushes that become a woodland,
Woods that turn to forest,
Forest that grows thicker, darker,
Till you are walking through a tunnel made of trees.

When at last the forest thins,
Before you is a clearing.
In its center grows the greatest of all trees,
So vast you cannot see around it,
So tall it pierces the sky.
Walk around it . . . from its base wind many paths.
Move north and eastward.
Look around you. All the world is white,
Snow everywhere, the sky white with clouds.
And the air beneath the clouds—is that white too?
You shiver in the cold. Your breath, too, is white.
The cold crawls into your white bones;
Your white teeth chatter.

You feel frost forming in your lungs.
Something hits your head, hard.
Another blow, and another!
Something stings your forehead as it glances off.
And as you throw your arms up to shield your face,
Something strikes bare skin and sears it with cold.
Hail is falling all around you,
So cold that it burns your skin.
Stones big as eggs batter you as you run
Blindly through churning white blindness,
Trying to escape.

You look for shelter;
You see a shattered tree broken into kindling.
Seize a great flat piece like a board
And hold it over your head as you run:
It drums in the hail.
Branches and strips of bark cling to it.

Even with this, you cannot stand still:
If you stand, you will freeze to a statue.
Running makes the blood move,
Makes the heart pound,
Builds fire in the blood to warm you.
Ahead you hear a roaring.
Hail is rebounding from something,
Though there is nothing but whiteness to be seen.
But there, whiteness moves—
Piles of hail shivering and stirring—
The hail leaps back from a cliff of ice.
Turn, run along the edge; run, through roaring white.
At last you hear, more than see, a cave in the cliff.
The hollow echoes the clamor around you.
Follow your ears through blind brightness
Into the cave.
The drumming above your head stops,
Darkness rests your eyes,
But you are still cold. A freezing breath chills you.
Something cold moves in the dark.
You must have light!
You must have warmth! You must have FIRE!

With fumbling fingers you fashion a fire drill,
Whittle a point on the tree branch, set it into soft bark
Where dry moss grew on the living log.
Twist your bowstring around it
And cap it with a piece of bark.
Draw the bow across the plane of the drill
Till it turns like a spindle.
Again . . . and again . . . the task seems endless. . . .
You are spinning the stick,
You are spinning the spindle.
You are spinning for yourself a future. . . .
The bow draws the image of NAUDHIZ;
The friction of your Need will kindle the flame.

And now, at last
A pale thread of smoke twines upward!
You scent scorched wood, and there—
A spark—blinks for a moment in the dark.
It fades, but you have hope now.
Faster and faster you spin.

The spark blinks again, your breath fans it.
A finger flicks moss and it grows!
Now drill and log both become fuel for the baby flame.

Trolls and etins gather.
Their freezing breath chills you,
But the fire grows, and they flee.
The fire grows, and you begin to warm.
Now you can see the drifted hailstones
At the mouth of the cave.
Pick up one of them.
Hold it up and see the six crossed planes
Of the crystalline form—
The shape of HAGALAZ!
Turn it on edge and see the "H" form
In the ice layered there.

Now it is so hot
That the icy walls of the cave itself are melting.
In the back wall the ice grows thin and clear—
And now it melts away and you can see . . .
Darkness beyond. . . . Is that black gap
A consuming maw or welcoming door?
The cave plunges deep into Earth's body;
The place where you sit is only an entry.
A vast cavern opens below you,
Lit by a glimmer of reflected flame
That shows the shapes of three dark figures there.
From the hand of one dangles a rod
That spins like your fire drill,
But from its shaft a thread is forming. . . .
This is the thread of your life.
Look at it, and remember all the strands
That have been twisted together
To make you who you are. . . .

A second figure takes up the thread
And measures it out.
This is the thread of your life.
Look at it, and see the shape of your life now. . . .

A third figure cuts it.
This is the thread of your life.
Look at it and understand your true way—

The purpose for which past and present
Are preparing you. . . .
Now they look up. They see you. You hear them. . . .

(1st speaker): Who is the shaft that whirls life and light
    into being?
(2nd speaker): Who is the answer to the riddle that you
    must solve?
(3rd speaker): Who is the crossroad where all paths
    meet and diverge once more?
(All three): I am. I am. I am. Come in who dares. . . .

Dare the darkness. Go down into the cave.
The third figure holds out your measure,
Glowing faintly in the gloom.
Take it. Your fate is in your own hands.
Your life is in your control now.
Take it into your being.
Let this knowledge be part of you.
Guard it safely. Use it well.

Now light grows behind you.
Turn and make your way back out of the cave.
Everywhere, the ice is melting.
Green things spring up through the drifted hailstones.
The land rejoices beneath a lovely sun.

Make your way through the meadows.
The path you follow curves.
You see the great Tree once more.
You have been walking around it.
There before you is the path by which you came.
Follow it. Go back through the tunnel of trees.
Come out into the light again.
Look ahead—there is the place that you know.

Sit down, feel the weight of your flesh,
The solid ground below.
Sink down into your body.
Remember what you have learned.
Now breathe in and out, in and out again.
(Read more quickly from here.)
Sigh and stretch. Open your eyes.
You are in the sacred enclosure once more.

CHANGING FATE

Ye who have faced your fates,
Know now the need that drives you.
HAGALAZ hallows all hard destinies.
Will you demand the doom that will transform you?

(All): We Will.
'Tis time to sing at the Seat of Thul,
At the well of Urdh to welcome wisdom.
Norns now we summon, need is upon us,
To foresee what fate has fashioned—
What has been, what is being, and becoming.
Be there truth in our seeing, truth in our saying,
Understanding in the ears that hear!
Bestowers of blessings,
From our words breed good fortune.

(Urdh): I am the shaft that whirls life and light into being.
I am the Fate that found you when you were born.
I am all that you have been. . . .

(Rises, makes the ᛉ rune over the circle.)

(Verdandi): I am the answer to the riddle that you must solve.
My Being is the Web into which you are woven.
I am what you are now. . . .

(Rises, makes the ᛉ rune over the circle.)

(Skuld): I am the crossroad where all paths meet
And diverge once more.
I am the Necessity that drives you forward.
I am what you shall be. . . .

(Rises, makes the ᛉ rune over the circle.)

(All): Light the fire and cast the spell,
Read the runes of fortune well.
What we need the Nornir know.
Change and chance and choice now show!

Light the fire and cast the spell, read the runes of fortune well.
What we need, the Nor - nir know.... Chance and change and
choice now show....

*(As all chant or intone the runes, the leader or Norns move
around the circle with the runes. The leader offers the rune cup.
Each person asks "What do I need to change?" and draws a rune.
The leader names and interprets it.)*

FEAST

(Assistant brings in ice cream.)
**Audhumla it was who in ancient days
Licked life into the ice-locked world.
Her sweet milk, spreading on the snow
Is holy food for Hagalaz.**
*(Dish ice cream into bowls and pass it around. Assistant brings in
mulled cider.)*

**The needfire flares, the ice is melted.
Thus—the flaming rod transforms it!**
(Thrust hot poker into pot.)

**Fire and water well are wedded.
This drink delights the wight who downs it.**
(Ladle cider into cups and pass it around.)

RETURNING TO THE WORLD

Thank Powers

**Nornir, now comes the time for leaving.
Fare well we bid and beg your blessing—**

Urdh:
With the blessing of Fate
I bless you — ᛣ
May you make peace with what is past.

Verdandi:
With the blessing of Being
I bless you — ᛣ
May your hearts be opened to That Which Is.

Skuld:
With the blessing of Necessity
I bless you — ᛣ
May you follow your bliss.

Open Circle

Starting facing north and turning to the left, visualize the rune ring fading
and sinking into the ground.

Chapter 7

ISA / JERA:
Melting the Ice

THE RITUAL FOR ISA AND JERA INVOKES the forces of winter and summer
and explores the Old Norse myth of the world's creation in the interaction
of primal elements. It is interesting to consider ways in which this story
might serve as a metaphor to express the process of cosmic evolution as
hypothesized by scientists. Certainly the encounter between the cold of
Niflheim and the fires of Muspel suggests the chemical reactions that led
to the evolution of the planetary surface and its atmosphere. Thorsson's

mystical interpretations of this process in *Futhark* are also worth considering.

Once the process of creation has begun, however, the forces of ice and fire must exist in equilibrium. Achieving this balance is the focus of the ritual. Before beginning, divide participants into "Winterspeakers" and "Summerspeakers," either by splitting the north and south sides of the room, or by having all those born between October and April be Winterspeakers, and between April and October Summerspeakers.

For the ceremony you will need:

- A copy of the Younger Edda

- A bowl of ice chips

- A warm moist washcloth

- Candles

- A pitcher of milk

- Bread

- A basket of golden apples

You may decorate the altar with green and bare branches.

ESTABLISHING SACRED SPACE

Participants stand in a circle, facing the north. Intone the runes, inscribing each rune in the air as it is chanted and turning to the right, so that by the time the whole futhark has been called everyone has turned in a complete circle.

ᚠ FEHU	ᚺ HAGALAZ	ᛏ TIWAZ
ᚢ URUZ	ᚾ NAUDHIZ	ᛒ BERKANO
ᚦ THURISAZ	ᛁ ISA	ᛖ EHWAZ
ᚨ ANSUZ	ᛃ JERA	ᛗ MANNAZ
ᚱ RAIDHO	ᛇ EIHWAZ	ᛚ LAGUZ
ᚲ KENAZ	ᛈ PERTHRO	ᛜ INGWAZ
ᚷ GEBO	ᛉ ELHAZ	ᛞ DAGAZ
ᚹ WUNJO	ᛋ SOWILO	ᛟ OTHALA

THE CREATION OF THE WORLD

The powers to whom we pray are present;
In Midgard may we meet them all.
Between the worlds to wend our way,
We gather here in hallowed hall.

Hear how the gods answered Gangleri
When he asked about the Creation:

*(Reader reads the description of creation at the beginning of the
"Deluding of Gylfi" in the Younger Edda from "Just-as-high said:
'That part of Ginnungagap which turned northwards. . ." to "The
man was called Ask and the woman Embla, and from them have
sprung the races of men who were given Midgard to live in.")*

MEDITATION

Pass around a bowl of ice chips, and this time, tell everyone to take and keep
one. Read slowly, allowing time for visualizations to build.

You are at ease, still and silent,
Centered upon the earth.
Breathe in . . . and out . . . in . . . and out . . .
(4 beats in, hold 2, 4 beats out, hold 2)
Let the cares of the world of men be gone.
You are relaxed, at peace, you sit in safety.
Safely you will fare forward, safely you will return.
You will remember all you need to know.

As you relax, feel the solid earth supporting you.
Let your awareness sink downward, inward,
Deep into earth's core . . . now draw it up again,
Fill yourself with its power. . . .

Move out of your body now.
See a place that you know well.
Look at the ground; is it grass or stones?
Feel the texture, hear the sounds around.
As you gaze, you see the beginnings of a path.
Follow it away from the fields you know,
Through bushes that become a woodland,
Woods that turn to forest,
Forest that grows thicker, darker,
Till you are walking through a tunnel made of trees.

When at last the forest thins,
Before you is a clearing.
In its center grows the greatest of all trees,
So vast you cannot see around it,

So tall it pierces the sky.
Walk around it . . . from its base wind many paths.
The path that draws you leads northward.
Cold mist swirls around you.
A drizzle of icy drops is congealing from the air;
From your lips you lick salty rime.
As it strikes the path the moisture freezes.
Frost crunches beneath your feet,
But still you go onward.
Colder and colder it grows.
In the air ice crystals hang suspended.
A white wall stretches before you
As far as you can see.
Look around you—
Whiteness overwhelms the world. . . .

This is the primal ice; you have touched it before.
Ice surrounds you, the ice is within you.
You cannot move, you do not wish to—
You are without motion, without volition,
Without desire. . . .

Your eyes are blinded by this cold radiance;
Your ears are deafened by a silence
Louder than sound.
Here is no need for striving,
Nothing for senses to perceive.
In this stillness, awareness of all else falls away. . . .

Now, you have only to BE. . . .
You are yourself, the essential "I."
Nothing and no one do you need. . . .

What would Another be like?
Stuck in stillness, is there anything to desire?
Knowing Nothing, can you ask for motion?
Only by act of will can you do it,
When you know no need.
In the center of your silence, ask for change. . . .

Time passes—that is new.
Time passes, and something is different.
You can feel your face—the ice is melting.

You shudder with awareness
As a warm, rough tongue scours the ice away.
Inch by inch your form is uncovered.
Your head emerges; once more you can see and hear.
Shoulders and torso, arms and hands and fingers,
That huge warm tongue licks warmth back into you.
Now you can sense once more
The shape of your body.
The warmth of that mother tongue recreates you—
Thighs are freed, calves and feet unfrozen.
Where the moist breath blows, the hoarfrost is melted.
You stand upright,
Whole and perfect in form and function.
All around you,
The dark earth is becoming hazed with green.
To the south great fires are burning;
Heat blazes before you; behind you cold chills.

As you turn from one to the other
Your body is balanced.
You are the model of humankind, newly created.
Stillness and motion, warmth and primal ice,
All the turning world is potential in you.

You see the ice behind you and the world before,
The paths and the Tree,
And the road that leads homeward.
Breathe in, and out. Stretch your newborn body.
You are at the center of all the worlds.

Now open your eyes. . . . Stand . . .
And face the others. . . .

THE YEAR WHEEL TURNS

The priest or priestess goes around the circle, wiping everyone's hands with
a warm washcloth. The drummer begins a slow rhythm as he or she helps
each one to stand up, and positions half the group at one end of the room,
half at the other. The group forms two lines, facing each other.

(Winterspeakers): I am the winter, worst of all seasons!
—Enthralling the earth in endless ice—
No strife of men disturbs my stillness,
The world's preserved in pristine peace.
(Summerspeakers): I am the summer, fairest of seasons!
I am the warmth that remakes the world!
Growth and gladness are my glory,
To hearten men, a harvest hoard!
(Winterspeakers): Children of Löge, my ice will freeze you—
(Summerspeakers): Food of Audhumla, my fire will ease you—
(Leader): Listen! There is no reward in this warfare!
Separate, summer and winter both suffer—
Only in motion shall each find expression—
Warmth and cold turning on the wheel of the year!

*(The leader leads the winter line to join the summer line, leads
them in a spiral that becomes a circle as all sing the following
chant by Deborah Bender to the tune of "Hi Ho, Anybody Home?")*

(All): Sun come, Moon come,
Seed time, dry time, fog and rain,
Sowing, growing, reaping, resting,
Sun come, Moon come, etc . . .

Sun come, moon come, seed-time, dry-time, fog and rain,
sow-ing, grow-ing, rea-ping, res-ting, sun come, moon come etc.

(When the dance is done, all are seated.)

FEAST

The following was provided by Laurel Mendes.

Behold the milk of Audhumla,
(Pour milk into horn. ♫)
Who licks life from the primal ice
And nourishes the world!
(Pass it around circle.)

Behold the holy harvest,
(Hold up round bread. 𝄍)
The bread of life
That puts heat in the bodies of men!
(Pass it around circle.)

Behold the apples of Idunna,
(Hold up basket of apples. 𝄎)
Ripened riches, youth restoring!
(Pass it around circle.)

(All): The blossom becomes the fruit
Becomes the seed, becomes the tree . . .

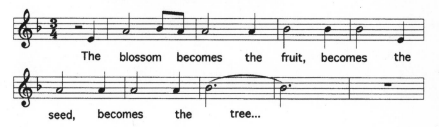

The   blossom   becomes   the   fruit,   becomes   the

seed,   becomes   the   tree...

RETURNING TO THE WORLD

For a moment, close your eyes.
The ice is behind you, and the world before,
Bright and blossoming.
The Tree is behind you.
There before you is the path by which you came.
Follow it. Go back through the tunnel of trees.
Come out into the light again.
Look ahead—there is the place that you know.

Sit down, feel the weight of your flesh,
The solid ground below.
Sink down into your body.
Remember what you have learned.
Now breathe in and out, in and out again.
(Read more quickly from here.)
Sigh and stretch. Open your eyes.
You are back within our hall.

Open Circle

Starting facing north and turning to the left, visualize the rune ring fading and sinking into the ground.

Chapter 8

EIHWAZ / PERTHRO:
The Tree and the Well

WHEN WE ADDRESS EIHWAZ AND PERTHRO, we explore the relationship between self-sacrifice and self-knowledge, between death and birth. The central part of this rite is initiatory in function (a very minor initiation, but with symbolism that is powerful all the same), in the sense that people will be asked to make a commitment to the search for wisdom. Explain that a rope will be briefly placed around the neck and that participants will need to trust the leader, and know that the danger is more in the surprise than the act itself. Those who don't feel ready to make this kind of commitment at this time (or at short notice) may stay in the "temple" and wait for the others. Be careful not to imply any judgments about those who choose not to participate in this part of the ritual—such experiences must be accepted freely and at the right time for each individual or they mean nothing.

The ritual is arranged to be conducted by a priest and priestess, but the invocations can be assigned as desired. The lullaby can be sung by one of them or another designated singer. The last person to enter the room before "The Tree" section should assist the priest and priestess with the rope and questions.

For the ritual, you will need the following:

- Pictures or images of Odin and Frigga

- Two votive candles

- A yard of rope or thick cord

- A basket of yew or evergreen twigs

- A bowl of water

- A horn or chalice and spring water

- A bowl of berries (optional: can be fresh or frozen and thawed)

- A platter with fruit- or seed-bread

Optional: Before the ritual, play some gloomy and portentous music, such as Sibelius's *Tapiola*, or Bax's *The Tale the Pine Trees Told*. Instruct those who don't wish to make a commitment to stay seated when the others line up.

ESTABLISHING SACRED SPACE

Participants stand in a circle, facing the north. Intone the runes, inscribing each rune in the air as it is chanted and turning to the right, so that by the time the whole futhark has been called everyone has turned in a complete circle.

ᚠ FEHU	ᚺ HAGALAZ	↑ TIWAZ
ᚢ URUZ	ᚾ NAUDHIZ	ᛒ BERKANO
ᚦ THURISAZ	ᛁ ISA	ᛖ EHWAZ
ᚨ ANSUZ	ᛃ JERA	ᛗ MANNAZ
ᚱ RAIDHO	ᛇ EIHWAZ	ᛚ LAGUZ
ᚲ KENAZ	ᛈ PERTHRO	◇ INGWAZ
ᚷ GEBO	ᛉ ELHAZ	ᛞ DAGAZ
ᚹ WUNJO	ᛋ SOWILO	ᛟ OTHALA

INVOCATIONS

To Odin

The following was provided by Leigh Ann Hussey.

> *(Priest)*: Ye who stand encircled in the sacred hall,
> Bright with the balefire's blaze,
> Hear, and see now, feel and know
> The presence of the As-priest.
> He is tree-rider, teller of riddles, teacher of runes.
> Black is the pit of his lost eye,
> Deep as the well for which he gave it.
> The sound of his steed's hooves
> Is the step of the dirge and the shaman's drum.
> Spear-shaker is he, and shape-shifter,
> Sacrificer and sacrificed.
> Gray-cowled comes the wanderer,
> In grim company of wolves,
> Crossroads-god, god of the quest,
> Cunning in council.
> He is mead-winner, mighty in skald-craft,
> Maker of magicks,
> He is hanging one and high-flier,
> Who gives the inspiring ale from his mouth.
> *(Light candle before image.)*

To Frigga

> *(Priestess)*: Ye who stand encircled in the sacred hall,
> Bright with the hearthfire's blaze,
> Open your hearts to the Queen of Asgard:
> She knows all fates, and yet keeps silence.
> Need-yarn that Norns spin, strings her loom.
> She is the womb of wisdom, she is the well-ward,
> Godmother, Worldmother, throne of kings.
> White-robed comes the Wise One
> With bright maidens around her:
> Gift-giver and healer of souls,
> The one who hears vows, who knows all history,
> Guardian of secrets, who knows what is hidden,
> The goddess who allows love to flourish,
> Defender of the Threshold, Soaring One.

She is the Mother of mothers
Who gives birth blessings to the newborn.
(Light candle before image.)

THE TREE

(Priestess): "Tell me, Fjölsvidh [Wide of Wisdom]—   I have to
  ask—
This I have to know—
What do you call that tree   whose broad limbs spread
Over all the land?

(Priest): Mimameith is its name   and no one can say
From what roots it rises;
As for what shall bring it down,   who knows?
Neither fire nore iron will make it fall.

(Priestess): Tell me, Fjölsvidh—   I have to ask—
This, I have to know—
What happens to the fruit   of that broad-limbed tree,
Since fire and iron cannot make it fall?

(Priest): If you take the fruit   from the tree to the fire
To roast for women in extremity,
Then out will come   what was hidden within,
Such power among men   has that fruit."

(Svipsdagmál: 19–22)

(Priestess): The Forest in which Mimameith grows is wild and
  deep.
There are many trees there, and many deceptions.
Those who would seek the Tree of Life must have courage;
They must be willing to face fear and danger;
They must conquer themselves;
They must be willing to pass through darkness
In order to reach the light.
Let all who would dare this quest go now to the place of waiting
Until it is time for the journey to begin.

FACING DEATH

(Priestess): Let those who are willing come forward
To make their commitment

To the sacrifice of self to self for wisdom.
(Those who wish to make this pledge line up at the entrance to the room. As each passes through the door, the Priest asks his questions.)

(Priest): Are you willing to ride the Steed of Ygg?
(Student): I am.
(Priest): Are you willing to sacrifice yourself to yourself
For the sake of wisdom?
(Student): I am.
(Priest): Are you willing to face death, that you may be born?
(Student): I am.

(The Priestess briefly places a rope around each student's neck, with just a little pressure, then releases.)

(Priestess): Pass then, and may this sprig from the Worldtree Guide you on your way.

(She gives each one a spring of yew or evergreen. Students then take their places for Meditation.)

TRANSFORMATION

Meditation

Read slowly, allowing time for visualizations to build.

You are at ease, still and silent,
Centered upon the earth.
Breathe in . . . and out . . . in . . . and out . . .
(4 beats in, hold 2, 4 beats out, hold 2)
Let the cares of the world of men be gone.
You are relaxed, at peace, you sit in safety.
Safely you will fare forward, safely you will return.
You will remember all you need to know.

As you relax, feel the solid earth supporting you.
Let your awareness sink downward, inward,
Deep into earth's core . . . now draw it up again.
Fill yourself with its power. . . .

Move out of your body now.
See a place that you know well.
Look at the ground; is it grass or stones?
Feel the texture, hear the sounds around.
As you gaze, you see the beginnings of a path.
Follow it away from the fields you know
Through bushes that become a woodland,
Woods that turn to forest,
Forest that grows thicker, darker,
Till you are walking through a tunnel made of trees.

When at last the forest thins,
Before you is a clearing.
Dusk has fallen but the sky still glows.
In the midst of Midgard grows the greatest of all trees,
So vast you cannot see around it,
So tall it pierces the sky.
Its trunk is gnarled and rough;
Its branches darkly furred
With needles of deepest green.
It is called Yggdrasil; it is called Worldtree.
Walk around it . . . from its base winds a stony path.
To either side, the dark humps of grave mounds
Swell from the ground.
The path curves northward; cold gray mist
From damp earth rises; the world grows gloomy;
Descending through dim Niflheim, you shiver with chill.
Then you turn eastward,
And a sharp wind blows the mist away.
Bracing air fills you with energy.
Upon the icy peaks you see stone fortresses,
The giants' homes in Jotunheim;
An immense Eagle claps wind from his wings.
Continue onward, and the world grows warmer.
Air blazes with brightness,
The sons of Muspel dance in the flames.
Onward winds the way of the wanderer.
Now the air is moist with the breath of the sea.
Seasurge and birdcall, and sweet over billows
Comes a breath of distant orchards
Where the Vanir play.

And now once more you stand at the center.
Something stirs in the branches,

A squirrel sprints upward—
Swiftly it passes through the realm of the Light Elves.
Beyond, the light of Asgard blazes still brighter.
There, the Tree is called Laeradh.
A rainbow shimmers on upper branches.
Dark needles quiver as the squirrel darts downward,
Veiling Asgard's light.
At the base of the trunk gapes an opening;
The squirrel scuttles through,
And careful, you follow it into the darkness.

The path curves into the depths beneath Midgard.
Once more you breathe the cold mists of Niflheim,
And hear the bubbling waters of the Well, Hvergelmir.
Through the dim shades of Svartalfheim you wander;
From here, the road to Hel curves downward.
But you take another path,
Squeezing beneath the root of the Tree.
You can hear nearby the roaring of a mighty river.
The mist drifts and eddies; turning, you follow
And glimpse, white with rime,
The roots of the Worldtree.
The Well of Urdh lies beneath them,
Mirror-dark in the shadows.
Deep is that well, from which the Norns drink daily,
And weave the world's fate at the base of the Tree.

But your pathway passes onward,
Away to the eastward.
Rime edges roots in covering of crystal.
Frost crunches beneath footsteps,
But a glassy glitter of open water gleams below;
The Well of Mimir waits with its wisdom.
A tracery of branches nets the silver surface.
Here, Mimameith is the name of the Tree.
Carefully you draw closer, look into the Well. . . .

The bright surface dims,
Depths draw vision downward.
Deep in that darkness a point of radiance glows—
The light of the bright Eye of Odin blazes,
Burns in your brain; in pain knowledge kindles,
Too bright, too great, a brilliance beyond bearing. . . .

The image shatters, radiant shards shimmer—
The bright berry that broke them floats in the water.
Fair is the fruit that from Mimameith is fallen;
Pluck the berry from the water, taste of its sweetness.

A swirl of memory whirls the years backward:
You remember today and its troubles,
The week that preceded, and last year, and others,
Farther and faster memories are unreeling.
You see the long road that has led you to this day. . . .
Other days, other lives, all are linked in a pattern
That has brought you from birth to rebirth.
What are you? WHO are you? What is your name?

The wind in the branches above begins to murmur.
The whisper grows louder,
Stirs the surface of the water.
Lean forward, listening; loud roars the well—
You hear, you remember— a word . . . a name . . .
A word that is your own. . . .

Water surges wildly; a wave overwhelms you;
The surge of the stream bears you strongly away.
Wave upon wave rolls; the well expels you.
You are squeezed out through darkness . . .
And come to rest . . . on solid ground . . .
At the base of the Tree. . . .

Solid strength behind and beneath you,
The Tree upholds you;
Rest, breathe, feel power flowing through it,
Linking Midgard with all the worlds.
Feel the depths from which you have come—
The heights into which you gaze—
The middle, where you are. . . .
Now, you remember what has been.
You accept what is.
With every breath you see what is coming into being:
Past, present, future, all part of one stream.

Rest, relax, you are safe here, and secure.
The Tree is your cradle.
Newborn, you will wake to new life in the world.

BIRTH

A singer sings a lullaby and if possible plays softly on an instrument while Priest and Priestess "awaken" each one with an embrace and a kiss on the forehead, asking softly:

> *(Priestess)*: Child of the Tree, what is the word you have been given?
> Child of the Well, what is your name?
> *(Student answers.)*
>
> *(Priest)*: _____ *(Name), with water from the holy well*
> To thee this name I fasten, *(Sprinkles with water.)*
> And receive you now as clan and kin!
>
> *(Priestess)*: Welcome, my son/daughter.
> With the gift of Mimameith I bless you— *(Feeds a berry.)*
> May you grow strong in spirit!

FEAST

When all have been blessed, Priest and Priestess return to consecrate food.

> *(Priestess)*: Water from the holy well, *(Bless horn. ᛉ)*
> Into which the berries fell,
> Water of the womb and sea,
> In Frigga's name now blessed be!
>
> *(Priest)*: Bread risen from the rooted grain, *(Bless cake. ᛚ)*
> And fruit that swelled and fell again,
> Staff of life and Tree of Power
> By Hár be hallowed in this hour!

RETURNING TO THE WORLD

Thank the Gods

> *(Priestess)*: For all we have been given, we thank the gods—
> For _____ *(Each one adds thanks for some blessing of heredity or environment.)*
> Our thanks to Frigga Allmother—

Womb of wisdom, weaver of fate.
Mother, we are grateful to thee and thy handmaidens,
For the blessings of birth and rebirth
You have given us.

(Priest): Honor and thanks to Odin the High One—
Treerider, Runegiver, Winner of Wisdom,
Allfather, our thanks to thee
For the gifts thy sacrifice has given us.

Return to World

For a moment, close your eyes.
The Tree is behind you.
There before you is the path by which you came.
Follow it. Go back through the tunnel of trees.
Come out into the light again.
Look ahead—there is the place that you know.

Sit down, feel the weight of your flesh,
The solid ground below.
Sink down into your body.
Remember what you have learned.
Now breathe in and out, in and out again.
(Read more quickly from here.)
Sigh and stretch. Open your eyes.
You are back in the Midgard that lies without.

Open Circle

Starting facing north and turning to the left, visualize the rune ring fading and sinking into the ground.

Chapter 9

ELHAZ / SOWILO: Safe on the Sun Road

IN THIS RITUAL, THE EARTH POWER OF ELHAZ and the sky power of SOWILO work together so that protection may be given and received. The altar should be decorated with symbols of both the elk and the sun. One way to do this is to place a box on the altar to create a two-tiered altar and cover both box and table with a cloth. The sun symbols are placed on the upper level, the elk symbols on the lower. Another approach is to create the sun altar on a card table whose white or gold-colored cloth covers the top only, and place the ELHAZ symbols on a black or brown cloth beneath it on the floor. Use a white or gold candle or votive holder for SOWILO and a brown or green candle or glass for ELHAZ.

Appropriate sun symbols could include a straw wreath, a brass disk, or one of cardboard covered with gold foil. Gold disks on which sun symbols have been inscribed can also be used. If possible, wedge a sun disk upright in a small boat or wagon. ELHAZ symbols could include a set of antlers, a disk with the rune inscribed on it, animal furs and skins, figures of animals or Valkyries.

For the feast, choose mead, a golden wine, or apple juice for the drink and a round, flat sourdough loaf or Norwegian cracker bread.

Sacred space is established at the beginning of the rite by simulating the daily round of the sun. Carrying fire around a territory to claim it is traditional; in this ritual that sunwise circuit becomes the sun's journey from dawn to dawn. The sun's action during each part of the day is symbolized by lighting a candle in the appropriate aett (based on Icelandic day-marks).

The procession and invocations with which the ritual opens therefore create a ritual space that is outside of time because within it all times exist simultaneously. In the closing sequence, the process is reversed; the eight lights and the taper are extinguished, returning us to the linear time of the world, in which the sun appears in only one place at any time.

The second action of the ritual is to balance the energies of earth and heaven as explained in the discussion of individual working. At this time the ELHAZ and SOWILO candles on the upper and lower altars should be lit. The balancing creates (or recreates) a kinesthetic awareness of the energy flow that will be used in the meditation, in which the individual seeks a protecting guide or ally (the fylgja) and, with its assistance, defends the sun from the wolf that pursues her. The meeting with the fylgja will probably be more powerful for those who have already done individual work of this kind; however, those who meet their guardian for the first time in this meditation can do individual work later on to develop the relationship.

After the inner work of the meditation, the group directs its energy outward in the dance of the sun. The movement is clockwise and begins with individual dancing. It is advisable to begin slowly, to give everyone a chance to warm up. Some may wish to thank their fylgjas by "dancing" them—letting them manifest in the tangible world by dancing in imitation of their movements or letting them use the bodies of those they are protecting. During this individual phase, each person may contact the power of the sun by jumping over its symbol, a practice portrayed on Bronze Age rock carvings in Scandinavia. This is essentially the same practice as jumping over the Beltane or Midsummer fire, but much safer to do in a living room.

The feast allows everyone to recover from the dancing and is followed by the self-blessing. The self-blessing is a simplified version of an Anglo-Saxon journey spell collected in Storms's *Anglo-Saxon Magic*. The lengthy invocation of Christian saints and prophets in the original has been replaced by a commendation to the landspirits and the High One, and instead of the blessings of saints, the mystical armor protecting the traveler consists of the powers of the gods. When invoking them, pause to draw the rune on your body as indicated.

Transposing the translation into poetry (which makes it more forceful and easier to remember) has required taking some liberties with the meaning; however, in structure and substance (especially the first half) it is essentially the same. The word *sig* is left in the original rather than being translated as "victory" for reasons of meter and to preserve its additional connotations. When invoking the Sig-galdor and so on, draw the SOWILO rune in each direction, turning clockwise. It is important to pace the wording slowly enough so that everyone has a chance to make the rune signs.

Talk the group through the ritual before beginning. In particular, it is useful to demonstrate the body movements for the balancing section, to describe the options for the dancing, and to demonstrate the coordination of the runes with the self-blessing.

ESTABLISHING SACRED SPACE

Participants stand in a circle, facing the north. Intone the runes inscribing each rune in the air as it is chanted and turning to the right, so that by the time the whole futhark has been called everyone has turned in a complete circle.

ᚠ FEHU	ᚺ HAGALAZ	ᛏ TIWAZ
ᚢ URUZ	ᚾ NAUDHIZ	ᛒ BERKANO
ᚦ THURISAZ	ᛁ ISA	ᛗ EHWAZ
ᚨ ANSUZ	ᛃ JERA	ᛉ MANNAZ
ᚱ RAIDHO	ᛇ EIHWAZ	ᛚ LAGUZ
ᚲ KENAZ	ᛈ PERTHRO	◇ INGWAZ
ᚷ GEBO	ᛉ ELHAZ	ᛞ DAGAZ
ᚹ WUNJO	ᛋ SOWILO	ᛟ OTHALA

(Eight participants move to the eight directions, holding unlit candles.)
(Leader): Let the holy flame be kindled —
Sunfire shining in the shadows;
Lightning lance from earth to heaven,
Blaze the way to climb the Worldtree —
SOWILO I summon thee, show us our road!
(Light the taper.)
In the old days they marked time
By the passage of the sun around the sky.
In each of these day-marks there is a blessing
That brings us into harmony with the world.

(The leader, carrying a lit taper (and followed, if available, by someone carrying a sun disk), goes to each position in turn, while the drummer drums. At each aett, all ask the question. The person in that position answers, and the leader lights the candle.)

(All, facing east): What is the mark?
(Eastern candle holder): It is Morning, a blessing of energy;
A new day, a new birth,
A new hope for the world. . . .

(All, facing southeast): What is the mark?
(Southeastern candle holder): It is Day, a blessing of growth;
Sun strengthens, hearts lift, life begins. . . .

(All, facing south): What is the mark?
(Southern candle holder): It is Midday, a blessing of power;
Light fills the sky, the fire of life, the heart. . . .

(All, facing southwest): What is the mark?
(Southwestern candle holder): It is Afternoon, a blessing of
    mastery;
Power and skill rightly applied bring victory. . . .

(All, facing west): What is the mark?
(Western candle holder): It is Eventide, a blessing of fulfillment;
Deeds are done, desires attained at last. . . .

(All, facing northwest): What is the mark?
(Northwestern candle holder): It is Night, a blessing of
    knowledge;
Contemplation of action brings understanding.

(All, facing north): What is the mark?
(Northern candle holder): It is Midnight, a blessing of mystery;
For darkness is the womb of a new world. . .

(All, facing northeast): What is the mark?
(Northeastern candle holder): It is the Outtide, a blessing of rest;
When heart and soul and body are renewed. . . .

(All sing): Sun wheel shine to show the way,
Drawn from darkness into day!
Sunwise stride the sacred ground,
Safe the circle shields us round!

"Sun-wheel Day"   words, music, Diana L. Paxson

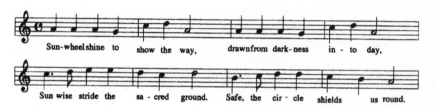

(When the circuit is completed, all take places within circle, facing the altar. Set the sun disk and taper on the altar.)

BALANCING OF FORCES

Sink down and touch the earth. . . .
(All sit or kneel.)
Feel its firm support, sense the depths below . . .
Place your palms on the floor.
Let your awareness move downward, inward—
Down to the roots of the world.
(Light candle on Underworld altar.)
Touch the power at the heart of things
And slowly draw it upward,
Up through the earth, through the floor,
Through your spine as you straighten,
Balanced and secure.
Find the center of your being.
Here is the place where your fylgja dwells.
Greet that patient, protecting power.
In silence invoke the guardian of your spirit,

In whatever shape it may appear.
Ask it to come to you—
Ask it to bless you—
Ask it to be with you tonight. . . .
Rise now and stand upon your feet.
Lift your arms in salutation,
(Stand with arms raised in ELHAZ stance.)
And release the power that fills you to the skies. . . .
(Stand upright with arms uplifted saluting heaven.
Take taper and light candle on Sky altar.)
The wind and the wide welkin,
And the shining shield of the sun.
Hail her as Sól and as Sunna,
Glory of Elves and Dwalin's bane,
Everglow and Elfgleam,
Mundilfari's daughter, Fair Wheel of the skies,
Her splendor surrounds you,
Her brightness embraces you;
You breathe in, and you are filled with light.
From your crown down your spine it travels,
Tingling, transforming. . . . .
Bring down your arms, bring down the light,
Bend to earth, adoring eastward,
Bow down and give the sunpower to the earth again.
(Bow down and touch the floor.)
(Everyone sits down.)

MEDITATION

You are at ease, still and silent,
Centered upon the earth.
Breathe in . . . and out . . . in . . . and out . . .
(4 beats in, hold 2, 4 beats out, hold 2)
Let the cares of the world of men be gone.
You are relaxed, at peace, you sit in safety.
Safely you will fare forward, safely you will return.
You will remember all you need to know.

As you relax, feel the solid earth supporting you.
Let your awareness sink downward, inward,
Deep into earth's core . . . now draw it up again.
Fill yourself with its power. . . .
Move out of your body now.

See a place that you know well.
Look at the ground; is it grass or stones?
Feel the texture, hear the sounds around.
As you gaze, you see the beginnings of a path.
Follow it away from the fields you know,
Through bushes that become a woodland,
Woods that turn to forest,
Forest that grows thicker, darker,
Till you are walking through a tunnel made of trees.
When at last the forest thins, before you is a clearing.
Chill mist swirls past.
You glimpse the greatest of all trees,
So vast you cannot see around it,
So tall it pierces the sky.
But frost clings to the rough trunk.
Each twig and needle is sheathed in ice.
Carefully you move across the glittering ground
Eastward, around the Tree.
The world is hushed and waiting
In the chill gray hour before dawn.
When will the sun rise? Will it rise at all?
Or will the world be prisoned in this dim existence
That is neither night nor day?

Facing eastward, lift your arms—
Pray to the sun to bring light into the world.
Remember her radiance,
Find the answering spark within you.
Call to her, and feel light growing within. . . .
Without and within light grows and gathers;
The eastern sky is brightening, from gray to palest rose.
From rose to coral the color changes,
Ever lighter and brighter, now the sky grows gold.
And there, through the mist, a shield of light is rising;
It glitters in every drop of mist,
Blazes from the ice that sheaths the Tree,
Glistens on the ground. . . .

You bow down in adoration at the dawning of the day.
Ice crackles around you, tinkles as it falls.
Light coruscates from a thousand rainbows,
And then, suddenly, they all are gone.
A shining lake laps the shore before you;

The sun road lies across it, shimmering gold.
Sharp sedges surrounding sway in the morning breeze.
They shiver, and a horned head
Rises from among them,
The mightiest horns in Midgard
Etch a rune of protection against the sky.
Then the Elk returns to his feeding,
And something pale moves out from among the reeds;
A silver swan glides slowly sunward, white on gold.

The swan shows you the way across the water,
Beyond it stretches a lovely land—
You want to go there, but how will you find your way?
If danger threatens, who will protect you?
Once more the Elk lifts his heavy head,
His thought comes to you—
"Look around you, Child of Ask and Embla—
See with your heart, and listen with your soul
And your guardian will come to you. . . ."

You gaze around you, waiting for movement.
Are there animals here, or birds,
Or creatures of the deep?
Totem beast or radiant spirit, what do you see?
(Allow extra time here.)
Something stirs, comes to you,
Once, twice, three times, it waits for you. . . .
(Allow extra time here.)
Greet it, ask for a name; will it be your guide on the sun road?
(Allow extra time here.)
Together, you turn to follow the sun's bright pathway.
Here, your eyes see clearly—
Above, two radiant horses pull a shining chariot;
The fairest of all maidens urges them on,
Shaking the golden reins.
Swiftly you follow through the forest,
And all that would harm you
Are driven off by your guide.
But overhead a shadow passes—
A black shape comes leaping—
Jaws open and slavering with desire
For the sun he pursues.
Fast as she flies,

Still the wolf is coming faster.
If he catches her, all light will leave the world.

Only you can help them, if your guide will help you.
Together you rise, you ride, you fly toward the sun. . . .
(Allow extra time here.)
Now you are near, but how quickly the wolf comes.
Quickly you grasp the shield that goes before the chariot.
Its radiance holds the wolf back, but still it follows.
To drive it away, something more is needed;
Earth strength, rising, summons sky power.
From your ally draw strength, stretch out your arm.
Power strikes through you
As earth reaches for heaven;
A sword of lightning blazes in your hand!

The wolf snarls and slavers
But your will does not falter;
All your being is focused through that shining blade.
It points toward your foe; brightness blazes outward.
Light leaps!
Bright blade strikes sharp!
Sparks flare!
The wolf recoils, is whirled away behind.
You straighten, watching it grow small in the distance,
But you and your ally, with sword and shield,
Guard Sunna's chariot to the end of the sky.
The horses plunge down
Toward the darkness of treetops.
The Grove of Night is waiting to give them rest.
But you and your ally turn downward and inward
Seeking the Tree at the center of the world.

You find yourself at dusk, by the Tree in the clearing;
Your ally is with you, it is time to say farewell.
But you know if you call now, your ally will find you,
And safely will keep you
Through all the roads of the world.
Every day of the world the sun sets and rises —
But she shines within you now and forever. . . .

There before you is the way by which you came.
Go back through the tunnel of trees

> Into the light again.
> And see the place that you know.
> Sit down, feel the weight of your flesh,
> The solid ground below.
> Sink down into your body.
> Remember what you have learned.
> Now breathe in and out, in and out again.
> *(Read more quickly from here.)*
> Sigh and stretch. Open your eyes.
> You are in the sacred enclosure once more.

When the meditation ends, the drummer should drum slowly but insistently to bring everyone back to focus. Allow sufficient time for everyone to get back in touch with their bodies before beginning the dance.

SUN DANCE

> Dance the sacred sun wheel round,
> Dance the dance of victory;
> All evil end, all bane be bound,
> As we have willed, so will it be!

The leader places the sun disk in the center of the room, and the drummer begins a lively beat. All dance clockwise around it to affirm divine order, imitate movements of fylgja, or simply move to the drumbeat. Jump over the sun for luck. After individuals have danced for a time, gather all into a circle, dancing round, bring the dance to a climax, then slow and stop. Allow everyone time to catch their breaths before starting the feast.

FEAST

> Sacred Sunna, now we thank thee,
> Glorious goddess whose golden warmth,
> Radiant, ripens the fruit of the Tree.
> Thy spirit burns in this brimming horn!
> *(Hold up horn, bless ᛋ.)*
>
> Grain that grew in golden fields,
> By wind and water, sun and soil
> Was blest, and then baked into bread.
> Shield and strengthen us, in Sunna's name!

(Hold up round loaf of bread, bless Υ.)

JOURNEY CHARM

The dance is done, the feast is ended.
Now from the hallowed hall we must be gone.
But before we go, let us share a blessing:

(All): By this rod, I'm circled round,
By wardings of the gods I'm bound.
(Draw circle around self.)
Against sore stitch, against sore bite,
Against all horrors that haunt the night,
'Gainst dread that folk fear everywhere,
And loathly things that here would fare.
Sig-Galdor, I chant, a sig rod is my stay,
(Turning sunwise, draw Ⴗ in each of the directions.)
Word-sig and work-sig me ward today.
No nightmare mire me, no foe harm.
In my life may no fear alarm.

Help me holy wights of land,
The High One hold me in his hand.
Ye Alfs and Aesir, Vanir aid.
From your power my protection's made.
Wodan, my helm, Tyr's sword I wield,
(Draw ᚱ on crown, ↑ on right arm.)
Freya, my byrnie, Thor, my shield.
(Draw ᚠ on breast, ▶ on left arm.)
Nor wight nor weather threatens me,
From danger defended will I be.
I bid the good gods victory give,
Guarded so, safe shall I live.
(Draw ELHAZ/SOWILO bindrune on forehead.)

Now by ELHAZ and SOWILO we are warded.
Though their flame be put out,
In us their power shall live.
(Priestess puts out ELHAZ candle; priest puts out SOWILO candle.)

RETURN TO THE WORLD

Take Down Sun Circle

All follow the priest and priestess around the circle as the eight candles are blown out. They then complete the circuit and say or sing:

(All): **Sun wheel shining ever bright,**
Drawn from daytime into night!
Safely leave this sacred ground
As widdershins the ward's unbound!

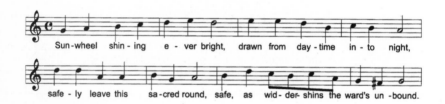

Sun-wheel shin-ing e - ver bright, drawn from day-time in - to night,

safe - ly leave this sa-cred round, safe, as wid-der-shins the ward's un-bound.

Open Circle

Starting facing north and turning to the left, visualize the rune ring fading and sinking into the ground.

Chapter 10

TIWAZ / BERKANO: The Tree of Tyr

IN THIS RITUAL, THE BIRCH TREE, a protecting power in the wilderness, becomes the Irminsul, which stands as the center of the community. Rather than experiencing the meditation within the context of the ritual, this time we find in it the means by which the transition is made from the chaos of wilderness to safety. It is therefore presented as the opening of the ritual.

Before the ritual begins, everyone except the priest and priestess should gather outside the room in which the rite is being held. For the first part of the ritual it will be helpful if you can play a tape of the howling of wolves, or failing that, music that suggests chaos or a storm. You will also need a pole—ideally it should be a real birch limb. If this is not available, a pole of some other natural wood, or even a length of dowel painted white, will do.

You will also need enough birch twigs for everyone to have one, a substantial glove (right hand), such as a fencer's gauntlet or a gardening glove, and if possible a Christmas-tree stand or bucket of sand in which the pole can stand upright. For the sacred enclosure, you will need a large enough skein of red yarn to make a rectangle around the participants, and four candles (preferably in glass). Other requirements are a taper, a horn of some appropriate drink such as cranberry juice or bull's blood wine, and a platter with a loaf of bread.

ESTABLISHING SACRED SPACE

Participants stand in a circle, facing the north. Intone the runes, inscribing each rune in the air as it is chanted and turning to the right, so that by the time the whole futhark has been called everyone has turned in a complete circle.

ᚠ FEHU	ᚺ HAGALAZ	↑ TIWAZ
ᚢ URUZ	ᚾ NAUDHIZ	ᛒ BERKANO
ᚦ THURISAZ	ᛁ ISA	ᛗ EHWAZ
ᚨ ANSUZ	ᛃ JERA	ᛗ MANNAZ
ᚱ RAIDHO	ᛇ EIHWAZ	ᛚ LAGUZ
ᚲ KENAZ	ᛕ PERTHRO	◇ INGWAZ
✕ GEBO	ᛉ ELHAZ	ᛞ DAGAZ
ᚹ WUNJO	ᛋ SOWILO	ᚷ OTHALA

UTGARD

Everyone sits down. Put the lights out; play a tape of wolves howling. Take a few moments of silence to center.

(Leader): Imagine that you are standing upon the barren earth;
The chill breath of the glacier freezes your bones.
You are far from home, alone and lonely,
All around is wasteland,

A chaos of rock and snow and stunted growing things.
You wander aimlessly, starting at shadows;
The only sound is the howling wind—
Or is it wind? Surely it carries voices—
Wolf voices . . . wolfsong is the music of the waste. . . .

Why are you alone? Why do you fear the shadows?
Is it because they might be wolves,
They might be trolls or draugrs;
They might be worse things still—they might be men?
This is Utgard . . . outside the boundaries;
This is the wilderness the outlier wanders;
This is the land of folk without law.

Why are you here, wolf's head, outlaw?
What crimes have set you apart from humankind?
Are you an oathbreaker? Does rage consume you?
Are you the prey of selfishness or fear?

Driven by memory, you wander on.
Surely somewhere there must be comfort. . . .
Ahead you see a blurring at the edge of the glacier.
Green-hazed branches tremble in a breeze
With a hint of summer.
White as the ice, the gleaming trunks of birch trees
March out across the land.
Here at least is some shelter,
You make your way toward them.
Beyond are more trees, branches twist and tangle,
You seek to go back,
But the way has closed behind you.
You can only go onward,
Seeking to find a pattern in the maze,
Seeking a path.
What do you want? Companionship? Order?
Something crashes in the brush behind you—
You whirl—is it a wolf or a man?

Light sparks,
(Light candle, turn off tape.)
The torch shows people around you.
Suspicious, you eye each other.
They look dangerous. Can you trust them?

Do they want the same things as you?
Where will you find the knowledge
To show you the way?
(Assistant steps forward, holding the "birch" pole.)

(Female Voice): I am the Mother Tree—
I am BERKANO; I am Ask and Embla;
My leaves hide Lif and Lithrasir.
When Audhumla licked the ice from Ymir's body,
I was the first to arise.
Winter snowfall wraps my whiteness;
Buds bless branches with green in spring;
In summer I shine in the midst of the forest.
My limbs are whipped by autumn winds.
My path is the passage of the seasons;
Only by changing am I sustained.
I am the seed buried in the ground;
I am the Tree bowing to the breeze.
My truth survives all transformations;
Through storms and seasons I endure.
Receive my gift and use it wisely;
I shield the spirit that is pure.

(Leader passes around a bundle of birch twigs; each one strikes
self a few times and passes it on.)

(All): Birch tree's blows set blood to singing,
Sting with strength to face the foe.
Mother tree be now my mainstay.
Leave me luck of leaf below!

(Leader): Luck of leaf with love I give you.
Holy herb defends from danger.
(Leader unties bundle and distributes twigs.)
The Tree comes up in my hand, let us take it with us;
Together we stumble forward.
(Group moves toward entrance.)
One pushes a branch aside;
Another steps on a limb so that others can pass.
Together we make our way through the forest;
We can seek justice, and a way to live among men.
But we have been wolves—
We must be willing to undergo transformation

To follow the way of the warrior within the community.
(Lights are turned up, person holding birch pole leads way into temple.)

THE ALTHING

(Leader): Listen, my kindred, we have come together,
But how shall we make order?
How shall we know what is outside and what is within?
Let us make walls against the darkness
And mark out the boundaries:
From east to south—
(Two participants unroll red yarn from corner to corner.)
From south to west—
From west to north—
From north to east—

Let us call upon the old powers of the earth to protect them:
Nordhri—
Austri—
Sudhri—
Vestri—
Let us carry fire around the boundaries
To claim all that lies within.
(Leader takes a candle from the altar and circles clockwise within bounds, lighting candles at the four corners.)

We have made walls against chaos,
But where is our center?
Bring forth the birch tree,
That we may take root in the world!
(The pole is brought to the center and held.)
Behold the Tree of Life,
The ancestors dwell beneath her roots
In the depths of darkness.
The gods dwell on the heights
Where her crown brushes heaven.
In the plane for which her trunk is the axis
Lies the world of humankind.

We have found our center,
But where shall we find Law to govern us?
Bring forth the Hand of Tyr,

Beneath whose protection we shall prosper.
*(Leader brings a gauntlet and slips it over the end of the pole,
then the pole is leaned against the wall or set in a stand.)*

(All): The glove is up!

(Leader): The Glove is up, the god is with us!
Let all within these boundaries live by law!
All hail the holy Irminsul!

FEAST

Let us feast, and celebrate our community!
(Bless horn. ↑)
Here's the holy drink of heroes—
Hallow the horn and hail the victor!
Sig-Tyr, hail, and share thy spirit
That to thy task we may be faithful!
(Pass the horn around the circle.)

Holy Mother Tree we thank thee,
(Bless bread. ᛒ)
Giving us thy fruits to nourish
Soul and body, bless this bread now,
That birth and rebirth may be blessed!
(Pass the bread around the circle.)

RETURNING TO THE WORLD

Now comes the time when we must uproot the tree
And take down the enclosure,
But though these symbols be dismantled,
We continue to carry their protection within.
(Take up pole and remove the glove.)
Hail Berkano!
(Leader holds up pole.)
Hail Tyr!
(Holds up glove.)

*(Those who laid out the boundary cord roll it up, moving counter-
clockwise, while the leader follows, carrying the candle. At each
corner, blow out the candle there.)*

The barrier that's here unbound
Firm-built within us still is found:
The safety set within this hall
Reigns still in hearts of one and all.
Let us carry that protection with us into the world!

Open Circle

Starting facing north and turning to the left, visualize the rune ring fading and sinking into the ground.

Chapter 11

EHWAZ / MANNAZ:
A Ritual of Union

IN THIS RITUAL, WHICH EXPLORES the story of Ríg to help you in communicating with yourself and others, as well as with the gods, the meditation is
a variation on the form you are used to. When it is time, participants will be
asked to pair off, and tell each other a question that they would like to ask
Heimdall. Periodically, as the meditation progresses, space will be left for the
partners to tell each other what they are seeing, until when they reach

Heimdall's hall, they, rather than the narrator, are providing the details. The narrator or another experienced person should keep track of what is going on, and if one of a pair seems to be having difficulties (or appears to have gone to sleep), help out by gently questioning and assisting him to focus, or if necessary, taking the person's place.

This process works like an interactive story, in which one partner provides a detail, the other elaborates on it and continues, and so forth. By working together, the intuitive power of each is amplified. The things they see, find, and hear are for each other, culminating with the question to be asked of the god.

You will need the following:

- A mirror (for the person acting as priest of Lodhur)

- A drinking horn and mead (for the priest of Hoenir to offer and for the feast)

- An eye patch and a pot with burning incense (for the priest of Odin)

- A staff for making the circle

- A platter with whole grain bread

- An image of a white horse (a statuette or a banner)

ESTABLISHING SACRED SPACE

Participants stand in a circle, facing the north. Intone the runes, inscribing each rune in the air as it is chanted and turning to the right, so that by the time the whole futhark has been called everyone has turned in a complete circle.

ᚠ FEHU	ᚺ HAGALAZ	↑ TIWAZ
ᚾ URUZ	ᚼ NAUDHIZ	ᛒ BERKANO
ᚦ THURISAZ	I ISA	ᛗ EHWAZ
ᚠ ANSUZ	ᚬ JERA	ᛙ MANNAZ
ᚱ RAIDHO	ᛝ EIHWAZ	ᚱ LAGUZ
ᚲ KENAZ	ᛆ PERTHRO	◇ INGWAZ
✕ GEBO	ᛉ ELHAZ	ᛞ DAGAZ
ᚹ WUNJO	ᛋ SOWILO	ᛦ OTHALA

INVOCATIONS

Landspirits

Now to Landspirits we lift our praise
And hail the powers who uphold and protect us.
Upon our work we ask your blessing.
Within your ward we work our magic.

THE GIFT OF LIFE

"Then from among   the holy people,
Fared three Aesir, kind and mighty,
They found on the shore,   two lifeless logs,
Ash and Elm,   without destiny.

Breath they had not   Brain they had not,
Neither being nor movement;   nor good looks.
Odin gave them önd,   Hoenir gave them odh,
Life gave Lodhurr   and good looks."

("Völuspá": 17–18)

(Three participants, representing Lodhur, Hoenir, and Odin, go from person to person around the circle, all three cloaked and hooded. Odin has an eye patch and fan; Lodhur, the mirror; Hoenir carries a horn of mead.)

("Lodhur"): **"Ash"** *(if male)*/**"Elm"** *(if female)*, I name thee.
Thyself, to thyself, thus do I show thee—*(Holds up mirror)*
Lá, and Litr, and Læti I leave thee:
Face and form and manner and motion. *(Blesses with* ᚾ. *)*

("Hoenir"): **"Ash"**/**"Elm,"** this marvelous mead,
Bragi's brew from Odhroerir I bring.
Odhr I offer, the soul's inspiration, *(Offers mead horn.)*
Drink deep, my child, of ecstasy! *(Blesses with* ᚹ. *)*

("Odin"): **"Ash"**/**"Elm,"** cherished child,
The breath of life to thee I blow. *(Fans vigorously.)*
Önd I offer, wind of the spirit.
Breathe deep, that life may leap within! (Blesses with ᚠ. *)*

(The gods return to the altar and bless each other.)

THE KIN OF RÍG

The lines are based on "Rígsthula." The leader may speak all the lines, or assign sections a, b, c, and d to four different speakers.

a. Great-Grandfather and Great-Grandmother

Long ago, a wise god wandered Midgard's ways. Full of might and power, Ríg walked unwearied through the wild lands until he came to a house. Though the door was shut it opened for him. An old man and an old woman sat by the hearth, their hair white as hoarfrost, with hoods in the olden style. Ríg knew how to talk to them. He sat down between them, and they fed him what they had. When bedtime came, he slept between them on a straw mattress in the hall. Three nights he stayed there, then went on his way. Nine moons passed and Great-Grandmother bore a boy child. They sprinkled him with water and named him Thrall.
(Stands forth and points around circle.)
You are Thrall and Thir,
You make ropes and gather wood,
You build fences, fertilize fields,
Fatten swine and herd goats
And cut the peat to feed the fire.
Thus do I bless you!
(Blesses with ᛗ.)

b. Grandfather and Grandmother

Ríg strode onward through the wilderness until he came to another hall. The door was ajar and he went in. Busy by the fire sat a man and his wife. He fashioned a loom pole while she spun the yarn. Well-dressed they were and made him welcome. Ríg knew how to talk to them and when the time came to sleep, he lay between them in the good bed in the hall. Three nights he stayed there, then went on his way. Nine moons passed, and Grandmother bore a boy. They sprinkled him with water and and wrapped him in linen and gave him the name of Carl.
(Stands forth and points around circle.)
You are Carl and Snoer.
You tame oxen and temper ploughshares,
Timber houses and barns for hay,
Fashion carts and follow the plow,
Spin and weave and stock the larder.

Thus do I bless you!
(Blesses with ᛗ. *)*

c. Father and Mother

Ríg took up his staff and fared forward till he came to a hall with
a door on the south. The door stood open and he went in. There
was straw on the floor and a bench by the hearth. Man and wife
sat there, fingers entwined, gazing into each other's eyes.
Mother laid the table with linen and silver and fed the guest
well. Ríg knew how to talk to them and when night came, he lay
between them for three nights long. Then he fared forth on the
wilderness ways. Nine moons passed, and Mother bore a bright-
eyed boy. They sprinkled him with water and swaddled him in
silk and gave him the name of Earl.
(Stands forth and points around circle.)
You are Earl and Erna.
You wield the buckler and fasten the bowstring,
Hurl the spear and speed the lance,
Hunt with the hounds and ride horses,
Brandish swords and swim in the sea.
You rule the house and embroider linen.
Thus do I bless you!
(Blesses with ᛗ. *)*

d. Earl and Erna

Earl's children grew up in the hall, but the youngest boy, Kon,
was the only one who could carve the runes. Age runes and life
runes he knew. In runelore he came to rival Ríg; with their wits
they battled and the boy knew them better. So he got the name
of Ríg himself and with that wisdom, ruled the land.
(Stands forth and points around circle.)
You are Kon and Kona
You carve the life-giving runes;
To bring forth babes, dull edge of sword and calm the sea.
Fowls' speech you know, fires you quench,
Sorrow soothe, the sick mind heal.
Ríg have you matched in wit and wisdom—
You shall be Kings and Queens of Creation.
Thus do I bless you! *(Blesses with* ᛗ. *)*

COMPLETING THE CIRCLE

Hear the words of the High One, oh children of Heimdall—
"When I was young   I travelled alone,
And wandered off the marked way;
Rich I thought myself   when another I found,
Humans are man's comfort."

("Hávamál": 47)

(Each one turns to the next, hails him/her as friend.)
When the world was young, the god's white horses
Harnessed together, hauled his holy cart.
Guided by the god, the way they would go,
Showed priests and people the prosperous path.
We are the kin of Ríg! We are one tribe, one people.
Behold the White Horse! Hither let her lead us.
Two by two let us travel together.
*(Leader brings forth the White Horse, and he or she and another
pair off, carrying it, followed by the others, two by two, with arms
crossed and linked in folk-dance fashion. The procession marches
in a circle around the room.)*

INTERACTIVE MEDITATION

Now it is time to divide into pairs *(or threes, and sit or lie down,
spaced so you cannot hear the other groups)*. Each of you should
decide on a question for Ríg and tell your partner what it is. I will
guide you to Midgard, and then you will help each other envision
the journey. Maintain a light trance, in which you can speak to
your companion when I instruct you.

You are at ease, still and silent,
Centered upon the earth.
Breathe in . . . and out . . . in . . . and out . . .
(4 beats in, hold 2, 4 beats out, hold 2)
Let the cares of the world of men be gone.
You are relaxed, at peace, you sit in safety.
Safely you will fare forward, safely you will return.
You will remember all you need to know.

As you relax, feel the solid earth supporting you.
Let your awareness sink downward, inward,
Deep into earth's core . . . now draw it up again.

Fill yourself with its power. . . .
Move out of your body now.
See a place that you know well.
Look at the ground; is it grass or stones?
Feel the texture, hear the sounds around.
Very near, you hear the sound of breathing—
You are not alone. Seek now for the companion
Who will journey with you between the worlds.
Clasp hands. . . . Greet each other now. . . .
Promise to help each other upon your way. . . .

Both of you see the beginnings of a path.
Follow it away from the fields you know,
Through bushes that become a woodland,
Woods that turn to forest,
Forest that grows thicker, darker.
Together, make your way through the tunnel of trees.

When at last the forest thins,
Before you is a clearing.
In its center grows the greatest of all trees,
So vast you cannot see around it,
So tall it pierces the sky.
Walk together around it . . .
From its base wind many paths.
Westward a gray fog flows in from the sea.
A path leads thither, across marsh and meadow. . . .

Mist swirls around you, cool as a kiss of blessing.
It shimmers with color; the shadows are fleeing.
The glimmering glory grows greater—gaze upward—
The radiance rises, color streams in a rainbow
From the heights of the heavens
To the roots of the Tree.
Bifrost! Bifrost! Behold the bridge of beauty,
An arch is arising; only the Aesir may ascend it,
Or those who can summon a steed
That can make the journey.
But to seek Heimdall, you must help each other.
Stare into the mist; call a steed for your companion
That can cross the gulf between man and god.
See it taking shape from the mist, find out its name.
And when you know it, describe it for your companion.

(Allow time for partners to talk to each other.)

Mount now the helper
That your friend has found for you.
Boldly fare forward, to glory you're guided.
The bridge curves through the clouds that
Cluster below.
Mighty slopes soar skyward, glimmering with light,
The road of radiance now ride nearer
And nearer still until you touch solid stone.
What do you see? Speak now to your companion,
Describing your vision, hearing it echoed
And amplified.
Help each other see until you reach the ramparts
Of Asgard,
And then, together, find the way to Himinbjorg—
Heimdall's hall on the cliffs of heaven!

What do you see? How is that hall fashioned?
Its roof and its walls, its rafters and doorways?

(Allow time for partners to describe Himinbjorg. . . .)

Seek now the fairest of gods,
The master of Himinbjorg,
Heimdall, Ríg, called Father of Men.
Through the shadows see him shining,
Describe for your companion
What you see, what he says when you greet him.

(Allow time for partners to tell what they are hearing.)

Now remember the question
That haunts your companion.
Ask the god, and in the silence of your heart,
Hear his answer, or accept the gift he gives.

*(Allow time for partners to tell what they are hearing or
receiving.)*

Heimdall blesses you, then he departs.
It is time for you to return to Midgard together.
Outside the door of Himinbjorg,

You see Bifrost glimmer.
Hard it is to leave heaven, but your home is waiting.
Summon your steeds, call those that will carry you.
Broad is the bridge to bear you boldly earthward,
Fare onward and downward, hastening toward home.
Describe for each other the journey,
Till you reach Midgard again.

(Allow time for partners to describe journey to each other.)

Now the mists are rising, gray cloud engulfs you,
Cool cloud caresses, heaven now is hidden.
You step onto solid earth. Steady you stand.
Say farewell to the steeds
That so safely have carried you.

Seek now the way that leads back to the Tree.
There before you is the path by which you came.
Follow it. Go back through the tunnel of trees.
Emerge into daylight, your companion beside you.
Look ahead—there is the place that you know.

Sit down, feel the weight of your flesh,
The solid ground below.
Sink down into your body.
Remember what you have learned.
Now breathe in and out, in and out again.
(Read more quickly from here.)
Sigh and stretch, mortal sight wakens,
Welcome ye wanderers to the world returning.

FEAST

In Heimdall's name, this holy horn
I hallow for the use of humankind!
(Blesses with ᛗ.)
Companions, share the cup of kindness.
Let the kin of Ríg carouse together!
*(Leader pours a little onto the hearth, or offering bowl, drinks,
then offers it to the person to his or her left. Each person in turn
thereafter drinks and blesses the horn for the one sitting next to
him or her.)*

Holy Horse, to you I offer
Golden grain your heart to gladden.
(Blesses the bread. ᛗ*)*
Sacred Stallion, share this seed;
Mare of Magic, make us mighty!
White Horse, show your people the way of the gods!
*(Leader places a piece of bread before the White Horse, eats a
piece, then breaks off another and offers it to the first person to
the left. Each person in turn thereafter eats and breaks off and
blesses a piece for the one sitting next to him or her.)*

RETURNING TO THE WORLD

Let us now thank the Powers which have protected us:

Landspirits

Landspirits, alas, now you must leave us,
Wights of wind and earth and water
And fire, farewell, till next we call you!

Open Circle

Starting facing north and turning to the left, visualize the rune ring fading
and sinking into the ground.

Chapter 12

LAGUZ / INGWAZ: The Mysteries of Yngvi and Erde

IN THIS RITUAL WE HONOR YNGVI/FRODHI/SCEAF, the harvest god who comes out of and returns to the sea, and Nerthus, or Erde, the goddess of the earth and the waters. On the altar they might be represented by images, or by pictures of a wheat field and a lake or the sea.

This time, the meditation frames the ritual, the first part being read when all are gathered but before the ceremony, and the second part to bring everyone back to ordinary reality.

The ritual itself celebrates the interaction of god and goddess throughout the life cycle of the divine marriage, followed by death and transformation into a god, leading finally to rebirth as the divine child. If this seems reminiscent of Wiccan practice, it is because we are working with the Vanir, elements of whose worship may well have survived in English country places to become part of modern Wicca. If the group has begun its meetings in January, the INGWAZ/LAGUZ meeting will be taking place the following December, a time that supports the symbolism of the ritual. However, with some changes it can be done at any time of the year.

The group leader and someone of the opposite sex should take the roles of priest and priestess for this ritual.

You will need:

- A drum

- A large red candle

- A cauldron or large iron pot and a slab of dry ice (or a bowl of ice cubes or a quartz crystal)

- A substantial chair

- A gray or earth-colored cloth or cloak

- A round shield or platter, votive candle in glass, a small sheaf of wheat (available at floral supply stores) and a doll swaddled in a plain cloth

- A platter, bread, drinking horn, and a bottle of spring water

ESTABLISHING SACRED SPACE

Participants stand in a circle, facing the north. Intone the runes, inscribing each rune in the air as it is chanted and turning to the right, so that by the time the whole futhark has been called everyone has turned in a complete circle.

ᚠ FEHU	ᚺ HAGALAZ	↑ TIWAZ
ᚾ URUZ	ᚾ NAUDHIZ	ᛒ BERKANO
ᚦ THURISAZ	ᛁ ISA	ᛗ EHWAZ
ᚠ ANSUZ	ᚻ JERA	ᛗ MANNAZ
ᚱ RAIDHO	ᛏ EIHWAZ	ᚱ LAGUZ
ᚲ KENAZ	ᚲ PERTHRO	◇ INGWAZ
☓ GEBO	ᛉ ELHAZ	ᛗ DAGAZ
ᚹ WUNJO	ᛋ SOWILO	ᚷ OTHALA

MEDITATION: PART 1

(All sit comfortably. No drumbeat until end.)
You are at ease, still and silent,
Centered upon the earth.
Breathe in . . . and out . . . in . . . and out . . .
(4 counts in, hold 2, 4 out, hold 2)
As you relax, feel the solid earth supporting you.
Let your awareness sink downward, inward,
Deep into earth's core . . . now draw it up again.
Fill yourself with its power. . . .

Move out of your body now.
See a place that you know well.
Look at the ground; is it grass or stones?
Feel the texture, hear the sounds around.
As you gaze, you see the beginnings of a path.
Follow it away from the fields you know,
Through bushes that become a woodland,
Woods that turn to forest,
Forest that grows thicker, darker,
Till you are walking through a tunnel made of trees.

When at last the forest thins,
Before you is a clearing.
In its center grows the greatest of all trees,
So vast you cannot see around it,
So tall it pierces the sky.
Walk around it . . . from its base wind many paths.
Take one that leads to the east,
To a land where once the forest ruled.

As you walk, you see the needles of the pines
Are growing yellow,
From the branches of oaks and beeches
Flutter skeletons of leaves.
Dun colored clouds obscure the sun;
The cold air is acrid.
You push onward,
Stepping over the scabrous corpses of trees.
Somewhere ahead you can hear water—
You follow the sound.
The stream is before you.

Brown waters gurgle as they flow downstream.
But the banks are choked with debris
And scum floats on the waters.
There is no life in this river, and at its edges
Only a faint and struggling band of green.
The forest ends. Barren fields stretch before you
To a town where gray cement is stained black
By the plumes of black smoke that drift from burning towers.

What folk can live here,
Where no beast burrows or fishes swim
And in the forests no birds sing?
WE live here, if not today, then tomorrow.
It is our brothers and sisters
Who have laid waste to this land.
Be still, and listen,
Has earth herself a voice to call you?
Be silent, open your ears and your heart.

Faintly at first, you hear a murmur,
Like the voice of ancient waters,
The wind in vanished trees.
Stronger and louder the sound comes to you.
"Oh ye who are lost; oh ye who are orphaned,
Look for the lake at the heart of the world.
Call me, and I will arise from the waters.
Call my lover to me, and I will bring life to the land.
I offer myself to the one
Who knows how to make the offering.
Open the way and ready my wagon.
From the world before time I will come,
To the place between the worlds."

The children of a barren world
Creep among shadows
Trying to remember how to restore the land.
But now from the world before time,
The knowledge comes to you
Of the drama of life and death,
Of the rite that renews the world.
As the play is performed,
So awareness will awaken.
As the light is reborn, so comes enlightenment.

As above, so below—as it is done in the Dreamtime,
It shall come to pass in the world of everyday.

Deep within you feel earth's pulse pound;
(Begin soft drumbeat.)
As you breathe, the sound grows stronger.
Is it a heartbeat, or a drum
Whose beating wakes you to a new reality?
Listen, and know that you are not alone.
Others have been drawn to this place
By this need, for this purpose.
Open your eyes and see them around you.
Rise and stand together.
Together you will call the holy powers
To bring healing.
Together you will make a circle between the worlds,
Through which the fertile force
Of the god and the goddess can flow.

CREATING THE WORLD

The following was provided by Leigh Ann Hussey.

*(The priest lights a candle and lifts it; the priestess pours water
over dry ice in a cauldron so that vapor rises or holds up the bowl
of ice or the crystal. Together they say:)*
Fire thaws frost, Ice fixes flame.
Waxed were the worlds in this wise.
Fixing and flowing all things form,
So work we this world from the worlds.

THE RITE OF RENEWAL

(Men): Lady of the lake whose waters upwelling,
Lend life to the land, Erda, we hail thee.
Womb of the world,
Bestow now thy bounty.
Come from thy island, oh Mother of Many.
Come to the call of the kin of Ríg!

*(The priest leads the priestess around the circle. All surround her
and chant.)*

(All): La-gu . . . La-gu . . . La-gu . . . . .

(The priest makes the rune ᛉ over the priestess, assists her to sit before the hearth on the throne while an assistant holds the script. The priest goes to the other side of the circle.)

(Priestess): Erde am I, of all goddesses eldest,
Nerthus my name, Nehalennia also,
And Audhumla, whose tongue
Touched the ice into motion,
The lake and the land and the waters within it.
Unborn and undying, uneasy my sleeping,
Awaiting the ecstasy love will awaken.
Where is the warrior, holiest of heroes,
Whose seed will spark light
From the depths of the darkness?

(Women): Help we beseech
From the holiest of heroes,
Glory of men who gives life to the goddess.
The land longs for loving,
The womb for the warrior.
Where is the strong son of Ríg
Who will serve her?

(Priest): *(He moves slowly toward priestess.)*
The birds that sing at dawning
Set a fate upon my soul.
Where is the wondrous woman
Whose embrace will make me whole?

(Priestess): Within my dream of darkness
I hear a distant call.
Oh hasten, my beloved,
And I will give you all!

(Priest): The sun strikes sparks of splendor
From the surface of the sea.
The ship fares well and swiftly,
That carries me to Thee.

(Priestess): The gleam of light on water
Stirs sweetness in my heart,

The frozen depths are melting,
How can we stay apart?

(Priest): The fertile fields are sprouting
With the first faint haze of green.
The sacred grove admits me
As I come to claim my queen!

(He kneels before priestess and salutes her.)

(Priestess): To passion thou didst stir me
When first I saw thy face,
Now awaken life within me
With the power of thy embrace!

(She raises him, they kiss, then he escorts her around circle and she blesses everyone.)

(Priest): In byre and barn bound up is the harvest.
Now in the northland the nights grow long.
Through the bright days of the summer
I have served thee,
And I become weary—oh my beloved.
Upon thy soft breast let me rest in the darkness.
Let me sink into sleep . . . let me drown . . .
Let me die. . . .

(She embraces him, drawing her cloak around him, and as he relaxes, slowly lowers him to the floor in front of her throne and covers him completely.)

(Women): Now over sea
Shall the ship safely bear him.
Hid in the howe the hero must lie.
The lord is laid low
And the land left in darkness.
Weep, oh ye women!
Weep for the warrior!
Yng-vi . . . Yng-vi . . . Yng-vi . . .

(Priestess draws the rune ◇ over the mound, sits.)

(Priest): (He sits up with cloth draped around him and over lap of priestess.)
Yngvi am I, earthgod most enduring,
Frodhi and Freyr, lord and landmaster.
From light through night I make my journey;
Bound in the mound, in darkness hidden
The secret seed of life lies sleeping.
Slain, I serve to feed the living,
Sacrificed, fulfill the cycle.
Men, I make your fields grow fertile,
And fill with fruit the wombs of women.

(One by one, people come up, kneel before the priest, and receive his blessing.)

(Men): Home is the hero; here the warrior
Rules a realm beneath the ground.
From the mound the king
His kin may counsel.
But where is a lord to lead the living?

(Priestess): I am the sea and the ship that moves o'er it.
I am the well and the waterfall flowing,
The water of life and the womb that contains it,
Silent streams stirring beneath the earth's darkness.
I cradled the life of my love in my cauldron,
In the vessel of life through the year's waning bore him.
(In Fall or Winter, say:)
Now comes the longest night—
Now let the spark of light
(OR in Spring or Summer say:)
Now when the days grow long,
Now as the sun grows strong,
(In all seasons say:)
From the tomb of my womb
Be released and reborn!

(Women): By sheaf and by shield,
By fire and by field,
May the ship of Ullr
Bear the babe safely to shore!
(Priestess brings shield with child, etc. out from under the throne, passes it around the circle.)

(Priest and Priestess): Behold the sacred sheaf
From the earth arising.
Behold the light of life
In the darkness shining!
Behold the holy child
From the realm of death returning!

FEAST

(Priest): *(Draws ◇ rune over bread.)*
The fruitful field is filled with a golden harvest.
Behold the seed of Ing, may it feed your body!

(Priestess): *(Draws ⌐ rune over horn.)*
The sparkling lake brims with sweet water.
Behold the water of life, may it restore your spirit!
(All sing "The Corn that Springeth Green")

Now the green blade ris - eth from the bur - ied grain,
Corn that in the dark earth many days has lain,
Love lives again, that with the dead has been:
Love is come again, like corn that springeth green.

(All): Hail the turning sun.
Hail to the continuing clan.
Hail to Yngvi and Erde,
Lord and Lady of Love and Life!

RETURNING TO THE WORLD

(Priest and Priestess hold up candle and ice and say:)
What has been Fixed, let flow.
What was in flux, let firm.
We wind this world back into the worlds.
The circle of life is shaped anew.

(Priest blows out candle. All sit down again for conclusion of the meditation that frames the ritual.)

MEDITATION, PART 2

The ritual is over.
(drum)
The god and the goddess
Have given new life to the world.
Close your eyes now, let your breathing slow.
Remember the way by which you came.
See once more around you the wasteland.
The waters of the goddess have washed it clean.
As the newborn sun rises,
You see that through the soil
The seed of the god is sprouting, vigorous and green.
Go back through the forest, and look at the trees—
On each branch new buds are bursting,
The waters run clean and sparkling
And in their depths tiny creatures swim.
Above, you hear the song of returning birds.

Deeper and deeper move into the forest.
The path you follow curves.
You see the great Tree once more.
You have been walking around it.
There before you is the path by which you came.
Follow it. Come out into the light again.
Look ahead—there is the place that you know.

Sit down, feel the weight of your flesh,
The solid ground below.
Sink down into your body.
The world of everyday re-forms around you.
Now breathe in and out, in and out again.

(Read more quickly from here.)
Sigh and stretch. Open your eyes.
You are home.

Open Circle

Starting facing north and turning to the left, visualize the rune ring fading and sinking into the ground.

Chapter 13

DAGAZ / OTHALA:
Kinship and Awakening

WHEN THESE TWO RUNES ARE TAKEN together, the understanding to which one is awakened by DAGAZ is the meaning of OTHALA, kinship and one's true home. This point is established at the beginning by the challenge. In the course of the ritual, each member of the group claims kin right in the community by bringing to it his or her gifts of skill and spirit. They recognize each other as kindred and extend that recognition to the other beings with whom we share the land. This is the awareness that leads to awakening and allows us to form a real family.

The entire ritual can be led by a single person, or, as usual, you may divide up the lines. The invocation to the house spirit, however, should be said by the person in whose home the meeting is being held.

For the ritual you will need a votive light in a holder for each participant, a horn of mead or cider, and a platter of bread. The altar may be decorated with contributions representing each member of the group.

Before the end of the meeting, discuss plans for the final meeting and ritual with the group. Ask each member to create something that demonstrates his or her mastery of the runes—a poem for one of the runes (or all of them), a painting, or a ritual item incorporating runic symbolism. Decide on a token of achievement to be given out (see the instructions for the ritual at the end of the next chapter). They should also bring their rune sets.

ESTABLISHING SACRED SPACE

Challenge

> *(Keep lights dim.)*
> *(Leader)*: Who comes here to the holy home?
> Wanderer, what clan and kin do you claim?
>
> *(Keep lights dim.)*
> *(Each person)*: From the kin of Ríg am I descended,
> from the womb of Erda was I born.
>
> *(Leader)*: Enter then, for all Ríg's kindred are one clan,
> and all Earth's children welcome here.

Participants stand in a circle, facing the north. Intone the runes, inscribing each rune in the air as it is chanted and turning to the right, so that by the time the whole futhark has been called everyone has turned in a complete circle.

ᚠ FEHU	ᚺ HAGALAZ	↑ TIWAZ
ᚢ URUZ	ᚾ NAUDHIZ	ᛒ BERKANO
ᚦ THURISAZ	ᛁ ISA	ᛗ EHWAZ
ᚨ ANSUZ	ᚻ JERA	ᛗ MANNAZ
ᚱ RAIDHO	ᛇ EIHWAZ	ᛚ LAGUZ
ᚲ KENAZ	ᛈ PERTHRO	◇ INGWAZ
ᚷ GEBO	ᛉ ELHAZ	ᛞ DAGAZ
ᚹ WUNJO	ᛋ SOWILO	ᛟ OTHALA

HOME AND HERITAGE

(Leader): Behold, we stand together.
But is this place our home?
Dark lies the land, by shadow dimmed.
The home we need by night is hidden.
How shall the descendants of Ríg
Recognize their kindred?
How shall the children of Mannus find their heritage?
Draw the rune of illumination between your brows. ᛞ
Be still, and seek the inheritance that hides within.

MEDITATION

(All sit comfortably. Do not begin drumming until indicated.)
Breathe in . . . and out . . . in . . . and out . . .
(4 beats in, hold 2, 4 beats out, hold 2)
You are relaxed, at peace, you sit in safety.
Safely you will fare forward, safely you will return.
You will remember all you need to know.
As you relax, feel the solid earth supporting you.
Let your awareness sink downward, inward,
Deep into earth's core . . . now draw it up again.
Fill yourself with its power. . . .

Move out of your body now.
See a place that you know well.
It is night, the world is hid by shadow.
Feel the texture of the ground beneath you;
Listen to the rustlings in the dark.
Dimly you make out the beginnings of a path.

Follow it away from the fields you know
Till you are walking through the deeper darkness
Of a tunnel made of trees.

When at last the forest thins,
Before you is a clearing.
In its center grows the greatest of all trees,
So vast you cannot see around it,
So tall it pierces the sky.
It glows with its own light, center post of the world.
Walk around it . . . the path spirals outward.
You move through Midgard in an expanding circle,
Through a realm whose outer seeming
Is always smaller than what lies within.

But it is dark here.
You wander through a land of shadow.
Where will you find kindred or companions?
Where you will you find shelter?
There are sounds in the darkness—
The wind whispers softly,
Invisible creatures are stirring,
Or is it the land itself that is turning in its sleep?
Before you now a greater darkness opens;
You scent the moist-earth smell of a cave.
You can see nothing, but here, at least,
You will be out of the wind.
Cautiously you enter; the air grows warmer.
Exhausted, you sink down
And feel yourself cradled and secure.

Presently you become aware of a regular rhythm—
Is it your own heartbeat?
(Soft drumbeat begins.)
It shakes your body, but it is deeper;
That rhythm pulses through the very stone.
A gentle breath of wind sighs through the darkness;
The earth is breathing around you—
Mother Earth is stirring,
SHE is stirring, your first ancestor,
You lie safe in her womb.
This earth does not belong to you,
But you belong to the land.

Your bones, your flesh—
All are part of Mother Earth
And must return to her in the end.
Feel the earthpower flowing through you. . . .
Here is your home. . . .

You blink as a red glow flickers
On curving walls of stone.
From a crack in the earth firelight is flickering.
Figures spring into bold relief
On the walls of the cavern—
Shaggy mammoths and sturdy horses,
Elk with branching antlers
And aurochs with twisting horns.
Bear and wolf snarl from the shadows,
A mouse darts across the floor,
From the ceiling soar swan and eagle,
Serpents coil in the shadows,
Fish gleam where water runs down the stone.

The painted creatures quiver in the firelight,
Or is it a fire?
Now the light seems to come from some distance—
In the east a pink glow is growing,
And cavern walls have turned to rocks and trees.
The animals around you fade into the wilderness,
The birds soar skyward, reptiles seek their holes,
The fish leave a trail of silver bubbles
On the surface of the stream.
You stand and face the east
And draw the rune DAGAZ.
Suddenly light leaps into the heavens.
Radiance overwhelms you;
Suddenly everything is clear.
You are surrounded by living beings.
The beasts are your brothers,
Part of the Earth, and part of you.

Now the sky grows bright;
The sun fills the sky with radiance.
DAGAZ drives the chill of night from your bones.
She too is of your kindred.
Without the fire of the sun to warm you,

You would freeze.
Earth is Sun's daughter—
Without her, she would be solid, unmoving,
Without the sun, time too would freeze.
In that eternity of frozen time, nothing would happen.
But this is our day, brief but full.
How shall we fill it?

Beyond the trees you can see open country.
Ahead someone is singing—move toward the sound.
Pause at the edge of the forest.
Ahead you see cleared fields.
The growing light shows you the shapes of dwellings.
Look carefully—what are they made of?
People are emerging to greet the dawning.
What do they look like? What do they wear?

Someone calls—they have seen you.
Suddenly a laughing crowd surrounds you,
Bringing you into the village.
The light grows, and you realize
That you look and are dressed the same.
These are your clan and kindred.
To the largest dwelling they bring you,
And there sits a woman, old, but beautiful.
She is your mother.
You embrace her and know that this is your home. . . .

As the sun rolls through the sky,
The scene changes around you.
The shapes of the houses alter,
The faces of the people change,
And their colors and costumes.
With each change of scene,
You gain new skills, new understanding.
But always you know that they are your kinfolk,
The children of your ancient mother,
Everchanging, and always the same.
Look upon them, love them, remember them. . . .
These are your kindred, and your homes.

Now you see the house of your grandparents,
And then the place where you grew up,

The faces of those you last called father and mother.
The sun is overhead.
Light fills the air;
You see everything with perfect clarity.
You remember things
They told you about their families;
You see now the gifts that they have given you,
Your inheritance in this lifetime,
And your understanding of home.

All days are one day, through which we strive.
Evil times may come, but they shall pass,
And who will care a thousand years from now?
Cattle die and kinsfolk die
And soon you yourself will pass
But reputation never dies,
Nor the learning of a thousand lifetimes,
The inheritance bred into blood and bone.
Who are you?
What is your heritage?
Where is your true home?

The light brightens till it transcends human vision.
You are lit from within,
And everything around you grows luminous.
The place in which you are dwelling
Becomes fair beyond mortal imagination.
Look at it, touch it,
Wander through its courts and chambers,
Memorize the furnishings of your spirit's home.
Find one thing that you will take with you
Back into the waking world.

There are others here with you—
In this fair light you see their true faces,
And in the waters of a pool
You see your own transformation.
You are the true child of your mother.
You see her in the face in the mirror,
And in the faces of your kin.
Light fills you, light rays out around you,
And then it fades.

You are the self you know once more,
But all that you have learned you will remember.
Before you the great Tree rises.
Beyond it is the path by which you came.
Follow it. Go back through the tunnel of trees.
Come out into the light again.
Look ahead—there is the place that you know.

Sit down, feel the weight of your flesh,
The solid ground below.
Sink down into your body.
Remember what you have learned.
Now breathe in and out, in and out again.
(Read more quickly from here.)
Sigh and stretch. Open your eyes.
You are in the sacred enclosure once more.

BUILDING A NEW HOME

Day dawns! Darkness is gone!
(ᛗ *Light candle, hold high.*)
Let holy light with blessing bright
This sacred ground with sunfire bound!
(Carry candle clockwise around circle.)

In every age the offspring of Ríg
Are left a legacy of land and people.
Heimdall's godchildren, what gifts got you
Of body and spirit from clan and kinfolk?
What have you learned? What powers are in you?
What do you bring to build our home?

(Each person): Day dawns, darkness is gone!
These are the gifts I bring—

*(Each one in turn lights candle from the person next to him or her,
then describes inherited qualities—physical or mental traits,
national or cultural inheritance, etc., personal gifts that can contribute to astral clanhold.)*

Behold the dawning of a new day!
The light of life our home illumines!
Behold the bright eyes of your brothers.

Hail your sisters and the sibs of your spirit!
Here is your clan and here your kindred,
The human family with whom you share the sacred ground—

(Each person clasps crossed arms with those to either side, being careful of the candles.)

We are the light-born, of Life and Life-longing.
We are the wights who are fed by the Worldtree,
Midgard the home which we inherit.
A new day is dawning out of the darkness.
With what kin shall we share the land,
What clans shall we claim in time to come?

Wide-winged wind riders, Four-footed furred ones,
Swimmers in the sea, and deep earth dwellers—
Now I honor.

(Each one in turn names a creature with which he or she feels especial kinship, such as "All the cats . . .")

(All respond): As kin we claim you on Midgard's ground!
(When everyone has spoken—)
(All): "Hail to thee Day, and Day's bright boy,
Hail to the Night and her daughter's joy.
With eyes that bless us may you see
And grant to those here, victory.
The goddesses and gods we call
And holy earth, who gives to all—
Give us here wise words and weal,
And in this life, the hands that heal!"

("Sigdrifumál": 2, freely translated)

FEAST

(All sit down, set candles carefully in circle.)
Behold the liquid light of heaven
(Bless horn with ᛗ.)
Spirit that the sun has given,
Sweetness from earth's flowers distilling,
All of Life's desire fulfilling.
(Pass horn.)
Behold the golden corn that's growing,

(Bless bread with ᛉ.)
Sprung in fields of no man's sowing,
The children of the Tree to nourish,
So that the clan of life may flourish.
(Pass bread.)

(Owner of place where meeting is): **Hail to the spirit of our home.**
Hallow the hall and hold it in safety!
Holy one, to thee this food and drink I offer—
(He or she offers juice and bread to the housespirit in the rock by the hearth or heater and passes the horn and platter around the circle.)

RETURNING TO THE WORLD

Darkness descends! Daylight ends,
(All put out candles.)
But holy light with blessing bright
Remains within this round, unbound!

Open Circle

Starting facing north and turning to the left, visualize the rune ring fading and sinking into the ground.

Chapter 14

DESCENDING THE TREE

YOUR STUDY OF THE RUNES BEGAN with a ritual; performing a similar rite at the end of the sequence will provide closure for this stage of your runic education. But there is a reason that similar ceremonies are called "commencement," "graduation," or "initiation." Although such ceremonies take place at the end of a period of study, they recognize that this is a rite of passage into the next phase of life or learning. This graduation ritual will give you all a chance to honor the bond that has developed among you, and either release the group identity, or prepare to move on to anotherstage of study.

Before the ritual, each participant should be assigned to create a poem, short essay, or a piece of art or craftwork expressing what he or she has learned about one of the runes.

It can be rewarding to mark this achievement by the presentation of some piece of jewelry—a disk of copper or leather inscribed with all of the runes, a bag to carry a rune set, or a ring. William Thorpe of Future Relics makes silver rune-rings which are very appropriate. He can be reached at 48 East Maine Rd., Johnson City, New York 13790 (607-7948-0873).

You will also need cookies with runes drawn on them in icing, cards or candles bearing each rune, a horn and mead to put in it, and if possible, an image of Odin.

ESTABLISHING SACRED SPACE

Participants stand in a circle, facing the north. Intone the runes, inscribing each rune in the air as it is chanted and turning to the right, so that by the time the whole futhark has been called everyone has turned in a complete circle.

ᚠ FEHU	ᚺ HAGALAZ	ᛏ TIWAZ
ᚢ URUZ	ᚾ NAUDHIZ	ᛒ BERKANO
ᚦ THURISAZ	ᛁ ISA	ᛖ EHWAZ
ᚨ ANSUZ	ᛃ JERA	ᛗ MANNAZ
ᚱ RAIDHO	ᛇ EIHWAZ	ᛚ LAGUZ
ᚲ KENAZ	ᛈ PERTHRO	◊ INGWAZ
ᚷ GEBO	ᛉ ELHAZ	ᛞ DAGAZ
ᚹ WUNJO	ᛋ SOWILO	ᛟ OTHALA

INVOCATION

(Leader): Honor we now Odin All-father,
Tree-Rider, Rune-winner, giver of good rede.
The Way of Wisdom we have walked.
The road to rune-might we have ridden.
Within our hearts we now would hold them—
Galdrfather, give to us your blessing.

(All sing "Odin Welcome")

(Solo): Open a way between the worlds—
(All): Behold, the ravens fly,
(Solo): Open a way into our hall—
(All): For Allfather draws nigh!
(Solo): His gifts to us are wit and will, His wisdom sets us free,
(All): A horn we raise in welcome to the god of ecstasy!

(Solo): Nine worlds there are upon the Tree,
(All): Behold, the ravens fly,
(Solo): Who knows the secrets of them all?
(All): The wanderer draws nigh!
(Solo): He knows the darkness and the light, the heavens and
    the sea,
(All): A horn we raise in welcome to the god of ecstasy!

(Solo): The Rider of the Tree draws near;
(All): Behold the ravens fly,
(Solo): The Runes of Power flare forth in might,
(All): For Galdor-father's nigh!
(Solo): The patterns of our lives laid out in sacred signs we see—
(All): A horn we raise in welcome to the god of ecstasy

"Odin Welcome"   words, music, Diana L. Paxson

O - pen a way be - tween the worlds BE- HOLD THE RA ˉ VENS   FLY!

O - pen a way in ˉ to our hall, FOR ALL- FA - THER DRAWS NIGH! His

gifts to us are wit and will, his wis - dom sets us free, A

HORN WE RAISE IN WEL- COME TO THE GOD OF EC - STA - SY!

TEACHING

(Leader): Hear what Odin says of the runes in the "Hávamál":
"'Tis time to sing at the seat of Thul,
At the Well of Wyrd.
I watched but said nothing,   I watched and thought,
I heard Hár's lore.
I heard men speaking   of the runes,
In the hall of Hár   I heard them say—"

                                                                    (111)

"Runes you must seek   and staves of counsel,
Most mighty staves,
Strongest staves,
That Fimbulthulr stained   that the great gods fashioned,
That were graven and be-spelled by Hrópt."

                                                                    (141)

Hear now the words of the High One—

"I know I was hanged   on the windy tree
For nine full nights,
Stabbed by a spear,   offered to Odin,
Sworn by myself to myself,
Upon that Tree   that no man knows
From what roots it rises.
No bread did they bear to me   nor horn handed,
Into the deep I gazed—
I took up the runes, took them up, screaming,
Then fell back again."

                                                                    (138–139)

Will you seek the wisdom of Odin?
Is it your will to receive the runes?
(All): It is.

MEDITATION

You are at ease, still and silent,
Centered upon the earth.
Breathe in . . . and out . . . in . . . and out . . .
(4 beats in, hold 2, 4 beats out, hold 2)
Let the cares of the world of men be gone.

You are relaxed, at peace, you sit in safety.
Safely you will fare forward, safely you will return.
You will remember all you need to know.

As you relax, feel the solid earth supporting you.
Let your awareness sink downward, inward,
Deep into earth's core . . . now draw it up again.
Fill yourself with its power. . . .

Move out of your body now.
See a place that you know well.
Look at the ground; is it grass or stones?
Feel the texture, hear the sounds around.
As you gaze, you see the beginnings of a path.
Follow it away from the fields you know,
Through bushes that become a woodland,
Woods that turn to forest,
Forest that grows thicker, darker,
Till you are walking through a tunnel made of trees.

When at last the forest thins,
Before you is a clearing.
In its center grows the greatest of all trees,
So vast you cannot see around it,
So tall it pierces the sky.

Three great roots plunge through the soil.
Beneath the nearest, a passage opens.
You pass within and find a dim, featureless light
That shows you the way.
From the north to the east you fare,
Spiraling downward,
And from the east to the south again.
As you turn westward,
A cool mist swirls around you, veils of mist,
Moist and soothing
Drawing a curtain to separate you from the world.

You float in the mist, midway
Between earth and heaven,
And hear nearby the roaring of a mighty river,
Water that rushes over rocks and rapids
Booms as it falls, mist swirls and you see

The Thunderflood's fury, and in the depths flashing
A fish-swift flickering reflection of sunlight.
The mist drifts and eddies. Turning, you follow
And glimpse, white with rime,
The roots of the Worldtree.
A well lies beneath them, mirror-dark in the shadows.
Deep is that well, from which the Norns drink daily,
And weave the world's fate at the base of the Tree.

The Tree rises high from its roots in the depths.
The bark of its trunk is all slabbed and twisted,
Easy to climb for the one who has need.
Above, the wood is worn and use-smoothed.
See there the spot where for nine nights, alone,
The High One hung between the worlds.

Would you seek the runes?
Ask a blessing of Odin before ascending.
Then, moving carefully, clamber upward.
Let its branches embrace your body. . . .
Sink back, oh seeker, upon the Tree,
Hanging between earth and heaven.
Sense the abyss that opens below you,
The immensity above, the roots and the branches,
The nine worlds and the spine of spirit that links them.

Wind whispers past you, ravens wing round;
Croaking their wisdom, they perch in the Tree.
Suspended, your own stillness deepens;
Your body is bound but your spirit flies freely.
Summon now the sacred runes!
Let the symbols soar before you.
As each is named, you must see it,
Accept it,
Make it your own!
Open your eyes, for that place is this place,
And what is done in this place
Is accomplished in all the worlds. . . .

*(Leader lights appropriate candle, displays the rune, and all
intone the rune. The individual who has prepared that rune then
makes a one minute presentation. At end, the rune is intoned
again, and all draw it on their foreheads. Leader allows a few
moments more for internalization, then lights next candle, etc.)*

Be still, think on the things you've learned:
"These runes now you know, which kings and queens
Know not, nor any earthly wight,
Of help to the sons of men,
Of harm to the sons of the Jotnar;
Hail to whoever spoke them,
Hail to whoever knows them!
Gain they who grasp them,
Happy they who heed them!"

("Hávamál": 142, 146, 165, adapted)

The runes you have won will remain with you.
Now close your eyes,
See the branches of the Tree around you.
Carefully from the Tree climb downward—
The bark of the trunk is all slabbed and twisted.
Easily you will descend
Until midst tangled roots you're standing
Beside the well where wait the Norns.
Offer your gratitude to Odin.

Now the mists are rising, gray cloud engulfs you,
Cool cloud caresses, root and pool are hidden.
Turn and make your way upward,
From the west to the south,
From the south to the east and north once more.
You emerge from beneath the arching root
And see the Tree rising above you.
There before you is the path by which you came.
Follow it. Go back through the tunnel of trees.
Come out into the light again.
Look ahead—there is the place that you know.

Sit down, feel the weight of your flesh,
The solid ground below.
You step onto solid earth. Steady you stand now.
All here is darkness.
Sink down into your body.
Remember what you have learned.
Now breathe in and out . . . in and out again . . .
Welcome rune-wielders, to the world returning.

APPLICATION

Everyone takes out his or her rune set. The person sitting closest to the North (A) turns to the person to his or her left (B) and asks a question. "A" then draws three runes from "B's" bag. "B" must now divine an answer to the question from reading those three runes. If the group is small, others may be invited to offer their own comments and interpretations once "B" has finished.

When the divination is done, "B" turns to the person on his or her left— "C," and the process is repeated all the way around the room, until everyone has asked a question and divined an answer.

FEAST

(Hold up horn of mead.)
"Beer I bring thee,   thou 'tree-of-battle,'
Mixed with might,   mingled with honor,
Full of spells   and songs of power
With goodly charms   and runes of joy."

("Sigdrifumál": 6)

"Often were shaved off   those runes that were scratched on,
And mixed into the holy mead,
And sent everywhere,
Some to the Aesir,   some to the Alfar,
Some to the wise Vanir,
And some to mortal men."

("Sigdrifumál": 18)

(The leader carries the horn around the circle and say to each:)
Drink deeply, wise one,
Since runes you have won here.
(Name) Runemistress/master
Now do I name thee.
(Then bless the plate of rune cookies.)
As you have taken the runes into your hearts,
Take this rune into your body,
And with it a blessing.
(Symbols of achievement can also be presented at this time.)

RETURNING TO THE WORLD

All-father Odin, now we thank thee—
High One, hear us, our hearts are grateful.
The runes we've won may we well remember.
Though these symbols we lose,
In our hearts they live.
Thy wisdom, wanderer, we bear into the world.

Open Circle

All sing the "Futhark Song" as you visualize the rune ring fading and sinking into the ground. Rune candles or cards are blown out or taken down.

Chapter 15

A RUNIC INITIATION

ONE MAY WALK THE WAY OF THE RUNES for many reasons—to learn how to use the runes in divination or magic, or as a key to the culture and worldview of the North, or as an introduction to the gods. For most students, study and meditation of the kind described in this book will be sufficient, but there may be some who feel the need to test themselves and their commitment. Such a testing should not be considered a prerequisite to working with the runes, but for those who feel compelled to do so, here is a procedure that, in our experience, can have a profound impact.

Like other rituals of commitment, an initiation to the runes is not to be entered into lightly. It is certainly not a shortcut to knowledge. The impact of the experience is in fact directly proportional to the amount of preparation and the depth of understanding that the initiate brings to it. Therefore, unless you have spent at least a year in serious study and can already name and discuss the significance of all the runes without looking them up, all you will get out of it is an uncomfortable night. For this reason, you may want to spend some time after completing this course of study and going through the "graduation" rite, applying what you have learned, and undergo the runic initiation only when you feel you have completed the journeyman stage of your study.

You should already have considerable experience in sustained and focused meditation—contemplation of a chosen subject—and the ability to move between different levels of trance at will. The mind must be sufficiently disciplined to visualize on cue, and to keep focused and awake with minimal physical stimuli. The experience of hanging on the Tree is the focus at the beginning and end of the meditation; however, most of the energy is directed toward internalizing and learning about each rune.

It may help if you articulate some specific goals, such as identifying one new way to apply the energy of each rune in your life, or a format, such as contemplating the action of the rune at the archetypal, legendary, social, and natural levels. The other requirement is an appropriate setting and at least two dependable friends, at least one of whom knows the runes well enough to pronounce them properly and is experienced enough to make sure you do not get into any trouble.

Essentially, the ritual consists of spending the night bound to a tree, during which the runes are presented at regular intervals. The initiate remains in a state of light trance for an extended period, during which it becomes possible to contemplate all of the runes simultaneously and to understand the connections between them.

To do this, you will need a tree located somewhere protected from the sights and sounds of humanity. These conditions can usually be met only on extended private land or at a public park with camping facilities during a time when it is not too crowded.

A more dramatic version of this ritual is described in my novel *The Wolf and the Raven*; however, the Walkyriun in the book were accustomed to enduring a rather higher level of hardship than most modern runesters. For most of us, simply spending the night awake in the woods is quite uncomfortable enough. The tree should be chosen carefully, straight enough to provide some support and close enough to the campsite so that your helpers can come and go without too much difficulty. Check to be sure it is not bleeding sap. You can place a small folding stool against it. You will need a heavy cloak or blanket to wrap up in and enough rope to tie you to the tree.

Your helpers will need a flashlight or candle lantern, a set of runes drawn in red on white paper or several sticks of incense, a small vial of aromatic oil, and a drum. A cane or staff is also helpful to steady them over rough ground. They should have somewhere comfortable to wait, and since they will not be in trance, enough coffee to keep them awake. Two helpers are necessary not only to watch the initiate, but to keep an eye on each other. The initiate goes through the night without being aware of the passage of time, and often with minimal awareness of the physical body. The helpers, on the other hand, must stay conscious enough to negotiate a difficult trail twenty-five times without falling.

PREPARATION

Ideally, the initiate should fast during the day before the ritual and spend as much time as possible in contemplation. At some time during the day, select your tree, make an offering (pour some mead or juice onto its roots) and ask its cooperation, set up your seat, and bless the space. The site selected should be a short walk from the place where the guide(s) will be waiting, by a path that can be negotiated easily in the dark. Set up the seat in front of the tree and test it for comfort. Padding the seat with a cushion or fur is a good idea. Prepare the ropes ahead of time as well—one for your neck, one to go around the upper arms, and one around the waist.

The purpose is not to test your ability to endure pain, but to create a situation that will facilitate deep and sustained, focused concentration. Cold and insect bites can be seriously distracting, therefore dress warmly, including a head covering, preferably with a hood that can be drawn down over your face. Use insect repellent on exposed areas of skin. The main problem with sitting without moving for a long period is muscle cramps—a few calcium lactate tablets will help prevent this. A cup of strong coffee or tea will also help, but don't drink too much liquid and visit the lavatory before you begin.

THE RITUAL

The ritual begins at midnight. The guide and assistant escort the initiate to the tree, one carrying the ropes, the other beating softly on a drum. The guide asks the local landspirits to allow this ritual to take place in their

territory, and to protect the initiate. He or she asks the tree to lend its help
and inscribes it with EIHWAZ (ᛇ). The guide may smudge the tree and the
initiate as well. Facing the initiate, the guide then says:

> *(Guide)*: Hear now the words of the High One—
> "I know I was hanged   on the windy tree
> For nine full nights,
> Stabbed by a spear,   offered to Odin,
> Sworn by myself to myself,
> Upon that Tree   that no man knows
> From what roots it rises.
> No bread did they bear to me   nor horn handed,
> Into the deep I gazed—
> I took up the runes, took them up, screaming,
> Then fell back again."
>
> ("Hávamál": 138–39)

> Will you, _____, seek the wisdom of Odin?
> Is it your will to be bound to the Tree?

> *(Initiate)*: It is.

> *(The initiate prays to Odin to ask his permission while the guide
> offers a prayer to Odin, asking his blessing on the initiate. The
> guide then wraps the initiate warmly and binds him or her to the
> tree, with a noose around the neck, and the ropes around arms
> and waist tight enough to lean on, but loose enough so that
> small adjustments of position are possible, and in an emergency
> the initiate could free him- or herself. The ideal is enough discom-
> fort to prevent the initiate from falling asleep, but not so much as
> to be distracting.)*

> *(Guide)*: This is the Tree of Life,
> The link between earth and heaven,
> The axis of all the worlds.
> This tree is your support;
> This tree is your torment;
> This tree shall teach you wisdom.
> Sink down, sink inward,
> Become one with the Tree.

> *(The guide or assistant begins to drum and continues for some
> minutes to allow deepening of trance. [Negotiate with initiate*

*whether he or she would like a trance induction or simply an
extended drumming sequence, what speed and rhythm work
best, etc.])*

(Guide): **"Runes you must seek   and staves of counsel
Most mighty staves
Strongest staves
That Fimbulthulr stained   that the great gods fashioned
That were graven and spelled by Hrópt."**

("Hávamál": 141)

Here is the first of those runes that he took up from the Tree.
*(The guide holds up the first rune card (FEHU) so that the light
shines through or on it, and intones the rune name. An alternate
method is to draw the rune in the air with a lighted incense stick
or cigarette. Note that the rune must be drawn backwards from
the point of view of the guide, in order to be seen correctly by the
initiate. Guide then draws the rune on the initiate's forehead with
the holy oil. After this, the guide and assistant withdraw, leaving
the initiate alone in the darkness to meditate on its meaning.
Following the same procedure, the Guide brings and displays
another rune every ten to fifteen minutes (depending on when
you started). The intervals should be as precise as possible so
that the initiate can internalize the timing. The regular stimulation
of light and sound keep the initiate from falling asleep or going
too deeply into trance. The result is a regular pattern of deepen-
ing and lightening trance that can be maintained for an extended
period. The guide and assistant may both stay awake the entire
night, or, if both are experienced with the runes, they may divide
it into two shifts. The process concludes at dawn (approximately
6 a.m.) with DAGAZ and OTHALA. Allow fifteen minutes more, then
bring a horn of warm herb tea with a dash of whiskey or mulled
cider or mead.*
*When the guide returns with the drink, he or she should call the
initiate by name to return to the Midgard of humankind. If sufficiently focused, the initiate may reply with Sigdrifa's prayer:)*

(Initiate): **"Hail to thee Day, and Day's bright boy,
Hail to the Night and her daughter's joy.
With eyes that bless us may you see
And grant to those here, victory.
The goddesses and gods we call
And holy earth, who gives to all—**

Give us here wise words and weal,
And in this life, the hands that heal!"

("Sigdrifumál": 2, freely translated)

(Guide): "Beer I bring thee,   thou 'tree-of-battle,'
Mixed with might,   mingled with honor,
Full of spells   and songs of power
With goodly charms   and runes of joy."

("Sigdrifumál": 6)

"Often were shaved off   those runes that were scratched on,
And mixed into the holy mead,
And sent everywhere,
Some to the Aesir,   some to the Alfar,
Some to the wise Vanir,
And some to mortal men."

("Sigdrifumál": 18)

Drink deeply, wise one,
Since runes thou hast won here.
(Name) Runemistress/master
Now do I name thee.

(The guide holds the horn so that the initiate can drink, then unties him or her from the tree. While the initiate recovers, the guide should thank Odin for sustaining and teaching, and thank the tree and the local landspirits for their support and protection.)

PRONUNCIATION GUIDE

The following notes should help you with the sounds of Old Norse and Anglo-Saxon.

OLD NORSE: emphasis on first syllable of words.

a = ah, **á** = aow, **au** = oy, **æ** = aye (a before ng is á)
e = eh, **é** = ieh, **ei** = ay (ayeh)
i = ih, **í** = ee, **oe** = aye
o = aw, **ó** = oh, **œ/ ö/ø** = eu
u = uh, **ú** = ooh
y = iy, **´y** = ee

þ "th" as in <u>th</u>ing
ð = dh, or th as in <u>the</u>
ll = tl
f between vowels = v
g can be soft ("j") or hard (as in "go")
j = ye
r before n hardly pronounced
r trilled

terminal n, l, s, all double in nominative = Oðinn
-R ends other nominatives
plurals: **ir, ar, ur**

ANGLO-SAXON (OLD ENGLISH): emphasis (stress) is usually heaviest on the first syllable or root, though in compound words, the root syllable of the second element has a secondary stress. Prefixes are usually unstressed.

a - or ´ above a letter means that the vowel is long (or occasionally indicates a stressed syllable)
a = "á" as in "ah" or "a" = "o" as in "pot"
æ = "a" as in "hat"
"æ" = "a" as in "mare" ("eh")

e = "é" as in "see" and "e" as in "egg"

i = "í" as in "machine" and "i" as in "bid"

o = "ó" as in "boat" and "o" as in "not"

u = "ú" as "oo" and "u" as in "bush"

y is a kind of "eu" sound, like the u in the French "reçu" (short) or "lune" (long)

f, s, þ/ð are soft initially but voiced between vowels, cf. "sits" versus "raisin", or "think" versus "other" or "five" versus "over"

h is hard initially, as in "hail," but in the middle or end of a word is like the "ch" in "loch"

r is slightly trilled or rolled

k is sometimes used instead of c to begin a word

c is pronounced "k" before a, o, or u (usually)
         or "ch" (as in "cheap") before i, y, or ea

g before a consonant or back vowel is hard, as in "goat"; before a front vowel it is a "ye" or "w" sound ("dragan" = "drawen")

sg is pronounced like a soft G or "dg" as in "judge"

sc or **sh** are both as in "ship"

All letters are voiced, even consonant combinations as in "writan" = *eritan*, or "cnihten" = *kuhni'hten*

British letters and letters used for Old English sounds:

w	p (wynn), uo, w = "w"
d	ð, (eth) or Ð = "th" as in "the"
T	þ (thorn) = "th" as in "this"
A	æ (ash)= "a" as in "hat"
	(yogh) or G = "gh"

BIBLIOGRAPHY

Arthen, Inanna. "The Theory and Practice of Weatherworking." *Fireheart* (Spring/Summer 1989).

Antonsen, Elmer H. 1975. *A Concise Grammar of the Older Runic Inscriptions*. Tübingen, Germany: Max Niemeyer Verlag.

Aswynn, Freya. 1990. *Leaves of Yggdrasil* (reissued as *Northern Mysteries and Magic*). Minneapolis, MN: Llewellyn.

Bauschatz, Paul C. 1982. *The Well and the Tree: A Study of the Concepts of Cosmology and Time in Early Germanic Culture*. Amherst: University of Massachusetts Press.

Bellows, Henry Adams, trans. 1969. *The Poetic Eddas*. New York: Biblo & Tannen.

Briggs, Katherine. 1976. *An Encyclopedia of Fairies*. New York: Pantheon.

Burns, Thomas. 1984. *A History of the Ostrogoths*. Bloomington: Indiana University Press.

Castleman, Michael. 1991. *The Healing Herbs*. Emmaus, PA: Rodale Press.

Cleasby, Richard, and Gudbrand Vigfusson. 1957. *Icelandic-English Dictionary*, 2nd ed. Oxford: Clarendon Press.

Culpepper, Nicholas. 1990. *Culpepper's Complete Herbal*. Glenwood, IL: Meyerbooks.

Cunningham, Scott. 1991. *Encyclopedia of Magical Herbs*. Minneapolis, MN: Llewellyn.

Ellis-Davidson, H. R. Ellis. 1964. *Gods and Myths of Northern Europe*. New York: Penguin. (Reissued as *Gods and Myths of the Viking Age*, Barnes & Noble, 1996.)

———. 1988. *Myths and Symbols of Pagan Europe*. Syracuse, NY: Syracuse University Press.

———. 1943. *The Road to Hel*. Cambridge: Cambridge University Press.

———. 1969. *Scandinavian Mythology*. London: Paul Hamlyn. (Reissued as *Viking and Norse Mythology*, Barnes & Noble, 1996.)

Dumézil, Georges. 1973.*Gods of the Ancient Northmen*. Berkeley: University of California Press.

Eliade, Mircea. 1964. *Shamanism*. Princeton: Princeton University Press.

Finch, R. G., trans. 1965. *The Saga of the Volsungs*. London: Thomas Nelson & Sons.

Francis, Dick. 1979. *Whip Hand*, New York: Pocket Books.

Frazer, Sir James. 1959. *The New Golden Bough*. Ed. Theodor Gaster. New York: Doubleday & Co.

Friedrich, Johannes. 1957. *Extinct Languages*. New York: Dorset Press.

Gelling, Peter, and Hilda Ellis-Davidson. 1969. *The Chariot of the Sun*. London: J.M. Dent & Sons Ltd.

Glosecki, Stephen. 1989. *Shamanism and Anglo-Saxon Poetry*. New York: Garland Publishing.

———. "The Thing about Thorns." 1992, April. Paper presented at the Old English Colloquium, University of California, Berkeley.

Griffiths, Bill, trans. 1993. *The Battle of Maldon*. Middlesex, England: Anglo-Saxon Books.

Grimm, Jacob. 1966. *Teutonic Mythology*. New York: Dover Publications.

Gundarsson, Kveldúlf. 1990. *Teutonic Magic*. Minneapolis, MN: Llewellyn.

———. 1993. *Teutonic Religion*. Minneapolis, MN: Llewellyn. (Also available as e-book from: http://www.aswynn.co.uk/ebooks.html)

Gundarsson, Kveldúlf, ed. 1993. *Our Troth*. Berkeley, CA: The Troth. (Available online at www.thetroth.org.)

Halsall, Maureen. 1981. *The Old English Rune Poem* (Appendix B, The Norse Rune Poems). Toronto: University of Toronto Press.

Hamer, Richard, trans. 1970. *A Choice of Anglo-Saxon Verse* ("The Seafarer," "The Wanderer," "The Battle of Maldon," "Deor's Lament"). London: Faber & Faber.

Harner, Michael. 1980. *The Way of the Shaman*. New York: Bantam.

Hastrup, Kirsten. 1985. *Culture and History in Medieval Iceland*. Oxford: Clarendon Press.

Haugen, Einar. 1985. "The Edda as Ritual: Odin and His Masks." In *Edda*, ed. Glendenning and Bessason. Winnipeg: University of Manitoba Press.

Hillenbrand, Laura. 2001. *Seabiscuit*. New York: Ballantine.

Hillman, James. 1980. *Facing the Gods*. Putnam, CT: Spring Publications.

Hollander, Lee M., trans. 1986. *The Poetic Edda*. Austin: University of Texas.

Kallir, Alfred. 1980. *Sign and Design: The Psychogenetic Source of the Alphabet*. N.p.: Vernum.

Kelchner, Georgia. 1935. *Dreams in Old Norse Literature*. Cambridge: Cambridge University Press.

Kodratoff, Yves. 2003. *Nordic Magic Healing*. N.p.: Universal Publishers. (Available via www.nordic-life.org/nmh/)

Kutin, Siegfried. 1977. "Pytheas of Massilia: The Epic Sea-Voyage of Discovery to Northwestern Europe as Reported and Discussed by Ancient Authors." Research Paper presented to the faculty of the Division of Library Science, San Jose University.

Lopez, Barry. 1978. *Of Wolves and Men*. New York: Scribners.

Malone, Kemp. 1964. *The Literary History of Hamlet*. New York: Haskell House, 1923,

McKinnell, John, trans. 1972. *Viga-Glum's Saga with the Tales of Ogmund Bash and Thorvald Chatterbox*. Edinburgh: Canongate.

Osborn, Marijane, and Stella Longland. 1964. *Rune Games*. London: Routledge & Kegan Paul.

Oxenstierna, Erik. 1965. *The Norsemen*. Trans. Catherine Hutter. Greenwich, CT: New York Graphic Society.

Page, R. I. 1987. *Reading the Past: Runes*. London: British Museum Publications.

Patch, Howard. 1950. *The Other World*. Cambridge, MA: Harvard University Press.

Paxson, Diana L. 1994. *The Wolf and the Raven*, book one of *Wodan's Children* trilogy. New York: William Morrow.

———. 1995. *The Dragons of the Rhine*, book two of *Wodan's Children* trilogy. New York: AvonNova.

———. 1996. *The Lord of Horses*, book three of *Wodan's Children* trilogy. New York: AvonNova.

Pennick, Nigel. 1989. *Games of the Gods*. York Beach, ME: Weiser.

Peterson, James. 1988. *The Enchanted Alphabet*. Wellingborough, England: Aquarian Press.

Phillpotts, B. S. 1991. "Wyrd and Providence in Anglo-Saxon Thought." In *Interpretations of Beowulf*, edited by R. D. Fulk. Bloomington: Indiana University Press.

Rees, Alwin, and Brinley Rees. 1961. *Celtic Heritage*. London: Thames & Hudson.

Rohan, Michael Scott. 1989–90. *The Winter of the World*. 3 vols. New York: Avon Books.

Saxo Grammaticus. 1979. *Gesta Danorum*. Trans. Peter Fisher, ed. H. R. Ellis-Davidson. Cambridge: D.S. Brewer.

Schwartz, Martin. 1992, April. "Wodanaz." Paper presented at the Old English Colloquium, University of California, Berkeley.

Shakespeare, William. (1952). *Hamlet*. Complete Works edition. Edited by G. B. Harrison. New York: Harcourt, Brace and Co.

Sibley, Jane. 1989. Workshop on the Runes at Esotericon. Conference in Providence, RI.

Simpson, Jacqueline. 1967. *Everyday Life in the Viking Age*. New York: Dorset.

Storms, Godfrid. 1975. *Anglo-Saxon Magic*. New York: Gordon Press.

Snorri Sturluson 1990. *Heimskringla*. New York: Dover Publications.

———. 1987. *Edda*. Trans. Anthony Faulkes. London: J.M. Dent & Sons.

———. 1954. *The Prose Edda*. Trans. Jean Young. Berkeley: University of California Press.

Sweet, Henry. (1987). *The Student's Dictionary of Anglo-Saxon*. Oxford: Clarendon Press.

Tacitus. 1942. *The Complete Works of Tacitus*. Ed. Moses Hadas. New York: Modern Library.

Thorsson, Edred. 1984. *Futhark: A Handbook of Rune Magic*. York Beach, ME: Samuel Weiser, Inc.

———. 1987. *Runelore*. York Beach, ME: Samuel Weiser, Inc.

———. 1989. *At the Well of Wyrd*. York Beach, ME: Samuel Weiser, Inc.

Tolkien, J.R.R. 1955. *The Lord of the Rings*. Boston: Houghton Mifflin.

Viherjuuri, H. J. (1965). *Sauna, the Finnish Bath*. Brattleboro, VT: Stephen Greene Press.

Wardle, Thorolf. 1984 *Rune Lore*. London: Odinic Rite.

Willis, Tony. 1980. *The Runic Workbook*. London: Aquarian Press.

Wolfram, Herwig. 1988. *History of the Goths*. Berkeley: University of California Press.

Wright, David, trans. 1957. *Beowulf*. New York: Penguin.

Zimmer, Carl. 2004. "Whose Life Would You Save?" Discover 25:4, April.

Zimmer, Paul Edwin. 1994. *The Wine of Kvasir*. Privately published from Greyhaven in Berkeley.

ABOUT THE AUTHOR

Diana Paxson is the author of more than two dozen historical novels with strong spiritual themes including *The White Raven* and *The Serpent's Tooth*. Her novels on Germanic themes include *Brisingamen* (1984) and the Wodan's Children Trilogy: *The Wolf and the Raven, The Dragons of the Rhine,* and *The Lord of Horses.* She is also coauthor, with Marion Zimmer Bradley, of *Priestess of Avalon* and has continued the immensely popular Mists of Avalon series on her own. Diana is gydhja of Hrafnar kindred, which she founded in 1988. She is also an elder in the Troth. She served as steerswoman of the Troth from 1999 to 2002, and still edits its magazine, *Idunna.*

Visit Diana at *www.hrafner.org.*

TO OUR READERS

Weiser Books, an imprint of Red Wheel/Weiser, publishes books across the entire spectrum of occult and esoteric subjects. Our mission is to publish quality books that will make a difference in people's lives without advocating any one particular path or field of study. We value the integrity, originality, and depth of knowledge of our authors.

Our readers are our most important resource, and we appreciate your input, suggestions, and ideas about what you would like to see published. Please feel free to contact us, to request our latest book catalog, or to be added to our mailing list.

Red Wheel/Weiser, LLC
with offices at
500 Third Street, Suite 230
San Francisco, CA 94107
www.redwheelweiser.com